Springer Finance

Springer

New York
Berlin
Heidelberg
Barcelona
Hong Kong
London
Milan
Paris
Singapore
Tokyo

Springer Finance

Risk-Neutral Valuation: Pricing and Hedging of Financial Derivatives
N.H. Bingham and Rüdiger Kiesel
ISBN 1-85233-001-5 (1998)

Visual Exploration in Finance with Self-Organizing Maps
Guido Deboeck and Teuvo Kohonen (Editors)
ISBN 3-540-76266-3 (1998)

Mathematics of Financial Markets
Robert J. Elliott and P. Ekkehard Kopp
ISBN 0-387-98553-0 (1999)

Mathematical Models of Financial Derivatives
Y.-K. Kwok
ISBN 981-3083-25-5 (1998)

Robert J. Elliott and P. Ekkehard Kopp

Mathematics of
Financial Markets

 Springer

Robert J. Elliott
AF Collins Professor of Finance
Department of Finance and Management Science
  and Department of Mathematical Sciences
University of Alberta
Edmonton, Alberta TG 2G1
Canada
e-mail: R.Elliott@UAlberta.ca

P. Ekkehard Kopp
Department of Mathematics
University of Hull
Hull HU6 7RX
UK
e-mail: P.E.Kopp@maths.hull.ac.uk

Mathematics Subject Classification (1991): 60H30, 90A09

With 6 figures.

Library of Congress Cataloging-in-Publication Data
Elliott, Robert James.
    Mathematics of financial markets / Robert J. Elliott, P. Ekkehard
  Kopp.
      p.   cm.   1002119425
    Includes bibliographical references and index.
    ISBN 0-387-98553-0 (alk. paper)
    1. Investments—Mathematics.   2. Stochastic analysis.   3. Options
  (Finance)—Mathematical models.   4. Securities—Prices—Mathematical
  models.   I. Kopp, P.E., 1944–   . II. Title.
  HG4515.3.E37   1998
  332.6′01′51—dc21   98-8540

Printed on acid-free paper.

Production managed by Francine McNeill; manufacturing supervised by Thomas King.
Typeset by The Bartlett Press, Inc., Marietta, GA.
Printed and bound by Edwards Brothers, Inc., Ann Arbor, MI.
Printed in the United States of America.

9 8 7 6 5 4 3 2 (Corrected second printing, 2000)

ISBN 0-387-98553-0 Springer-Verlag New York Berlin Heidelberg   SPIN 10756679

Preface

This work is aimed at an audience with a sound mathematical background wishing to learn about the rapidly expanding field of mathematical finance. Its content is suitable particularly for graduate students in mathematics who have a background in measure theory and probability.

The emphasis throughout is on developing the mathematical concepts required for the theory within the context of their application. No attempt is made to cover the bewildering variety of novel (or 'exotic') financial instruments that now appear on the derivatives markets; the focus throughout remains on a rigorous development of the more basic options that lie at the heart of the remarkable range of current applications of martingale theory to financial markets.

The first five chapters present the theory in a discrete-time framework. Stochastic calculus is not required, and this material should be accessible to anyone familiar with elementary probability theory and linear algebra.

The basic idea of pricing by arbitrage (or, rather, by nonarbitrage) is presented in Chapter 1. The unique price for a European option in a single-period binomial model is given and then extended to multi-period binomial models. Chapter 2 introduces the idea of a martingale measure for price processes. Following a discussion of the use of self-financing trading strategies to hedge against trading risk, it is shown how options can be priced using an equivalent measure for which the discounted price process is a martingale. This is illustrated for the simple binomial Cox–Ross–Rubinstein pricing models, and the Black–Scholes formula is derived as the limit of the prices obtained for such models. Chapter 3 gives the 'fundamental theorem of asset pricing', which states that if the market does not contain arbitrage opportunities there is an equivalent martingale measure. Explicit constructions of such measures are given in the setting of finite market models. Completeness of markets is investigated in Chapter 4; in a complete market, every contingent claim can be generated by an admissible self-financing strategy (and the martingale measure is unique). Stopping times, martingale convergence results, and American options are discussed in a discrete-time framework in Chapter 5.

The second five chapters of the book give the theory in continuous time. This begins in Chapter 6 with a review of the stochastic calculus. Stopping times, Brownian motion, stochastic integrals, and the Itô differentiation rule are all defined and discussed, and properties of stochastic differential equations developed.

The continuous-time pricing of European options is developed in Chapter 7. Girsanov's theorem and martingale representation results are developed, and the Black–Scholes formula derived. Optimal stopping results are applied in Chapter 8 to a thorough study of the pricing of American options, particularly the American put option.

Chapter 9 considers selected results on term structure models, forward and future prices, and change of numéraire, while Chapter 10 presents the basic framework for the study of investment and consumption problems.

Acknowledgments

Sections of the book have been presented in courses at the Universities of Adelaide and Alberta. The text has consequently benefited from subsequent comments and criticism. Our particular thanks go to Monique Jeanblanc-Piqué, whose careful reading of the text and valuable comments led to many improvements. Many thanks are also due to Volker Wellmann for reading much of the text and for his patient work in producing consistent TeX files and the illustrations.

Finally, the authors wish to express their sincere thanks to the Social Sciences and Humanities Research Council of Canada for its financial support of this project.

Edmonton, Alberta, Canada   Robert J. Elliott
Hull, United Kingdom   P. Ekkehard Kopp

Contents

List of Figures

1
Pricing by Arbitrage

1.1   Introduction: Pricing and Hedging

The 'unreasonable effectiveness' of mathematics is evidenced by the frequency with which mathematical techniques that were developed without thought for practical applications find unexpected new domains of applicability in various spheres of life. This phenomenon has customarily been observed in the physical sciences; in the social sciences its impact has perhaps been less evident. One of the more remarkable examples of simultaneous revolutions in economic theory and market practice is provided by the opening of the world's first options exchange in Chicago in 1973, and the ground-breaking theoretical papers on preference-free option pricing by Black and Scholes [18] (quickly extended by Merton [188]) which appeared in the same year, thus providing a workable model for the 'rational' market pricing of traded options.

From these beginnings financial derivatives markets worldwide have become one of the most remarkable growth industries, and now constitute a major source of employment for graduates with high levels of mathematical expertise. The principal reason for this phenomenon has its origins in the simultaneous stimuli described previously, and the explosive growth of these secondary markets (whose levels of activity now frequently exceed the underlying markets on which their products are based) continues unabated, with total trading volume in 1996 being estimated at some 35 trillion dollars. The variety and complexity of new financial instruments is often bewildering, and much effort goes into the analysis of the (ever more complex) mathematical models on which their existence is predicated.

In this book we present the necessary mathematics, within the context of this field of application as simply as possible, in an attempt to dispel some of the mystique which has come to surround these models and at the same time to exhibit the essential structure and robustness of the underlying theory. Since making choices and decisions under conditions of *uncertainty* about their outcomes is inherent in all market trading, the area of mathematics that finds the most natural applications in finance theory is the modern theory of *probability and stochastic processes*, which has itself undergone spectacular growth into the past five decades. Given our current preoccupations, it seems entirely appropriate that the origins of probability, as well as much of its current motivation, lie in one of the earliest and most pervasive indicators of 'civilised' behaviour: *gambling*.

Contingent Claims

A *contingent claim* represents the potential liability inherent in a *derivative security*; that is, in an asset whose value is determined by the values of one or more underlying variables (usually securities themselves). The analysis of such claims, and their *pricing* in particular, forms a large part of the modern theory of finance. Decisions about the prices appropriate for such claims are made contingent on the price behaviour of these underlying securities (often simply referred to as the *underlying*) and the theory of derivatives markets is primarily concerned with these relationships, rather than with the economic fundamentals that determine the prices of the underlying.

While the construction of mathematical models for this analysis often involves very sophisticated mathematical ideas, the *economic* insights that underlie the modelling are often remarkably simple and transparent. In order to highlight these insights we first develop rather simplistic mathematical models based on discrete time (and, frequently, finitely generated probability spaces) before showing how the analogous concepts can be used in the more widely known continuous models based on diffusions and *Itô processes*. For the same reason we do not attempt to survey the range of contingent claims now traded in the financial markets, but concentrate on the more basic *stock options* before attempting to discuss only a small sample of the multitude of more recent, and often highly complex, financial instruments that finance houses place on the markets in ever greater quantities.

Before commencing the mathematical analysis of market models and the options based upon them, we outline the principal features of the main types of financial instruments and the conditions under which they are currently traded, in order to have a benchmark for the mathematical idealisations that characterise our modelling. We briefly consider the role of *forwards, futures, swaps,* and *options*.

Forward Contracts

A *forward contract* is simply an agreement to buy or sell a specified asset S at a certain future time T for a price K that is specified now (which we take to be time 0). Such contracts are not normally traded on exchanges, but are agreements reached between two sophisticated institutions, usually between a financial institution such as a bank and one of its corporate clients. The purpose is to share risk: one party assumes a *long position* by agreeing to buy the asset, the other takes a *short position* by agreeing to sell the asset for the *delivery price* K at the *delivery date* T. Initially neither party incurs any costs in entering into the contract, and the *forward price* of the contract at time $t \in [0, T]$ is the delivery price that would give the contract zero value. Thus at time 0, the forward price is K, but at later times movement in the market value of the underlying commodity will suggest different values. The *payoff* to the holder of the long position at time T is simply $S_T - K$, and for the short position it is $K - S_T$. Thus, since both parties are obliged to honour the contract, in general one will lose and the other gain the same amount.

On the other hand, trading in forwards is not closely regulated, and the market participant bears the risk that the other party may default—the instruments are not traded on an exchange, but 'over-the-counter' (OTC) worldwide, usually by electronic means. There are no price limits (as could be set by exchanges), and the object of the transaction is delivery; that is, the contracts are not usually 'sold on' to third parties. Thus the problem of determining a 'fair' or rational price, as determined by the collective judgement of the market makers or by theoretical modelling, appears complicated.

However, the simple assumption that investors will always prefer having more to having less (this is what constitutes 'rational behaviour' in the markets) and cognisance of the 'time-value of money' (i.e., using continuous compounding to keep track of increase under a riskless interest rate r) already allows us to price a forward contract that provides no dividends or other income: let S_t be the *spot price* of the underlying asset S (i.e., its price at time $t \in [0, T]$); then the forward price $F(t, T)$ at that time must be $F(t, T) = S_t e^{r(T-t)}$. To see this, consider the alternatives: if the forward price is higher, we can borrow S_t for the interval $[t, T]$ at rate r, buy the asset, and take a short position in the forward contract. At time T we need $S_T e^{r(T-t)}$ to repay our loan, but will realise the higher forward price from the forward contract, and thus make a riskless profit. For $F(t, T) < S_t e^{r(T-t)}$ we can similarly make a sure gain by shorting the asset (i.e., 'borrowing' it from someone else's account, a service that brokers will provide, subject to various market regulations) and taking a long position in the contract. Thus simple 'arbitrage' considerations, in other words, that we cannot expect riskless profits, or a 'free lunch', lead to a definite forward price at each time t.

Forward contracts can be used for reducing risk (*hedging*): for example, large corporations regularly face the risk of currency fluctuations, and may be willing to pay a price for greater certainty. A company facing the need to make a large fixed payment in a foreign currency at a fixed future date may choose to enter into a forward contract with a bank to fix the rate now, in order to lock in the exchange rate. The bank, on the other hand, is acting as a *speculator*, since it will benefit from an exchange rate fluctuation that leaves the foreign currency below the value fixed today. Equally, a company may speculate on the exchange rate going up more than the bank predicts, and take a long position in a forward contract to lock in that potential advantage—while taking the risk of losses if this prediction fails. In essence, it is betting on future movements in the asset. The advantage over actual purchase of the currency now is that the forward contract involves no cost at time 0, and only potential cost if the gamble does not pay off. In practice, financial institutions will demand a small proportion of the funds as a deposit to guard against default risk; nonetheless the *gearing* involved in this form of trading is considerable.

Both types of trader, *hedgers* and *speculators*, are thus required for forward markets to operate. The third group, *arbitrageurs*, enter two or more markets simultaneously, trying to exploit local or temporary disequilibria (i.e., *mispricing* of certain assets) in order to lock in riskless profits. The fundamental economic assumption that (ideal) markets operate in equilibrium makes this a hazardous undertaking, requiring rapid judgements (and hence well-developed underlying mathematical models) for sustained success—their existence means that assets do not remain mispriced for long, or by large amounts. Thus it is reasonable to build models and calculate derivative prices that are based on the assumption of the absence of arbitrage, and this is our general approach.

Futures Contracts

Futures contracts involve the same agreement to trade an asset at a future time at a certain price, but the trading takes place on an exchange, and is subject to regulation. The parties need not know each other, so the exchange needs to bear any default risk—hence the contract requires standardised features, such as daily settlement arrangements, known as *marking to market*. The investor is required to pay an initial deposit, and this *initial margin* is adjusted daily to reflect gains and losses, since the *futures price* is determined on the floor of the exchange by demand and supply considerations. The price is thus paid over the life of the contract in a series of instalments that enable the exchange to balance long and short positions and minimise its exposure to default risk. Futures contracts often involve commodities whose quality cannot be determined with certainty in advance, such as cotton, sugar, or coffee, and the delivery price thus has reference points which guarantee that the asset quality falls between agreed limits, as well as specifying contract size.

The largest commodity futures exchange is the Chicago Board of Trade, but there are many different exchanges trading in futures around the world; increasingly, financial futures have become a major feature of many such markets. Futures contracts are written on stock indices, on currencies, and especially on the movements in interest rates. Treasury bills and Eurodollar futures are among the most common instruments.

Futures contracts are traded heavily, and only a small proportion are actually delivered before being sold on to other parties. Prices are known publicly and so the transactions conducted will be at the best price available at that time. We consider futures contracts only in the context of interest rate models, in Chapter 9.

Swaps

A more recent development, dating from 1981, is the exchange between two partners of future cash flows according to agreed prior criteria that depend on the values of certain underlying assets. Swaps can thus be thought of as portfolios of forward contracts, and the initial value as well as the final value of the swap is zero. The cash flows to be exchanged may depend on interest rates. In the simplest example (a *plain vanilla* interest rate swap) one party agrees to pay the other cash flows equal to interest at a fixed rate on a notional principal, at each payment date. The other party agrees to pay interest on the same notional principal and in the same currency, but the cash flow is based on a floating interest rate. Thus the swap transforms a floating rate loan into a fixed rate one, and vice versa. The floating rate used is often LIBOR (the London Interbank Offer Rate), which determines the interest rate used by banks on deposits from other banks in Eurocurrency markets; it is quoted on deposits of varying duration—one month, three months, and so on. LIBOR operates as a reference rate for international markets: three-month LIBOR is the rate underlying Eurodollar futures contracts, for example.

There is now a vast range of swap contracts available, with *currency swaps* (whereby the loan exchange uses fixed interest rate payments on loans in different currencies) among the most heavily traded. We do not study swaps in any depth in this book; see [197] or [262] for detailed discussions. The latter text focuses on options that have derivative securities, such as forwards, futures, or swaps, as their underlying assets; in general, such instruments are known as *exotics*.

Options

An *option* on a stock is a contract giving the owner the right, but not the obligation, to trade a given number of shares of a common stock for a fixed price at a future date (the *expiry date T*). A *call* option gives the owner the right to buy stocks, and a *put* option confers the right to sell, at the fixed *strike price* K. The option is *European* if it can only be exercised at the fixed expiry date T; the option is *American* if the owner can exercise his right to trade at any time up to the expiry date. Options are the principal financial instruments discussed in this book.

In Figures 1.1 and 1.2, we draw the simple graphs that illustrate the *payoff* function of each of these options: in every transaction there are two parties, the *buyer* and the seller, more usually termed the *writer*, of the option. In the case of a European call option on a stock (S_t) with strike price K at time T, the payoff equals $S_T - K$ if $S_T > K$ and 0 otherwise. The payoff for the writer of the option must balance this quantity; that is, it should equal $K - S_T$ if $S_T < K$ and 0 otherwise.

Fair Prices and Hedge Portfolios

The problem of *option pricing* is to determine what value to assign to the option at a given time (e.g., at time 0). It is clear that a trader can make a riskless profit (at least in the absence of inflation) unless she has paid an 'entry fee' which allows her the chance of exercising the option favourably at the expiry date. On the other hand, if this 'fee' is too high, and the stock price seems likely to remain close to the strike price, then no sensible trader would buy the option for this fee. As we saw previously, operating on a set $\mathbb{T}$ of possible *trading dates* (which may typically be a finite set of natural numbers of the form $\mathbb{T} = \{0, 1, 2, \ldots, T\}$, or, alternatively, a finite interval $[0, T]$ on the real line), the buyer of a European call option on a stock with price process $(S_t)_{t \in \mathbb{T}}$ will have the opportunity of receiving a payoff at time T of $C_T = \max(S_T - K, 0)$; since she or he will exercise the option if, and only if, the final price of the stock S_T is greater than the previously agreed strike price K.

With the call option price set at C_0, we can draw the graph of the gain (or loss) in the transaction for both buyer and writer of the option. In this section we assume for simplicity that the riskless interest rate is 0 (the 'value of money' remains constant); in later sections we drop this assumption, and then account must be taken of the rate at which money held in a savings account would accumulate: for example, with continuous compounding over the interval $\mathbb{T} = [0, T]$ the price C_0 paid for the option at time 0 would be worth $C_0 e^{rT}$ by time T. With the rate $r = 0$, the buyer's gain from the call option will be $S_T - K - C_0$ if $S_T > K$ and $-C_0$ if $S_T \leq K$. The writer's gain is given by $K - S_T + C_0$ if $S_T > K$ and C_0 if $S_T \leq K$. Similar arguments hold for the buyer and writer of a European put option with strike K and option price P_0. The payoff and gain graphs are given in Figures 1.1 and 1.2.

Determining the option price entails an assessment of a price to which both parties would logically agree. One way of describing the *fair price* for the option is as the *current* value of a portfolio that will yield exactly the

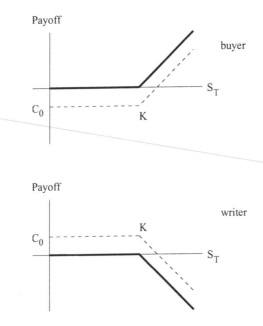

FIGURE 1.1. Payoff and gain for European call option

same return as does the option by time T. Strictly, this price is fair only for the writer of the option, who can calculate the fair price as the smallest initial investment that would allow him to *replicate* the value of the option throughout the time set $\mathbb{T}$ by means of a portfolio consisting of stock and a riskless *bond* (or savings account) alone. The buyer, on the other hand, will want to cover any potential losses by borrowing the amount required to buy the option (the buyer's option price) and to invest in the market in order to reduce this liability, so that at time T the option payoff at least covers the loan. In general, the buyer's and seller's option prices will not coincide—it is a feature of *complete market models*, which form the main topic of interest in this book, that they do coincide, so that it becomes possible to refer to *the* fair price of the option. Our first problem is to determine this price uniquely.

When option replication is possible, the replicating portfolio can be used to offset, or *hedge*, the risk inherent in writing the option, that is, the risk that the writer of the option may have to sell the share S_T for the fixed price K even though, with small probability, S_T may be much larger than K. Our second problem is therefore to construct such a *hedge portfolio*.

Call–Put Parity

The next market assumption enables us to concentrate our attention on call options alone. Once we have dealt with these, the solutions of the

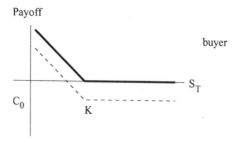

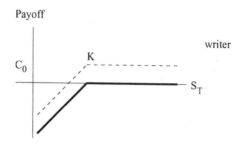

FIGURE 1.2. Payoff and gain for European put option

corresponding problems for the European put option can be read off at once from those for the call option. The crucial assumption that ensures this is that our market model rules out *arbitrage*; that is, no investor should be able to make riskless profits, in a sense that we will shortly make more precise. This assumption is basic to option pricing theory, since there can be no market *equilibrium* otherwise. (In fact, it has been argued that the very existence of 'arbitrageurs' in real markets justifies the assumption: in general, markets will quickly adjust prices so as to eliminate disequilibrium, and hence will move to eliminate arbitrage.)

So let C_t (resp., P_t) be the value at time t of the European call (resp., put) option on the stock (S_t). We continue to assume that the 'value of money' remains constant throughout (i.e., the riskless interest rate is 0). Writing

$$x^+ = \begin{cases} x & \text{if } x > 0 \\ 0 & \text{if } x \leq 0 \end{cases}$$

we can write the payoff of the European call as $(S_T - K)^+$ and that of the corresponding put option as $(K - S_T)^+$.

It is obvious from these definitions that at the expiry date T:

$$C_T - P_T = (S_T - K)^+ - (K - S_T)^+ = S_T - K.$$

We claim that, in order to avoid arbitrage, the call and put prices must satisfy this relation throughout $\mathbb{T}$; that is, for all $t \in \mathbb{T}$:

$$C_t - P_t = S_t - K. \tag{1.1}$$

To see this, suppose we make the following trades. At time $t \in \mathbb{T}$, buy a share S_t and a put P_t and sell a call C_t, each with strike price K and exercise date T. The balance of these transactions is $C_t - P_t - S_t$. Now consider what happens at time T: if $S_T > K$, then the call will be exercised, yielding a cash sum K in return for the share. We will not exercise the put, since we would be selling the share for less than its value S_T. Hence at time T the total value of the assets resulting from our transactions will be K. On the other hand, if $S_T < K$, then we exercise the put (our buyer will not exercise the call) and we gain K for our share, so again the final value of our assets is K. Consequently, buying a share and a put, and selling a call, provides a sure, riskless way of obtaining an amount K at time T; that is,

$$P_T + S_T - C_T = K.$$

Since the interest (or discount) rate is zero we must also have, at each $t \in \mathbb{T}$,

$$P_t + S_t - C_t = K.$$

If $C_t - P_t \neq S_t - K$, there is room for riskless profits, accruing either to ourselves or our trading partner. This verifies the *call–put parity relation* (1.1).

Exercise 1.1.1. Suppose that $\mathbb{T} = \{0, 1, 2, \dots, T\}$ for some $T \in \mathbb{N}$ and that the riskless rate of return per period is $r > 0$, so that the values of assets are discounted at rate $\beta = (1+r)^{-1}$. Show that the call–put parity relation now reads: $C_t - P_t = S_t - \beta^{T-t} K$.

1.2   Single-Period Option Pricing Models

Risk-Neutral Probability Assignments

In our first examples we restrict attention to markets with a single trading period, so that the time set $\mathbb{T}$ contains only the two trading dates 0 and T. The mathematical tools needed for contingent claim analysis are those of probability theory: in the absence of complete information about the time evolution of the risky asset (S_t) it is natural to model its value at some future date T as a random variable defined on some probability space $(\Omega, \mathcal{F}, P)$. Similarly, any contingent claim H that can be expressed as a function of S_T or, more generally, (S_t), is a non-negative random variable on $(\Omega, \mathcal{F}, P)$.

The probabilistic formulation of option prices allows us to attack the problem of finding the fair price H_0 of the option in a different way: since we do not know in advance what value S_T will take, it seems logical to estimate H by $E(\beta H)$, using some discount factor β; that is, we estimate H by its average discounted value. (Here $E = E_P$ denotes mathematical expectation relative to the probability measure P.)

This averaging technique has been known for centuries, and is termed the 'principle of equivalence' in actuarial theory; there it reflects the principle that, on average, the (uncertain) discounted future benefits should be equal in value to the present outlay. We are left, however, with a crucial decision: how do we determine the probability measure P? At first sight it is not clear that there is a 'natural' choice at all; it seems that the probability measure (i.e., the assignment of probabilities to every possible event) must depend on investors' risk-preferences.

However, in particular situations one can obtain a 'preference-free' version of the option price: the theory that has grown out of the mathematical modelling initiated by the work of Black and Scholes [18] provides a framework in which there *is* a natural choice for P, namely, a measure under which the (discounted) price process is a *martingale*. Economically, this corresponds to a market in which the investors' probability assignments show them to be 'risk-neutral' in a sense made more precise later. Although this framework depends on some rather restrictive conditions, it provides a firm basis for mathematical modelling as well as being a testbed for more 'economically realistic' market models. To motivate the choice of the particular models currently employed in practice, we first consider a simple numerical example.

Example 1.2.1. We illustrate the connection between the 'fair price' of a claim and a replicating (or 'hedge') portfolio that mimics the value of the claim. For simplicity we again set the discount factor $\beta \equiv 1$; that is, the riskless interest rate (or 'inflator') r is set at 0. The only trading dates are 0 and T, so that any portfolio fixed at time 0 is held until time T. Suppose a stock S has price 10 (dollars, say) at time 0, and takes one of only two possible values at time T:

$$S_T = \begin{cases} 20 & \text{with probability } p, \\ 7.5 & \text{with probability } 1-p. \end{cases}$$

Consider a European call option $H = (S_T - K)^+$ with strike price $K = 15$, written on the stock. At time T, the option H yields a profit of 5 dollars if $S_T = 20$, and 0 otherwise. The probability assignment is $(p, 1-p)$, which, in general, depends on the investor's attitude to risk: an inaccurate choice could mean that the investor pays more for the option than is necessary. We look for a 'risk-neutral' probability assignment $(q, 1-q)$, that is, one under which the stock price S is constant on average. Thus, if Q denotes the probability measure given by $(q, 1-q)$, then the expected value of S under Q should be constant (i.e., $E_Q(S_T) = S_0$), which we can also write as $E_Q(\Delta S) = 0$, where $\Delta S = S_T - S_0$. (This makes S into a 'one-step martingale.') In our example we obtain:

$$10 = 20q + 7.5(1 - q)$$

so that $q = 0.2$. With the probability assignment $(0.2, 0.8)$ we then obtain the option price $\pi(H) = 5q = 1$.

To see why this price is the *unique* 'rational' one, consider the hedge portfolio approach to pricing: we attempt to replicate the final value of the option by means of a portfolio (θ_0, θ_1) of cash and stock alone, and determine what initial capital is needed for this portfolio to have the same time T value as H in all contingencies. The portfolio (θ_0, θ_1) can then be used by the option writer to insure, or *hedge*, perfectly against all the risk inherent in the option.

Recall that the discount rate is 0, so that the bank account remains constant. The *value* of our portfolio is $V_t = \theta_0 + \theta_1 S_t$ $(t = 0, T)$. Here we use 1 dollar as our unit of cash, so that the value of cash held is simply θ_0, while θ_1 represents the *number* of shares of stock held during the period. Changes in the value of the portfolio are due solely to changes in the value of the stock. Hence the *gain* from trade is simply given by $G = \theta_1 \Delta S$, and $V_T = V_0 + G$. By the choice of the measure Q we also have:

$$V_0 = E_Q(V_0) = E_Q(V_T - G) = E_Q(V_T),$$

since $E_Q(\theta_1 \Delta S) = \theta_1 E_Q(\Delta S) = 0$. To find a hedge (θ_0, θ_1) which replicates the option yields the equations:

$$
\begin{aligned}
5 &= \theta_0 1 + \theta_1(20), \\
0 &= \theta_0 1 + \theta_1(7.5).
\end{aligned}
$$

These have the solution $\theta_0 = -3$, $\theta_1 = 0.4$. Substituting into $V_0 = \theta_0 + \theta_1 S_0$ gives $V_0 = -3 + 0.4(10) = 1$.

The *hedging strategy* implied by the preceding is the following: At time 0, sell the option in order to obtain capital of 1 dollar, and borrow 3 dollars, in order to invest the sum of 4 dollars in shares. This buys $\frac{4}{10} = 0.4$ shares of stock. At time T, there are two possible outcomes:

(i) $S_T = 20$. The option is exercised at a cost of 5 dollars; we repay the loan (cost 3 dollars) and sell the shares (gain $0.4 \times 20 = 8$ dollars).

Net balance of trade: 0.

(ii) $S_T = 7.5$. The option is not exercised (cost 0); we repay the loan (cost 3 dollars) and sell the shares (gain $0.4 \times 7.5 = 3$ dollars).

Net balance of trade: 0.

Thus selling the option and holding the hedge portfolio exactly balances out in each case, *provided* the initial price of the option is set at $\pi(H) = 1$.

It is clear that no other initial price has this property: if $\pi(H) > 1$ we can make a riskless profit by selling the option in favour of the portfolio (θ_0, θ_1), and gain $(\pi(H) - 1)$, while if $\pi(H) < 1$ we simply exchange roles with the buyer in the same transaction! Moreover, since $\pi(H) = 5q = 1$, the natural (risk-neutral) probability is given by $q = 0.2$ as before.

Remark 1.2.2. This example shows that the risk-neutral valuation of the option is the unique one which prevents arbitrage profits, so that the price $\pi(H)$ will be fixed by the market in order to maintain market equilibrium. The preceding simple calculation depends crucially on the assumption that S_T can take only *two* values at time T: even with a three-splitting it is no longer possible, in general, to find a hedge portfolio (see Exercise 1.4.4). The underlying idea can, however, be adapted to deal with more general situations and to identify the *intrinsic risk* inherent in the particular market commodities. We illustrate this by considering a more general single-period model, where the investor has access to external funds and/or consumption.

1.3   A General Single-Period Model

We now generalise the hedge portfolio approach to option pricing by examining the *cost function* associated with various trading strategies and minimising its mean-square variation. Suppose that our stock price takes the (known) value S_0 at time 0 and the random value S_1 at time 1. (These are again the only trading dates in the model.) In order to express all values in terms of time-0 prices, we introduce a discount factor β and use the notation $\overline{X} = \beta X$ for any random variable X. So write $\overline{S}_1 = \beta S_1$ for the discounted value of the stock price.

The stock price S and a quite general contingent claim H are both taken to be random variables on some probability space $(\Omega, \mathcal{F}, P)$, and we wish to hedge against the obligation to honour the claim, that is, to pay out $H(\omega)$ at time 1. (Here we are assuming that the underlying probability P is known in advance.) To this end, we build a portfolio at time 0, consisting of θ shares of stock and η_0 units of cash. The initial value of this portfolio is $V_0 = \eta_0 + \theta S_0$. We place the cash in the savings account, where it accrues interest at some positive rate r, or, more generally, increases by a factor β^{-1} by time 1. We wish this portfolio to have value $V_1 = H$ at time 1; in discounted terms, $\overline{V}_1 = \overline{H}$.

Assuming that we have access to external funds this can be achieved very simply by adjusting the savings account from η_0 to the value $\eta_1 = H - \theta S_1$, since this gives the portfolio value $V_1 = \theta S_1 + \eta_1 = \theta S_1 + H - \theta S_1 = H$. Now H is given, so it simply remains to choose the constants θ and V_0 to determine our *hedging strategy* (θ, η) completely. The *cost* of doing this can be described by the process (C_0, C_1), where $C_0 = V_0$ is the initial investment required, and $\Delta C = C_1 - C_0 = \eta_1 - \eta_0$, since the only change at time 1 was to adjust η_0 to η_1. Finally, write $\Delta \overline{X} = \beta X_1 - X_0$ for any 'process' $X = (X_0, X_1)$, in order to keep all quantities in discounted terms. We obtain from the preceding:

$$\begin{aligned} \Delta \overline{C} &= \beta C_1 - C_0 = \beta \eta_1 - \eta_0 = \beta(V_1 - \theta S_1) - (V_0 - \theta S_0) \\ &= \overline{H} - (V_0 + \theta \Delta \overline{S}). \end{aligned} \tag{1.2}$$

This equation exhibits the discounted cost increment $\Delta \overline{C}$ simply as the difference between the discounted claim $\overline{H}$ and its approximation by *linear estimates* based on the discounted price increment $\Delta \overline{S}$. A rather natural choice of the parameters θ and V_0 is thus given by *linear regression*: the parameter values θ and V_0 that minimise the *risk function*

$$R := E((\Delta \overline{C})^2) = E((\overline{H} - (V_0 + \theta \Delta \overline{S}))^2)$$

are given by the *regression estimates*

$$\theta = \frac{\mathrm{Cov}(\overline{H}, \Delta \overline{S})}{\mathrm{Var}(\Delta \overline{S})}, \qquad V_0 = E(\overline{H}) - \theta E(\Delta \overline{S}) \tag{1.3}$$

In particular, $E(\Delta \overline{C}) = 0$, so that the *average* discounted cost remains constant at V_0. The minimal risk obtained when using this choice of the parameters is:

$$R_{\min} = \mathrm{Var}(\overline{H}) - \theta^2 \mathrm{Var}(\Delta \overline{S}_0) = \mathrm{Var}(\overline{H})(1 - \rho^2)$$

where $\rho = \rho(\overline{H}, \overline{S}_1)$ is the correlation coefficient. Thus the *intrinsic risk* of the claim H cannot be completely eliminated unless $|\rho| = 1$.

In general models, therefore, we cannot expect all contingent claims to be *attainable* by some hedging strategy that eliminates all the risk—where this *is* possible, we call the model *complete*. The essential feature which distinguishes complete models is a *martingale representation property*: it turns out that in these cases the (discounted) price process is a *basis* for a certain vector space of martingales.

The preceding discussion is of course much simplified by the fact that we have dealt with a single-period model. In the general case this rather sophisticated approach to option pricing (which is due to [108]; see [106] and [229] for its further development, which we do not pursue here) can only be carried through at the expense of using quite powerful mathematical machinery. In this chapter we consider in more detail only the much simpler situation where the probabilities arise from a binomial splitting.

1.4   A Single-Period Binomial Model

We look for pricing models in which we can take $\eta_1 = \eta_0 = \eta$, that is, where there is no recourse to external funds. Recall that in the general single-period model the initial holding is

$$V_0 = \eta + \theta S_0,$$

which becomes

$$V_1 = \eta + \theta S_1 = V_0 + \theta \Delta S$$

at time 1.

A simple complete model is found by taking ΔS as a *binomial* splitting; that is, S_1 is a random variable on a probability space $(\Omega, \mathcal{F}, P)$, and there are two real values a and b with $a < r < b$ (in order to avoid arbitrage opportunities) and $0 < p < 1$ such that

$$P\{S_1 = (1+b)S_0\} = p, \qquad P\{S_1 = (1+a)S_0\} = 1 - p. \tag{1.4}$$

For any contingent claim H we can find θ and V_0 so that $P(\overline{H} = V_0 + \theta \Delta \overline{S}) = 1$ as follows. Write h^b for the value of H when $S_1 = (1+b)S_0 = S^b$ and similarly for h^a. We need to choose θ and V_0 to satisfy

$$\begin{aligned} \beta h^b &= V_0 + \theta(\beta(1+b)S_0 - S_0), \\ \beta h^a &= V_0 + \theta(\beta(1+a)S_0 - S_0). \end{aligned} \tag{1.5}$$

Subtracting, we obtain

$$\theta = \frac{h^b - h^a}{(b-a)S_0} = \frac{h^b - h^a}{S^b - S^a} = \boxed{\frac{\delta V}{\delta S}}$$

where the last expression denotes the rate of change in V relative to the change in the stock price; although we have denoted it by θ (as our interest is in finding the hedge portfolio) this parameter is usually called the *delta of the contingent claim*.

We can determine the initial investment V_0 required for the hedging strategy from (1.5) as

$$\begin{aligned} V_0 &= \beta h^a - \left(\frac{h^b - h^a}{S^b - S^a}\right)(\beta S^a - S_0) \\ &= \beta\left(h^b \frac{\beta^{-1}S_0 - S^a}{S^b - S^a} + h^a \frac{S^b - \beta^{-1}S_0}{S^b - S^a}\right). \end{aligned} \tag{1.6}$$

In particular, when $\beta = (1+r)^{-1}$ we obtain:

$$V_0 = \frac{1}{1+r}\left(h^b \frac{(1+r)S_0 - S^a}{S^b - S^a} + h^a \frac{S^b - (1+r)S_0}{S^b - S^a}\right). \tag{1.7}$$

These choices of θ and V_0 provide a linear estimator with a perfect fit. The fair price V_0 for H therefore does not need to be adjusted by any risk premium, and is uniquely determined, irrespective of the investor's attitude to risk. Thus the binomial model constructed here allows preference-free or *arbitrage pricing* of the claim H. Since the cost function C has the constant value V_0 we say that the optimal strategy (θ, η) is *self-financing* in this special case, since no new funds have to be introduced at time 1. (Recall that $\eta = V_0 - \theta S_0$.) In our general single-period model we were only able to conclude that C is constant on average: in that case we say that the optimal strategy is *mean-self-financing* in the general single-period model (see [106]).

Note that the analysis leading to the general pricing formula (1.7) is valid for an arbitrary contingent claim. By way of example we examine the case of a European call option, where further analysis is possible.

*Example 1.4.1 (**European call option**).* Consider the special case when $H = (S_1 - K)^+$ is a European call with strike K; assume further that K lies between $(1+a)S_0$ and $(1+b)S_0$, and the riskless interest rate $r > a$ is constant, so that $\beta = (1+r)^{-1}$. Then we have

$$h^b = (1+b)S_0 - K, \qquad h^a = 0,$$

so that

$$\theta = \frac{h^b - h^a}{S_0(b-a)} = \frac{S_0(1+b) - K}{S_0(b-a)}.$$

From (1.6) we obtain the option price

$$V_0 = \frac{1}{1+r}\left(\frac{r-a}{b-a}\right)(S_0(1+b) - K).$$

Note that differentiation with respect to b and a, respectively, shows that in this special case the option price increases with b and decreases with a, which accords with our intuition.

Moreover, the 'variability' of the stock price S can be measured by the variance σ of the ratio $S_1/S_0 = 1+\xi$, where the Bernoulli random variable ξ takes the values b and a with probabilities p and $(1-p)$, respectively. The variance is therefore $\sigma^2 = (b-a)^2 p(1-p)$, which increases with $(b-a)$. We call σ the *volatility* of the stock.

However, contrary to what is asserted by various authors, the option price V_0 does *not* necessarily increase with σ, as the following simple example, due to M. Capinski, shows. Take $r = 0$, $S_0 = 1 = K$, so that $V_0 = -ab/(b-a)$. For $b = -a = 0.05$ we have $V_0 = 0.025$, $\sigma^2 = 0.1p(1-p)$, while for $b = 0.01$, $a = -0.19$ we obtain $V_0 = 0.0095$, $\sigma^2 = 0.2p(1-p)$.

Remark 1.4.2. If our main interest is in the trading strategy (θ, η), equations (1.5) can of course be solved directly for θ and η: in terms of these variables we have

$$\theta(1+b)S_0 + \eta\beta^{-1} = h^b,$$
$$\theta(1+a)S_0 + \eta\beta^{-1} = h^a,$$

which gives the same value of θ as previously, and

$$\eta = \beta \frac{(1+b)h^a - (1+a)h^b}{b-a}.$$

Note now that the preceding discussion does not involve the value of the probability parameter p defined by (1.4), or, more generally, on the choice of probability measure P. In the binomial case there is a natural candidate for a *risk-neutral* probability assignment, namely, that suggested by (1.6): if we set

$$q = \frac{\beta^{-1}S_0 - S^a}{S^b - S^a}, \qquad 1 - q = \frac{S^b - \beta^{-1}S_0}{S^b - S^a}, \tag{1.8}$$

then (1.6) states that $V_0 = E_Q(\overline{H})$, where Q is the probability measure defined by $Q(S_1 = S^b) = q$ and $Q(S_1 = S^a) = 1 - q$. Under Q the discounted price has constant expectation (i.e., $E_Q(\overline{S}_1) = S_0$), so that the fluctuation in the discounted price behaves like a 'fair game,' or a *martingale* under Q. (A more detailed discussion and definitions are given in Chapter 2.)

Thus by choosing the risk-neutral measure Q we can justify the long-standing actuarial practice of averaging the value of the discounted claim, at least for the case of our single-period binomial model. Moreover, we have shown that in this model *every* contingent claim can be *priced by arbitrage;* that is, there exists a (unique) self-financing strategy (θ, η) which replicates the value of H, so that the pricing model is *complete*. In a complete model the optimal choice of strategy completely eliminates the risk in trading H, and the fair price of H is uniquely determined as the initial value V_0 of the optimal strategy, which can be computed explicitly as the expectation of H relative to the risk-neutral measure Q.

Before leaving single-period models we review some of the preceding concepts in a modification of Example 1.2.1.

Example 1.4.3. Suppose that the stock price S_T defined in Example 1.2.1 can take three values: 20, 15, and 7.5. In this case there are an infinite number of risk-neutral probability measures for this stock: the risk-neutral probability assignment requires $E_Q(S_1) = S_0$ (since $\beta = 1$ in this example). This leads to the equations:

$$20q_1 + 15q_2 + 7.5q_3 = 10,$$
$$q_1 + q_2 + q_3 = 1,$$

which have solutions $(\lambda, \frac{1}{3}(1 - 5\lambda), \frac{1}{3}(2 + 2\lambda))$ for arbitrary λ. For nondegenerate probability assignments we need $q_i \in (0, 1)$ for $i = 1, 2, 3$, hence we require $0 < \lambda < \frac{1}{5}$. For each such λ we obtain a different risk-neutral probability measure Q_λ.

Let $X = (X_1, X_2, X_3)$ be a contingent claim based on the stock S. We show that there exists a replicating portfolio for X if and only if

$$3X_1 - 5X_2 + 2X_3 = 0. \tag{1.9}$$

To see this, recall that a hedge portfolio (η, θ) for X needs to satisfy $V_1 = \eta + \theta S_1 = X$ in all outcomes, so that:

$$\begin{aligned}
\eta + 20\theta &= X_1, \\
\eta + 15\theta &= X_2, \\
\eta + 7.5\theta &= X_3,
\end{aligned}$$

leading to

$$\theta = \frac{X_1 - X_3}{12.5} = \frac{X_2 - X_3}{7.5}; \qquad \text{that is,} \quad 3X_1 - 5X_2 + 2X_3 = 0.$$

Thus a contingent claim in this model is attainable if and only if equation (1.9) holds.

Finally, we verify that the value of an attainable claim X is the same under every risk-neutral measure: we have

$$\begin{aligned}
E_{Q_\lambda}(X) &= \lambda X_1 + \frac{1}{3}(1 - 5\lambda)X_2 + \frac{1}{3}(2 + 2\lambda)X_3 \\
&= \frac{1}{3}[\lambda(3X_1 - 5X_2 + 2X_3) + X_2 + 2X_3]
\end{aligned}$$

and this quantity is independent of λ precisely when the attainability criterion (1.9) holds.

Exercise 1.4.4. Extend the market defined in the previous example by adding a second stock S' with $S_0' = 5$ and $S_T' = 6$, 6 or 4, so that the vector of stock prices (S, S') reads:

$$(S_0, S_0') = (10, 5), \qquad (S_T, S_T') = \begin{cases} (20, 6) \\ (15, 6) \\ (7.5, 4) \end{cases}$$

with probabilities (p_1, p_2, p_3), respectively. Verify that in this case there is *no* risk-neutral probability measure for the market—recall that we would need $p_i > 0$ for $i = 1, 2, 3$. We say that this market is not *viable*, and it can be shown that in this situation it is possible to construct arbitrage opportunities.

1.5 Multi-Period Binomial Models

A One-Step Risk-Neutral Measure

Consider a binomial pricing model with trading dates $0, 1, 2, \ldots, T$ for some fixed positive integer T. By this we mean that the price of the stock takes values $S_0, S_1, S_2, \ldots, S_T$, and for each $t \leq T$, $S_t = (1 + b)S_{t-1}$ with probability p, and $S_t = (1 + a)S_{t-1}$ with probability $(1 - p)$, where, as before,

$r > 0$ is the riskless interest rate (so that $\beta = (1+r)^{-1}$) and $a < r < b$. Again assume that H is a contingent claim, to be evaluated at time T. Consider the current value of H at time $T - 1$, that is, one period before expiration. We can consider this as the initial value of a claim in the single-period model discussed previously, and so there is a hedging strategy (θ, η) which replicates the value of H on the time set $\{T - 1, T\}$, and a risk-neutral measure Q; we can therefore compute the current value of βH as its expectation under Q.

To be specific, assume that $H = (S_T - K)^+$ is a European call option with strike price K and expiry date T. Writing h^b for the value of H if $S_T = (1 + b)S_{T-1}$ and h^a similarly, then the current value of H is given by $E_Q(H/(1 + r))$, where the measure Q is given by $(q, 1 - q)$ as defined in (1.8); hence

$$V_{T-1} = \frac{1}{1+r}(qh^b + (1-q)h^a) \tag{1.10}$$

with (writing S for S_{T-1})

$$q = \frac{(1+r)S - (1+a)S}{(1+b)S - (1+a)S} = \frac{r-a}{b-a}.$$

This again illustrates why we called Q the 'risk-neutral' measure, since a risk-neutral investor is one who is indifferent between an investment with a certain rate of return and another whose uncertain rate of return has the same expected value: under Q the expectation of S_T, given that $S_{T-1} = S$, is given by

$$E_Q(S_T|S_{T-1} = S) = q(1+b)S + (1-q)(1+a)S = (1+r)S.$$

Two-Period Trading

Now apply this analysis to the value V_{T-2} of the call H at time $T - 2$: the stock, whose value S_{T-2} is now written as S, can take one of the three values $(1+b)^2S$, $(1+a)(1+b)S$, and $(1+a)^2S$ at time T; hence the call H must have one of three values at that time (see Figure 1.3). We write these values as h^{bb}, h^{ab}, and h^{aa}, respectively. From (1.6), and using the definition of q in (1.8), we can read off the possible values of V_{T-1} as $V^b = \beta(qh^{bb} + (1-q)h^{ab})$ and $V^a = \beta(qh^{ab} + (1-q)h^{aa})$, respectively. For each of these cases we have now found the value of the option at time $T - 1$, and can therefore select a hedging portfolio as before. The value of the parameters θ and η is determined at each stage exactly as in the single-period model. We obtain:

$$
\begin{aligned}
V_{T-2} &= \beta(qV^b + (1-q)V^a) \\
&= \beta\{q\beta(qh^{bb} + (1-q)h^{ab}) + (1-q)\beta(qh^{ab} + (1-q)h^{aa})\} \\
&= \beta^2\{ q^2[(1+b)^2 S - K]^+ + 2q(1-q)[(1+a)(1+b)S - K]^+ \\
&\quad + (1-q)^2[(1+a)^2 S - K]^+\}.
\end{aligned}
$$

Hence the current value of the claim is completely determined by quantities that are known to the investor at time $T - 2$.

The CRR Formula

We can continue this backward recursion to calculate the value process $V = (V_t)$ for each $t \leq T$.

In particular, with $\beta = (1+r)^{-1}$, the initial investment needed to replicate the European call option H is:

$$
\begin{aligned}
V_0 &= \beta^T \sum_{t=0}^{T} \frac{T!}{t!(T-t)!} q^t (1-q)^{T-t} [(1+b)^t (1+a)^{T-t} S_0 - K]^+ \\
&= S_0 \sum_{t=A}^{T} \frac{T!}{t!(T-t)!} q^t (1-q)^{T-t} [\frac{(1+b)^t (1+a)^{T-t}}{(1+r)^T}] \\
&\quad - K(1+r)^{-T} \sum_{t=A}^{T} \frac{T!}{t!(T-t)!} q^t (1-q)^{T-t}, \qquad (1.11)
\end{aligned}
$$

where A is the first integer k for which $S_0(1+b)^k(1+a)^{T-k} > K$.

Now observe that using $q = (r-a)/(b-a)$ and $q' = q(1+b)/(1+r)$ we obtain $q' \in (0,1)$ and $1 - q' = (1-q)(1+a)/(1+r)$, so that we can finally write the fair price for the European call option in this multi-period binomial pricing model as

$$
V_0 = S_0 \Psi(A; T, q') - K(1+r)^{-T} \Psi(A; T, q), \qquad (1.12)
$$

where Ψ is the complementary binomial distribution function; that is,

$$
\Psi(m; n, p) = \sum_{j=m}^{n} \frac{n!}{j!(n-j)!} p^j (1-p)^{n-j}.
$$

Formula (1.12) is known as the *Cox–Ross–Rubinstein* (or CRR, see [46]) binomial option pricing formula for the European call. We shall shortly give an alternative derivation of this formula by computing the expectation of H under the risk-neutral measure Q directly, utilising the martingale property of the discount stock price under this measure.

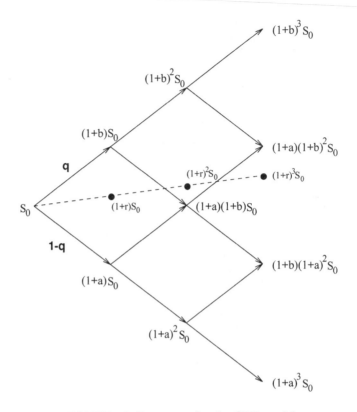

FIGURE 1.3. Event-tree for the CRR model

The event-tree that describes the behaviour of stock prices in the CRR model is depicted in Figure 1.3. Each arrow points 'up' with probability q and 'down' with probability $(1 - q)$. At each node there are only two branches, that is, one more than the number of stocks available. It is this simple splitting property which ensures that the model is complete, since it allows us to 'cover' the two random outcomes at each stage by adjusting the quantities θ and η.

The Hedge Portfolio

More generally, it is clear that the value V_t of the option at time $t \leq T$ is given similarly by the formula

$$V_t = S_t \Psi(A_t; T - t, q') - K(1 + r)^{-T-t} \Psi(A_t; T - t, q), \qquad (1.13)$$

where A_t is the first integer k for which $S_t(1 + b)^k (1 + a)^{T-t-k} > K$. An analysis similar to that outlined in Remark 1.4.2 provides the components of the trading strategy (θ, η): the portfolio $(\theta_{t-1}, \eta_{t-1})$ is held over the time interval $[t-1, t)$ and is required to replicate V_t; that is,

$$\theta_{t-1}S_t + \eta_{t-1}(1+r) = V_t.$$

Thus V_t is determined by S_{t-1} and the price movement in the time interval $[t-1, t)$, so that it takes two possible values, depending on whether $S_t = (1+b)S_{t-1}$ or $S_t = (1+a)S_{t-1}$. Writing V_t^b and V_t^a, respectively, for the resulting values, we need to solve the equations

$$\begin{aligned}
\theta_{t-1}(1+b)S_{t-1} + \eta_{t-1}(1+r) &= V_t^b, \\
\theta_{t-1}(1+a)S_{t-1} + \eta_{t-1}(1+r) &= V_t^a.
\end{aligned}$$

Again we obtain

$$\theta_{t-1} = \frac{V_t^b - V_t^a}{(b-a)S_{t-1}}, \qquad \eta_{t-1} = \frac{(1+b)V_t^a - (1+a)V_t^b}{(1+r)(b-a)}. \qquad (1.14)$$

Analogously with (1.6) we can write down binomial expressions for V_t^b and V_t^a, and this leads to the following explicit formulae for θ_t and η_t; the details are left to the reader.

$$\begin{aligned}
\theta_t &= \sum_{s=A_t}^{T-t} \frac{(T-t)!}{s!(T-t-s)!}(q')^s(1-q')^{T-t-s}, \\
\eta_t &= -K(1+r)^{-(T-t)} \sum_{s=A_t}^{T-t} \frac{(T-t)!}{s!(T-t-s)!}q^s(1-q)^{T-t-s}.
\end{aligned} \qquad (1.15)$$

1.6   Bounds on Option Prices

We conclude this chapter with a few simple observations concerning bounds on option prices. We restrict attention to call options, though similar arbitrage considerations provide bounds for other types of options. The bounds described here are quite crude, but are independent of the model used, relying solely on the assumption of 'no arbitrage.' In this section we denote the call price by C_0 and the put price by P_0.

It should be obvious that American options are, in general, more valuable than their European counterparts, since the holder has greater flexibility in exercising them. We can illustrate this by constructing a simple arbitrage. For example, if the price $C_0(E)$ of a European call with strike K and exercise date T were greater than the price $C_0(A)$ of an American option with the same K and T, then we would make a riskless profit by writing the European option and buying the American one, while pocketing the difference $C_0(E) - C_0(A)$. We keep this riskless profit by holding the American option until time T when both options have the same value. Thus, in the absence of arbitrage, the relations

$$0 \le C_0(E) \le C_0(A) \tag{1.16}$$

will always hold.

Both option prices must lie below the current value S_0 of the underlying share (and will in practice be much less): if $C_0(A)$ were greater than S_0 we could buy a share at S_0 and write the option. The profit made is secure, since the option liability is covered by the share. By (1.14) both option values are therefore less than S_0.

Call–put parity for European options (see Exercise 1.1.1) demands that $C_0(E) - P_0(E) = S_0 - \beta^T K$. As $P_0(E) \ge 0$, it follows that $C_0(E) \ge S_0 - \beta^T K$. We have therefore restricted the European call option price to lie in the interval $[\min(0, S_0 - \beta^T K), S_0]$. While this remains a crude estimate, it holds in all option pricing models.

These bounds provide a simple, but initially surprising, relationship between European and American call option prices for shares that (as here) pay no dividends; note first that

$$C_0(A) \ge C_0(E) \ge S_0 - \beta^T K \ge S_0 - K \tag{1.17}$$

since the discount factor β is less than or equal to 1. This means that the option price is, in either case, at least equal to the gain achieved by immediate exercise of the option. Hence (as long as our investor prefers more to less) the option will not be exercised immediately. But the same argument applies at any starting time $t < T$, so that the European option's value $C_t(E)$ at time t (which must be the same as that of an option written at t, with strike K and exercise date T) satisfies $C_t(E) \ge S_t - \beta^{T-t} K$, and, as previously, $C_t(A) \ge S_t - K$, which is *independent* of the time to expiry $T - t$. Consequently, *an American call option on a stock that pays no dividends will not be exercised before expiry*, so that in this case $C_0(E) = C_0(A)$.

Exercise 1.6.1. Derive the following bounds for the European put option price $P_0(E)$ by arbitrage arguments.

$$\max(0, \beta^T K - S_0) \le P_0(E) \le \beta^T K.$$

2

Martingale Measures

2.1 A General Discrete-Time Market Model

Information Structure

Fix a time set $\mathbb{T} = \{0, 1, 2, \ldots, T\}$, where the *trading horizon* T is treated as the terminal date of the economic activity being modelled, and the points of $\mathbb{T}$ are the admissible *trading dates*. We assume given a fixed probability space $(\Omega, \mathcal{F}, P)$ to model all 'possible states of the market'.

In most of the simple models discussed in Chapter 1, Ω is a *finite* probability space (i.e., has a finite number of points ω each with $P(\{\omega\}) > 0$). In this situation the σ-field $\mathcal{F}$ is the power set of Ω, so that every subset of Ω is $\mathcal{F}$-measurable.

Note, however, that the finite models can equally well be treated by assuming that, on a general sample space Ω, the σ-field $\mathcal{F}$ in question is finitely generated; that is, there is a finite partition $\mathcal{P}$ of Ω into mutually disjoint sets $A_1, A_2, \ldots, A_n$ whose union is Ω. Then $\mathcal{F}$ also contains only finitely many events and consists precisely of those events that can be expressed in terms of $\mathcal{P}$. In this case we further demand that the probability measure P on $\mathcal{F}$ satisfies $P(A_i) > 0$ for all i.

In both cases the only role of P is to identify the events that investors agree are *possible*; they may disagree in their assignment of probabilities to these events. We refer to models in which either of the preceding additional assumptions applies as *finite market models*. Although most of our examples are of this type, the following definitions apply to general market models. Real-life markets are, of course, always finite, thus the additional 'generality' gained by considering arbitrary sample spaces and σ-fields is a question of mathematical convenience rather than wider applicability!

The *information structure* available to the investors is given by an increasing (finite) sequence of *sub-σ-fields* of $\mathcal{F}$: we assume that $\mathcal{F}_0$ is trivial, that is, contains only sets of P-measure 0 or 1. We assume that $(\Omega, \mathcal{F}_0)$ is complete (so that any subset of a null set is itself null and $\mathcal{F}_0$ contains all P-null sets), and that $\mathcal{F}_0 \subset \mathcal{F}_1 \subset \mathcal{F}_2 \subset \ldots \subset \mathcal{F}_T = \mathcal{F}$. An increasing family of σ-fields is called a *filtration* $\mathbb{F} = (\mathcal{F}_t)_{t \in \mathbb{T}}$ on $(\Omega, \mathcal{F}, P)$ in modern probability theory. We can think of $\mathcal{F}_t$ as containing the information available to our investors at time t: investors learn without forgetting, but we assume that they are not prescient—insider trading is not possible. Moreover, our investors think of themselves as 'small investors,' in that their actions will not change the probabilities they assign to events in the market. Again, note that in a finite market model each σ-field $\mathcal{F}_t$ is generated by a minimal finite partition $\mathcal{P}_t$ of Ω, and that $\mathcal{P}_0 = \{\Omega\} \subset \mathcal{P}_1 \subset \mathcal{P}_2 \subset \ldots \subset \mathcal{P}_T = \mathcal{P}$. At time t all our investors know which cell of $\mathcal{P}_t$ contains the 'true state of the market', but none of them knows more.

Market Model and Numéraire

Fix a natural number d, the *dimension* of the market model, and assume given a $(d+1)$-dimensional stochastic process $S = \{S_t^i : t \in \mathbb{T}, 0 \le i \le d\}$ to represent the time evolution of the *securities price process*. The security labelled 0 is taken as a riskless (i.e., nonrandom) *bond* (or *bank account*) with price process S^0 while the d risky (i.e., random) stocks labelled $1, \ldots, d$ have price processes $S^1, S^2, \ldots, S^d$. The process S is assumed to be *adapted* to the filtration $\mathbb{F}$, so that for each $i \le d$, S_t^i is $\mathcal{F}_t$-measurable; that is, the prices of the securities at all times up to t are known at time t. Most frequently, we in fact take the filtration $\mathbb{F}$ as that generated by the price process $S = \{S^0, S^1, \ldots, S^d\}$. Then $\mathcal{F}_t = \sigma(S_u : u \le t)$ is the smallest σ-field such that all the $\mathbb{R}^{d+1}$-valued random variables $S_u = (S_u^0, S_u^1, \ldots, S_u^d)$, $u \le t$, are $\mathcal{F}_t$-measurable. In other words, at time t the investors know the values of the price vectors $(S_u : u \le t)$, but they have no information about later values of S.

The tuple $(\Omega, \mathcal{F}, P, \mathbb{T}, \mathbb{F}, S)$ is the *securities market model*. We require at least one of the price processes to be strictly positive throughout, that is, to act as a benchmark, known as the *numéraire*, in the model. As is customary, we assign this role to the bond price S^0, although in principle any strictly positive S^i could be used for this purpose.

Note on Terminology: The term 'bond' is the one traditionally used to describe the riskless security that we use here as numéraire, although 'bank account' or 'money market account' are becoming popular alternatives. We continue to use 'bond' in this sense until Chapter 9, where we discuss models for the evolution of interest rates; in that context the term 'bond' refers to a certain type of risky asset, as is made clear.

2.2 Trading Strategies and Arbitrage Opportunities

Value Processes

In keeping with tradition we have taken S^0 as a strictly positive *bond* or riskless security, and without loss of generality we assume that $S_0^0 = 1$, so that the initial value of the bond S^0 yields the units relative to which all other quantities are expressed. The *discount factor* $\beta_t = 1/S_t^o$ is then the sum of money we need to invest in bonds at time 0 in order to have 1 unit at time t. Note that we allow the discount *rate*, that is, the increments in β_t, to vary with t; this includes the case of a constant interest rate $r > 0$, where $\beta_t = (1+r)^{-t}$.

The securities $S^0, S^1, S^2, \ldots, S^d$ are traded at times $t \in \mathbb{T}$: an investor's *portfolio* at time $t \geq 1$ is given by the $\mathbb{R}^{d+1}$-valued random variable $\theta_t = (\theta_t^i)_{0 \leq i \leq d}$, with *value process* $V_t(\theta)$ given by

$$V_0(\theta) = \theta_1 \cdot S_0,$$

$$V_t(\theta) = \theta_t \cdot S_t = \sum_{i=0}^{d} \theta_t^i S_t^i \quad (t \in \mathbb{T}, \ t \geq 1).$$

The value $V_0(\theta)$ is the investor's initial endowment. The investors select their time t portfolio once the stock prices at time $t-1$ are known, and they hold this portfolio during the time interval $(t-1, t]$. At time t the investors can adjust their portfolios, taking into account their knowledge of the prices S_t^i for $i = 0, 1, \ldots, d$. They then hold the new portfolio (i.e., θ_{t+1}) throughout the time interval $(t, t+1]$.

Market Assumptions

We require, therefore, that the *trading strategy* $\theta = \{\theta_t : t = 1, 2, \ldots, T\}$ consisting of these portfolios is a *predictable* (vector-valued) stochastic process: for each $t < T$, θ_{t+1} should be $\mathcal{F}_t$-measurable, so θ_1 is $\mathcal{F}_0$-measurable, hence constant, as $\mathcal{F}_0$ is assumed to be trivial. We also assume throughout that we are dealing with a 'frictionless' market; that is, there are no transaction costs, unlimited short sales and borrowing are allowed (the random variables θ_t^i can take any real values), and the securities are perfectly divisible (the S_t^i can take any positive real values).

Self-Financing Strategies

We call the trading strategy θ *self-financing* if any changes in the value $V_t(\theta)$ result entirely from net gains (or losses) realised on the investments; the value of the portfolio after trading has occurred at time t and before stock prices at time $t + 1$ are known is given by $\theta_{t+1} \cdot S_t$. If the total value of the portfolio has been used for these adjustments (i.e., there are no withdrawals and no new funds are invested), then this means that for all $t = 1, 2, \ldots, T - 1$,

$$\theta_{t+1} \cdot S_t = \theta_t \cdot S_t. \quad \text{self-financing} \tag{2.1}$$

Writing $\Delta X_t = X_t - X_{t-1}$ for any function X on $\mathbb{T}$, we can rewrite this equation at once as

$$\begin{aligned} \Delta V_t(\theta) &= \theta_t \cdot S_t - \theta_{t-1} \cdot S_{t-1} \\ &= \theta_t \cdot S_t - \theta_t \cdot S_{t-1} = \theta_t \cdot \Delta S_t; \end{aligned} \tag{2.2}$$

that is, the gain in value of the portfolio in the time interval $[t-1, t]$ is the scalar product in $\mathbb{R}^d$ of the new portfolio vector θ_t with the vector ΔS_t of price increments. Thus, defining the *gains process* associated with θ by setting

$$G_0(\theta) = 0, \qquad G_t(\theta) = \theta_1 \cdot \Delta S_1 + \theta_2 \cdot \Delta S_2 + \ldots + \theta_t \cdot \Delta S_t, \tag{2.3}$$

we see at once that θ is self-financing if and only if

$$V_t(\theta) = V_0(\theta) + G_t(\theta) \tag{2.4}$$

for all $t \in \mathbb{T}$. This means that θ is self-financing if and only if the value $V_t(\theta)$ arises solely as the sum of the initial *endowment* $V_0(\theta)$ and the gains process $G_t(\theta)$ associated with the strategy θ.

We can write this relationship in yet another useful form: since $V_t(\theta) = \theta_t \cdot S_t$ for any $t \in \mathbb{T}$ and *any* strategy θ, it follows that we can write

$$\begin{aligned} \Delta V_t &= V_t - V_{t-1} = \theta_t \cdot S_t - \theta_{t-1} \cdot S_{t-1} \\ &= \theta_t \cdot (S_t - S_{t-1}) + (\theta_t - \theta_{t-1}) \cdot S_{t-1} \\ &= \theta_t \cdot \Delta S_t + (\Delta \theta_t) \cdot S_{t-1}. \end{aligned} \tag{2.5}$$

Thus the strategy θ is self-financing if and only if

$$(\Delta \theta_t) \cdot S_{t-1} = 0. \tag{2.6}$$

This means that for a self-financing strategy the vector of changes in the portfolio θ is orthogonal in $\mathbb{R}^{d+1}$ to the *prior* price vector S_{t-1}. This property is sometimes easier to verify than (2.1). It also serves to justify the terminology: the cumulative effect of the time t variations in the investor's holdings (which are made *before* the time t prices are known) should be to balance each other; for example, if $d = 1$, we need to balance $\Delta \theta_t^0 S_{t-1}^0$ against $\Delta \theta_t^1 S_{t-1}^1$, since by (2.6) their sum must be zero.

Numéraire Invariance

Trivially, (2.1) and (2.4) each have an equivalent 'discounted' form; in fact, given any numéraire (i.e., any process (Z_t) with $Z_t > 0$ for all $t \in \mathbb{T}$), it follows that a trading strategy θ is self-financing relative to S if and only if it is self-financing relative to ZS, since $(\Delta\theta_t) \cdot S_{t-1} = 0$ iff $(\Delta\theta_t) \cdot Z_{t-1}S_{t-1} = 0$ for $t \in \mathbb{T} \setminus \{0\}$.

Thus changing the choice of 'benchmark' security will not alter the class of trading strategies under consideration and thus will not affect market behaviour. This simple fact is sometimes called the 'numéraire invariance theorem'; in continuous-time models it is not completely obvious (see [80]).

Writing $\overline{X}_t = \beta_t X_t$ for the discounted form of the vector X_t in $\mathbb{R}^{d+1}$, it follows (using $Z = \beta$ in the preceding) that θ is self-financing if and only if $(\Delta\theta_t) \cdot \overline{S}_{t-1} = 0$, that is, if and only if

$$\theta_{t+1} \cdot \overline{S}_t = \theta_t \cdot \overline{S}_t, \tag{2.7}$$

or, equivalently, if and only if

$$\overline{V}_t(\theta) = V_0(\theta) + \overline{G}_t(\theta) \quad \text{for all } t \in \mathbb{T}. \tag{2.8}$$

To see the last equivalence, note first that (2.5) holds for any θ with $\overline{S}$ instead of S, so that for self-financing θ we have $\Delta\overline{V}_t = \theta_t \cdot \Delta\overline{S}_t$; hence (2.8) holds. Conversely, (2.8) implies that $\Delta\overline{V}_t = \theta_t \cdot \Delta\overline{S}_t$, so that $(\Delta\theta_t) \cdot \overline{S}_{t-1} = 0$ and so θ is self-financing.

Note finally that the definition of $\overline{G}(\theta)$ does not involve the amount θ_t^0 held in bonds (i.e., in the security S^0) at time t. Hence, if θ is self-financing, the initial investment $V_0(\theta)$ and the predictable real-valued processes θ^i $(1 \le i \le d)$ completely determine θ^0. In other words, given an $\mathcal{F}_0$-measurable function V_0 and predictable processes $\theta^1, \theta^2, \ldots, \theta^d$, the unique predictable process θ^0 that turns $\theta = (\theta^0, \theta^1, \ldots, \theta^d)$ into a self-financing strategy is found from the equation

$$\overline{V}_t(\theta) = \theta_t^0 + \theta_t^1 \overline{S}_t^1 + \ldots \theta_t^d \overline{S}_t^d = V_0 + \sum_{u=1}^{t}(\theta_u^1 \Delta\overline{S}_u^1 + \ldots + \theta_u^d \Delta\overline{S}_u^d)$$

which also shows that θ^0 is predictable, since we have, solving this equation for θ_t^0:

$$\theta_t^0 = V_0 + \sum_{u=1}^{t-1}(\theta_u^1 \Delta\overline{S}_u^1 + \ldots + \theta_u^d \Delta\overline{S}_u^d) - (\theta_t^1 \overline{S}_{t-1}^1 + \ldots + \theta_t^d \overline{S}_{t-1}^d). \tag{2.9}$$

Admissible Strategies

Let Θ be the class of all self-financing strategies. So far we have not insisted that a self-financing strategy must at all times yield nonnegative total wealth, that is, that $V_t(\theta) \geq 0$ for all $t \in \{0, 1, 2, \dots, T\}$. From now on, when we impose this additional restriction, we call such self-financing strategies *admissible*; they define the class Θ_a.

Economically this requirement has the effect of restricting certain types of short sales: although we can still borrow certain of our assets (i.e., have $\theta_t^i < 0$ for some values of i and t) the overall value process must remain nonnegative for each t. But the additional restriction has little impact on the mathematical modelling, as we show shortly.

We use the class Θ_a to define our concept of 'free lunch':

Definition 2.2.1. An *arbitrage opportunity* is an admissible strategy θ such that $V_0(\theta) = 0$, $V_t(\theta) \geq 0$ for all $t \in \mathbb{T}$, and $E(V_T(\theta)) > 0$.

In other words, we require $\theta \in \Theta_a$ with initial value 0 but final value strictly positive with positive probability.

Definition 2.2.2. The market model is *viable* if it does not contain any arbitrage opportunities; that is, if $\theta \in \Theta_a$ has $V_0(\theta) = 0$, then $V_T(\theta) = 0$ (P-almost surely).

'Weak Arbitrage Implies Arbitrage'

To justify the assertion that restricting attention to admissible claims has little effect on the modelling we call a self-financing strategy $\theta \in \Theta$ a *weak arbitrage* if $V_0(\theta) = 0$, $V_T(\theta) \geq 0$ and $E_P(V_T(\theta)) \geq 0$. The following calculation shows that if a weak arbitrage exists then it can be adjusted to yield an admissible strategy, that is, an arbitrage as defined in 2.2.1.

Suppose that θ is a weak arbitrage and that $V_t(\theta)$ is *not* non-negative a.s. for all t. Then there exists $t < T$, $a < 0$ and $A \in \mathcal{F}_t$ such that $(\theta_t \cdot S_t)(\omega) = a$ for $\omega \in A$ and $\theta_u \cdot S_u \geq 0$ a.s. whenever $u > t$. We amend θ to a new strategy ϕ by setting $\phi_u(\omega) = 0$ for all $u \in \mathbb{T}$ and $\omega \in \Omega \setminus A$, while on A we set $\phi_u(\omega) = 0$ if $u \leq t$, and for $u > t$ we define

$$\phi_u^0(\omega) = \theta_u^0(\omega) - \frac{a}{S_t^0(\omega)},$$

$$\phi_u^i(\omega) = \theta_u^i(\omega) \quad \text{for } i = 1, 2, \dots, d.$$

This strategy is obviously predictable. It is also self-financing: on $\Omega \setminus A$ we clearly have $V_u(\phi) \equiv 0$ for all $u \in \mathbb{T}$, while on A we need only check that $(\Delta\phi_{t+1}) \cdot S_t = 0$, by the preceding construction (in which $\Delta\theta_u$ and $\Delta\phi_u$ differ only when $u = t + 1$) and (2.6). We observe that $\phi_t^i = 0$ on A^c for $i \geq 0$, and that, on A :

$$\Delta\phi_{t+1}^0 = \phi_{t+1}^0 = \theta_{t+1}^0 - \frac{a}{S_t^0}, \qquad \Delta\phi_{t+1}^i = \theta_{t+1}^i.$$

Hence $(\Delta\phi_{t+1}) \cdot S_t = 1_A(\theta_{t+1} \cdot S_t - a) = 1_A(\theta_t \cdot S_t - a) = 0$ since θ is self-financing and $\theta_t \cdot S_t = a$ on A.

We show $V_u(\phi) \geq 0$ for all $u \in \mathbb{T}$, and $P(V_T(\phi) > 0) > 0$: first note that $V_u(\phi) = 0$ on $\Omega \setminus A$ for all $u \in \mathbb{T}$. On A we also have $V_u(\phi) = 0$ when $u \leq t$, but for $u > t$ we obtain

$$V_u(\phi) = \phi_u \cdot S_u = \theta_u^0 S_u^0 - \frac{aS_u^0}{S_t^0} + \sum_{i=1}^{d} \theta_u^i S_u^i = \theta_u \cdot S_u - a\left(\frac{S_u^0}{S_t^0}\right).$$

Since by our choice of t, $\theta_u \cdot S_u \geq 0$ for $u > t$, and $a < 0$ while $S^0 \geq 0$, it follows that $V_u(\phi) \geq 0$ for all $u \in \mathbb{T}$. Moreover, since $S_T^0 > 0$, we also see that $V_T(\phi) > 0$ on A.

This construction shows that the existence of what we have called weak arbitrage immediately implies the existence of an arbitrage opportunity. This fact is useful in the fine structure analysis for finite market models we give in the next chapter.

Uniqueness of the Arbitrage Price

Fix H as a contingent claim with maturity T. So H is a non-negative $\mathcal{F}_T$-measurable random variable on $(\Omega, \mathcal{F}_T, P)$. The claim is said to be *attainable* if there is an admissible strategy θ that *generates* (or *replicates*) it, that is, such that

$$V_T(\theta) = H.$$

We should expect the value process associated with a generating strategy to be given *uniquely*: the existence of two admissible strategies θ and θ' with $V_t(\theta) \neq V_t(\theta')$ would violate the *Law of One Price*, and the market would therefore allow riskless profits, and not be viable. (Pliska [205] provides a full discussion of these economic arguments.)

The next lemma shows, conversely, that in a viable market the *arbitrage price* of a contingent claim is indeed unique.

Lemma 2.2.3. *Suppose H is a contingent claim in a viable market model. Then the value processes of all generating strategies for H are the same.*

Proof. If θ and ϕ are admissible strategies with

$$V_T(\theta) = H = V_T(\phi)$$

but $V(\theta) \neq V(\phi)$, then there exists $t < T$ such that

$$V_u(\theta) = V_u(\phi) \quad (u < t), \quad V_t(\theta) \neq V_t(\phi).$$

The set $A = \{V_t(\theta) > V_t(\phi)\}$ is in $\mathcal{F}_t$ and we can assume $P(A) > 0$ without loss. The r.v. $X = V_t(\theta) - V_t(\phi)$ is $\mathcal{F}_t$-measurable and defines a self-financing strategy ψ as follows.

$$\psi_u(\omega) = \theta_u(\omega) - \phi_u(\omega) \text{ for } u \leq t \text{ on } A, \text{ and for all } u \in \mathbb{T} \text{ on } A^c$$
$$\psi_u^0 = \beta_t X, \psi_u^i = 0 \text{ for } i = 1, 2, \ldots, d \text{ on } A \text{ for } u > t.$$

It is clear that ψ is predictable. Since both θ and ϕ are self-financing, it follows that (2.1) also holds with ψ for $u < t$, while if $u > t$, $\psi_{u+1} \cdot S_u = \psi_u \cdot S_u$ on A^c similarly, whereas on A, $\psi_{u+1} = \psi_u$. Thus we only need to compare $\psi_t \cdot S_t = V_t(\theta) - V_t(\phi)$ and $\psi_{t+1} \cdot S_t = \mathbf{1}_{A^c}(\theta_{t+1} - \phi_{t+1}) \cdot S_t + \mathbf{1}_A \beta_t X S_t^0$. Now note that $S_t^0 = \beta_t^{-1}$ and that $X = V_t(\theta) - V_t(\phi)$; while on A^c the first term becomes $(\theta_t - \phi_t) \cdot S_t = V_t(\theta) - V_t(\phi)$, and the latter vanishes. Thus $\psi_{t+1} \cdot S_t = V_t(\theta) - V_t(\phi) = \psi_t \cdot S_t$.

Since $V_0(\theta) = V_0(\phi)$, ψ is self-financing with initial value 0. But $V_T(\psi) = \mathbf{1}_A(\beta_t X S_T^0) = \mathbf{1}_A \beta_t \beta_T^{-1} X$ is non-negative a.s. and is strictly positive on A, which has positive probability. Hence ψ is a weak arbitrage, and by the previous section the market cannot be viable. $\qquad\square$

We have shown that in a viable market it is possible to associate a unique time t value (or *arbitrage price*) to any attainable contingent claim H. However, it is not yet clear how the generating strategy, and hence the price, are to be found in particular examples. In the next section we characterise viable market models without having to construct explicit strategies, and derive a general formula for the arbitrage price instead.

2.3   Martingales and Risk-Neutral Pricing

Martingales and Their Transforms

We wish to characterise viable market models in terms of the behaviour of the *increments* of the discounted price process $\overline{S}$: to set the scene we first need to recall some simple properties of martingales. Only the most basic results needed for our purposes are described here; for more details consult, for example, [87], [169], [200], [258].

For these results, we take a general probability space $(\Omega, \mathcal{F}, P)$, together with any filtration $\mathbb{F} = (\mathcal{F}_t)_{t \in \mathbb{T}}$, where, as before, $\mathbb{T} = \{0, 1, 2, \dots, T\}$. Consider (stochastic) processes defined on this *filtered probability space* (also called *stochastic basis*) $(\Omega, \mathcal{F}, P, \mathbb{F}, \mathbb{T})$. Recall that a (stochastic) process $X = (X_t)$ is *adapted* to $\mathbb{F}$ if X_t is $\mathcal{F}_t$-measurable for each $t \in \mathbb{T}$.

Definition 2.3.1. An $\mathbb{F}$-adapted process $M = (M_t)_{t \in \mathbb{T}}$ is an $(\mathbb{F}, P)$-*martingale* if $E(|M_t|) < \infty$ for all $t \in \mathbb{T}$ and

$$E(M_{t+1}|\mathcal{F}_t) = M_t$$

for each $t < T$ in $\mathbb{T}$. If the equality is replaced by $\leq$ ($\geq$) we say that M is a *supermartingale (submartingale)*.

Note that M is a martingale if and only if $E(\Delta M_{t+1}|\mathcal{F}_t) = 0$ for all $t < T$. Thus, in particular, $E(\Delta M_{t+1}) = 0$, hence $E(M_{t+1}) = E(M_t)$ for all $t \in \mathbb{T}$, so that a martingale is 'constant on average.' Similarly, a submartingale increases, and a supermartingale decreases on average. Thinking of M_t

as representing the current capital of a gambler, a martingale therefore models a 'fair' game, while sub- and supermartingales model 'favourable' and 'unfavourable' games, respectively (as seen from the perspective of the gambler, of course!).

The linearity of the conditional expectation operator shows trivially that any linear combination of martingales is a martingale, and the tower property shows that M is a martingale if and only if $E(M_{s+t}|\mathcal{F}_s) = M_s$ for $t = 1, 2, \ldots, T - s$. Moreover, (M_t) is a martingale if and only if $(M_t - M_0)$ is a martingale, so we can assume $M_0 = 0$ without loss whenever convenient.

Many familiar stochastic processes are martingales. The simplest example is given by the successive conditional expectations of a single integrable random variable X. set $M_t = E(X|\mathcal{F}_t)$ for $t \in \mathbb{T}$, then by the tower property:

$$E(M_{t+1}|\mathcal{F}_t) = E(E(X|\mathcal{F}_{t+1})|\mathcal{F}_t) = E(X|\mathcal{F}_t) = M_t.$$

The values of the martingale M_t are successive best mean-square estimates of X, as our 'knowledge' of X, represented by the σ-fields $\mathcal{F}_t$, increases with t.

More generally, if we model the price process of a stock by a martingale M, the conditional expectation (i.e., our best mean-square estimate at time s of the future value M_t of the stock) is given by its current value M_s. This generalises a well-known fact about processes with independent increments: if the zero-mean process W is adapted to the filtration $\mathbb{F}$ and $(W_{t+1} - W_t)$ is independent of $\mathcal{F}_t$, then $E((W_{t+1} - W_t)|\mathcal{F}_t) = E(W_{t+1} - W_t) = 0$, hence W is a martingale.

Exercise 2.3.2. Suppose that the centred integrable random variables $(Y_t)_{t \in \mathbb{T}}$ are independent and let $X_t = \sum_{u \leq t} Y_u$ for each $t \in \mathbb{T}$. Show that X is a martingale for the filtration it generates. What can we say when the Y_t have positive means?

Note also that any *predictable* martingale is almost surely constant: if M_{t+1} is $\mathcal{F}_t$-measurable, we have $E(M_{t+1}|\mathcal{F}_t) = M_{t+1}$, hence M_t and M_{t+1} are a.s. equal for all $t \in \mathbb{T}$. This is no surprise: if at time t we know the value of M_{t+1} our best estimate of that value will be perfect.

The construction of the gains process associated with a trading strategy now suggests the following further definition:

Definition 2.3.3. Let $M = (M_t)$ be a martingale and $\phi = (\phi_t)_{t \geq 1}$ a predictable process defined on $(\Omega, \mathcal{F}, P, \mathbb{F}, \mathbb{T})$. The process $X = \phi \bullet M$ given for $t \geq 1$ by

$$X_t = \phi_1 \Delta M_1 + \phi_2 \Delta M_2 + \ldots + \phi_t \Delta M_t \qquad (2.10)$$

and $X_0 = 0$ is the *martingale transform* of M by ϕ.

Martingale transforms are the discrete analogues of the stochastic integrals in which the martingale M is used as the 'integrator.' The Itô Calculus based upon this integration theory forms the mathematical backdrop to martingale pricing in continuous time, which comprises the bulk of this book. An understanding of the technically much simpler martingale transforms provides valuable insight into the essentials of stochastic calculus and its many applications in finance theory.

The Stability Property

When ϕ is bounded and predictable, ϕ_{t+1} is $\mathcal{F}_t$-measurable and $\phi_{t+1}\Delta M_{t+1}$ remains integrable; hence we obtain that

$$E(\Delta X_{t+1}|\mathcal{F}_t) = E(\phi_{t+1}\Delta M_{t+1}|\mathcal{F}_t) = \phi_{t+1}E(\Delta M_{t+1}|\mathcal{F}_t) = 0$$

for each $t < T$; hence $X = \phi \bullet M$ is a martingale with $X_0 = 0$.

Similarly, if ϕ is also non-negative and Y is a supermartingale, then $\phi \bullet Y$ is again a supermartingale.

This stability under transforms provides a simple, yet extremely useful, characterisation of martingales.

Theorem 2.3.4. *An adapted real-valued process M is a martingale if and only if*

$$E((\phi \bullet M)_t) = E(\sum_{u=1}^{t} \phi_u \Delta M_u) = 0 \quad (t \in \mathbb{T}, \, t \geq 1)$$

for each bounded predictable process ϕ.

Proof. If M is a martingale, so is the transform $X = \phi \bullet M$, and $X_0 = 0$. Hence $E((\phi \bullet M)_t) = 0$ for all $t \geq 1$ in $\mathbb{T}$.

Conversely, if this equation holds for M and every predictable ϕ, take $s > 0$, let $A \in \mathcal{F}_s$ be given, and define a predictable process ϕ by setting $\phi_{s+1} = 1_A$, $\phi_t = 0$ for all other $t \in \mathbb{T}$. Then for $t > s$, we have

$$0 = E((\phi \bullet M)_t) = E(1_A(M_{s+1} - M_s)).$$

Since this holds for all $A \in \mathcal{F}_s$ it follows that $E(\Delta M_{s+1}|\mathcal{F}_s) = 0$, so M is a martingale. $\square$

2.4 Arbitrage Pricing with Martingale Measures

Equivalent Martingale Measures

With these preliminaries we return to our study of viable securities market models. Recall that we assume given an arbitrary complete measurable space $(\Omega, \mathcal{F})$, on which we consider various probability measures, as well as a filtration $\mathbb{F} = (\mathcal{F}_t)_{t \in \mathbb{T}}$ such that $(\Omega, \mathcal{F}_0)$ is complete, and $\mathcal{F}_T = \mathcal{F}$. Finally, we are given a $(d+1)$-dimensional stochastic process $S = \{S_t^i : t \in \mathbb{T}, 0 \leq i \leq d\}$, with $S_0^0 = 1$, and S^0 interpreted as a riskless bond providing a discount factor $\beta_t = 1/S_t^0$, and with S^i $(1 \leq i \leq d)$ interpreted as risky stocks. In the present section we do *not* assume that the resulting market model is finite or that the filtration $\mathbb{F}$ is generated by S.

Suppose that the discounted vector price process $\bar{S}$ happens to be a martingale under some probability measure Q; that is, $E_Q(\Delta \bar{S}_t | \mathcal{F}_{t-1}) = 0$ for $t \geq 1$ in $\mathbb{T}$. Let $\theta = \{\theta_t^i : i \leq d, t = 1, 2, \ldots, T\} \in \Theta_a$ be an admissible strategy, and recall from (2.8) that the discounted value process of θ has the form

$$
\begin{aligned}
\bar{V}_t(\theta) &= \theta_t \cdot \bar{S}_t = \sum_{i=0}^d \theta_t^i \bar{S}_t^i = V_0(\theta) + \bar{G}_t(\theta) \\
&= \theta_1 \cdot S_0 + \sum_{u=1}^t \theta_u \cdot \Delta \bar{S}_u = \sum_{i=1}^d [\theta_1^i S_0^i + (\sum_{u=1}^t \theta_u \Delta \bar{S}_u^i)].
\end{aligned}
$$

Thus the discounted value process $\overline{V}(\theta)$ is a constant plus a finite sum of martingale transforms and therefore it is a martingale with initial (constant) value $V_0(\theta)$. Hence we have $E(\overline{V}_T(\theta)) = E(V_0(\theta))$.

This precludes the possibility of arbitrage: if $V_0(\theta) = 0$ and $V_T(\theta) \geq 0$ a.s. (Q), but $E(\overline{V}_T(\theta)) = 0$, it follows that $V_T(\theta) = 0$ a.s. (Q). This remains true a.s. (P) provided that the probability measure Q has the same null sets as P (we say that Q and P are *equivalent measures*, and write $Q \sim P$). If such a measure can be found, then no self-financing strategy θ can lead to arbitrage; that is, the market is viable. This leads to an important definition.

Definition 2.4.1. A probability measure $Q \sim P$ is an *equivalent martingale measure* for S if the discounted price process $\overline{S}$ is a (vector) martingale under Q for the filtration $\mathbb{F}$. That is, for each $i \leq d$ the discounted price process $\overline{S}^i$ is an $(\mathbb{F}, Q)$-martingale (recall that $\overline{S}^0 \equiv 1$).

We have just seen that the existence of an equivalent martingale measure for S is *sufficient* for viability of the securities market model. In the next chapter we discuss the *necessity* of this condition. Mathematically, the search for equivalent measures under which the given process $\overline{S}$ is a martingale is often much more convenient than having to show that no arbitrage opportunities exist for $\overline{S}$.

Economically, we can interpret the role of the martingale measure as follows. The probability assignments that investors make for various events do not enter into the derivation of the arbitrage price; the only criterion is that agents prefer more to less, and would therefore become arbitrageurs if the market allowed arbitrage. The price we derive for the contingent claim

H must thus be the same for all risk preferences (probability assignments) of the agents, as long as they preclude arbitrage. In particular, an economy of risk-neutral agents will also produce the arbitrage price we derived previously. The equivalent measure Q, under which the discounted price process is a martingale, represents the probability assignment made in this risk-neutral economy, and the price that this economy assigns to the claim will simply be the average (i.e., expectation under Q) discounted value of the payoff H.

Thus the existence of an equivalent martingale measure provides a general method for pricing contingent claims, which we now derive.

Martingale Pricing

We summarise the role played by martingale measures in pricing claims.

Assume that we are given a viable market model $(\Omega, \mathcal{F}, P, \mathbb{F}, S)$ with equivalent martingale measure Q. Recall that a *contingent claim* in this model is a nonnegative ($\mathcal{F}$-measurable) random variable H, representing a contract that pays out $H(\omega)$ dollars at time T if $\omega \in \Omega$ occurs. Its time-0 value or (current) *price* $\pi(H)$ is then the value that the parties to the contract would deem a 'fair price' for entering into this contract.

In a viable model, an investor could hope to evaluate $\pi(H)$ by constructing an admissible trading strategy $\theta \in \Theta_a$ which exactly replicates the returns (cash-flow) yielded by H at time T. For such a strategy θ, the initial investment $V_0(\theta)$ would represent the price $\pi(H)$ of H. Recall that H is an *attainable claim* in the model if there exists a *generating strategy* $\theta \in \Theta_a$ such that $V_T(\theta) = H$, or, equivalently, $\overline{V}_T(\theta) = \beta_T H$. But as Q is a martingale measure for S, $\overline{V}(\theta)$ is, up to a constant, a martingale transform, and hence a martingale, under Q, it follows that for all $t \in \mathbb{T}$,

$$\overline{V}_t(\theta) = E_Q(\beta_T H | \mathcal{F}_t),$$

and thus

$$V_t(\theta) = \beta_t^{-1} E_Q(\beta_T H | \mathcal{F}_t) \tag{2.11}$$

for any $\theta \in \Theta_a$.

In particular,

$$\pi(H) = \overline{V}_0(\theta) = E_Q(\beta_T H | \mathcal{F}_0) = E_Q(\beta_T H). \tag{2.12}$$

Market models in which all contingent claims are attainable are called *complete*. These models provide the simplest class in terms of option pricing, since any contingent claim can be priced simply by calculating its (discounted) expectation relative to an equivalent martingale measure for the model.

Uniqueness of the EMM

Note that $\bar{V}_0(\theta) = E_Q(\beta_T H)$ holds for *every* equivalent martingale measure (EMM) Q in the model; hence if the claim H is attainable then its price $\pi(H)$ will be independent of the choice of the EMM Q. In a complete model, therefore, if Q and R are two EMMs, and H is any claim, we must have $E_Q(\beta_T H) = \pi(H) = E_R(\beta_T H)$. But this means (since $\beta_T > 0$) that the expectations of every non-negative random variable H are the same under Q and R. The same remains true for any random variable by considering its positive and negative parts separately.

Hence the measures Q and R are identical, and in a complete viable model there is therefore a *unique* EMM. We show in Chapter 4 that the converse also holds for finite market models.

Moreover, our argument again verifies that the *Law of One Price* (see Lemma 2.2.3) must hold in a viable model; that is, we cannot have two admissible trading strategies θ, θ' that satisfy $V_T(\theta) = V_T(\theta')$ but $V_0(\theta) \neq V_0(\theta')$. Our modelling assumptions are thus sufficient to guarantee consistent pricing mechanisms (in fact, this consistency criterion is strictly weaker than viability; see [205] for simple examples).

The Law of One Price permits valuation of an attainable claim H through the initial value of a self-financing strategy that generates H; the valuation technique using risk-neutral expectations gives the price $\pi(H)$ *without* prior determination of such a generating strategy. In particular, consider a single-period model and a claim H defined by

$$H(\omega) = \begin{cases} 1 & \text{if } \omega = \omega' \\ 0 & \text{otherwise} \end{cases},$$

where $\omega' \in \Omega$ is some specified state. If H is attainable,

$$\pi(H) = E_Q(\beta_T H) = \frac{1}{\beta_T} Q(\{\omega'\}).$$

This holds even when β is random, and the ratio $(Q(\{\omega'\}))/(\beta_T(\omega'))$ is known as the *state price* of ω'. In a finite market model, we can similarly define the change of measure density $\Lambda = \Lambda(\{\omega\})_{\omega \in \Omega}$, where $\Lambda(\{\omega\}) = (Q(\{\omega\}))/(P(\{\omega\}))$, as the *state price density*. See [205] for details of the role of these concepts.

2.5 Example: Martingale Formulation of the Binomial Market Model

We now take another look at the Cox-Ross-Rubinstein binomial model, which provides a very simple, yet powerful, example of the strength of the martingale methods developed so far.

The CRR Market Model

The Cox–Ross–Rubinstein binomial market model was described in Chapter 1. Recall that we assumed that $d = 1$; that is, there is single stock S^1, and a riskless bond S^0, which accrues interest at a fixed rate $r > 0$. Taking $S_0^0 = 1$ we have $S_t^0 = (1 + r)^t$ for $t \in \mathbb{T}$, and hence $\beta_t = (1 + r)^{-t}$. The *ratios* of successive stock values are Bernoulli random variables; that is, for all $t < T$, either $S_t^1 = S_{t-1}^1(1+a)$ or $S_t^1 = S_{t-1}^1(1+b)$, where $b > a > -1$ are fixed throughout, while S_0^1 is constant. We can thus conveniently choose the sample space

$$\Omega = \{1 + a, 1 + b\}^{\mathbb{T} \setminus \{0\}}$$

together with the natural filtration $\mathbb{F}$ generated by the stock price values; that is, $\mathcal{F}_0 = \{\emptyset, \Omega\}$, $\mathcal{F}_t = \sigma(S_u^1 : u \leq t)$ for $t > 0$. Note that $\mathcal{F}_T = \mathcal{F} = 2^\Omega$ is the σ-field of all subsets of Ω.

The measure P on Ω is that induced by the ratios of the stock values. More explicitly, we write S for S^1 for the rest of this section to simplify the notation, and set $R_t = S_t/S_{t-1}$ for $t > 0$. For $\omega = (\omega_1, \omega_2, \ldots, \omega_T)$ in Ω, define

$$P(\{\omega\}) = P(R_t = \omega_t, t = 1, 2, \ldots, T). \tag{2.13}$$

For any probability measure Q on $(\Omega, \mathcal{F})$, the relation $E_Q(\overline{S}_t | \mathcal{F}_{t-1}) = \overline{S}_{t-1}$ is equivalent to

$$E_Q(R_t | \mathcal{F}_{t-1}) = 1 + r,$$

since $\beta_t/\beta_{t-1} = 1 + r$. Hence if Q is an equivalent martingale measure for S it follows that $E_Q(R_t) = 1 + r$. On the other hand, R_t only takes the values $1 + a$ and $1 + b$; hence its average value can equal $1 + r$ only if $a < r < b$. We have proved:

Lemma 2.5.1. *For the binomial model to have an EMM we must have* $a < r < b$.

When the binomial model is viable, there is a *unique* equivalent martingale measure Q for S. We construct this measure by showing that:

Lemma 2.5.2. $\overline{S}$ *is a Q-martingale if and only if the random variables* (R_t) *are i.i.d., with* $Q(R_1 = 1 + b) = q$ *and* $Q(R_1 = 1 + a) = 1 - q$, *where* $q = (r - a)/(b - a)$.

Proof. To see this, note that, under independence, the (R_t) will satisfy

$$E_Q(R_t | \mathcal{F}_{t-1}) = E_Q(R_t) = q(1 + b) + (1 - q)(1 + a)$$
$$= q(b - a) + 1 + a = 1 + r.$$

Hence by our earlier discussion $\overline{S}$ is a Q-martingale.

Conversely, if $E_Q(R_t|\mathcal{F}_{t-1}) = 1 + r$, then, since R_t takes only the values $1 + a$ and $1 + b$, we have:

$$(1 + a)Q(\{R_t = 1 + a\}|\mathcal{F}_{t-1}) + (1 + b)Q(\{R_t = 1 + b\}|\mathcal{F}_{t-1}) = 1 + r,$$

while $Q(\{R_t = 1 + a\}|\mathcal{F}_{t-1}) + Q(\{R_t = 1 + b\}|\mathcal{F}_{t-1}) = 1$.

Letting $q = Q(\{R_t = 1 + b\}|\mathcal{F}_{t-1})$ we obtain:

$$(1 + a)(1 - q) + (1 + b)q = 1 + r,$$

hence $q = (r - a)/(b - a)$. The independence of the R_t follows by induction on $t > 0$, since for $\omega \in \Omega$, $\omega = (\omega_1, \omega_2, \dots, \omega_T)$ we see inductively that

$$Q(R_1 = \omega_1, R_2 = \omega_2, \dots, R_t = \omega_t) = \prod_{i=1}^{t} q_i,$$

where $q_i = q$ when $\omega_i = 1 + b$, and equals $1 - q$ when $\omega_i = 1 + a$. Thus the (R_t) are i.i.d. as claimed.   □

Remark 2.5.3. Note that $q \in (0, 1)$ if and only if $a < r < b$. Thus a viable binomial market model admits a *unique* equivalent martingale measure, given by Q as in the preceding.

The CCR Pricing Formula

The CRR pricing formula, obtained in Chapter 1 by an explicit hedging argument, can now be deduced from our general martingale formulation by calculating the Q-expectation of a European call option on the stock. More generally, the value of the call $C_T = (S_T - K)^+$ at time $t \in \mathbb{T}$ is given by (2.11); that is,

$$V_t(C_T) = \beta_t^{-1} E_Q(\beta_T C_T|\mathcal{F}_t).$$

Since $S_T = S_t \prod_{u=t+1}^{T} R_u$ (by definition of the (R_u)), we can calculate this expectation quite simply, as S_t is $\mathcal{F}_t$-measurable, and each R_u ($u > t$) is independent of $\mathcal{F}_t$:

$$V_t(C_T) = \beta_t^{-1} \beta_T E_Q((S_t \prod_{u=t+1}^{T} R_u - K)^+|\mathcal{F}_t)$$

$$= (1 + r)^{t-T} E_Q((S_t \prod_{u=t+1}^{T} R_u - K)^+|\mathcal{F}_t) = v(t, S_t), \quad (2.14)$$

where $v(t, x) = (1 + r)^{t-T} E_Q((x \prod_{u=t+1}^{T} R_u - K)^+)$

$$= (1 + r)^{-(T-t)} \sum_{u=0}^{T-t} \frac{(T - t)!}{u!(T - t - u)!} q^u (1 - q)^{T-t-u}$$

$$\times (x(1 + b)^u (1 + a)^{T-t-u} - K)^+.$$

In particular, the price at time 0 of the European call option $X = (S_T - K)^+$
is given by

$$
\begin{aligned}
\pi(X) &= v(0, S_0) \\
&= (1+r)^{-T} \sum_{u=A}^{T} \left[\frac{T!}{u!(T-u)!} q^u (1-q)^{T-u} \right. \\
&\qquad \left. \times (S_0(1+b)^u(1+a)^{T-u} - K) \right],
\end{aligned}
\tag{2.15}
$$

where A is the first integer k for which $S_0(1+b)^k(1+a)^{T+k} > K$. We have
rederived the CRR option pricing formula for the European call.

Exercise 2.5.4. Show that for the replicating strategy $\theta = (\theta^0, \theta^1)$ which
duplicates the value process of the European call X the stock portfolio θ^1
can be described in terms of the differences of the value function as follows.
$\theta_t^1 = \theta(t, S_{t-1})$, where

$$
\theta(t, x) = \frac{v(t, x(1+b)) - v(t, x(1+a))}{x(b-a)}.
$$

Exercise 2.5.5. Derive the call–put parity relation (see Chapter 1) by describing the values of the contingent claims involved as expectations relative
to Q.

2.6   From CRR to Black–Scholes

The Approximating Binomial Models

The binomial model contains all the information necessary to deduce the
famous Black–Scholes formula for the price of a European call option in a
continuous-time market driven by Brownian motion. A detailed discussion
of the underlying mathematics is deferred until Chapter 6, but we indicate
now how the 'random walks' performed by the binomial steps lead to Brownian motion as a limiting process when the step size decreases continually,
and how the CRR formula has a continuous-time Black–Scholes limit.
    Consider a price process $S = (S_t)$ defined on a finite time interval $[0, T]$
on the real line, and consider a European call with payoff function $f_T = (S_T - K)^+$ on this stock. We transform this into a discrete-time problem by
considering a binomial stock price that begins at S_0 and changes at a finite
number N of discrete time points in $(0, T]$, chosen a fixed distance $h = T/N$
apart; that is, we create the time set $\mathbb{T} = \{0, h, 2h, \dots, Nh\} \subset [0, T]$, and
consider the price C_0^N of a European call option in this setting. This price is
given by the expectation (2.11), specialised to the present case as in (2.15);

that is,

$$V_0^N = \beta_N E_Q((S_0 \prod_{n=1}^{N} R_n^N - K)^+)$$

$$= (1+R)^{-N} E_Q((S_0 \prod_{n=1}^{N} R_n^N - K)^+), \qquad (2.16)$$

where $R_n^N = S_{nh}^N / S_{(n-1)h}^N$ takes values of the form $(1+b)$ and $(1+a)$ for $n \geq 1$, where S^N is the Nth binomial stock price process and where a, b, and the 'riskless interest rate' R over $[0, h]$ must still be chosen. The latter will determine the measure Q, since, by Lemma 2.5.2, under Q the R_n^N are i.i.d. and

$$Q(R_1^N = 1 + b) = q = \frac{R-a}{b-a}.$$

Now fix $r \geq 0$ and let $R = rT/N$, so that the discrete-time riskless interest rate R over $[0, h]$ tends to zero as $N \to \infty$, and r acts as a constant 'instantaneous' interest rate at points of $[0, T]$. Note that $e^{rT} = \lim_{N \to \infty}(1+R)^N$.

For fixed $\sigma > 0$ (which will represent the volatility per unit of time of our stock price in continuous time) and fixed N we can now choose the parameters a and b in the Nth approximating binomial price process S^N by setting:

$$\log(\frac{1+b}{1+R}) = \sigma\sqrt{\frac{T}{N}} = \sigma\sqrt{h}, \qquad \log(\frac{1+a}{1+R}) = -\sqrt{\frac{T}{N}} = -\sigma\sqrt{h}. \quad (2.17)$$

Write $S_{nh}^{0,N} = (1+R)^n$ ($n \leq N$) for the associated bond price. The ratios of the discounted stock price process take the form $e^{\sigma \xi_n}$, where the i.i.d. random variables (ξ_n) take the values $\pm\sqrt{h}$, with probabilities q and $1-q$, respectively.

Convergence in Distribution

A simple form of the Central Limit Theorem (CLT, cf. [258]) ensures that, given an i.i.d. sequence $(Y_k^N)_{k \leq N}$ of random variables with mean μ_N such that $(N\mu_N)_N$ converges to a finite μ as $N \to \infty$, and whose variance has the form $\sigma^2/N + o(1/N)$, the sums $Z_N = \sum_{k=1}^{N} Y_k^N$ will converge in distribution to an $N(\mu, \sigma^2)$-distributed random variable Z.

(We recall some notation: $a_n \sim o(1/n)$ means that na_n tends to 0, while $b_n \sim O(1/n)$ means that nb_n converges to a non-zero limit as $n \to \infty$.)

This important result can be proved by considering the characteristic functions, and approximating the exponential by its first three terms, since the Y^N are i.i.d. and have second moment also of the form $(\sigma^2/N) +$

$o(1/N)$:

$$\phi_N(t) = E(\exp\{iuZ_N\}) = [E(\exp\{iuY_1^N\})]^N = [1 + \frac{it\mu}{N} - \frac{\sigma^2 t^2}{2N} + o(\frac{1}{N})]^N$$

which converges to $\exp(it\mu - \frac{1}{2}\sigma^2 t^2)$. But since this is the characteristic function of the normal law $N(\mu, \sigma^2)$ the result follows from the Lévy continuity theorem for characteristic functions (Fourier transforms). See [258], 18.1 for definitions and details.

To apply this to the price V_0^N in (2.16), we bring the factor $(1+R)^{-N} = (1+(rT/N))^{-N}$ into the expectation, and set

$$Y_n^N = \log(\frac{R_n^N}{1+R}), \qquad Z_N = \sum_{n=1}^{N} Y_n^N,$$

so that

$$(1 + R)^{-N} \prod_{n=1}^{N} R_n^N = (1+R)^{-N}(1+R)^N \exp(\sum_{n=1}^{N} Y_n^N) = e^{Z_N}.$$

Hence V_0^N takes the form:

$$V_0^N = E_Q[S_0 e^{Z_N} - (1 + \tfrac{rT}{N})^{-N}K]^+.$$

But R_n^N takes values $(1+b)$ and $(1+a)$, so Y_n^N takes values $\pm(\sigma\sqrt{T}/\sqrt{N}) = \pm\sigma\sqrt{h}$, hence its second moment is $\sigma^2 T/N$, while its mean μ_N equals

$$\sigma\sqrt{h}q - \sigma\sqrt{h}(1 - q) = (2q - 1)\sigma\sqrt{h} = \frac{2q - 1}{\sqrt{N}}\sigma\sqrt{T}.$$

To apply the CLT we need to show that $2q - 1$ is of order $1/\sqrt{N}$. This now follows directly from our choices for a, b, and R: note that $2q - 1 = q - (1-q)$, and both these probabilities converge to $\frac{1}{2}$ as $N \to \infty$. We need to estimate the rate at which this occurs. This is most quickly seen by computing

$$
\begin{aligned}
2q - 1 &= 1 - 2(1 - q) = 1 - 2(\frac{b - R}{b - a}) \\
&= 1 - 2\frac{(1 + R)e^{-\sigma\sqrt{h}} - 1 - R}{(1 + R)(e^{\sigma\sqrt{h}} - e^{-\sigma\sqrt{h}})} = 1 - 2(\frac{e^{-\sigma\sqrt{h}} - 1}{e^{\sigma\sqrt{h}} - e^{-\sigma\sqrt{h}}}) \\
&= 1 - \frac{[e^{-\sigma\sqrt{h}} - 1]}{\sinh(e^{\sigma\sqrt{h}})}.
\end{aligned}
$$

Expanding into Taylor series we find easily that $2q - 1 = -\frac{1}{2}\sigma\sqrt{(T/N)} + O(1/N)$, so that $N\mu_N \to -\frac{1}{2}\sigma^2 T$ as $N \to \infty$. Therefore the application of the CLT ensures as previously that $Z_N \to Z$ in distribution, and thus, because $(1 + (rT/N))^{-N} \to e^{-rT}$ also, V_0^N converges to

$$E(S_0 e^Z - e^{-rT} K)^+,$$

where the expectation is taken with respect to the distribution of $Z \sim N(-\frac{1}{2}\sigma^2 T, \sigma^2 T)$.

The Black–Scholes formula

Standardising Z, we see that the random variable $X = (1/\sigma\sqrt{T})(Z + \frac{1}{2}\sigma^2 T) \sim N(0, 1)$; that is, $Z = \sigma\sqrt{T} X - 1/2\sigma^2 T$, so that the limiting value of V_0^N is found by evaluating the integral

$$\int_{-\infty}^{\infty} [(S_0 e^{-(1/2)\sigma^2 T + \sigma\sqrt{T} x} - e^{-rT} K)^+] \frac{e^{-(1/2)x^2}}{\sqrt{2\pi}} \, dx.$$

To do this, observe that the integrand is non-zero only when $\sigma\sqrt{T} x - \frac{1}{2}\sigma^2 T > \log(K/S_0) - rT$, that is, on the interval (γ, ∞), where $\gamma = \left(\log(K/S_0) + (\frac{1}{2}\sigma^2 - r)T\right)/\sigma\sqrt{T}$. Thus the option price for the limiting pricing model reduces to

$$
\begin{aligned}
V_0 &= S_0 \int_\gamma^\infty e^{-(\sigma^2 T)/2} e^{\sigma\sqrt{T} x - x^2/2} \frac{dx}{\sqrt{2\pi}} \quad - K e^{-rT}(1 - \Phi(\gamma)) \\
&= S_0 \int_\gamma^\infty e^{-1/2(x - \sigma\sqrt{T})^2} \frac{dx}{\sqrt{2\pi}} \quad - K e^{-rT}(1 - \Phi(\gamma)) \\
&= S_0(1 - \Phi(\gamma - \sigma\sqrt{T})) - K e^{-rT}(1 - \Phi(\gamma)).
\end{aligned}
$$

(Here Φ denotes the cumulative normal distribution function.)

Note now that

$$\gamma - \sigma\sqrt{T} = \frac{\log(K/S_0) - (r + \frac{1}{2}\sigma^2)T}{\sigma\sqrt{T}}.$$

The symmetry of Φ gives $1 - \Phi(\gamma) = \Phi(-\gamma) = \Phi(d_-)$, and $1 - \Phi(\gamma - \sigma\sqrt{T}) = \Phi(d_+)$, where

$$d_\pm = \frac{\log(S_0/K) + (r \pm \frac{1}{2}\sigma^2)T}{\sigma\sqrt{T}} \tag{2.18}$$

Thus we have derived the familiar *Black–Scholes formula*, in which the time 0 price of the call option $f_T = (S_T - K)^+$ is given by

$$V_0(C) = V_0 = S_0 \Phi(d_+) - e^{-rT} K \Phi(d_-). \tag{2.19}$$

By replacing T by $T - t$ and S_0 by S_t we can read off the value process V_t for the option similarly; in effect this treats the option as a contract written at time t with time to expiry $T - t$:

$$V_t(C) = S_t \Phi(d_{t+}) - e^{-r(T-t)} K \Phi(d_{t-}), \qquad (2.20)$$

where $d_{t\pm} = \left(\log(S_t/K) + (r \pm \frac{1}{2}\sigma^2)(T - t)\right)/\sigma\sqrt{T - t}$.

The preceding derivation has not required us to study the dynamics of the 'limit stock price' S; it is shown in Chapter 7 that this takes the form

$$dS_t = S_t \mu dt + \sigma S_t dW_t, \qquad (2.21)$$

where W is a Brownian motion. The stochastic calculus necessary for the solution of such stochastic differential equations is developed in Chapter 6. However, we can already note one remarkable property of the Black-Scholes formula: it does not involve the mean return μ of the stock, but depends on the riskless interest rate r and the volatility σ. The mathematical reason for this lies in the change to a risk-neutral measure (which underlies the martingale pricing techniques described in this chapter), which eliminates the drift term from the dynamics.

Dependence of the Option Price on the Parameters

Write $C_t = V_t(C)$ for the Black–Scholes value process of the call option. By call–put parity applied to (2.20), the European put option with the same parameters in the Black–Scholes pricing model is given by

$$P_t = Ke^{-r(T-t)} \Phi(-d_{t-}) - S_t \Phi(d_{t+}).$$

We examine the behaviour of the prices C_t at extreme values of the parameters. (The reader may consider the put prices P_t similarly.)

Recall that

$$C_t = S_t \Phi(d_{t+}) - e^{-r(T-t)} K \Phi(d_{t-}),$$

where $d_\pm$ is given by (2.18); that is,

$$d_\pm = \frac{\log(S_0/K) + (r \pm \frac{1}{2}\sigma^2)T}{\sigma\sqrt{T}}.$$

When S_t increases, $d_{t\pm}$ grows indefinitely, so that $\Phi(d_{t\pm})$ tends to 1, and so C_t has limiting value $S_t - Ke^{-r(T-t)}$. In effect, the option becomes a forward contract with delivery price K, since it is 'certain' to be exercised at time T. Similar behaviour is observed when the volatility σ shrinks to 0, since again $d_{t\pm}$ become infinite, and the riskless stock behaves like a bond (or money in the bank).

When $t \to T$ (i.e., the time to expiry decreases to 0), and $S_t > K$, then $d_{t\pm}$ becomes $+\infty$ and $e^{-r(T-t)} \to 1$, so that C_t tends to $S_t - K$. On the other hand, if $S_t < K$, $\log(S_t/K) < 0$ so that $d_{t\pm} = -\infty$ and $C_t \to 0$. Thus, as expected, $C_t \to (S_T - K)^+$ when $t \to T$.

Remark 2.6.1. Note finally that there is a natural 'replicating strategy' given by (2.20), since this value process is expressed as a linear combination of units of stocks S_t and bonds S_t^0 with $S_0^0 = 1$ and $S_t^0 = \beta_t^{-1} S_0^0 = e^{rt}$. writing the value process $V_t = \theta_t \cdot S_t$ (where by abuse of notation $S = (S^0, S)$) we obtain:

$$\theta_t^0 = -Ke^{-rT}\Phi(d_{t-}), \qquad \theta_t^1 = \Phi(d_{t+}). \tag{2.22}$$

3

The Fundamental Theorem
of Asset Pricing

We saw in the previous chapter that the existence of a probability measure $Q \sim P$ under which the (discounted) stock price process is a martingale is sufficient to ensure that the market model is viable; that is, it contains no arbitrage opportunities. We now address the converse: whether for every viable model one can construct an equivalent martingale measure for S, so that the price of a contingent claim can be found as an expectation relative to Q.

3.1 The Separating Hyperplane Theorem in $\mathbb{R}^n$

To deal with the preceding question fairly fully, while avoiding difficult technical issues, we assume throughout this chapter (unless specifically indicated otherwise) that we are working with a *finite market model*, so each σ-field $\mathcal{F}_t$ is generated by a finite partition $\mathcal{P}_t$ of Ω. This restriction avoids recourse to the technically advanced functional-analytic arguments that are needed for the general case, although the basic ideas are almost all present in the special case we consider. In particular, we use the following standard separation theorem for compact convex sets in $\mathbb{R}^n$.

Theorem 3.1.1 (Separating Hyperplane Theorem). *Let L be a linear subspace of $\mathbb{R}^n$ and let K be a compact convex subset in $\mathbb{R}^n$, disjoint from L. Then we can separate L and K strictly by a hyperplane containing L; that is, there exists a (bounded) linear functional $\phi : \mathbb{R}^n \to \mathbb{R}$ such that $\phi(x) = 0$ for all $x \in L$ but $\phi(x) > 0$ for all $x \in K$.*

Proof. First, let C be any closed convex subset of $\mathbb{R}^n$ that does not contain the zero vector. We show that there is a linear functional ϕ on $\mathbb{R}^n$ whose kernel $\{x \in \mathbb{R}^n : \phi(x) = 0\}$ does not meet C. Denote by $B = B(0, r)$ the closed ball of radius r centred at the origin in $\mathbb{R}^n$ and choose $r > 0$ so that B intersects C. Then $B \cap C$ is non-empty and closed and bounded, hence compact, so that the continuous map $x \mapsto |x|$ attains its infimum over $B \cap C$ at some $z \in B \cap C$. (Here $|x|$ denotes the Euclidean norm of x in $\mathbb{R}^n$.) Since $|x| > r$ when $x \notin B$, it is clear that $|x| \geq |z|$ for all $x \in C$. In particular, since C is convex, $y = \lambda x + (1 - \lambda)z$ is in C whenever $x \in C$ and $0 \leq \lambda \leq 1$. So $|y| \geq |z|$, in other words,

$$|\lambda x + (1 - \lambda)z|^2 \geq |z|^2.$$

Multiplying out both sides of this inequality, and writing $a \cdot b$ for the scalar product in $\mathbb{R}^n$ we obtain

$$\lambda^2 x \cdot x + 2\lambda(1 - \lambda)x \cdot z + (1 - \lambda)^2 z \cdot z \geq z \cdot z$$

which simplifies at once to

$$2(1 - \lambda)x \cdot z - 2z \cdot z + \lambda(x \cdot x + z \cdot z) \geq 0.$$

This holds for every $\lambda \in [0, 1]$. Letting $\lambda \to 0$ we obtain

$$x.z \geq z \cdot z = |z|^2 > 0.$$

Defining $\phi(x) = x.z$ we have found a linear functional such that $\phi(x)$ is bounded below on C by the positive number $|z|^2$. (ϕ is also bounded above as any linear functional on $\mathbb{R}^n$ is bounded.)

Now let K be a compact convex set disjoint from the subspace L. Define $C = K - L = \{x \in \mathbb{R}^n : x = k - l$ for some $k \in K, l \in L\}$. Then C is convex, since K and L are, and C is closed; to see this, note that if $x_n = k_n - l_n$ converges to some $x \in \mathbb{R}^n$, then, as K is compact, (k_n) has a subsequence converging to some $k \in K$. Thus $x_{n_r} = k_{n_r} - l_{n_r} \to x$ as $r \to \infty$ and $k_{n_r} \to k$, so that $l_{n_r} = k_{n_r} - x_{n_r} \to k - x$ and hence $l = k - x$ belongs to L, since L is closed. But then $x = k - l \in C$, so that C is closed.

As C does not contain the origin, we can therefore apply the first part of the proof to C, to obtain a bounded linear functional ϕ on $\mathbb{R}^n$ such that $\phi(x) \geq |z|^2 > 0$ for z as previously. In other words, writing $x = k - l$, we have $\phi(k) - \phi(l) \geq |z|^2 > 0$. This must hold for all $x \in C$. Fix k and replace l by λl for arbitrary positive λ if $\phi(l) \geq 0$ or by λl for arbitrary negative λ if $\phi(l) < 0$. The vectors λl belong to L, as L is a linear space; since ϕ is bounded, we must have $\phi(l) = 0$; that is, L is a subspace of the hyperplane $\ker\phi = \{x : \phi(x) = 0\}$, while $\phi(K)$ is bounded below by $|z|^2 > 0$. This proves the theorem. $\square$

3.2 Construction of Martingale Measures

The preceding separation theorem applies to sets in $\mathbb{R}^n$. We can apply it to $\mathbb{R}^\Omega$, the space of all functions $\Omega \mapsto \mathbb{R}$, by identifying this space with $\mathbb{R}^n$ for a finite n, in view of the assumption that the σ-field $\mathcal{F}$ is finitely generated: this means that any $\mathcal{F}$-measurable real function on Ω takes only finitely many distinct values, so that n is simply the number of cells in the partition $\mathcal{P}$ that generates $\mathcal{F}$. In other words, we assume that $\Omega = D_1 \cup D_2 \cup \ldots \cup D_n$ with $D_i \cap D_j = \emptyset$ for $i \neq j$, and $P(D_i) = p_i > 0$ for $i \leq n$. Without loss we can take the (D_i) as atoms or 'points' ω_i of Ω, and we do so in the following.

With appropriate caution several of the next results hold without this restriction; we discuss the possible extensions briefly in Section 3.5.

Recall first (Definition 2.2.2) that the market model is *viable* if it contains no arbitrage opportunities, that is, if, whenever a strategy $\theta \in \Theta_a$ has initial value $V_0(\theta) = 0$, and final value $V_T(\theta) \geq 0$ P a.s., then $V_T(\theta) = 0$ P a.s.

Denote by C the *cone* (this just means that C is closed under vector addition and multiplication by non-negative scalars) in $\mathbb{R}^n$ of vectors with all non-negative and at least one strictly positive coordinate; that is,

$$C = \{Y \in \mathbb{R}^n : Y_i \geq 0 \ (i = 1, 2, \ldots, n), \exists i \ s.t. Y_i > 0\}.$$

For simplicity we identify the cells $(D_i)_{i \leq n}$ of the partition $\mathcal{P}$ with the points $(\omega_i)_{i \leq n}$ of Ω, so that for fixed $t \in \mathbb{T}$, the values $\{V_t(\theta)(\omega) : \omega \in \Omega\}$ and the gains $\{G_t(\theta)(\omega) : \omega \in \Omega\}$ of any trading strategy θ can be regarded as vectors in $\mathbb{R}^n$.

Then the no arbitrage assumption means that for every admissible strategy $\theta \in \Theta_a$ we have:

$$\text{if } V_0(\theta) = 0 \quad \text{then} \quad \bar{V}_T(\theta) = \bar{G}_T(\theta) \notin C.$$

Thus the discounted gains process $\bar{G}(\theta)$ for such a strategy θ cannot have a final value contained in C.

Recall from equation (2.9) that a self-financing strategy $\theta = (\theta^0, \theta^1, \ldots, \theta^d)$ is completely determined by the stock holdings $\hat{\theta} = (\theta^1, \ldots, \theta^d)$. Thus, given a predictable $\mathbb{R}^d$-valued process $\hat{\theta} = (\theta^1, \ldots, \theta^d)$, there is a unique predictable $\mathbb{R}^{d+1}$-valued process θ^0 such that the augmented process $\theta = (\theta^0, \theta^1, \ldots, \theta^d)$ has initial value $V_0(\theta) = 0$ and is self-financing. By a minor abuse of notation we define the discounted gains process associated with $\hat{\theta}$ as

$$\bar{G}_t(\hat{\theta}) = \sum_{u=1}^{t} \theta_u \cdot \Delta \bar{S}_u = \sum_{u=1}^{t} \left(\sum_{i=1}^{d} \theta_u^i \Delta \bar{S}_u^i \right)$$

for $t = 1, 2, \ldots, T$. Suppose that $\bar{G}_T(\hat{\theta}) \in C$. Then

$$V_T(\theta) = \beta_T^{-1} \bar{V}_T(\theta) = \beta_T^{-1}(V_0(\theta) + \bar{G}_T(\theta)) = \beta_T^{-1} \bar{G}_T(\hat{\theta})$$

is non-negative and is strictly positive with positive probability. So θ is a weak arbitrage, which contradicts the viability of the model. We have proved:

Lemma 3.2.1. *If the market model is viable, the discounted gains process associated with any predictable $\mathbb{R}^d$-valued process $\hat{\theta}$ cannot belong to the cone C.*

Since $\bar{G}_T(\hat{\theta})$ is a sum of scalar products $\theta_t \cdot \Delta \bar{S}_t$ in $\mathbb{R}^n$, and since any linear functional on $\mathbb{R}^n$ takes the form $x \mapsto x \cdot y$ for some $y \in \mathbb{R}^n$, the relevance of the Separation Theorem to these questions is apparent in the proof of the main result in this chapter.

Theorem 3.2.2. *A finite market model is viable if and only if there exists an equivalent martingale measure (EMM) for S.*

Proof. Since we have already shown (in Chapter 2) that the existence of an EMM ensures viability of the model, we need only prove the converse.

Suppose therefore the market model is viable. We need to construct a measure $Q \sim P$ under which the price processes are martingales relative to the filtration $\mathbb{F}$. Recall that C is the convex cone of all real random variables ϕ on $(\Omega, \mathcal{F})$ such that $\phi(\omega) \geq 0$ a.s. and $\phi(\omega_i) > 0$ for at least one $\omega_i \in \Omega = \{\omega_1, \omega_2, \dots, \omega_n\}$ (and by assumption $p_i = P(\{\omega_i\}) > 0$). We have shown that in a viable market we must have $G_T(\hat{\theta}) \notin C$ for all predictable $\mathbb{R}^d$-valued processes $\hat{\theta}$. On the other hand, the set defined by such gains processes, $L = \{G_T(\hat{\theta}) : \hat{\theta} = (\theta^1, \theta^2, \dots, \theta^d)$, with θ^i predictable for $i = 1, 2, \dots, d\}$, is a linear subspace of the vector space of all $\mathcal{F}$-measurable real-valued functions on Ω.

Since L does not meet C, we can separate L and the compact convex subset $K = \{X \in C : E_P(X) = 1\}$ of C by a linear functional f on $\mathbb{R}^n$ which is strictly positive on K and 0 on L. The linear functional has a representation in the form $f(x) = (x, q) = \sum_{i=1}^{n} x_i q_i$ for a unique vector $q = (q_i)$ in $\mathbb{R}^n$. Taking the vectors $\xi_i = (0, \dots, 0, 1/p_i, 0, \dots, 0)$ in turn, we see that $E_P(\xi_i) = p_i/p_i = 1$, so that $\xi_i \in K$, and hence $f(\xi_i) = q_i/p_i > 0$. Thus $q_i > 0$ for all $i \leq n$.

Now define a new linear functional $g = f/\alpha$, where $\alpha = \sum_{i=1}^{n} q_i > 0$. This is implemented by the vector p^* with $p_i^* = q_i/\alpha > 0$, so that $\sum_{i=1}^{n} p_i^* = 1$. Hence the vector p^* induces a probability measure P^* on $\Omega = \{\omega_1, \dots, \omega_n\}$ by setting $P^*(\{\omega_i\}) = p_i^* > 0$, so that $P^* \sim P$. Let E^* denote expectation relative to P^*. Since $g(x) = (1/\alpha)f(x) = 0$ for all $x \in L$ we have $E^*(\bar{G}_T(\hat{\theta})) = 0$ for each vector $\hat{\theta}$ of stock holdings creating a self-financing strategy θ with $V_0(\theta) = 0$. As $\bar{V}_T(\theta) = V_0(\theta) + \bar{G}_T(\theta)$, this implies $E^*(\bar{V}_T(\theta)) = 0$ for such θ. But by (2.9) we can generate such θ from any n-dimensional predictable process, in particular from $(0, \dots, 0, \theta^i, 0, \dots, 0)$, where the predictable real-valued process θ^i is given for $i \leq n$. Thus

$$E^*(\sum_{t=1}^{T} \theta_t^i \Delta \bar{S}_t^i) = 0$$

holds for every bounded predictable process θ^i, $i = 1, 2, \ldots, T$. By Theorem 2.3.4 this implies that each S^i is a martingale under P^*; hence P^* is the desired EMM for the price process S.   □

3.3   A Local Form of the 'No Arbitrage' Condition

The geometric origin of the preceding result is clear from the essential use that was made of the Separation Theorem. In this form it is specific to finite market models, although it can be extended in various forms to infinite-dimensional situations, where it follows from the Hahn–Banach Theorem in functional analysis (see [75], [121]).

A more directly geometric formulation of Theorem 3.2.2 can be based on the 'local' equivalent of the no arbitrage condition. In fact, although the definition of arbitrage involves only the initial and final values of a strategy, we show that the no arbitrage condition is an assumption about the *pathwise* behaviour of the value process. Although this discussion is somewhat detailed, it is included here for its value in providing an intuitive grasp of the ideas that underlie the more abstract proof of Theorem 3.2.2, and in giving a step-by step construction of the equivalent martingale measure. While our present discussion (which comes from [250]) remains restricted to the case where $\mathcal{F}$ is finitely generated, the ideas presented here prove useful when we briefly discuss the general case in Section 3.5.

The One-Stock Case

The idea behind the construction lies in the following simple observation. Consider a market model with a single bond and stock (i.e., $d = 1$) and assume that the bond price $S^0 \equiv 1$ for all trading dates. In particular, for any self-financing strategy $\theta = (\theta^0, \theta^1)$, the value process $V_t(\theta)$ has increments $\Delta V_t = \theta_t^1 \Delta S_t^1$, as $\Delta S_t^0 = 0$. These increments will be 'concentrated' to one side of the origin precisely when the same is true for the price increments ΔS_t^1.

Now suppose we *know* at some time $(t - 1) \in \mathbb{T}$ that the stock price S^1 will not decrease in the time interval $[t-1, t]$; that is, for some partition set $A \in \mathcal{P}_{t-1}$ we have $P(\{\Delta S_t^1 \geq 0\}|A) = 1$. Then we can buy stock S^1 at time $t - 1$, sell it again at time t, and invest the profit ΔS_t^1 in the riskless bond S^0 until the time horizon T. To prevent this arbitrage opportunity we need to have $P(\{\Delta S_t^1 = 0\}|A) = 1$; that is, S^1 (and hence also the value process

$V(\theta)$ associated with any admisssible strategy θ) is a 'one-step martingale' in the time interval $[t-1, t]$.

This idea can be extended to models with d stocks and hyperplanes in $\mathbb{R}^{d+1}$: we have

$$\Delta V_t(\theta) = \theta_t \cdot \Delta S_t = \sum_{k=1}^{d} \theta_t^k \Delta S_t^k,$$

so it is clear that Condition (i) in Proposition 3.3.1 expresses the fact that, along each sample path of the price process S, the support of the conditional distribution of the vector random variable ΔS_t, given $A \in \mathcal{P}_t$, cannot be wholly concentrated only on one 'side' of any hyperplane in $\mathbb{R}^{d+1}$.

Assume for the remainder of this section that $S_t^0 \equiv 1$ for all $t \in \mathbb{T}$.

Proposition 3.3.1. *If the finite market model* $S = (S^0, S^1, \ldots, S^d)$ *is viable, then, for all* $\theta \in \Theta$, $t > 0$, *and* $A \in \mathcal{P}_{t-1}$, *and with* $V_t = V_t(\theta)$, *the following hold.*

(i) $P(\Delta V_t \geq 0 | A) = 1$ *implies* $P(\Delta V_t = 0 | A) = 1$,

(ii) $P(\Delta V_t \leq 0 | A) = 1$ *implies* $P(\Delta V_t = 0 | A) = 1$.

Proof. Fix $t > 0$ and $\theta \in \Theta$. Suppose that $P(\Delta V_t \geq 0 | A) = 1$ for some $A \in \mathcal{P}_{t-1}$. We define ψ with $\psi_0 = 0$ as follows for $s > 0$,

for $\omega \notin A$ set $\psi_s(\omega) = 0$ for all $s = 1, 2, \ldots, T$;
for $\omega \in A$ set $\psi_s(\omega) = 0$ when $0 < s < t$; and
at time t set

$$\psi_t(\omega) = (\theta_t^0(\omega) - V_{t-1}(\theta)(\omega), \theta_t^1(\omega), \theta_t^2(\omega), \ldots, \theta_t^d(\omega))',$$

and for all $s > t$ set

$$\psi_s(\omega) = (V_t(\theta)(\omega), 0, 0, \ldots, 0)'.$$

(Note the similarity with the arbitrage constructed in Section 2.2.)

Under the strategy ψ we start with no holdings at time 0, and trade only from time t onwards, and then only if $\omega \in A$ (which we know by time $t-1$). In that case, we elect to follow the strategy θ in respect to stocks, and borrow an amount equal $(V_{t-1}(\theta) - \theta_0)$ in order to deal in stocks at $(t-1)$-prices, using the strategy θ for our stock holdings. For ω in A this is guaranteed to increase total wealth. At times $s > t$ we then maintain all wealth (i.e., our profits from these transactions) in the bond.

The strategy ψ is obviously predictable. To see that it is self-financing, we need only consider $\omega \in A$. Then we have:

$$
\begin{aligned}
(\Delta \psi_t) \cdot S_{t-1} &= (\theta_t^0 - V_{t-1}(\theta)) S_{t-1}^0 + \sum_{i=1}^{d} \theta_t^i S_{t-1}^i \\
&= \theta_t \cdot S_{t-1} - V_{t-1}(\theta) = \theta_{t-1} \cdot S_{t-1} - V_{t-1}(\theta) = 0
\end{aligned}
$$

since $S^0 \equiv 1$ and θ is self-financing. Hence ψ is also self-financing.

With this strategy we certainly obtain $V_T(\psi) \geq 0$. in fact, for $u \geq t$ we have $V_u(\psi) = \psi_t \cdot S_t = \Delta V_t(\psi) = \Delta V_t(\theta) \geq 0$ on A and 0 off A. Hence ψ defines a self-financing strategy with initial value 0 and $V_T(\psi) \geq 0$. If there is no arbitrage we must, therefore, conclude that $V_T(\psi) = 0$. Since $V_T(\psi) = 0$ off A and $V_T(\psi) = \Delta V_t(\theta)$ on A, this is equivalent to

$$0 = P(V_T(\psi) > 0) = P(\{V_T(\psi) > 0\} \cap A) = P(\{\Delta V_T(\theta) > 0\}|A)P(A),$$

that is, $P(\Delta V_t = 0|A) = 1$. This proves the first assertion. The proof of the second part is similar. □

The preceding formulation can be used to establish a further equivalent form of market model viability. In the following we write $\hat{S}$ for the $\mathbb{R}^d$-valued process obtained by deleting the 0th component of S, that is, where $S = (1, \hat{S})$.

Note. For the statement and proof of the next proposition we do *not* need the assumption that the filtration $\mathbb{F} = (\mathcal{F}_t)_{t \in \mathbb{T}}$ is finitely generated; it is valid in an arbitrary probability space $(\Omega, \mathcal{F}, P)$. It states, in essence, the 'obvious' fact that if there is an arbitrage opportunity for the model defined on the time set $\mathbb{T} = \{0, 1, 2, \ldots, T\}$, then there is an arbitrage opportunity in at least one of the single-period markets $[t - 1, t)$.

Proposition 3.3.2. *Let $(\Omega, \mathcal{F}, P, \mathbb{T}, \mathbb{F}, S)$ be an arbitrary discrete market model, where $(\Omega, \mathcal{F}, P)$ is a probability space, $\mathbb{T} = \{0, 1, 2, \ldots, T\}$ is a discrete time set, $\mathbb{F} = (\mathcal{F}_t)_{t \in \mathbb{T}}$ is a complete filtration, and $S = (S^i)_{i=0,1,2,\ldots,d}$ is a price process, as defined in Section 2.1.*

The following are equivalent.

(i) *The model allows an arbitrage opportunity.*

(ii) *For some $t = 1, 2, \ldots, T$ there is an $\mathcal{F}_{t-1}$-measurable $\phi : \Omega \mapsto \mathbb{R}^{d+1}$ such that $\phi \cdot \Delta S_t \geq 0$ and $P(\phi \cdot \Delta S_t > 0) > 0$.*

(iii) *For some $t = 1, 2, \ldots, T$ there is an $\mathcal{F}_{t-1}$-measurable $\hat{\phi} : \Omega \mapsto \mathbb{R}^d$ such that $\hat{\phi} \cdot \Delta \hat{S}_t \geq 0$ and $P(\hat{\phi} \cdot \Delta \hat{S}_t > 0) > 0$.*

Proof. The equivalence of (ii) and (iii) is obvious. If (ii) holds with ϕ and $A = \{\omega : (\phi \cdot \Delta S_t)(\omega) > 0\}$ then we can construct an arbitrage opportunity θ as follows. For $\omega \notin A$, set $\theta_u(\omega) = 0$ for all $u \in \mathbb{T}$; for $\omega \in A$, set $\theta_u(\omega) = 0$; for all $u < t$, set

$$\theta_t(\omega) = (-\Sigma_{i=1}^d \phi_i(\omega) S_{t-1}^i(\omega), \phi_1(\omega), \phi_2(\omega), \ldots, \phi_d(\omega))';$$

and finally, for all $u > t$, set $\theta_u(\omega) = (V_t(\theta)(\omega), 0, 0, \ldots, 0)'$. It is clear that θ is predictable by construction. (The strategy θ is a special case of ψ constructed in Proposition 3.3.1.) To see that it is also self-financing, note that the value process $V(\theta)$ only changes when $\omega \in A$, and then $\Delta V_u(\theta) = 0$ unless $u = t$. Moreover,

$$
\begin{aligned}
\Delta V_t(\theta)(\omega) &= \theta_t \cdot S_t(\omega) - \theta_{t-1} \cdot S_{t-1}(\omega) = \theta_t \cdot S_t(\omega) \\
&= -\sum_{i=1}^{d} \phi_i(\omega) S_{t-1}^i(\omega) + \sum_{i=1}^{d} \phi_i(\omega) S_t^i(\omega) = \theta_t \cdot \Delta S_t(\omega).
\end{aligned}
$$

Now $V_0(\theta) = 0$, while for $u > t$ we have $V_u(\theta) = 0$ on $\Omega \setminus A$, and, since $S^0 \equiv 1$, $V_u(\theta) = \Delta V_t(\theta) = \theta_t \cdot \Delta S_t = \phi_t \cdot \Delta S_t \geq 0$ on A. Hence $V_T(\theta) \geq 0$ P a.s. But by definition of A, $\{V_T(\theta) > 0\} = \{\Delta V_t(\theta) > 0\} \cap A$; hence θ is an arbitrage opportunity since $P(A) > 0$.

$G_T(\theta)$ is a.s. non-negative and strictly positive with positive probability, for some strategy $\theta \in \Theta$. Assume without loss that $(\theta \cdot S)_0 = 0$. There must be a first index $u \geq 1$ in $\mathbb{T}$ such that $(\theta \cdot S)_u$ is a.s. non-negative and strictly positive with positive probability. Consider $(\theta \cdot S)_{u-1}$: either $(\theta \cdot S)_{u-1} = 0$ a.s. or $A = \{(\theta \cdot S)_{u-1} < 0\}$ has $P(A) > 0$.

In the first case,

$$
(\theta \cdot S)_u = (\theta \cdot S)_u - (\theta \cdot S)_{u-1} = \theta_u \cdot \Delta S_u \geq 0
$$

since $(\theta_u - \theta_{u-1}) \cdot S_{u-1} = 0$, because θ is self-financing. For the same reason $P[\theta_u \cdot \Delta S_u > 0] > 0$; hence (ii) holds.

In the second case we have

$$
\theta_u \cdot \Delta S_u = (\theta \cdot S)_u - (\theta \cdot S)_{u-1} \geq -(\theta \cdot S)_{u-1} > 0
$$

on A, so that the predictable random variable $\phi = 1_A \theta_u$ will satisfy (ii). This completes the proof. $\qquad \square$

This result shows that the 'global' existence of arbitrage is equivalent to the existence of 'local' arbitrage at some $t \in \mathbb{T}$. To exploit this fact geometrically, we revert to the special case of finite market models. First we have the immediate

Corollary 3.3.3. *If a* finite *market model is viable, then for all $t > 0$ in $\mathbb{T}$ and all (non-random) vectors $x \in \mathbb{R}^d$ the following holds. $x \cdot \Delta \hat{S}_t(\omega) \geq 0$ P-a.s implies $x \cdot \Delta \hat{S}_t(\omega) = 0$ P-a.s.*

Geometric Interpretation of Arbitrage

We briefly review two well-known concepts and one basic result concerning convex sets in $\mathbb{R}^d$.

(i) Define the *relative interior* of a subset C in $\mathbb{R}^d$ as the interior of C when viewed as a subset of its *affine hull*. The affine hull and the *convex hull* of C are defined as follows.

$$\text{aff}(C) \;=\; \{x \in \mathbb{R}^d : x = \sum_{i=1}^{n} a_i c_i, c_i \in C, \sum_{i=1}^{n} a_i = 1\},$$

$$\text{conv}(C) \;=\; \{x \in \mathbb{R}^d : x = \sum_{i=1}^{n} a_i c_i, c_i \in C, a_i \geq 0, \sum_{i=1}^{n} a_i = 1\}.$$

The relative interior of C is then simply the set

$$\text{ri}(C) = \{x \in \text{aff}(C) : \exists \epsilon > 0, \; B_\epsilon(x) \cap \text{aff}(C) \subset C\},$$

where $B_\epsilon(x)$ is the Euclidean ϵ-ball centred at x. (See [209] for details.)
The following result is an easy consequence of the definitions.

(ii) The existence of a hyperplane separating two non-empty convex sets
is equivalent to the statement that their relative interiors are disjoint [209],
p. 96.

In the absence of arbitrage there is no hyperplane in $\mathbb{R}^d$ that properly
separates the origin from the convex hull $C_t(A)$ of the set $\hat{A} = \{\Delta \hat{S}_t(\omega) : \omega \in A\}$ for any given $A \in \mathcal{P}_{t-1}, t > 0$. Thus we have proved the first part
of

Proposition 3.3.4. *In a finite market model, the no arbitrage condition
is equivalent to the condition that for all $t \in \mathbb{T}$ and all $A \in \mathcal{P}_{t-1}$, 0 should
belong to the relative interior of $C_t(A)$. In other words, the finite market
model allows no arbitrage opportunities if and only if for each t and $A \in \mathcal{P}_{t-1}$, the value of S_{t-1} is a strictly convex combination of the values taken
by S_t on A.*

Proof. To prove the latter equivalence, suppose that $0 \in C_t(A)$. Since $A \in \mathcal{P}_{t-1}$ and S is adapted, $\hat{S}_{t-1}(\omega) = c \in \mathbb{R}^d$ is constant for $\omega \in A$. Any vector
in $C_t(A)$ thus takes the form $\sum_{i=1}^{m} \alpha_i(z_i - c)$, where $\alpha_i > 0$, $\sum_{i=1}^{m} \alpha_i = 1$,
and each $z_i = \hat{S}_t(\omega)$ for some $\omega \in A$. Thus $0 \in C_t(A)$ if and only if
$c = \sum_{i=1}^{m} \alpha_i z_i$, where the vectors z_i are values of $\hat{S}_t$ on A, $\sum_{i=1}^{m} \alpha_i = 1$,
and all $\alpha_i > 0$. $\square$

Constructing the EMM

The last result can in turn be interpreted in terms of conditional probablil-
ities: for each fixed $A \in \mathcal{P}_{t-1}$ we can redistribute the conditional probabilities to ensure that under this new mass distribution (probability measure)
the price increment vector $\Delta \hat{S}_t$ has zero conditional expectation on A. Piec-
ing together these conditional probabilities we then construct an equivalent
martingale measure for S.

More precisely, fix t, let $A = \bigcup_{k=}^{n} A_k$ be a minimal partition of A, and let $M = (a_{ik})$ be the $d \times n$ matrix of the values taken by the price *increments* $\Delta \hat{S}_t^i$ on the cells A_k. By Proposition 3.3.4 the vector 0 in $\mathbb{R}^d$ lies in the relative interior of $C_t(A)$, and hence can be expressed as a strictly convex combination of elements of $C_t(A)$.

This means that the equation $Mx = 0$ has a strictly positive solution $\alpha = (\alpha_k)$ in $\mathbb{R}^n$.

It is intuitively plausible that the coordinates of the vector α should give rise to an EMM for the discounted prices. To see this we first need to derive a useful 'matrix' version of the Separation Theorem, for which we also have use in Chapter 4.

Lemma 3.3.5 (Farkas' Lemma (1902)). *If A is an $m \times n$ matrix and $b \in \mathbb{R}^m$, then exactly one of the following alternatives holds.*

(i) *there is a non-negative solution $x \geq 0$ of $Ax = b$;*

(ii) *the inequalities $y \cdot A \leq 0$, $y \cdot b > 0$ have a solution $y \in \mathbb{R}^m$.*

Proof. The columns $a_j = (a_{ij})$ $(j \leq n)$ of A define a convex polyhedral cone K in $\mathbb{R}^m$, each of whose elements is given in the form $k = \sum_{j=1}^{n} x_j a_j$ for scalars $x_j \geq 0$. Thus $Ax = b$ for some $x \geq 0$ iff the vector $b \in \mathbb{R}^m$ belongs to K. Now if $b \notin K$, we can separate it from K by a linear functional f on $\mathbb{R}^m$ such that $f(b) > 0$, $f(k) \leq 0$ for $k \in K$ (this is an easy adaptation of the first part of the proof of Theorem 3.1.1). Now implement f by $f(z) = y \cdot z$ for some $y \in \mathbb{R}^m$. Then $y \cdot a_j \leq 0$ for $j \leq n$; hence $y \cdot A \leq 0$, and $y \cdot b > 0$, as required. $\qquad\square$

The next reformulations of the lemma follow without much difficulty and are used in the sequel. The proof is left to the reader.

Lemma 3.3.6. (i) *For a given $m \times n$ matrix M exactly one of the following holds.*
  (α) *$Mx = 0$ has a solution $x \in \mathbb{R}^n$ with $x > 0$;*
  (β) *there exists $y \in \mathbb{R}^m$ such that $y \cdot M \geq 0$, and $y \cdot M$ is not identically 0.*
(ii) *For a given matrix M and $b \in \mathbb{R}^m$ exactly one of the following holds.*
  (a) *$Mx = b$ has a solution in $\mathbb{R}^n$;*
  (b) *there exists $z \in \mathbb{R}^m$ with $z \cdot M = 0$ and $z \cdot b > 0$.*

Applying the alternatives $(\alpha), (\beta)$ in (i) to the matrix $M = (a_{ik})$, we see that the existence of a strictly positive solution $\alpha = (\alpha_k)$ of the equation $Mx = 0$ is what precludes arbitrage; otherwise there would be a $\theta \in \mathbb{R}^d$ with $\theta \cdot M \geq 0$ and not identically 0. Such a θ would yield an arbitrage strategy.

We proceed to use the components (α_k) of this positive solution to build a one-step 'conditional EMM' for this model, restricting attention to the fixed set $A \in \mathcal{P}_{t-1}$: first denote by $\mathcal{A}_A$ the σ-field of subsets of A generated by the cells $A_1, A_2, \ldots, A_n$ of $\mathcal{P}_t$ that partition A, and let P_A be the restriction to $\mathcal{A}_A$ of the conditional probabilities $P(\cdot|A)$. Now construct a probability measure Q_A on the measurable space $(A, \mathcal{A}_A)$ by setting $Q_A(A_k) = \alpha_k/|\alpha|$ for $k = 1, 2, \ldots, n$, where $|\alpha| = \sum_{i=1}^{n} \alpha_k$.

Clearly $Q_A \sim P_A$. As $\mathcal{A}_A$ is generated by $(A_k)_{k \leq n}$ any $\mathcal{A}_A$-measurable vector random variable $Y : A \mapsto \mathbb{R}^d$ takes constant values $Y(\omega) = y_k \in \mathbb{R}^d$ on each of the sets A_k. Hence its expectation under Q_A takes the form

$$E_{Q_A}(Y) = \sum_{k=1}^{n} y_k Q_A(A_k) = \frac{1}{|\alpha|} \sum_{k=1}^{n} y_k \alpha_k.$$

In particular, taking $Y = \Delta \hat{S}_t$ yields $y_k = (a_{ik})_{i \leq d}$ for each $k \leq n$, where the a_{ik} are the entries of the matrix M defined previously, so that $0 = M\alpha = \sum_{k=1}^{n} y_k \alpha_k$. Thus $E_{Q_A}(\Delta \hat{S}_t \mathbf{1}_A) = 0$. Since S^0 is constant by hypothesis, it follows that $E_{Q_A}(\Delta S_t \mathbf{1}_A) = 0$ (in $\mathbb{R}^{d+1}$) also.

Conversely, suppose we are given a probability measure Q_A on $\mathcal{A}_A$ with $E_{Q_A}(\Delta S_t \mathbf{1}_A) = 0$. Setting $\alpha_k = Q_A(A_k)$ for $k \leq n$, the preceding calculation shows that $M\alpha = 0$, so that the zero vector in $\mathbb{R}^d$ can be expressed as a strictly convex combination of vectors in $C_t(A)$, hence the condition of Proposition 3.3.4 is satisfied. We have proved:

Proposition 3.3.7. *For a finitely generated filtration $\mathbb{F}$, the following are equivalent.*

(i) *For all $t > 0$ and $A \in \mathcal{P}_{t-1}$, the zero vector in $\mathbb{R}^d$ can be expressed as a strictly convex combination of vectors in the set $C_t(A) = \{\Delta \hat{S}_t(\omega) : \omega \in A\}$,*

(ii) *for all $t > 0$ in $\mathbb{T}$ and all $\mathcal{F}_{t-1}$-measurable random vectors $x \in \mathbb{R}^d$ we have $x \cdot \Delta \hat{S}_t \geq 0$ P a.s. implies $x \cdot \Delta \hat{S}_t = 0$ P a.s.,*

(iii) *there is a probability measure $Q_A \sim P_A$ on $(A, \mathcal{A}_A)$ with $E_{Q_A}(\Delta S_t \mathbf{1}_A) = 0$.*

Finally, we can put it all together to obtain three conditions, each describing the viability of the market model. Note, in particular, that Condition (ii) is not affected by an equivalent change of measure. However, our proof of the steps described in Proposition 3.3.7 crucially used the fact that the filtration $\mathbb{F}$ was taken to be finitely generated.

Theorem 3.3.8. *The following are equivalent.*

(i) *The securities market model is viable.*

(ii) *For all $t > 0$ in $\mathbb{T}$ and all $\mathcal{F}_{t-1}$-measurable random vectors $x \in \mathbb{R}^d$ we have $x \cdot \Delta \hat{S}_t \geq 0$ P a.s. implies $x \cdot \Delta \hat{S}_t = 0$ P-a.s.*

(iii) *There exists an equivalent martingale measure Q for S.*

Proof. That (i) implies (ii) was shown in Corollary 3.3.3, and that (iii) implies (i) was shown in Section 2.4. This leaves the proof that (ii) implies (iii), in which we make repeated use of Proposition 3.3.7. The family

$$\{P_A : A \in \mathcal{P}_t, \, t < T\}$$

determines P, since all the σ-fields being considered are finitely generated. Thus for each $\omega \in \Omega$ we can find a unique sequence of sets $(B_t)_{t \in \mathbb{T}}$ with $B_t \in \mathcal{P}_t$ for each $t < T$, and such that

$$\Omega = B_0 \supset B_1 \supset B_2 \supset \ldots \supset B_{T-1} \supset B_T = \{\omega\}.$$

By the law of total probability we can write

$$P(\{\omega\}) = P_{B_0}(B_1)P_{B_1}(B_2)\ldots P_{B_{T-1}}(\{\omega\}).$$

Now if (ii) holds, we can use Proposition 3.3.7 successively with $t = 1$ and $A \in \mathcal{P}_0$ to construct a probability measure Q_A, then repeat for $t = 2$ and sets in $\mathcal{P}_t$, and so on. In particular this yields probability measures Q_{B_t} for each $t < T$, defined as in the discussion following Lemma 3.3.6. Setting

$$Q(\{\omega\}) = Q_{B_0}(B_1)Q_{B_1}(B_2)\ldots Q_{B_{T-1}}(\{\omega\})$$

we obtain a probability measure $Q \sim P$ on the whole of $(\Omega, \mathcal{F})$. For any fixed $t > 0$ and $A \in \mathcal{P}_{t-1}$ the conditional probability is just

$$Q(\{\omega\}|A) = \mathbf{1}_A(\{\omega\})Q_A(B_t)Q_{B_t}(B_{t+1})\ldots Q_{B_{T-1}}(\{\omega\}).$$

Therefore for $\omega \in A$, $E_Q(\Delta S_t|\mathcal{F}_{t-1})(\omega) = 0$, and thus Q is an equivalent martingale measure for S.   □

3.4   Two Simple Examples

Example 3.4.1. The following binomial tree example, which is adapted from [205], illustrates the step-wise construction of the EMM and also shows how viability of the market can break down even in very simple cases.

Let $\Omega = \{\omega_1, \omega_2, \omega_3, \omega_4\}$ and $T = 2$. Suppose that the evolution of a stock price S^1 is given by the requirements:

$S_0^1 = 5,$
$S_1^1 = 8$ on $\{\omega_1, \omega_2\}$ and $S_1^1 = 4$ on $\{\omega_3, \omega_4\}$,
$S_2^1 = 9$ on $\{\omega_1\}$, $S_2^1 = 6$ on $\{\omega_2, \omega_3\}$, and $S_2^1 = 3$ on $\{\omega_4\}$.

Note that $\mathcal{F}_0 = \{\emptyset, \Omega\}$ and that the partition $\mathcal{P}_1 = \{\omega_1, \omega_2\} \cup \{\omega_3, \omega_4\}$ generates the algebra $\mathcal{F}_1 = \{\emptyset, \{\omega_1, \omega_2\}, \{\omega_3, \omega_4\}, \Omega\}$, while $\mathcal{F}_2 = \mathcal{P}(\Omega)$.

Although the stock price S_2^1 is the same in states ω_2 and ω_3, the histories (i.e., *paths*) of the price process allow us to distinguish between them, hence the investor knows by time 2 exactly which state ω_i has been realised. For the present we take $S^0 \equiv 1$; that is, the discount rate $r = 0$.

To find an EMM $Q = \{q_i\}_{i=1,2,3,4}$ directly, we need to solve the equations $E_Q(S_u^1|\mathcal{F}_t) = S_t^1$ for all t and $u > t$. This leads to the equations:

$$
\begin{aligned}
t = 0, \quad u = 1 \quad & 5 = 8(q_1 + q_2) + 4(q_3 + q_4), \\
t = 0, \quad u = 2 \quad & 5 = 9q_1 + 6(q_2 + q_3) + 3q_4, \\
t = u = 1, \quad S_1^1 = 8 \quad & 8 = \frac{1}{q_1 + q_2}(9q_1 + 6q_2), \\
t = u = 1, \quad S_1^1 = 4 \quad & 4 = \frac{1}{q_3 + q_4}(6q_3 + 3q_4).
\end{aligned}
\tag{3.1}
$$

Solving any three of these (dependent) equations together with $\sum_{i=1}^4 q_i = 1$ yields the unique solution $q_1 = \frac{1}{6}$, $q_2 = \frac{1}{12}$, $q_3 = \frac{1}{4}$, $q_4 = \frac{1}{2}$.

On the other hand, it is simpler to construct q_i step by step, as indicated in the previous section. Here this means that we must calcuate the one-step conditional probabilities at each node of the tree for $t = 0$ and $t = 1$. When $S_0^1 = 5$, this requires $5 = 8p + 4(1 - p)$; that is, $p = \frac{1}{4}$.

For $S_1^1 = 8$ we solve $8 = 9p' + 6(1 - p')$, (i.e., $p' = \frac{2}{3}$), while for $S_1^1 = 4$ we need $4 = 6p'' + 3(1 - p'')$ (i.e., $p'' = \frac{1}{3}$.) According to the proof of Theorem 3.3.8 this yields the q_i as: $q_1 = \frac{1}{4}\cdot\frac{2}{3}$, $q_2 = \frac{1}{4}\cdot\frac{1}{3}$, $q_3 = \frac{3}{4}\cdot\frac{1}{3}$, $q_4 = \frac{3}{4}\cdot\frac{2}{3}$. This agrees with the values we found previously.

It is instructive to examine the effect of discounting on this example: suppose instead that $S_t^0 = (1 + r)^t$ for each t, with $r \geq 0$. The left-hand sides of the equations (3.1) then become $5(1 + r)$, $5(1 + r)^2$, $8(1 + r)$, and $4(1 + r)$, respectively.

This yields the solution for the q_i (using the one-step method, which greatly simplifies the calculation!) in the form:

$$
q_1 = \left(\frac{1 + 5r}{4}\right)\left(\frac{2 + 8r}{3}\right), \quad q_2 = \left(\frac{1 + 5r}{4}\right)\left(\frac{1 - 8r}{3}\right), \quad q_3 = \left(\frac{3 - 5r}{4}\right)\left(\frac{1 + 4r}{3}\right)
$$

and $q_4 = ((3 - 5r)/4)((2 - 4r)/3)$, as the reader can verify readily.

This time the requirement that Q be a probability measure is not automatically satisfied; when $r \geq \frac{1}{8}$, q_2 becomes nonpositive. Hence Q is an EMM for $S = (S^0, S^1)$ only if $0 \leq r < \frac{1}{8}$, that is, if the riskless interest rate is less than 12.5%. If $r \geq \frac{1}{8}$ there is no EMM for this process, and if we observe $S_1^1 = 8$, an arbitrage opportunity can be constructed, since we know in advance that the discounted stock price $\overline{S}_2^1$ will be lower than $\overline{S}_1^1 = 8/(1 + r)$ in each of the states ω_1 and ω_2.

Example 3.4.2. Consider a pricing model with two stocks, S^1, S^2, and a riskless bond S^0, with tree structure as shown in Figure 3.1. This example is taken from [260].

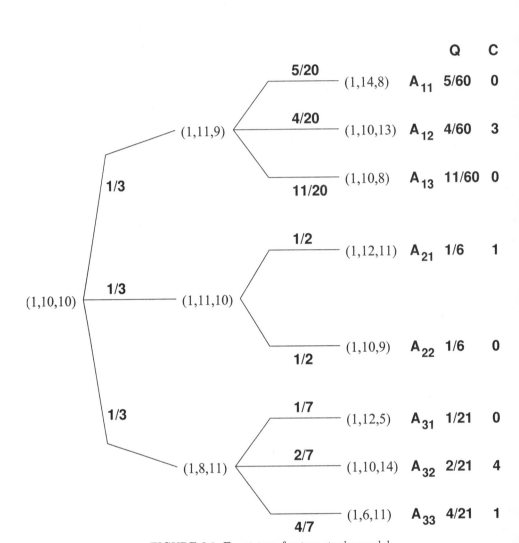

FIGURE 3.1. Event-tree for two-stocks model

The partitions giving the filtration $\mathbb{F}$ are:

$$\begin{aligned}
\mathcal{P}_0 &= \{\Omega\}, \\
\mathcal{P}_1 &= \{A_1, A_2, A_3\}, \\
\mathcal{P}_2 &= \{A_{11}, A_{12}, A_{13}, A_{21}, A_{22}, A_{31}, A_{32}, A_{33}\}.
\end{aligned}$$

We take $T = 2$ and the various probabilities are as shown in Figure 3.1. (Note that we again keep $S^0 \equiv 1$ here.) Note that in each case the one-step transition includes both 'up' and 'down' steps, so that by Theorem 3.3.8 the model is viable and an EMM Q can be constructed for $S = (S^0, S^1, S^2)$. The calculation of Q proceeds as in the previous example (using the one-step probabilities), so that, for example, $Q(A_{13}) = pq$, where p is found by solving the equations

$$\begin{aligned}
10 &= 11p + 11p' + 8(1 - p - p'), \\
10 &= 9p + 10p' + 11(1 - p - p'),
\end{aligned}$$

which yields $p = \frac{1}{3}$, while q must satisfy

$$\begin{aligned}
11 &= 10q + 10q' + 14(1 - q - q'), \\
9 &= 8q + 13q' + 8(1 - q - q'),
\end{aligned}$$

which yields $q = \frac{11}{20}$, and hence $Q(A_{13}) = \frac{11}{60}$.

To use the measure Q to calculate the price of a European call option C on stock S^2 with strike price 10, we simply find the time 0 value of C as

$$E_Q(C) = 0. \frac{5}{60} + 3. \frac{4}{60} + 0. \frac{11}{60} + 1. \frac{1}{6} + 0. \frac{1}{6} + 0. \frac{1}{21} + 4. \frac{2}{21} + 1. \frac{4}{21} = \frac{197}{210}.$$

3.5 Equivalent Martingale Measures for Discrete Market Models

The Fundamental Theorem of Asset Pricing

The detailed construction of the EMM Q for the price process S that we undertook in Section 3.3 relies heavily on the assumption that the filtration $\mathbb{F}$ is finitely generated. In recent years several authors have produced variants of Theorem 3.2.2 in more general contexts. The sought-after equivalence between conditions of 'no arbitrage type' and the existence of an equivalent (local) martingale measure has become known as the *Fundamental Theorem of Asset Pricing*: it provides the vital link between the economically significant 'no arbitrage' condition and the mathematically important reason for equating the class of admissible stock price processes with the class of P-semimartingales, thus allowing the fullest use of the well-developed theory of semimartingales and the general stochastic calculus.

The extensions of Theorem 3.2.2 to models based on general filtered probability spaces and with more general (infinite) time lines all turn on ensuring that the preceding equivalence is *essentially* maintained. This, however, allows considerable scope for interpretation of precisely what is meant by 'essentially,' and this has given rise to a number of modifications of the 'no arbitrage' assumption (see [59] for a detailed discussion).

Nonetheless, for discrete-time models, based on a general probability space $(\Omega, \mathcal{F}, P)$, and a *finite discrete time set* $\mathbb{T} = \{0, 1, 2, \ldots, T\}$, Theorem 3.2.2 has been proved in the form stated, *without* assuming that the filtration in question is finitely generated. To be precise:

Theorem 3.5.1. *Let $(\Omega, \mathcal{F}, P)$ be a probability space, and define the finite discrete time set $\mathbb{T} = \{0, 1, 2, \ldots, T\}$. Assume given a filtration $\mathbb{F} = (\mathcal{F}_t)_{t \in \mathbb{T}}$ and an $\mathbb{R}^{d+1}$-valued process $S = (S_t)_{t \in \mathbb{T}}$, adapted to $\mathbb{F}$. We assume further that the first component $S^0 \equiv 1$, and that for $i \leq d$ and $t \in \mathbb{T}$ we have $S_t^i > 0$ P-a.s. Then the following are equivalent.*

(i) *There is a probability $Q \sim P$ such that $(S_t, \mathcal{F}_t)_{t \in \mathbb{T}}$ is a Q-martingale.*

(ii) *There are no arbitrage opportunities; that is, for every self-financing trading strategy $\theta = (\theta_t^0, \theta_t^1, \ldots, \theta_t^d)_{t \in \mathbb{T}}$, with gains process $G(\theta)$ defined by $G_t(\theta) = \Sigma_{u=1}^t \theta_u \cdot \Delta S_u$ $(t \in \mathbb{T})$, we have $G_T(\theta) \geq 0$ P-a.s. implies $G_T(\theta) = 0$ P a.s.*

If either (i) or (ii) holds, then Q can be found with bounded Radon–Nikodym derivative dQ/dP.

In this generality the result was first proved in [54]; alternative proofs have appeared in [224] and [211]. As with the propositions leading to Theorem 3.3.8, Q is constructed inductively over the elements of $\mathbb{T}$. The major difficulty is to construct the 'one-step' conditional probabilities corresponding to $P_{B_{t-1}}(B_t)$ used in the proof of Theorem 3.3.8: when attempting a 'pathwise' approach to this construction one must ensure that the various choices can be made *measurably*. These technical issues do not arise in the finitely generated situation discussed in Sections 3.2 and 3.3.

Outline of the Proof

A detailed proof of Theorem 3.5.1 would therefore lead us too far afield. The main ideas of the proof advanced in [211] can however be stated reasonably simply: we consider how to build a one-step conditional probability, much as we did for a finite market. Take $\mathbb{T} = \{0, T\}$, and write $X = \Delta S = S_T - S_0$. *Assume* for the moment that this $\mathbb{R}^d$-valued random variable has support that is not contained in any proper subspace of $\mathbb{R}^d$. that is, for any $a \in \mathbb{R}^d$ the set $D_a = \{\omega \in \Omega : a \cdot X(\omega) \neq 0\}$ has positive P-measure.

We are looking for a probability measure $Q \sim P$ under which $E_Q(X) = 0$. Consider a strictly concave, strictly increasing function $U : \mathbb{R} \mapsto (-\infty, 0)$

with continuous derivative U' (note that we will have $U' > 0$; $U(x) = -e^{-x}$ is an example that will satisfy our requirements). Set $\bar{U}(a) = E_P(U(a \cdot X))$ for $a \in \mathbb{R}^d$. Then $\bar{U}$ is bounded above by 0. We again have two alternatives, just as in the discussion preceding Proposition 3.3.7:

either $\bar{U}$ attains its supremum at some $a^* \in \mathbb{R}^d$;
or we can find $\theta \neq 0$ in $\mathbb{R}^d$ such that $\bar{U}(t\theta) = E_P(U(t\theta \cdot X))$ remains bounded at $t \to \infty$.

The second alternative implies that $P(\theta \cdot X < 0) = 0$, and since by hypothesis $P(D_\theta) > 0$, it follows that $P(\theta \cdot X > 0) > 0$, so that (cf. Proposition 3.3.2) θ is an arbitrage opportunity in this single-period model.

Thus in the absence of arbitrage the first alternative must hold (just as we had a strictly positive solution to $Mx = 0$ in the finite case, which then allowed us to construct the conditional probability Q_A). At its maximum point a^*, the function $\bar{U}$ satisfies the first-order condition $E_P X(U'(a \cdot X) = 0$. Normalising to obtain a probability, we can use $U'(a \cdot X) > 0$ as the change of measure 'density' which provides the measure $Q \sim P$ for which $E_Q(X) = 0$.

This very sketchy outline is, of course, only a plausibility argument, and not a proof. Care must be taken to ensure that the hypothesis on the support of X can be justified, that the choices made previously can be made measurably, and that the induction procedure hinted at can be accomplished. The interested reader is referred to [211] for these details, or to the alternative proofs given in [54] (see also [205] for an exposition of their argument) and [224]. Each of these deals with the considerable subtleties of the problem in slightly different ways.

4

Complete Markets and Martingale Representation

4.1   Uniqueness of the EMM

Our objective in this chapter is to study *completeness* of the market model. We continue to restrict attention to *finite* market models: although our initial results can be stated in a more general framework, the proofs we give rely heavily on the finite nature of the model, and we show in the later sections that completeness depends strongly on the fine structure of the filtrations, a feature that is not easily formulated for more general models.

As before, let $S = (S^i : i = 0, 1, 2, \ldots, d)$ be a strictly positive $\mathbb{R}^{d+1}$-valued stochastic process, representing the price vector of one riskless security with $S_0^0 = 1, S_t^0 = \beta_t^{-1} S_0^0$, and d risky securities $\{S_t^i : i = 1, 2, \ldots, d\}$ for each $t \in \mathbb{T} = \{0, 1, \ldots, T\}$.

Let X be a contingent claim, that is, a nonnegative $\mathcal{F}$-random variable $X : \Omega \mapsto \mathbb{R}$. Recall that X is said to be *attainable* if there exists an admissible trading strategy θ that *generates* X, that is, whose value process $V(\theta) \geq 0$ satisfies $V_T(\theta) = X$ P-a.s.

Remark 4.1.1. Note that, in a viable market model, the requirements on θ can be relaxed without loss: if the generating strategy for X only satisfies $\theta \in \Theta$ (i.e., $V_T(\theta) = X$, but $V(\theta)$ is not required a priori to be non-negative) then for any EMM Q we have

$$V_t(\theta) = \beta_t^{-1} E_Q(\bar{V}_T(\theta)|\mathcal{F}_t) = \beta_t^{-1}\beta_T E_Q(X|\mathcal{F}_t) \geq 0 \qquad (4.1)$$

for all $t \in \mathbb{T}$, since $X \geq 0$. Thus the generating strategy θ is automatically admissible.

We saw in Chapter 2 that the Cox–Ross–Rubinstein binomial market model is both viable and complete. In fact, we were able to construct the equivalent martingale measure Q for S directly, and showed that in this model there is a *unique* equivalent martingale measure. We now show that this property characterises completeness in the class of viable finite market models.

Theorem 4.1.2. *A viable finite market model is complete if and only if it admits a unique equivalent martingale measure.*

Proof. $\Longrightarrow$: The following is a variant of the argument already given in Section 2.4. Suppose the model is viable and complete, and that Q and Q' are martingale measures for S, with $Q' \sim P \sim Q$. Let X be a contingent claim, and let $\theta \in \Theta_a$ generate X. Then by (2.8),

$$\beta_T X = \overline{V}_T(\theta) = V_0(\theta) + \sum_{t=1}^{T} \theta_t \cdot \Delta \overline{S}_t. \tag{4.2}$$

Since each discounted price process $\overline{S}^i$ is a martingale under both Q and Q', the preceding sum has zero expectation under both measures. Hence $E_Q(\beta_T X) = V_0(\theta) = E_{Q'}(\beta_T X)$; in particular, $E_Q(X) = E_{Q'}(X)$.

This holds for every $\mathcal{F}$-measurable random variable X, as the model is complete. In particular, it holds for $X = \mathbf{1}_A$, where $A \in \mathcal{F}$ is arbitrary, so $Q(A) = Q'(A)$. Hence $Q = Q'$ and so the equivalent martingale measure for this model is unique.

$\Longleftarrow$: Conversely, suppose that the market model is viable but not complete, so that there exists a nonnegative random variable X that cannot be generated by an admissible trading strategy. By Remark 4.1.1 this means that X cannot be generated by any self-financing strategy $\theta = \{\theta^0, \theta^1, \dots, \theta^d\}$, and by (2.9) we can even restrict attention to predictable processes $\{\theta^1, \dots, \theta^d\}$ in $\mathbb{R}^d$, as these determine θ^0 up to constants.

Therefore, define $L = \{c + \sum_{t=1}^{T} \theta_t \cdot \Delta \overline{S}_t : \theta \text{ predictable}, c \in \mathbb{R}\}$. Then L is a linear subspace of the vector space $L^0(\Omega, \mathcal{F}, P)$ of all real random variables on Ω (note that this is again just $\mathbb{R}^n$, where the minimal $\mathcal{F}$-partition of Ω has n members) and since this space is finite-dimensional, L is closed. Suppose $\beta_T X \in L$; that is, $\beta_T X = c + \sum_{t=1}^{T} \theta_t \cdot \Delta \overline{S}_t$ for some $\mathbb{R}^d$-valued predictable process θ. By (2.9) we can always extend θ to a self-financing strategy with initial value c; in other words, X would be attained by this strategy. Hence we cannot have $\beta_T X \in L$ and so L is a proper subspace of L^0, and thus has a non-empty orthogonal complement, $L^\perp$.

Thus, for any EMM Q, there exists a non-zero random variable $Z \in L^0$ such that

$$E_Q(YZ) = 0 \tag{4.3}$$

for all $Y \in L$. Again because L^0 is finite-dimensional, Z is bounded. Note that $E_Q(Z) = 0$ since $Y \equiv 1$ is in L (take $\theta^i \equiv 0$ for $i \geq 1$).

Define a measure $Q' \sim Q$ by $(Q'(\omega))/(Q(\omega)) = R(\omega)$, where $R(\omega) = 1 + ((Z(\omega))/(2\|Z\|_\infty))$ and $\|Z\|_\infty = \max\{|Z(\omega)| : \omega \in \Omega\}$.

Then Q' is a probability measure, since $Q'(\{\omega\}) > 0$ for all ω and $Q'(\Omega) = E_Q(R) = 1$, as $E_Q(Z) = 0$. Moreover,

$$E_{Q'}(Y) = E_Q(RY) = E_Q(Y) + \frac{1}{2\|Z\|_\infty} E_Q(YZ) = c$$

for each $Y = c + \sum_{t=1}^T \theta_t \cdot \Delta \bar{S}_t \in L$ and in particular $E_{Q'}(Y) = 0$ when Y has $c = 0$. Thus for any predictable process $\theta = \{\theta_t^i : t = 1, 2, \dots, T, 1 = 1, 2, \dots, d\}$ we have

$$E_{Q'}\left(\sum_{t=1}^T \theta_t \cdot \Delta \bar{S}_t\right) = 0. \tag{4.4}$$

Again using $\theta = (0, 0, \dots, \theta^i, 0, \dots, 0)$ successively for $i = 1, 2, \dots, d$ in (4.4), it is clear that Theorem 2.3.4 implies that $\bar{S}$ is a Q'martingale. We have therefore constructed an equivalent martingale measure distinct from Q. Thus in a viable incomplete market the EMM is not unique. This completes the proof of the theorem. $\qquad\square$

4.2 Completeness and Martingale Representation

Let $(\Omega, \mathcal{F}, P, \mathbb{T}, \mathbb{F})$ be a complete market model with unique EMM P^*. This is equivalent to the following martingale representation property. The discounted price $\bar{S}$ serves as a *basis* (under martingale transforms) for the space of $(\mathbb{F}, P^*)$-martingales on $(\Omega, \mathcal{F})$. More precisely:

Proposition 4.2.1. *The viable finite market model* $(\Omega, \mathcal{F}, \mathbb{T}, \mathbb{F}, P)$ *with EMM* P^* *is complete if and only if each real-valued* $(\mathbb{F}, P^*)$-*martingale* $M = (M_t)_{t \in \mathbb{T}}$ *can be represented in the form*

$$M_t = M_0 + \sum_{u=1}^t \gamma_u \cdot \Delta \bar{S}_u = M_0 + \sum_{i=1}^d (\sum_{u=1}^t \gamma_u^i \Delta \bar{S}_u^i) \tag{4.5}$$

for some predictable processes γ^i $(i = 1, \dots, d)$.

Proof. Suppose the model is complete and (since every martingale is the difference of two positive martingales) assume without loss that $M = (M_t)$ is a non-negative $(\mathbb{F}, P^*)$-martingale. Let $C = M_T S_T^0$ and find a strategy $\theta \in \Theta_a$ that generates this contingent claim, so that $V_T(\theta) = C$, and hence $\bar{V}_T(\theta) = M_T$. Now since the discounted value process is a P^*-martingale, we have

$$\bar{V}_t(\theta) = E^*(\bar{V}_T(\theta)|\mathcal{F}_t) = E^*(M_T|\mathcal{F}_t) = M_t.$$

Thus the martingale M has the form

$$M_t = \overline{V}_t(\theta) = V_0(\theta) + \sum_{u=1}^{t} \theta_u \cdot \Delta \overline{S}_u = M_0 + \sum_{u=1}^{t} \theta_u \cdot \Delta \overline{S}_u$$

for all $t \in \mathbb{T}$. Hence we have proved (4.5) with $\gamma_u = \theta_u$ for all $u \in \mathbb{T}$.

Conversely, fix a contingent claim C, and define the martingale $M = (M_t)$ by setting $M_t = E^*(\beta_T C | \mathcal{F}_t)$. By hypothesis the martingale M has the representation

$$M_t = M_0 + \sum_{u=1}^{t} \gamma_u \cdot \Delta \overline{S}_u.$$

So define a strategy θ by setting $\theta_t^i = \gamma_t^i$ for $i \geq 1$ and $\theta_t^0 = M_t - \gamma_t \cdot \overline{S}_t$ for $t \in \mathbb{T}$. We show that θ is self-financing by verifying that $(\Delta \theta_t) \cdot S_{t-1} = 0$. To see this, fix $t \in \mathbb{T}$ and compute

$$
\begin{aligned}
(\Delta \theta_t) \cdot S_{t-1} &= S_{t-1}^0 [\Delta M_t - \Delta(\sum_{i=1}^{d} \gamma_t^i \overline{S}_t^i)] + \sum_{i=1}^{d} S_{t-1}^i \Delta \gamma_t^i \\
&= \sum_{i=1}^{d} [S_{t-1}^0 \{(\gamma_t^i \Delta \overline{S}_t^i) - (\gamma_t^i \overline{S}_t^i - \gamma_{t-1}^i \overline{S}_{t-1}^i)\} + S_{t-1}^i \Delta \gamma_t^i] \\
&= \sum_{i=1}^{d} S_{t-1}^i (\Delta \gamma_t^i - \Delta \gamma_t^i) = 0.
\end{aligned}
$$

Moreover, $V_t(\theta) = \theta_t \cdot S_t = M_t S_t^0$ for all $t \in \mathbb{T}$, hence in particular we obtain $C = V_T(\theta)$, as required. Thus the market model is complete. □

Remark 4.2.2. Note that, unlike Theorem 4.1.2, Proposition 4.2.1 does not depend on the finiteness of the model, but holds in general for discrete-time market models, since it just involves a trivial reinterpretation of the value process $V(\theta)$. (Indeed, the extension to continuous-time models, using stochastic integrals to replace martingale transforms, is equally straightforward.) The significant connection is that between the uniqueness of the EMM P^* and the martingale representation property (4.5), and we explore this relationship further in the following sections.

4.3   Martingale Representation in the CRR-Model

Again the Cox–Ross–Rubinstein model provides a good testbed for the ideas developed previously. We saw in Section 2.5 that this model is complete, by an explicit construction of the unique EMM as a product of one-step probabilities. We explore the content of the martingale representation result (Proposition 4.2.1) in this context, and use it to provide a more precise description of the generating strategy for a fairly general contingent claim.

Recall that the bond price in this model is $S_t^0 = (1+r)^t$ for $t \in \mathbb{T} = \{0, 1, \ldots, T\}$, where $r > 0$ is fixed, and that the stock price S satisfies $S_t = R_t S_{t-1}$, where R_t takes the values $(1+b)$ and $(1+a)$ with probability $q = (r-a)/(b-a)$ and $1-q = (b-r)/(b-a)$, respectively. Here we assume that $-1 < a < r < b$ to ensure that the market is viable, and that the sample space can be taken as $\Omega = \{1+a, 1+b\}^{\mathbb{T}\backslash\{0\}}$, so that the i.i.d random variables $\{R_t : t = 1, \ldots, T\}$ describe the randomness in the model. The unique EMM Q then takes the form $Q(R_t = \omega_t : s = 1, \ldots, T) = \Pi_{t \leq T} q_t$, and $q_t = q$ if $\omega_t = 1+b$, $q_t = 1-q$ if $\omega_t = 1+a$.

In such simple cases a direct proof of the martingale representation theorem is almost obvious, and does not depend on the nature of the sample space, since the (R_t) contain all the relevant information.

Proposition 4.3.1. *Suppose that $(\Omega, \mathcal{F}, Q)$ is a probability space and $(R_t)_{t=1,\ldots,T}$ is a finite sequence of i.i.d. random variables, taking the two values u, v with probabilities q and $1 - q$, respectively. Suppose further that $E[R_1] = w$, where $-1 < v < w < u$ and $q = (w - v)/(u - v)$, while $m_t = \sum_{s=1}^{t}(R_t - w)$, $\mathcal{F}_0 = \{\emptyset, \Omega\}$, $\mathcal{F}_t = \sigma(R_s : s \leq t)$ for all $t = 1, 2, \ldots, T$.*

Then $m = (m_t, \mathcal{F}_t, Q)$ is a centred martingale and every $(\mathcal{F}_t, Q)$-martingale $(M_t, \mathcal{F}_t, Q)$ with $E_Q(M_0) = 0$ can be expressed in the form

$$M_t = \sum_{s \leq t} \theta_s \Delta m_s, \qquad (4.6)$$

where the process $\theta = (\theta_t)$ is $(\mathcal{F}_t)$-predictable.

Proof. We follow the proof given in [258], 15.1 (see also [49], [243]). It is obvious that m is a martingale relative to $(\mathcal{F}_t, Q)$. Since M_t is $\mathcal{F}_t$-measurable, it has the form

$$M_t(\omega) = f_t(R_1(\omega), R_2(\omega), \ldots, R_t(\omega))$$

for all ω in Ω. If (4.6) holds, then the increments of M take the form $\Delta M_t(\omega) = \theta_t(\omega)\Delta m_t(\omega)$, so that, if we set $f_t^u(\omega) = f_t(R_1(\omega), R_2(\omega), \ldots, R_{t-1}(\omega), u)$ and $f_t^v(\omega) = f_t(R_1(\omega), R_2(\omega), \ldots, R_{t-1}(\omega), v)$, then (4.6) reduces to showing that

$$f_t^u - f_{t-1} = \theta_t(u - w), \qquad f_t^v - f_{t-1} = \theta_t(v - w).$$

In other words, θ_t would need to take the form

$$\theta_t = \frac{f_t^u - f_{t-1}}{u - w} = \frac{f_t^v - f_{t-1}}{v - w}. \qquad (4.7)$$

To see that this is indeed the case, we simply use the martingale property of M: as $E_Q(\Delta M_t | \mathcal{F}_{t-1}) = 0$, we have

$$q f_t^u + (1 - q) f_t^v = f_{t-1} = q f_{t-1} + (1 - q) f_{t-1}$$

which reduces to $(f_t^u - f_{t-1})/(1 - q) = (f_t^v - f_{t-1})/q$, and this is the same as (4.7), since $q = (w - v)/(u - v)$ and $1 - q = (u - w)/(b - v)$. $\qquad \square$

Valuation of General European Claims

We showed in Section 2.5 that the value process $V_t(C) = (1 + r)^{-(T-t)} E_Q(C | \mathcal{F}_t)$ of a European call option C in the Cox–Ross–Rubinstein model can be expressed more concretely in the form $V_t(C) = v(t, S_t)$, where

$$v(t, x) = (1 + r)^{-(T-t)} \sum_{u=0}^{T-t} \left[\frac{(T - t)!}{u!(T - t - u)!} q^u (1 - q)^{T-t-u} \right.$$
$$\left. \times (x(1 + b)^u (1 + a)^{T-t-u} - K)^+ \right].$$

This Markovian nature of the European call (i.e., the fact that the value process depends only on the *current* price and not on the *path* taken by the process S) can be exploited more generally to provide explicit expressions for the value process and generating strategies of a European contingent claim (i.e., a claim $X = g(S_T)$). In the CRR model we know that the evolution of S is determined by the ratios (R_t), which take only two values, $1 + b$ and $1 + a$. For any path ω, the value $S_T(\omega)$ is thus determined by the initial stock price S_0 and the *number* of 'upward' movements of the price on $\mathbb{T} = \{0, 1, 2, \ldots, T\}$. To express this more simply, note that $R_t = (1 + a) + (b - a)\delta_t$, where δ_t is a Bernoulli random variable taking the value 1 with probability q. Hence we can consider, generally, claims of the form $X = h(u_T)$, where $u_T(\omega) = \sum_{t \leq T} \delta_t(\omega)$.

Recall from Proposition 4.3.1 that the martingale $M_t = E_Q(X | \mathcal{F}_t)$ can be represented in the form $M_t = M_0 + \sum_{u \leq t} \theta_u \Delta m_u$. But $m_u = R_u - (1+r)$ in the CRR setting (we use $v = 1 + a$, $w = 1 + r$, $u = 1 + b$ in applying Proposition 4.3.1) so that

$$\Delta m_u = (1 + a) - (b - a)\delta_u - (1 + r)$$
$$= (b - a)[\delta_u - \frac{r - a}{b - a}] = (b - a)(\delta_u - q).$$

Thus the representation of M can also be written in the form $M_t = \sum_{u \leq t} \alpha_u(\delta_u - q)$, where $\alpha_u = (b - a)\theta_u$.

Consider the identity $\Delta M_t = \alpha_t(\delta_t - q)$; exactly as in the proof of Proposition 4.3.1 this leads to a description of α.

$$
\begin{aligned}
\alpha_t &= \frac{E_Q(M_T|\delta_u, u < t, \delta_t = 1) - E_Q(M_T|\delta_u, u < t)}{1 - q} \\
&= \frac{E_Q(h(u_T)|\delta_u, u < t, \delta_t = 1) - E_Q(h(u_T)|\delta_u, u < t)}{1 - q}.
\end{aligned}
$$

Restrict attention to the set $A = \{\omega : u_{t-1}(\omega) = x, \delta_t = 1\}$. On this set we obtain, using the independence of the (R_t),

$$
\begin{aligned}
E_Q(h(u_T)|\mathcal{F}_t) &= E_Q(h(x + 1 + (u_T - u_t))), \\
E_Q(h(u_T)|\mathcal{F}_{t-1}) &= E_Q(h(x + (u_T - u_{t-1}))) \\
&= qE_Q(h(x + 1 + (u_T - u_t))) \\
&\quad + (1 - q)E_Q(h(x + (u_T - u_t))).
\end{aligned}
$$

Thus, on the set A, the difference

$$
\begin{aligned}
&E_Q(h(u_T)|\mathcal{F}_t) - E_Q(h(u_T)|\mathcal{F}_{t-1}) \\
&= (1 - p)E_Q[h(x + 1 + (u_T - u_t)) - h(x + (u_T - u_t))]
\end{aligned}
$$

and the final expectation is just

$$
\sum_{s=0}^{T-t}[h(x + 1 + s) - h(x + s)] \sum_{s=1}^{T-t} \frac{(T - t)!}{u!(T - t - u)!}q^s(1 - q)^{T-t-s}.
$$

We have therefore shown that

$$
\alpha_t = H_{T-t}(u_{t-1}; q),
$$

where

$$
H_s(x; q) = \sum_{\tau=0}^{s}[h(x + 1 + \tau) - h(x + \tau)]\frac{s!}{\tau!(s - \tau)!}q^\tau(1 - q)^{s-\tau}.
$$

For a European claim $X = g(S_T)$ this can be taken further, using the explicit form of the martingale representation given in Proposition 4.2.1. We leave the details (which can be found in [243]) to the reader, and simply note here that the function h given previously now takes the form

$$
h(x) = (1 + r)^{-T}f(S_0(1 + b)^x(1 + a)^{T-x}),
$$

which leads to the following ratio for the time t stock holdings

$$
\alpha_t = (1 + r)^{-(T-t)}\frac{F_{T-t}(S_{t-1}(1 + b); q) - F_{T-t}(S_{t-1}(1 + a); q)}{S_{t-1}(b - a)}, \qquad (4.8)
$$

where

$$F_t(x;p) = \sum_{s=0}^{t} f(x(1+b)^s(1+a)^{t-s}) \frac{t!}{s!(t-s)!} p^s (1-p)^{t-s}.$$

Note that for a *nondecreasing* f we obtain $\alpha_t \geq 0$ for all $t \in \mathbb{T}$. Hence the hedge portfolio can be obtained without ever having to take a short position in the stock—though clearly we may have to borrow cash to finance the position at various times.

Exercise 4.3.2. Use formula (4.7) to obtain an explicit description of the strategy that generates the European call option of strike K, expiry T, in the CRR model.

4.4 The Splitting Index and Completeness

Harrison and Kreps [120] introduced the notion of the *splitting index* for viable finite market models, as a means of identifying event trees that lead to complete models. This idea is closely related to the concept of extremality of a probability measure among certain convex sets of martingale measures, and in this setting, the ideas also extend to continuous-time models (see [250], [122]).

Fix a finite market model $(\Omega, \mathcal{F}, Q, \mathbb{T}, \mathbb{F}, S)$ with $S_t = (S_t^i)_{0 \leq i \leq d}$. We assume that the filtration $\mathbb{F} = (\mathcal{F}_t)$ is generated by minimal partitions $(\mathcal{P}_t)$. The *splitting index* $K(t, A)$ of a set $A \in \mathcal{P}_{t-1}$ is then the number of branches of the event tree that begin at node A; that is, for $t = 1, 2, \ldots, T$,

$$K(t, A) = \text{card}\{A' \in \mathcal{P}_t : A' \subset A\}. \tag{4.9}$$

It is intuitively clear that this number will serve to characterise completeness of the market, since we can reduce our consideration to a single-period market (as we have seen in Chapter 3) with A as the new sample space: in order to construct a hedging strategy which we use to 'span' all the possible states of the market at time t by means of a linear combination of securities (i.e., a linear combination of the prices $(S_t^i(\omega))_{0 \leq i \leq d}$) then clearly the number of different possible states should not exceed $(d+1)$. Moreover, it is possible that some of the prices can be expressed as linear combinations of the remaining ones, hence are 'redundant' in the single-period market, so that, as before, what matters is the *rank* of the matrix of prices (which correspond to the price *increments* in multi-period models). Recalling finally that the 0th security (the bond) is held constant as numéraire, the following result becomes plausible; we only outline the proof.

Proposition 4.4.1. *A viable finite market model is complete if and only if for every* $t = 1, 2, \ldots, T$ *and* $A \in \mathcal{P}_{t-1}$ *we have*

$$\dim(\text{span}\{\Delta \bar{S}_t(\omega) : \omega \in A\}) = K(t, A) - 1. \tag{4.10}$$

In particular, if the market contains no redundant securities (i.e., there is no $\alpha \neq 0$ in $\mathbb{R}^{d+1}$, $t > 0$, in $\mathbb{T}$ and $A \in \mathcal{P}_{t-1}$ such that $Q(\alpha \cdot S_t = 0 | A) = 1$), then $K(t, A) = d + 1$.

Outline of Proof. (See [250] for details, and refer to the notation introduced in the discussion following Lemma 3.3.6.) We can reduce this situation to the one-step conditional probabilities as in Chapter 3, and finally 'paste together' the various steps. We also assume without loss that $S^0 \equiv 1$ throughout, so that $S_t = \bar{S}_t$ for all $t \in \mathbb{T}$.

Fix $A \in \mathcal{P}_{t-1}$ and consider the set $\mathcal{M}$ of all probability measures on the space $(A, \mathcal{A}_A)$, where $\mathcal{A}_A$ is the σ-algebra generated by the sets A_i, $i \leq n$, in $\mathcal{P}_t$ that partition A. Consider an element Q_A of the convex set $\mathcal{M}_0 = \{Q'_A \in \mathcal{M} : E_{Q'_A}(\Delta S_t \mathbf{1}_A) = 0\}$. If Q_A is in $\mathcal{M}_0$ and assigns positive mass to $A_1, A_2, \ldots, A_m$, while giving zero mass to the other A_i, then we can write the price increment on the set A_j, $j \leq m$, as $\Delta S_t(\omega) = y_i - y$, where $S_{t-1}(\omega) = y$ is constant on A, since S is adapted. The condition that Q_A cannot be expressed as a convex combination of measures in $\mathcal{M}_0$ now translates simply to the demand that the vectors $(y_i - y)$ are linearly independent, in other words, that the matrix of price increments has linearly independent columns. But we have already seen that nonsingularity of the matrix of price increments is equivalent to completeness in the single-period model. The proof may now be completed by pasting together the steps to construct the unique EMM.   □

Example 4.4.2. The binomial random walk model is complete: we know this already by virtue of the uniqueness of the EMM, but our interest here is the splitting index. Recall that the price process S has the form $S_t = \Pi_{u=1}^t R_t$, where the return process R_t takes only the values $u = 1 + b$ and $d = 1 + a$, and is independent of $\mathcal{F}_{t-1}$, so that we can describe the price dynamics by an event tree, as in Figure 1.3.

Clearly there are only two branches at each node, so that $K(t, A) = 2$, while

$$\dim(\mathrm{span}\{\Delta S_t(\omega) : \omega \in A\}) = 1$$

for each $A \in \mathcal{P}_t$, $t \in \mathbb{T}$: $\Delta S^0 \equiv 0$, and $\Delta S_t^1(\omega) = S_{t-1}^1(\omega)(R_t(\omega) - 1)$ takes the values $bS_{t-1}^1(\omega)$ and $aS_{t-1}^1(\omega)$, both of which are multiples of $S_{t-1}^1(\omega)$, which remains constant throughout A.

Example 4.4.3. For $d \geq 2$, however, the d-dimensional random walk composed of independent copies of one-dimensional walks *cannot* be complete: we have $K(t, A) = 2^d$, and this equals $d + 1$ only when $d = 1$.

We can easily construct an infinite number of EMMs for the two-dimensional (also known as *two-factor*) random walk model; in the preceding example we have a price process $S = (1, S^1, S^2)$ with stock return processes R^1, R^2, which we assume to take the values $(1 \pm a_1)$ and $(1 \pm a_2)$, respectively (so that we make the 'up' and 'down' movements symmetrical in each coordinate). Suppose that $a_1 = \frac{1}{2}$ and $a_2 = \frac{1}{4}$, and define, for each $\lambda \in (0, \frac{1}{2})$, a probability measure Q_λ by fixing, at each $t = 1, 2, \ldots, T$, the return probabilities as follows.

$$Q_\lambda(R_t^1 = 1 + a_1, R_t^2 = 1 + a_2) = \lambda = Q_\lambda(R_t^1 = 1 - a_1, R_t^2 = 1 - a_2)$$

$$Q_\lambda(R_t^1 = 1 + a_1, R_t^2 = 1 - a_2) = \frac{1}{2} - \lambda = Q_\lambda(R_t^1 = 1 - a_1, R_t^2 = 1 + a_2).$$

It is straightforward to check that each Q_λ is an EMM; that is,

$$E_{Q_\lambda}(R_t^i | \mathcal{F}_{t-1}) = E_{Q_\lambda}(R_t^i) = 1 \quad \text{for all } t \geq 1.$$

It can be shown (much as we did in Chapter 2) that the multi-factor Black–Scholes model is a limit of multi-factor random walk models *and* is complete. Consequently, it is possible to have a complete continuous-time model that is a limit (in some sense) of incomplete discrete models. If one is interested in 'maintaining completeness' along the approximating sequence, then one is forced to use *correlated* random walks; see [49], [123] for details.

Filtrations in Complete Finite Models

The completeness requirement in finite models is very stringent; fixing the degree of linear dependence among the values of the price increments ΔS_t on any partition set $A \in \mathcal{P}_{t-1}$ in terms of the number of cells into which $\mathcal{P}_t$ 'splits' the set A. It also ensures that the *filtration* $\mathbb{F} = (\mathcal{F}_t)$ which is determined by these partition sets is in fact the *minimal* filtration $\mathbb{F}^S$; that is, the σ-field $\mathcal{F}_t = \mathcal{F}_t^S = \sigma(S_u : u \leq t)$ for each t.

To see this, let Q denote the unique EMM in the complete market model and suppose that, on the contrary, the filtration $\mathbb{F} = (\mathcal{F}_t)$ strictly contains $\mathbb{F}^S$. Then there is a least $u \in \mathbb{T}$ such that $\mathcal{F}_u$ strictly contains $\mathcal{F}_u^S$. This means that some fixed $A \in \mathcal{P}_u^S$ (the minimal partition generating $\mathcal{F}_u^S$) can be split further into sets in the partition $\mathcal{P}_u$ generating $\mathcal{F}_u$; that is, $A = \cup_{i=1}^n A_i$ for some $A_i \in \mathcal{P}_u$ ($n \geq 2$).

Note that S_u is constant on $A = \cup_{i=1}^n A_i$. There is a unique set $B \in \mathcal{P}_{u-1} = \mathcal{P}_{u-1}^S$ that contains A. The partition $\mathcal{P}_u$ then contains disjoint sets $\{A_i : i = 1, 2, ..., m\}$ whose union is B, and since $A \subset B$, we can assume (re-ordering if needed) that $m \geq n$ and the sets $A_1, \ldots, A_n$ defined previously comprise the first n of these.

Let Q^* be a probability measure on $(\Omega, \mathcal{F})$ such that $Q^*(\cdot | B)$ defines different conditional probabilities with $Q^*(A_i | B) > 0$ for all $i \leq n$, and such that

$$\sum_{i=1}^n Q^*(A_i | B) = Q(A | B),$$

while

$$Q^*(A_j | B) = Q(A | B) \quad \text{for } j = n+1, \ldots, m,$$

and agreeing with Q otherwise. There are clearly many choices for such Q^*. Since ΔS_u is constant on $A = \bigcup_{i=1}^n A_i$, it follows that

$$E_{Q^*}(\Delta S_u|\mathcal{F}_{u-1})(\omega) = E_Q(\Delta S_u|\mathcal{F}_{u-1})(\omega) = 0$$

holds for all $\omega \in B$ and hence throughout Ω. Hence Q is not the only EMM in the model, which contradicts completeness.

Thus in a complete *finite* market model there is no room for 'extraneous information' that does not result purely from the past behaviour of the stock prices. This severely restricts their practical applicability, as Kreps [170], page 228 has observed: the presence of other factors (Kreps lists 'differential information, moral hazard and individual uncertainty about future tastes' as examples) that are not fully reflected in the security prices will destroy completeness. Nonetheless, in the more general setting of continuous-time finance these are the principal market models in which we are able to apply martingale techniques (and martingale representation in particular) to the full, in order to obtain precise solutions to the problems of option pricing and hedging.

4.5 Characterisation of Attainable Claims

More generally, we can characterise attainable claims in finite models. For this we also return briefly to a single-period setting, with prices $(S^i)_{0 \leq i \leq d}$ and $\mathbb{T} = \{0, 1\}$, defined, on a finite sample space $\Omega = \{\omega_i : 1 \leq i \leq k\}$, with $P(\{\omega_i\}) > 0$ for all $i \leq k$. Consider the $k \times (d+1)$ matrix $M = (S_1^i(\omega_j))_{1 \leq j \leq k, 0 \leq i \leq d}$ of security prices at time 1. The single-period model is complete if and only if for every given $X = (x_j)$ in $\mathbb{R}^k$, the equation $M\theta = X$ has a solution $\theta = (\theta^i)_{0 \leq i \leq d}$. This occurs if and only if the matrix M has rank k. In particular, if $k > (d+1)$ the model *cannot* be complete: this confirms our intuition that the number k of random outcomes cannot be 'spanned' by the $(d+1)$ security prices.

While this condition is not so easily checked for multi-period markets, it allows us to generalise our discussion to include the characterisation of attainable claims.

Proposition 4.5.1. *In a viable finite market model a contingent claim X is attainable if and only if the expectation $E_Q(\bar{X})$ is constant over all EMMs Q.*

Proof. We know that if X is attainable then $E_Q(\bar{X})$ takes the same value for every EMM Q. Thus we only need to prove the converse.

First consider the single-period model discussed previously. If X is not attainable, the matrix equation $M\theta = X$ has no solution $\theta \in \mathbb{R}^{d+1}$. Thus X does not belong to the subspace of $\mathbb{R}^k$ spanned by the columns $(S_1^i(\omega_j))_{j \leq k}$ $(0 \leq i \leq d)$ of M, so that its orthogonal projection X_M onto this subspace does not equal X. Hence taking the vector $y = (y_j)_{j \leq k}$ given by $y = X - X_M$ (or $X_M - X$ if necessary), we have found $y \in \mathbb{R}^k$ which is orthogonal to each column of M (written $y \cdot M = 0$) and $y \cdot X > 0$.

Now choose any EMM Q_1 and let $\delta > 0$ be small enough to ensure that $Q_2(\omega_j) = Q_1(\omega_j) + \delta y_j S_1^0(\omega_j) > 0$ for every $j \leq k$. (This is possible because all the $Q_1(\{\omega_j\}) > 0$.) We show that Q_2 is also an EMM for $\bar{S}$:

y annihilates the columns of M, hence

$$\sum_{j=1}^{k} y_j S_1^0(\omega_j) = 0, \quad \text{so that} \quad \sum_{j=1}^{k} Q_2(\omega_j) = \sum_{j=1}^{k} Q_1(\omega_j) = 1,$$

and so Q_2 is a probability measure equivalent to Q_1. Moreover, for $1 \leq i \leq d$,

$$\begin{aligned}
E_{Q_2}(\bar{S}_1^i) &= \sum_{j=1}^{k} Q_2(\omega_j) \bar{S}_1^i(\omega_j) = \sum_{j=1}^{k} Q_1(\omega_j) \bar{S}_1^i(\omega_j) + \delta \sum_{j=1}^{k} y_j S_1^i(\omega_j) \\
&= E_{Q_1}(\bar{S}_1^i) = \bar{S}_0^i,
\end{aligned}$$

since y also annihilates the ith column of M and since Q_1 is an EMM for S. Hence Q_2 is also an EMM for S. However, since $y \cdot X = a > 0$, it follows that $E_{Q_2}(\bar{X}) = E_{Q_1}(\bar{X}) + \delta a \neq E_{Q_1}(\bar{X})$.

This proves the converse for the case of single-period models. The remainder of the proof is a familiar application of the step-wise approach adopted in Chapter 3: given a nonattainable claim X in the finite model, there is no generating strategy, so any attempt to build such a strategy backwards from time T will break down at one of the stages of the underlying single-period models in the event tree. Two conditional one-step probabilities can be constructed as previously for this step, and they will lead to EMMs whose expectations differ on $\bar{X}$. This completes the proof of the proposition. □

Remark 4.5.2. Note that the same considerations lead to a simple proof that completeness of a finite market model implies uniqueness of the EMM.

First, it is now clear that a viable finite market model is complete if and only if each underlying single-period model in the event tree is complete. Hence we can restrict attention to single-period models. Now suppose that every claim X in such a model is attainable, but that there are two EMMs, Q_1 and Q_2 for the model. These must differ at some $\omega* \in \Omega$ (recall that we assume that neither measure has non-empty null set) and we can define the claim $X(\omega) = S^0(\omega*)\mathbf{1}_{\{\omega=\omega*\}}$. Thus

$$E_{Q_1}(\bar{X}) = Q_1(\{\omega*\}) \neq Q_2(\{\omega*\}) = E_{Q_2}(\bar{X})$$

and by Proposition 4.5.1 the claim X is not attainable, contrary to our assumption. Hence the EMM must be unique, as asserted.

5

Stopping Times and American Options

5.1   Hedging American Claims

Random Exercise Dates

American options differ fundamentally from their European counterparts, since the exercise date is now at the holder's disposal, and not fixed in advance. The only constraint is that the option ceases to be valid at time T and thus cannot be exercised *after* the expiry date T.

We model discrete-time options on a given filtered probability space $(\Omega, \mathcal{F}, P, \mathbb{T}, \mathbb{F})$ with time set $\mathbb{T} = \{0, 1, 2, \ldots, T\}$, and filtration $\mathbb{F} = (\mathcal{F}_t)_{t \in \mathbb{T}}$ as before on the probability space $(\Omega, \mathcal{F}, P)$. We wish to develop general market models, and the restriction to finite models does not apply in this chapter, unless specifically indicated otherwise. At the same time, the pricing problem for American options is more complex than those considered up to now, and we need to develop appropriate mathematical concepts to deal with it.

First, we clearly require a concept of 'random exercise dates' to reflect that the option holder can choose different dates at which to exercise the option, depending on her perception of the random movement of the underlying stock price. The exercise date τ is therefore no longer the constant T, but becomes a function on Ω with values in $\mathbb{T}$, that is, a *random variable* $\tau : \Omega \mapsto \mathbb{T}$. It remains natural to assume that investors are not prescient, so that the decision whether to exercise at time t when in state ω depends only on information contained in the σ-field $\mathcal{F}_t$. Hence our exercise dates should satisfy the requirement that $\{\tau = t\} \in \mathcal{F}_t$. Recalling that the $(\mathcal{F}_t)$ increase with t, it is not difficult to complete the following.

Exercise 5.1.1. Show that the following requirements on a random variable $\tau : \Omega \mapsto \mathbb{T}$ are equivalent.
   (i) for all $t \in \mathbb{T}$, $\{\tau = t\} \in \mathcal{F}_t$;
   (ii) for all $t \in \mathbb{T}$, $\{\tau \leq t\} \in \mathcal{F}_t$.

We also discuss significant aspects of martingale theory and optimal stopping—these often require care about measurability problems. The greater technical complexity is offset by wider applicability of our results, and they provide good practice for the unavoidable technicalities that we encounter in the continuous-time setting. Throughout, however, it is instructive to focus on the underlying ideas, and it may be advantageous, in this and the following chapters, to skip lightly over some technical matters at a first reading.

Hedging Constraints

Hedge portfolios also require a little more care than in the European case, since the liability inherent in the option may face the writer at any time in $\mathbb{T}$. More generally, an American contingent claim is a function of the whole *path* $t \mapsto S_t(\omega)$ of the price process under consideration, for each $\omega \in \Omega$, not just a function of $S_T(\omega)$. We again assume that $S = \{S_t^i : i = 0, 1, \ldots, d; t \in \mathbb{T}\}$ where $S_t^0 = \beta_t^{-1}$ is a (nonrandom) riskless bond, and the stock price S^i is a random process indexed by $\mathbb{T}$ for each $i = 1, \ldots, d$.

Accordingly, let $f = (f_t(S))_{t \in \mathbb{T}}$ denote an American contingent claim, so that f is a *sequence* of non-negative random variables, each depending, in general, on $\{S_i(\omega) : 0 \leq i \leq d\}$ for every $\omega \in \Omega$. A *hedge portfolio* with initial investment $x > 0$ for this claim will then be a self-financing strategy $\theta = \{\theta_t^i : i = 0, 1, \ldots, d; t \in \mathbb{T}\}$, producing a value process $V(\theta)$ that satisfies the hedging constraints:

$$V_0(\theta) = \theta_1 \cdot S_0 = x$$
$$V_t(\theta)(\omega) \geq f_t(S_0(\omega), S_1(\omega), \ldots, S_T(\omega)) \tag{5.1}$$

for all $\omega \in \Omega$ and $t > 0$ in $\mathbb{T}$.

The hedge portfolio θ is *minimal* if, for some random variable τ with $\{\omega : \tau(\omega) = t\} \in \mathcal{F}_t$ for all $t \in \mathbb{T}$ we have:

$$V_{\tau(\omega)}(\theta)(\omega) = f_{\tau(\omega)}(S_0(\omega), \ldots, S_T(\omega)). \tag{5.2}$$

Since the times at which the claim f takes its greatest value may vary with ω, the hedge portfolio θ must enable the seller (writer) of the claim to 'cover his losses' in all eventualities. The hedge portfolio thus no longer 'replicates' the value of the claim in general, but it may never be less than this value.

This raises several questions for the given claim f.

(i) Do such self-financing strategies exist for a given value of the initial investment $x > 0$?

(ii) Do minimal self-financing strategies always exist for such x?

(iii) What is the optimal choice of the random exercise time τ?

(iv) How should the 'rational' time-0 *price* of the option be defined?

These questions are examined in this chapter. To deal with them, however, we first need to develop the necessary mathematical tools.

5.2   Stopping Times and Stopped Processes

The preceding considerations lead us to study 'random times,' which we call *stopping times*, for (discrete) stochastic processes more generally. While our applications often have a finite time horizon, it is convenient to take the study further, to stopping times that take values in the set $\bar{\mathbb{N}} = \{0, 1, 2, \ldots, \infty\}$. This extension requires us to deal with questions of martingale convergence, which are also needed in later chapters. The well-known martingale convergence theorems are discussed briefly; refer to other texts (e.g., [87], [169], [258]) for detailed proofs.

The idea of stopping times for stochastic processes, while intuitively obvious, provides perhaps the most distinguishing feature of the techniques of probability theory that we use in this book. At its simplest level, a stopping time τ should provide a gambling strategy for a gambler seeking to maximise his winnings; since martingales represent 'fair' games, such a strategy should not involve prescience, and therefore the decision to 'stop' the adapted process $X = (X_t)$ representing the gambler's winnings at time t should only involve knowledge of the progress of the winnings up to that point; that is, if state ω occurs, the choice $\tau(\omega) = t$ should depend only on $\mathcal{F}_t$. Generally, suppose we are given a filtration $\mathbb{F} = (\mathcal{F}_t)_{t \in \mathbb{N}}$ on $(\Omega, \mathcal{F}, P)$ with $\mathcal{F} = \mathcal{F}_\infty = \sigma(\bigcup_{t=0}^\infty \mathcal{F}_t)$, and such that $\mathcal{F}_0$ contains all P-null sets. We have:

Definition 5.2.1. A *stopping time* is a random variable $\tau : (\Omega, \mathcal{F}) \to \bar{\mathbb{N}}$ such that for all $t \in \mathbb{N}$, $\{\tau \le t\} \in \mathcal{F}_t$.

Remark 5.2.2. Exercise 5.1.1 shows that we could equally well have used the condition: for all $t \in \mathbb{N}$, $\{\tau = t\} \in \mathcal{F}_t$. Note, however, that this depends on the countability of $\mathbb{N}$. For continuous-time models the time set $\mathbb{T}$ is a finite or infinite interval on the positive halfline, and we have to use the condition, for all $t \in \mathbb{T}$, $\{\tau \le t\} \in \mathcal{F}_t$, in the definition of stopping times. In discrete-time models the condition $\{\tau = t\}$ is often much simpler to check.

Nevertheless, many of the basic results about stopping times, and their proofs, are identical in both set-ups, and the exceptions become clear from the following examples and exercises.

Example 5.2.3. (i)   Observe that if $\tau = t_0$ a.s., then $\{\tau = t_0\} \in \mathcal{F}_0 \subset \mathcal{F}_{t_0}$, so that each 'constant time' is a stopping time. It is similarly easy to see that $\tau + t_0$ is a stopping time for each stopping time τ and constant t_0.

(ii)   Suppose that σ and τ are stopping times. Then $\sigma \vee \tau := \max(\sigma, \tau)$ and $\sigma \wedge \tau := \min(\sigma, \tau)$ are stopping times, because $\{\sigma \vee \tau \leq t\} = \{\sigma \leq t\} \cap \{\tau \leq t\}$ and $\{\sigma \wedge \tau \leq t\} = \{\sigma \leq t\} \cup \{\tau \leq t\}$ and in both cases the sets on the right are in $\mathcal{F}_t$ since σ and τ are stopping times.

(iii)   Let $(X_t)_{t \in \mathbb{N}}$ be an $\mathbb{F}$-adapted process and let B be a Borel set. We now show that $\tau_B : \Omega \to \mathbb{N}$ defined by $\tau_B(\omega) = \min\{s \geq 1 : X_s \in B\}$ (where $\min \emptyset = \infty$) is an $\mathbb{F}$-stopping time. (We call τ_B the *hitting time* of B.)

To see this, note that each $X_s^{-1}(B) \in \mathcal{F}_s$ since X_s is $\mathcal{F}_s$-measurable, and that since $\mathbb{F}$ is increasing, $\mathcal{F}_s \subset \mathcal{F}_t$ when $s \leq t$. Hence for any $t \geq 0$, $\{\tau_B = t\} \in \mathcal{F}_t$, as

$$\{\tau_B = t\} = \bigcap_{s=0}^{t-1}\{\tau_B > s\} \cap X_t^{-1}(B) = \bigcap_{s=0}^{t-1}(\Omega \setminus X_s^{-1}(B)) \cap X_t^{-1}(B).$$

The continuous-time counterpart of this result is rather more difficult in general, and involves delicate measurability questions; in special cases, such as when B is an open set and $t \mapsto X_t(\omega)$ is continuous, it becomes much simpler (see, e.g., [169]).

Exercise 5.2.4. Suppose that (τ_n) is a sequence of stopping times. Extend the argument in Example (ii) to show that $\bigvee_{n \geq 1} \tau_n = \sup(\tau_n : n \geq 1)$ and $\bigwedge_{n \geq 1} \tau_n = \inf(\tau_n : n \geq 1)$ are stopping times. (Note that this uses the requirement that the σ-fields $\mathcal{F}_t$ are closed under *countable* unions and intersections.)

Fix a stochastic basis $(\Omega, \mathcal{F}, \bar{\mathbb{N}}, \mathbb{F}, P)$ with $\mathcal{F} = \mathcal{F}_\infty = \sigma(\cup_{t=0}^\infty \mathcal{F}_t)$. Recall that we assume throughout that the σ-fields $\mathcal{F}_t$ are *complete*. First we consider random processes 'stopped' at a *finite* stopping time τ, as most of our applications assume a finite trading horizon T.

Definition 5.2.5. If $X = (X_t)$ is an adapted process and τ is any a.s. *finite* stopping time, then we define the map $\omega \mapsto X_{\tau(\omega)}(\omega)$, giving the values of X at the stopping time τ, by the random variable $X_\tau = \sum_{t \geq 0} X_t \mathbf{1}_{\{\tau = t\}}$.

To see that X_τ is $\mathcal{F}$-measurable, note that, for any Borel set B in $\mathbb{R}$,

$$\{X_\tau \in B\} = \bigcup_{t \geq 0}(\{X_t \in B\} \cap \{\tau = t\}) \in \mathcal{F}. \tag{5.3}$$

Moreover, if we define the σ-field of *events prior to τ* by

$$\mathcal{F}_\tau = \{A \in \mathcal{F} : \text{for all } t \geq 1, \ A \cap \{\tau = t\} \in \mathcal{F}_t\} \tag{5.4}$$

then (5.3) shows that X_τ is $\mathcal{F}_\tau$-measurable, since $\{X_t \in B\}$ is in $\mathcal{F}_t$ for each t, so that $\{X_\tau \in B\} \in \mathcal{F}_\tau$. Trivially, τ itself is $\mathcal{F}_\tau$-measurable.

Exercise 5.2.6. Let σ and τ be stopping times.

(i) Suppose that $A \in \mathcal{F}_\sigma$. Show that $A \cap \{\sigma \le \tau\}$ and $A \cap \{\sigma = \tau\}$ belong to $\mathcal{F}_\tau$. Deduce that if $\sigma \le \tau$ then $\mathcal{F}_\sigma \subset \mathcal{F}_\tau$. (*Hint:* The continuous-time analogue of this result is proved in Theorem 6.1.8. Convince yourself that a virtually identical statement and proof applies here.)

Deduce that, for any σ, τ, $\mathcal{F}_{\sigma \wedge \tau} \subset \mathcal{F}_\sigma \subset \mathcal{F}_{\sigma \vee \tau}$.

(ii) Show that the sets $\{\sigma < \tau\}$, $\{\sigma = \tau\}$, and $\{\sigma > \tau\}$ belong to both $\mathcal{F}_\sigma$ and $\mathcal{F}_\tau$.

The next two results, which are extended considerably later, use the fact that stopping a martingale is essentially a special case of taking a martingale transform. They are used extensively in the rest of this chapter.

Theorem 5.2.7 (Optional Sampling for Bounded Stopping Times).
Let X be a supermartingale and suppose that σ and τ are bounded stopping times with $\sigma \le \tau$ a.s. Then

$$E(X_\tau | \mathcal{F}_\sigma) \le X_\sigma. \tag{5.5}$$

If X is a martingale, $E(X_\tau | \mathcal{F}_\sigma) = X_\sigma$.

Proof. Consider the process $\phi = (\phi_t)$, where $\phi_t = \mathbf{1}_{(\sigma < t \le \tau)}$. The random variable ϕ_t is $\mathcal{F}_{t-1}$-measurable for $t > 0$, since

$$\{\sigma < t \le \tau\} = \{\sigma < t\} \cap (\Omega \backslash \{\tau < t\}).$$

Thus ϕ is predictable and non-negative, and we consider the transform $\phi \bullet X$. Since τ is assumed to be bounded (by some $k \in \mathbb{N}$, say) we have

$$|(\phi \bullet X)_t| \le |X_0| + \ldots + |X_k|$$

for each t, so that each $Z_t = (\phi \bullet X)_t$ is integrable. Thus Z is a supermartingale, with $Z_0 = 0$ and $Z_k = X_\tau - X_\sigma$. So

$$0 = E(Z_0) \ge E(Z_k) = E(X_\tau - X_\sigma).$$

Now consider $A \in \mathcal{F}_\sigma$ and apply the preceding to the bounded stopping times σ', τ', where σ' equals σ on A, and k otherwise, with a similar definition for τ'. (The reader should check carefully, using (5.4) and Exercise 5.2.6(i), that these are indeed stopping times!)

This yields $\int_A X_\tau dP \le \int_A X_\sigma dP$, hence the result follows, using Exercise 5.2.6(ii). $\qquad\square$

Definition 5.2.8. Let X be a stochastic process on $(\Omega, \mathcal{F}, P, \mathbb{T}, \mathbb{F})$, σ any stopping time. Define the *process X^σ, stopped at time σ* by $X_t^\sigma = X_{\sigma \wedge t}$ for all $t \in \mathbb{T}$.

Then X^σ is again a transform $\phi \cdot X$, with $\phi_t = \mathbf{1}_{\{\sigma \geq t\}}$. To complement Theorem 5.2.7 we have

Theorem 5.2.9 (Optional Stopping Theorem). *If X is a (super-) martingale and σ is a bounded stopping time, then X^σ is again a (super-) martingale for the filtration $\mathbb{F}$.*

Proof. We deal with the supermartingale case. For $t \geq 1$,

$$X_{t \wedge \sigma} = X_0 + \sum_{s \leq t} \phi_s \Delta X_s,$$

where we have set $\phi_s = \mathbf{1}_{\{s \leq \sigma\}}$, which is predictable. Hence X^σ is adapted to $\mathbb{F}$ and $\phi_s \geq 0$. Hence X^σ is a supermartingale. The martingale case is then obvious. □

Note carefully that $(t, \omega) \mapsto X_t^{\sigma(\omega)}(\omega) = X_{t \wedge \sigma(\omega)}(\omega)$ is a *process*, while $\omega \mapsto X_{\sigma(\omega)}(\omega)$ is a *random variable*.

5.3 Uniformly Integrable Martingales

In order to deal with unbounded stopping times we need to develop a little of the convergence theory for a particularly important class of martingales indexed by $\mathbb{N}$, namely, uniformly integrable martingales. These also feature prominently in the continuous-time situation.

Definition 5.3.1. A family $\mathcal{C}$ of random variables is *uniformly integrable (UI)* if, given $\epsilon > 0$, there exists $K > 0$ such that

$$\int_{\{|X|>K\}} |X| dP < \epsilon \quad \forall X \in \mathcal{C}. \tag{5.6}$$

In other words, $\sup_{X \in \mathcal{C}} \int_{\{|X|>K} |X| dP \to 0$ as $K \to \infty$, which explains the terminology. Such families are easy to find.

Examples of UI Families

(i) If $\mathcal{C}$ is bounded in $L^p(\Omega, \mathcal{F}, P)$ for some $p > 1$, then $\mathcal{C}$ is UI.

To see this, choose A such that $E(|X|^p) < A$ for all $X \in \mathcal{C}$ and fix $X \in \mathcal{C}$, $K > 0$. Write $Y = |X| \mathbf{1}_{\{|X|>K\}}$. Then $Y(\omega) \geq K > 0$ for all $\omega \in \Omega$ and since $p > 1$ it is clear that $Y \leq K^{1-p} Y^p$. Thus

$$E(Y) \leq K^{1-p} E(Y^p) \leq K^{1-p} E(|X|^p) \leq K^{1-p} A.$$

But K^{1-p} decreases to 0 when $K \to \infty$, so (5.6) holds.

(ii) If $\mathcal{C}$ is UI, then it is bounded in L^1, but the converse is false (*Exercise: Prove this!*). A useful additional hypothesis is domination in L^1: if there exists $Y \geq 0$ in L^1 such that $|X| \leq Y$ for all $X \in \mathcal{C}$, then $\mathcal{C}$ is UI. (See, e.g., [258] for a simple proof.)

(iii) To illustrate why uniform integrability is so important for martingales, we have the following.

Proposition 5.3.2. *Let* $X \in L^p$, $p \geq 1$. *The family*

$$\mathcal{C} = \{E(X|\mathcal{G}) : \mathcal{G} \text{ is a sub-}\sigma\text{-field of } \mathcal{F}\}$$

is UI.

We prove the case $p > 1$ (which is all we need in the sequel) and refer to [258], Theorem 13.4 for the case $p = 1$. First we need an important inequality, which is used frequently.

Proposition 5.3.3 (Jensen's Inequality). *Suppose* $X \in L^1$. *If* $\phi : \mathbb{R} \mapsto \mathbb{R}$ *is convex and* $\phi(X) \in L^1$, *then*

$$E(\phi(X)|\mathcal{G}) \geq \phi(E(X|\mathcal{G})). \tag{5.7}$$

Proof. Any convex function $\phi : \mathbb{R} \mapsto \mathbb{R}$ is the supremum of a family of affine functions, so there exists a sequence (ϕ_n) of real functions with $\phi_n(x) = a_n x + b_n$ for each n, such that $\phi = \sup_n \phi_n$. Therefore $\phi(X) \geq a_n X + b_n$ holds a.s. for each (and hence all) n. So by the posititivity of $E(\cdot|\mathcal{G})$, $E(\phi(X)|\mathcal{G}) \geq \sup_n(a_n E(X|\mathcal{G}) + b_n) = \phi(E(X|\mathcal{G}))$ a.s.

The proposition follows easily, since with $\phi(x) = |x|^p$ the inequality implies that $|E(X|\mathcal{G})|^p \leq E(|X|^p|\mathcal{G})$, and taking expectations and pth roots on both sides we obtain

$$||E(X|\mathcal{G})||_p \leq ||X||_p$$

for all $\mathcal{G} \subset \mathcal{F}$. Thus the family $\mathcal{C}$ is L^p-bounded, hence UI. □

Remark 5.3.4. (i) Note that the Jensen inequality shows that the conditional expectation operator is a *contraction* on L^p. The same is true for L^1, since with $\phi(x) = |x|$ we obtain $|E(X|\mathcal{G})| \leq E(|X||\mathcal{G})$, and hence $||E(X|\mathcal{G})||_1 \leq ||X||_1$.

(ii) Jensen's inequality also shows that given $p > 1$ and an L^p-bounded martingale $(M_t, \mathcal{F}_t)_{t \in \mathbb{T}}$, the sequence $(N_t, \mathcal{F}_t)$ is a *sub*martingale, where $N_t = |M_t|^p$; this follows upon taking $\phi(x) = |x|^p$, so that by (5.7), with $t \geq s$,

$$E(N_t|\mathcal{F}_s) = E(|M_t|^p|\mathcal{F}_s) \geq |E(M_t|\mathcal{F}_s)|^p = |M_s|^p = N_s.$$

Here the integrability of N_t, which is required for the application of (5.7) follows from the L^p-boundedness of M_t. Similar results follow upon applying (5.7) with $\phi(x) = x^+$ or $\phi(x) = (x-K)^+$, with suitable integrability assumptions.

Martingale Convergence

We now review briefly the principal limit theorems for martingales. The role of uniform integrability is evident from:

Proposition 5.3.5. *Suppose* (X_n) *is a sequence of integrable random variables and X is integrable. The following are equivalent.*

(i) $\|X_n - X\|_1 = E(|X_n - X|) \to 0$;

(ii) *the sequence* (X_n) *is UI and $X_n \to X$ in probability.*

See [87] or [258] for the proof of this standard result. Since a.s. convergence implies convergence in probability, we have

Corollary 5.3.6. *If (X_n) is UI and $X_n \to X$ a.s., then $X \in L^1$ and $X_n \to X$ in L^1-norm (i.e., $\|X_n - X\|_1 \to 0$).*

Thus to prove that a UI martingale converges in L^1-norm, the principal task is showing a.s. convergence. Doob's original proof of this result remains instructive and has been greatly simplified by the use of martingale transforms. We outline here the beautifully simple treatment given in [258], to which we refer for details.

Let $t \mapsto M_t(\omega)$ denote the sample paths of a random process M defined on $\mathbb{N} \times \Omega$ and interpret $\Delta M_t = M_t - M_{t-1}$ as 'winnings' per unit stake on game t. The total winnings ('gains process') can be represented by the martingale transform $Y = C \bullet M$ given by a playing strategy C, in which we stake one unit as soon as M has taken a value below a, continue placing unit stakes until M reaches values above b, after which we do not play until M is again below a, and repeat the process indefinitely. It is 'obvious' (and can be shown inductively) that C is predictable.

Let $U_T[a, b](\omega)$ denote the number of 'upcrossings' of $[a, b]$ by the path $t \mapsto M_t$, that is, the maximal $k \in \mathbb{N}$ such that there are $0 \leq s_1 < t_1 < s_2 < \ldots < t_k < T$ for which $M_{s_i}(\omega) < a$ and $M_{t_i}(\omega) > b$ $(i = 1, 2, \ldots, k)$. Then

$$Y_T(\omega) \geq (b - a)U_T[a, b](\omega) - (M_T(\omega) - a)^- \tag{5.8}$$

since Y increases by at least $(b - a)$ during each upcrossing, while the final term overestimates the potential loss in the final play.

Now suppose that M is a supermartingale. Since C is bounded and non-negative, the transform Y is again a supermartingale (the results of Chapter 2 apply here as everything is restricted to the finite time set $\{0, 1, 2, \ldots, T\}$). Thus $E(Y_T) \leq E(Y_0) = 0$. Then (5.8) yields:

$$(b - a)E(U_T[a, b]) \leq E(M_T - a)^-. \tag{5.9}$$

If, moreover, $M = (M_t)_{t \in \mathbb{N}}$ is L^1-bounded, $K = \sup_t \|M_t\|_1$ is finite, so that $(b - a)E(U_T[a, b]) \leq |a| + K$. The bound is independent of T, so monotone convergence implies that $(b - a)E(U_\infty[a, b]) < \infty$, where $U_\infty[a, b] = \lim_{T \to \infty} U_T[a, b]$.

Hence $\{U_\infty[a, b] = \infty\}$ is a P-null set; that is, every interval is 'upcrossed' only finitely often by almost all paths of M. Now the set $D \subset \Omega$ on which $M_t(\omega)$ does *not* converge to a finite *or* infinite limit can be written as

$$D = \bigcup_{\{a, b \in \mathbb{Q} : a < b\}} D_{a,b},$$

where $D_{a,b} = \{\omega : \liminf_t M_t(\omega) < a < b < \limsup_t M_t(\omega)\}$, and $D_{a,b} \subset \{\omega : U_\infty[a, b] = \infty\}$, so that D is also P-null.

Thus the a.s. limit M_∞ exists a.s.(P) in $[-\infty, \infty]$ and by Fatou's lemma

$$||M_\infty||_1 = E(\liminf |M_t|) \leq \liminf ||M_t||_1 \leq K$$

so that M_∞ is in L^1 and thus a.s. finite.

Finally, if the family $(M_t)_{t \in \mathbb{N}}$ is a martingale and is also UI (we simply say that M is a UI martingale), then it follows at once from Corollary 5.3.6 that $M_t \to M_\infty$ in L^1−norm. Moreover the martingale property 'extends to the limit'; that is, for all t,

$$M_t = E(M_\infty | \mathcal{F}_t). \tag{5.10}$$

To see this, note that for $A \in \mathcal{F}_t$ and $u \geq t$, the martingale property yields $\int_A M_u dP = \int_A M_s dP$, while

$$|\int_A M_t dP - \int_A M_\infty dP| \leq \int_A |M_t - M_\infty| dP \leq ||M_t - M_\infty||_1 \to 0$$

as $t \to \infty$. This proves (5.10).

We say that the limit random variable M_∞ *closes* the martingale M whenever (5.10) holds.

To summarise:

Theorem 5.3.7 (Martingale Convergence Theorems).   (i) *If* M *is an* L^1-*bounded supermartingale,* $M_\infty(\omega) = \lim_{t \to \infty} M_t(\omega)$ *exists a.s.* (P) *and the random variable* M_∞ *is integrable.*

(ii) *If* M *is a UI martingale,* $M_t \to M_\infty$ *a.s. and in* L^1-*norm, and* M_∞ *closes the martingale* M*; that is, for all finite* t*,* $M_t = E(M_\infty | \mathcal{F}_t)$ *a.s.*

(iii) *If* $X \in L^1$ *and* $M_t = E(X | \mathcal{F}_t)$ *for all* $t \in \mathbb{N}$*, then* M *is a UI martingale and* $M_t \to E(X | \mathcal{F}_\infty)$ *a.s and in* L^1*.*

(Only the final statement still requires proof; this can be found in [258], 14.2. Note that if $\mathcal{F} = \mathcal{F}_\infty$ (as we assume) then $M_t \to X$.)

The preceding results have been proved for discrete-time martingales, but have identical counterparts in continuous time for right-continuous processes. They are therefore used in both settings in the sequel.

One immediate consequence of the convergence theorems is that for UI martingales we can extend Definition 5.2.5 to general stopping times: given a UI martingale M and any stopping time τ, then $M_\tau(\omega) = M_{\tau(\omega)}(\omega)$ is now also well-defined on the set $\{\tau = \infty\}$, on which set $M_\tau = M_\infty$.

We extend Theorems 5.2.7 (Optional Sampling) and 5.2.9 (Optional Stopping) to general stopping times when M is a UI martingale—first we have

Theorem 5.3.8. *Let M be a UI martingale and τ a stopping time. Then*

$$E(M_\infty | \mathcal{F}_\tau) = M_\tau \ a.s.(P) \tag{5.11}$$

Proof. As M_∞ closes M, $M_t = E(M_\infty | \mathcal{F}_t)$ for all t, and as $\tau \wedge t$ is a bounded stopping time, Theorem 5.2.7 yields $M_{\tau \wedge t} = E(M_t | \mathcal{F}_{\tau \wedge t})$. Hence $E(M_\infty | \mathcal{F}_{\tau \wedge t}) = M_{\tau \wedge t}$.

Let $A \in \mathcal{F}_\tau$. The set $B_t = A \cap \{\tau \leq t\}$ is in $\mathcal{F}_t$ by definition and in $\mathcal{F}_\tau$ since τ is $\mathcal{F}_\tau$-measurable. Hence $B_t \in \mathcal{F}_{\tau \wedge t}$ and so

$$\int_{B_t} M_\infty dP = \int_{B_t} M_{\tau \wedge t} dP = \int_{B_t} M_\tau dP. \tag{5.12}$$

Assume without loss that M_∞ (and hence each M_t) is non-negative, and let $t \uparrow \infty$. Then (5.12) shows that

$$\int_{A \cap \{\tau < \infty\}} M_\infty dP = \int_{A \cap \{\tau < \infty\}} M_\tau dP$$

and since $M_\tau = M_\infty$ trivially on $\{\tau = \infty\}$, the result follows.   □

Corollary 5.3.9.   (i) *Optional Sampling: If M is UI martingale and $\sigma \leq \tau$ are stopping times, then*

$$E(M_\tau | \mathcal{F}_\sigma) = M_\sigma a.s.(P). \tag{5.13}$$

(ii) *Optional Stopping: If M is a UI martingale and τ a stopping time, then $M_\tau \in L^1$ and M^τ is a UI martingale. In particular $E(M_\tau) = E(M_0)$.*

Doob Decomposition and Quadratic Variation

Again let $(\Omega, \mathcal{F}, P, \mathbb{N}, \mathbb{F})$ be a stochastic basis, and let $X = (X_t)_{t \in \mathbb{T}}$ be an adapted process. Since martingales describe what we might call 'purely random' behaviour, it is natural to ask to what extent the 'martingale part' of X can be isolated from the 'long-term trends' that X exhibits. In discrete time this is easily accomplished; remarkably there is also such a decomposition in continuous time (the *Doob-Meyer decomposition*, see [87], [169]) and this fact underlies the success of general stochastic integration and the success of martingale methods in continuous-time finance.

Definition 5.3.10. Given an adapted sequence $X = (X_t)$ of random variables on $(\Omega, \mathcal{F}, P)$, define processes M, A by

$$
\begin{aligned}
M_0 &= 0, & \Delta M_t &= M_t - M_{t-1} = X_t - E(X_t|\mathcal{F}_{t-1}) \quad (t > 0), \\
A_0 &= 0, & \Delta A_t &= A_t - A_{t-1} = E(X_t|\mathcal{F}_{t-1}) - X_{t-1} \quad (t > 0).
\end{aligned}
\tag{5.14}
$$

It is clear that A_t is $\mathcal{F}_{t-1}$-measurable, so that A is *predictable*. M is a *martingale* null at 0, since $E(\Delta M_t|\mathcal{F}_{t-1}) = 0$. Thus we have, for all $t > 0$:

$$
E(\Delta X_t|\mathcal{F}_{t-1}) = \Delta A_t.
\tag{5.15}
$$

By construction, $\Delta M_t + \Delta A_t = \Delta X_t$ for all $t > 0$. Adding terms for $s \leq t$, it is clear that $X_t = X_0 + M_t + A_t$ for all $t \geq 0$. We call this the *Doob decomposition* of the adapted process X.

The Doob decomposition is unique in the following sense. If we also have $X - X_0 = M' + A'$ for some martingale M' and predictable process A', then $M + A = X - X_0 = M' + A'$, so that $M - M' = A' - A$ is a predictable martingale. Such a process must be constant, as we saw in Chapter 2. Hence (up to some fixed P-null set N, for all $t \in \mathbb{N}$) $X_t = X_0 + M_t + A_t$ is the *unique* decomposition of an adapted process X into the sum of its initial value, a martingale, and a predictable process A, both null at 0.

When X is a submartingale, (5.15) shows that $\Delta A_t \geq 0$, so that $t \mapsto A_t(\omega)$ is *increasing* in t, for almost all $\omega \in \Omega$. This increasing predictable process A therefore has an a.s. limit A_∞ (which can take the value $+\infty$ in general.)

Now consider the special case where $X = M^2$ and M is an L^2-bounded martingale with $M_0 = 0$; then M^2 is a submartingale, by Jensen's inequality (5.7) (see Remark 5.3.4(ii)). The Doob decomposition $M^2 = N + A$ consists of a UI martingale N and a predictable increasing process A, both null at 0. Define $A_\infty = \lim_{t \uparrow \infty} A_t$ (a.s.). We have $E(M_t^2) = E(N_t) + E(A_t) = E(A_t)$ for all $t \in \mathbb{N}$, and these quantities are bounded precisely when $A_\infty \in L^1$.

Observe, using (5.15), that, since M is a martingale,

$$
\begin{aligned}
\Delta A_t &= E((M_t^2 - M_{t-1}^2)|\mathcal{F}_{t-1}) \\
&= E((M_t - M_{t-1})^2|\mathcal{F}_{t-1}) = E((\Delta M_t)^2|\mathcal{F}_{t-1})
\end{aligned}
\tag{5.16}
$$

For this reason we call A the *quadratic variation of M* and write $A = \langle M \rangle$. We have shown that *an L^2-bounded martingale has integrable quadratic variation.*

Remark 5.3.11. In Chapters 6 through 8 we make fuller use of the preceding results in the continuous-time setting. The translation of the convergence theorems so that they apply to continuous-time UI martingales is relatively straightforward (though somewhat tedious), once one has established that such a martingale M, with time set $[0, T]$ or $[0, \infty)$, always possesses a 'version' almost all of whose paths $t \mapsto M_t(\omega)$ are right-continuous and have left limits. (This enables one to use countable dense subsets to approximate the path behaviour and use the results just presented; see [87], [169] for details.) With the interpretation of $\mathbb{T}$ as an interval in $\mathbb{R}^+$ the convergence theorems and the optional sampling and optional stopping results proved in the foregoing go over verbatim to the continuous-time setting, and we assume this in Chapter 6 and beyond.

Of particular importance in continuous time is the analogue of the Doob decomposition, the *Doob–Meyer decomposition* of a sub- (or super-) martingale; we briefly outline its principal features without proof (see [87], Chapter 8 for a full treatment).

If $\mathbb{T} = [0, \infty)$ and $X = (X_t)$ is a supermartingale with right-continuous paths $t \mapsto X_t(\omega)$ for P-almost all $\omega \in \Omega$, then we say that X *is of class D* if the family $\{X_\tau : \tau$ is a stopping time$\}$ is UI. (If X is a UI martingale this is automatic from Theorem 5.3.8, but this is not generally so for supermartingales.) Every such supermartingale has decomposition $X_t = M_t - A_t$, where M is a UI martingale and the increasing process A has $A_0 = 0$ and is *predictable*. (This means that A is measurable with respect to the σ-field $\mathcal{P}$ on $[0, \infty) \times \Omega$ that is generated by the continuous processes.) This decomposition is unique up to indistinguishability (see Definition 6.1.12) and the process A is integrable.

Given an L^2-bounded (hence UI) martingale M, the decomposition again defines a quadratic variation for the submartingale $M^2 = N + A$, and we write $A = \langle M \rangle$. Note that since M is a martingale, (5.16) also holds in this setting, which justifies the terminology. Of particular interest to us are martingales whose quadratic variation is nonrandom; we find (Chapter 6) that Brownian Motion W is a martingale such that $\langle W \rangle_t = t$.

5.4 Optimal Stopping: The Snell Envelope

American Options

We return to our consideration of American options on a finite discrete time set: consider a price process $S = (S^0, S^1)$ consisting of a riskless bond $S_t^0 = (1 + r)^t$ and a single risky stock $(S_t^1)_{t \in \mathbb{T}}$, where $\mathbb{T} = \{0, 1, 2, \ldots, T\}$ for finite $T > 0$ and $r > 0$, defined on a probability space $(\Omega, \mathcal{F}, P)$. We have seen that the holder's freedom to choose the exercise date (without prescience) requires the option writer (seller) of an American call option with strike K, to hedge against a liability of $(S_\tau^1 - K)^+$ at a (random) stopping time $\tau : \Omega \mapsto \mathbb{T}$. Thus, if the system is in state $\omega \in \Omega$, and if $\tau(\omega) = t$, the liability is $(S_t^1(\omega) - K)^+$, and in general this *varies* with ω. We write $\mathcal{T} = \mathcal{T}_{\mathbb{T}}$ for the class of all $\mathbb{T}$-valued stopping times. Since $\mathbb{T}$ is assumed finite, we can restrict attention to *bounded* stopping times for the present, and hence Theorems 5.2.7 and 5.2.9 apply to this situation.

Suppose that the writer tries to construct a hedging strategy $\theta = (\theta^0, \theta^1)$ to guard against the potential liability. This will generate a value process $V(\theta)$ with

$$V_t(\theta) = V_0(\theta) + \sum_{u \le t} \theta_u \cdot \Delta S_u = V_0(\theta) + \sum_{u \le t} (\theta_u^0 \Delta S_u^0 + \theta_u^1 \Delta S_0^1).$$

The strategy should be self-financing, so we also demand that $(\Delta \theta_t) \cdot S_{t-1} = 0$ for $t \ge 1$.

We assume that the model is viable, and that Q is an EMM for S. Then the discounted value process $M = \overline{V}(\theta)$ is a martingale under $(\mathbb{F}, Q)$ and by Theorem 5.2.7 we conclude that

$$V_0(\theta) = M_0 = E_Q(\overline{V}_\tau(\theta)) = E_Q((1+r)^{-\tau} V_\tau(\theta)). \qquad (5.17)$$

Note that since τ is a random variable we cannot now take the term $(1+r)^{-\tau}$ outside the expectation, as in the case of European options.

Hence if the writer is to hedge successfully against the preceding liability, the initial capital required for this portfolio is $E_Q((1+r)^{-\tau} V_\tau(\theta))$. This holds for every $\tau \in \mathcal{T}$. But since we need $V_\tau(\theta) \ge (S_\tau - K)^+$, the initial outlay x with which to form the strategy θ must satisfy

$$x \ge \sup_{\tau \in \mathcal{T}} E_Q((1+r)^{-\tau}(S_\tau^1 - K)^+). \qquad (5.18)$$

More generally, given an American option, we saw in Section 5.1 that its payoff function is a random *sequence* $f_t = f_t(S^1)$ of functions which (in general) depend on the *path* taken by S^1. The initial capital x needed for a hedging strategy satisfies $x \ge \sup_{\tau \in \mathcal{T}} E_Q((1+r)^{-\tau} f_\tau)$. If we can find a self-financing strategy θ *and* a stopping time $\tau^* \in \mathcal{T}$ such that $V_{\tau^*}(\theta) = f_{\tau^*}$ almost surely, then the initial capital required is exactly

$$x = \sup_{\tau \in \mathcal{T}} E_Q((1+r)^{-\tau} f_\tau) = E_Q((1+r)^{-\tau^*} f_{\tau^*}). \qquad (5.19)$$

Recall from Section 5.1 that a hedging strategy (or simply a *hedge*) is a self-financing strategy θ which generates a value process $V_t(\theta) \ge f_t$ Q-a.s. for all $t \in \mathbb{T}$, and we say that the hedge θ is *minimal* if there exists a stopping time τ^* with $V_{\tau^*}(\theta) = f_{\tau^*}$ Q-a.s. Thus (5.19) is *necessary* for the existence of a minimal hedge θ, and we show that it is also *sufficient*. This justifies calling x the *rational price* of the American option with payoff function f.

To see how the value process $V(\theta)$ changes in each underlying single-period model we again consider the problem faced by the option writer, but work backwards in time from the expiry date T. since f_T is the value of the option at time T, the hedge must yield at least $V_T = f_T$ in order to cover exercise at that time. At time $T - 1$ the option holder has the choice either to exercise immediately or to hold the option until time T. The time $T - 1$ value of the latter choice is $(1 + r)^{-1} f_T = S^0_{T-1} E_Q(\bar{f}_T | \mathcal{F}_{T-1})$; recall that we write $\overline{Y}_t = \beta_t Y_t = (S^0_t)^{-1} Y_t$ for the discounted value of any quantity Y_t. Thus the option writer needs income from the hedge to cover the potential liability $\max(f_{T-1}, S^0_{T-1} E_Q(\bar{f}_T | \mathcal{F}_{T-1}))$, so this quantity is a rational choice for $V_{T-1}(\theta)$. Inductively, we obtain:

$$V_{t-1}(\theta) = \max(f_{t-1}, S^0_{t-1} E_Q(\bar{f}_t | \mathcal{F}_{t-1})). \tag{5.20}$$

In particular, if $\beta_t = (1 + r)^t$ for some constant interest rate $r > 0$, this simplifies for each $t > 0$ in $\mathbb{T}$ to

$$V_{t-1}(\theta) = \max(f_{t-1}, (1 + r)^{-1} E_Q(f_t | \mathcal{F}_{t-1})). \tag{5.21}$$

The option writer's problem is to construct such a hedge.

The Snell Envelope

Adapting the treatment given in [200] we now solve this problem in a more abstract setting in order to focus on its essential features; given a *finite* adapted sequence $(X_t)_{t \in \mathbb{T}}$ of *non-negative* random variables on $(\Omega, \mathcal{F}, Q)$, we show that the optimisation problem of determining $\sup_{\tau \in \mathcal{T}} E_Q(X_\tau)$ can be solved by the inductive procedure suggested previously, and that the optimal stopping time $\tau^* \in \mathcal{T}$ can be described in a very natural way.

Definition 5.4.1. Given $(X_t)_{t \in \mathbb{T}}$ with $X_t \geq 0$ a.s. for all t, define a new adapted sequence $(Z_t)_{t \in \mathbb{T}}$ by backward induction as follows.

$$\begin{aligned} Z_T &= X_T; \\ \text{if } T \geq t > 0, \quad Z_{t-1} &= \max(X_{t-1}, E_Q(Z_t | \mathcal{F}_{t-1})). \end{aligned} \tag{5.22}$$

Note that (Z_t) is defined 'backwards in time.' It is instructive to read the definition with a 'forward' time variable, using the *time to maturity* $s = T - t$. Then the definitions become, for $s = 0, 1, \ldots, T : Z_T = X_T$,

$$\begin{aligned} Z_{T-1} &= \max(X_{T-1}, E_Q(X_T | \mathcal{F}_{T-1})), \\ Z_{T-2} &= \max(X_{T-1}, E_Q(Z_{T-1} | \mathcal{F}_{T-2})), \end{aligned}$$

and in general, $Z_{T-s} = \max(X_{T-s}, E_Q(Z_{T-s+1} | \mathcal{F}_{T-s}))$ for $s \geq 0$.

The sequence (Z_t) is clearly adapted to the filtration $\mathbb{F} = (\mathcal{F}_t)_{t \in \mathbb{T}}$. We call Z the *Snell envelope* of the finite sequence (X_t). In the following we give a more general definition, applicable also to infinite sequences. We examine the properties of the process Z.

Proposition 5.4.2. *Let (X_t) and (Z_t) be given as previously. Then:*

(i) *Z is the smallest $(\mathbb{F}, Q)$supermartingale dominating X.*

(ii) *The random variable $\tau^* = \min(t \geq 0 : Z_t = X_t)$ is a stopping time, and the stopped process Z^{τ^*} defined by $Z_t^{\tau^*} = Z_{t \wedge \tau^*}$ is an $(\mathbb{F}, Q)$-martingale.*

Proof. (i) By definition $Z_{t-1} = \max(X_{t-1}, E_Q(Z_t|\mathcal{F}_{t-1}))$ dominates each of the terms in the maximum, that is, for $Z_t \geq X_t$ for $t < T$, and $Z_T = X_T$ by definition. So Z dominates X. Since $Z_{t-1} \geq E_Q(Z_t|\mathcal{F}_{t-1})$ for all $t \leq T$, Z is a supermartingale.

To see that it is the *smallest* such supermartingale, we argue by backward induction: suppose that $Y = (Y_t)$ is any supermartingale with $Y_t \geq X_t$ for all $t \in \mathbb{T}$. Then $Y_T \geq X_T = Z_T$. Now if for a fixed $t \leq T$, $Y_t \geq Z_t$, then we have $Y_{t-1} \geq E_Q(Y_t|\mathcal{F}_{t-1})$ since Y is a supermartingale, so that $Y_{t-1} \geq E_Q(Z_t|\mathcal{F}_{t-1})$ follows from the positivity of the conditional expectation operator. On the other hand, Y dominates X; hence $Y_{t-1} \geq X_{t-1}$. Therefore $Y_{t-1} \geq \max(X_{t-1}, E_Q(Z_{t-1}|\mathcal{F}_{t-1})) = Z_{t-1}$, which completes the induction step. Hence (i) follows.

(ii) Note that $Z_0 = \max(X_0, E_Q(Z_1|\mathcal{F}_0))$, and $\{\tau^* = 0\} = \{Z_0 = X_0\} \in \mathcal{F}_0$, since both random variables are $\mathcal{F}_0$-measurable. For $t \geq 1$, the definition of τ^* shows that

$$\{\tau^* = t\} = \bigcap_{s=0}^{t-1} \{Z_s > X_s\} \cap \{Z_t = X_t\}$$

and this set belongs to $\mathcal{F}_t$, since X and Z are adapted. Thus τ^* is a stopping time. Note that $\tau^*(\omega) \leq T$ a.s.

To see that the stopped process $Z_t^{\tau^*} = Z_{t \wedge \tau^*}$ defines a martingale, we again use a martingale transform, as in the proof of Theorem 5.2.9: define $\phi_t = \mathbf{1}_{\{\tau^* \geq t\}}$; then ϕ is predictable ($\{\tau^* \geq t\} = \Omega \setminus \{\tau^* < t\}$) and

$$Z_t^{\tau^*} = Z_0 + \sum_{u=1}^{t} \phi_u \Delta Z_u.$$

Now $Z_t^{\tau^*} - Z_{t-1}^{\tau^*} = \phi_t(Z_t - Z_{t-1}) = \mathbf{1}_{\{\tau^* \geq t\}}(Z_t - Z_{t-1})$, and if $\tau^*(\omega) \geq t$, then $Z_{t-1}(\omega) > X_{t-1}(\omega)$, so that $Z_{t-1}(\omega) = E_Q(Z_t|\mathcal{F}_{t-1})(\omega)$ on this set. For all $t \leq T$,

$$E_Q((Z_t^{\tau^*} - Z_{t-1}^{\tau^*})|\mathcal{F}_{t-1}) = \mathbf{1}_{\{\tau^* \geq t\}} E_Q((Z_t - E_Q(Z_t|\mathcal{F}_{t-1}))|\mathcal{F}_{t-1}) = 0.$$

Thus the stopped process Z^{τ^*} is a martingale on $(\Omega, \mathbb{F}, Q)$. Recall that we assume that the σ-field $\mathcal{F}_0$ is trivial, so that it contains only Q-null sets and their complements (in the case of a finite market model this reduces to $\mathcal{F}_0 = \{\emptyset, \Omega\}$). Therefore X_0 and Z_0 are a.s. constant, since both are $\mathcal{F}_0$-measurable. $\qquad\square$

Definition 5.4.3. We call a stopping time $\sigma \in \mathcal{T} = \mathcal{T}_{\mathbb{T}}$ *optimal for* (X_t) if

$$E_Q(X_\sigma) = \sup_{t \in \mathcal{T}} E_Q(X_\tau). \tag{5.23}$$

Proposition 5.4.4. *The stopping time* $\tau^* = \min\{t \geq 0 : Z_t = X_t\}$ *is optimal for* (X_t), *and*

$$Z_0 = E_Q(X_{\tau^*}) = \sup_{\tau \in \mathcal{T}} E_Q(X_\tau). \tag{5.24}$$

Proof. Z^{τ^*} is a martingale, so that

$$Z_0 = Z_0^{\tau^*} = E_Q(Z_T^{\tau^*}) = E_Q(Z_{\tau^*}) = E_Q(X_{\tau^*}),$$

where the final equality follows from the definition of τ^*. On the other hand, given any $\tau \in \mathcal{T}$, we know that Z^τ is a supermartingale by Proposition 5.4.2. Hence

$$Z_0 = E_Q(Z_0^\tau) \geq E_Q(Z_\tau) \geq E_Q(X_\tau)$$

since Z dominates X. □

Characterisation of Optimal Stopping Times

We are now able to describe how the martingale property characterises optimality more generally.

Proposition 5.4.5. *The stopping time* $\sigma \in \mathcal{T}$ *is optimal for* (X_t) *if and only if the following two conditions hold.*

(i) $Z_\sigma = X_\sigma$ Q-a.s.;

(ii) Z^σ *is an* $(\mathbb{F}, Q)$-*martingale.*

Proof. If Z^σ is a martingale, then

$$Z_0 = E_Q(Z_0^\sigma) = E_Q(Z_T^\sigma) = E_Q(Z_\sigma) = E_Q(X_\sigma),$$

where the final step uses (i). On the other hand, for $\tau \in \mathcal{T}$, Z^τ is a supermartingale; hence as Z dominates X,

$$Z_0 = E_Q(Z_0^\tau) \geq E_Q(Z_T^\tau) = E_Q(Z_\tau) \geq E_Q(X_\tau).$$

Since $\sigma \in \mathcal{T}$, it follows that σ is optimal.

Conversely, suppose σ is optimal. Since by (5.24), $Z_0 = \sup_{\tau \in \mathcal{T}} E_Q(X_\tau)$, it follows that $Z_0 = E_Q(X_\sigma) \leq E_Q(Z_\sigma)$, as Z dominates X. However, Z^σ is a supermartingale, so $E_Q(Z_\sigma) \leq Z_0$. In other words, for any optimal σ, $E_Q(X_\sigma) = Z_0 = E_Q(Z_\sigma)$. But Z dominates X, thus $X_\sigma = Z_\sigma$ Q-a.s., proving (i).

To prove (ii) observe that we have $Z_0 = E_Q(Z_\sigma)$ as well as

$$Z_0 \geq E_Q(Z_{\sigma \wedge t}) \geq E_Q(Z_\sigma)$$

because Z^σ is a supermartingale. Hence

$$E_Q(Z_{\sigma \wedge t}) = E_Q(Z_\sigma) = E_Q(E_Q(Z_\sigma | \mathcal{F}_t)).$$

Again because Z is a supermartingale, we also have, by Theorem 5.2.7, that

$$Z_{\sigma \wedge t} \geq E_Q(Z_\sigma | \mathcal{F}_t),$$

so that again $Z_{\sigma \wedge t} = E_Q(Z_\sigma | \mathcal{F}_t)$, which means that Z^σ is in fact a martingale, so that (ii) holds. □

Remark 5.4.6. From Proposition 5.4.5 it is clear that τ^* is the *smallest* optimal stopping time for (X_t), since by definition it is the smallest stopping time satisfying (i). To find the *largest* optimal stopping time for X we look for the first time that the increasing process A in the Doob decomposition of Z 'leaves zero,' that is, the time ν at which the stopped process Z^ν ceases to be a martingale.

Since Z is a supermartingale, its Doob decomposition $Z = Z_0 + N + B$ has N as a martingale and B as a predictable *decreasing* process, both null at 0. Let $M = Z_0 + N$, which is a martingale, since Z_0 is a.s. constant, and set $A = -B$, so that $A = (A_t)_{t \in \mathbb{T}}$ is increasing, with $A_0 = 0$, and $Z = M - A$.

Definition 5.4.7. Define a random variable $\nu : \Omega \mapsto \mathbb{T}$ by setting

$$\nu(\omega) = \begin{cases} T & \text{if } A_T(\omega) = 0 \\ \min\{t \geq 0 : A_{t+1} > 0\} & \text{if } A_T(\omega) > 0 \end{cases}.$$

To see that $\nu \in \mathcal{T}$, simply observe that A_{t+1} is $\mathcal{F}_t$-measurable, hence

$$\{\nu = t\} = \bigcap_{s \leq t} \{A_s = 0\} \cap \{A_{t+1} > 0\}$$

is in $\mathcal{F}_t$. Thus ν is a stopping time, and it is clearly $\mathbb{T}$-valued, and therefore bounded.

Proposition 5.4.8. ν *is optimal for* (X_t) *and it is the largest optimal stopping time for* (X_t).

Proof. Let Z denote the Snell envelope of X. For $s \leq \nu(\omega)$, $Z_s(\omega) = M_s(\omega) - A_s(\omega)$, hence Z^ν is a martingale, so that (ii) in Proposition 5.4.5 holds for ν. To verify (i), that is, $Z_\nu = X_\nu$, let us write Z_ν in the form

$$Z_\nu = \sum_{s=0}^{T-1} \mathbf{1}_{\{\nu = s\}} Z_s + \mathbf{1}_{\{\nu = T\}} Z_T$$

$$= \sum_{s=0}^{T-1} \mathbf{1}_{\{\nu = s\}} \max(X_s, E(Z_{s+1} | \mathcal{F}_s)) + \mathbf{1}_{\{\nu = T\}} X_T.$$

Now $E(Z_{s+1}|\mathcal{F}_s) = E(M_{s+1} - A_{s+1}|\mathcal{F}_s) = M_s - A_{s+1}$. On the set $\{\nu = s\}$ we have $A_s = 0$, $A_{s+1} > 0$, hence $Z_s = M_s$. This means that $E(Z_{s+1}|\mathcal{F}_s) < Z_s$ a.s. on this set, and therefore that $Z_s = \max(X_s, E(Z_{s+1}|\mathcal{F}_s)) = X_s$ on the set $\{\nu = s\}$. This verifies that $Z_\nu = X_\nu$ a.s. and hence that ν is optimal.

It is now clear that ν is the *largest* optimal time for (X_t): if $\tau \in \mathcal{T}$ has $\tau \geq \nu$ and $Q(\tau > \nu) > 0$, then we have

$$E(Z_\tau) = E(M_\tau) - E(A_\tau) = E(Z_0) - E(A_\tau) < E(Z_0) = Z_0$$

and so by (5.24) τ cannot be optimal. $\qquad\square$

Extension to Unbounded Stopping Times

We need to consider value processes at *arbitrary* times $t \in \mathbb{T}$, since the holder's possible future actions from time t onwards will help to determine those processes. So let $\mathcal{T}_t$ denote the set of stopping times $\tau : \Omega \mapsto \mathbb{T}_t = \{t, t+1, \dots, T\}$ and consider instead the optimal stopping problem $\sup_{\tau \in \mathcal{T}_t} E(X_\tau)$. Although the stopping times remain bounded, an immediate difficulty in attempting to transfer the results we have for $t = 0$ to more general $t \in \mathbb{T}$ is that we made use in our proofs of the fact that Z_0 was a.s. constant—this followed from our assumption that $\mathcal{F}_0$ contained only null sets and their complements, and it led us to establish (5.24), which has been used throughout.

In the general case we are obliged to replace expectations $E_Q(Z_\tau)$ by *conditional* expectations $E_Q(Z_\tau|\mathcal{F}_t)$. We thus face the problem of defining the supremum of a family of random variables, rather than real numbers. We need to ensure that we obtain this supremum as an $\mathcal{F}-measurable$ function, even for an uncountable family, and we use the opportunity to extend the definition of the Snell envelope, in preparation for a similar extension to continuous-time situations needed in Chapter 8.

Proposition 5.4.9. *Let $(\Omega, \mathcal{F}, P)$ be a probability space. Let $\mathcal{L}$ be a family of $\mathcal{F}$-measurable functions $\Omega \mapsto [-\infty, \infty]$. There exists a unique $\mathcal{F}$-measurable function $g : \Omega \mapsto [-\infty, \infty]$ with the following properties.*

(i) *$g \geq f$ a.s for all $f \in \mathcal{L}$;*

(ii) *given an $\mathcal{F}$-measurable function h such that $h \geq f$ a.s. for all $f \in \mathcal{L}$, then $h \geq g$ a.s.*

We call g the *essential supremum* of $\mathcal{L}$ and write $g = \operatorname{ess\,sup}_{f \in \mathcal{L}} f$. There exists a sequence (f_n) such that $g = \sup_n f_n$. If $\mathcal{L}$ is upward filtering (i.e., if for given f', f'' in $\mathcal{L}$ there exists $f \in \mathcal{L}$ with $f \geq \max(f', f'')$), then the sequence (f_n) can be chosen to be increasing, so that $f = \lim_n f_n$.

Proofs of this result can be found in [169], [200]. The idea is simple: identify the closed intervals $[0, 1]$ and $[-\infty, \infty]$, for example, via the increasing bijection $x \mapsto e^x$. Any countable family $\mathcal{C}$ in $\mathcal{L}$ has a well-defined

$\mathcal{F}$-measurable ($[0, 1]$-valued) f_C, which thus has finite expectation under P. Define $\alpha = \sup\{E(f_C) : C \subset \mathcal{L},$ countable$\}$ and choose a sequence (f'_n, C_n) with $E(f'_n) \to \alpha$. Since $\mathcal{K} = \bigcup_n C_n$ is countable and $E(f'_{\mathcal{K}}) = \alpha$ we can set $g = f'_{\mathcal{K}}$. The sequence (f'_n) serves as an approximating sequence, and $f_0 = f'_0$, $f_{n+1} \ge f_n \vee f'_{n+1}$ will make it increasing with n.

Definition 5.4.10. Let $(\Omega, \mathcal{F}, \mathbb{T}, \mathbb{F}, P)$ be a stochastic base with $\mathbb{T} = \mathbb{N}$. Given an adapted process $(X_t)_{t \in \mathbb{T}}$ such that $X^* = \sup_t X_t \in L^1$, define $\mathcal{T}_t$ as the family of $\mathbb{F}$-stopping times τ such that $t \le \tau < \infty$. (We call $\tau \in \mathcal{T}_t$ a *t-stopping rule*.)

The *Snell envelope* of (X_t) is the process $Z = (Z_t)$, where

$$Z_t = \operatorname*{ess\,sup}_{\tau \in \mathcal{T}_t} E(X_\tau | \mathcal{F}_t). \tag{5.25}$$

This definition allows *unbounded* (but a.s. finite) stopping times. When X is UI, we can still use the optional stopping results proved earlier in this context. The martingale characterisation of optimal stopping times can be extended also; see [169] or [200] for details.

5.5   Pricing and Hedging American Options

Existence of a Minimal Hedge

Return to the set-up at the beginning of Section 5.4 and assume henceforth that the market model $(\Omega, \mathcal{F}, P, \mathbb{T}, \mathbb{F}, S)$ is viable and complete, with Q as the unique EMM.

Given an American option (f_t) in this model (e.g., an American call with strike K), where $f_t = (S^1_t - K)^+$, we saw that a hedging strategy θ would need to generate a value process $V(\theta)$ that satisfies (5.20); that is, $V_T(\theta) = f_T$ and (since $S^0_t = (1 + r)^{-t}$ for all $t \in \mathbb{T}$)

$$V_{t-1}(\theta) = \max(f_{t-1}, (1 + r)^{-1} E_Q(f_t | \mathcal{F}_{t-1})).$$

Moving to discounted values, $\bar{V}_t(\theta) = (1 + r)^{-t} V_t(\theta)$ is then the Snell envelope Z of the discounted option price $\bar{f}_t = (1 + r)^{-t} f_t$, so that $Z_T = \bar{f}_T$ and $Z_{t-1} = \max(\bar{f}_{t-1}, E_Q(\bar{f}_t | \mathcal{F}_{t-1}))$ for $t < T$. In particular, the results of the previous section yield

$$Z_t = \sup_{\tau \in \mathcal{T}_t} E_Q(\bar{f}_\tau | \mathcal{F}_t) \tag{5.26}$$

and the stopping time $\tau^*_t = \min(s \ge t : Z_s = \bar{f}_s)$ is optimal, so that the supremum in (5.26) is attained by τ^*_t. (We developed these results for $t = 0$, but with the extended definition of the Snell envelope they hold for general t.)

For $\tau^* = \tau_0^*$ and $\mathcal{T} = \mathcal{T}_0$ we have, therefore,

$$Z_0 = \sup_{\tau \in \mathcal{T}} E_Q(\bar{f}_\tau) = E_Q(\bar{f}_{\tau^*}) \tag{5.27}$$

and this *defines* the rational price of the option at time 0, and thus also the initial investment needed for the existence of a hedging strategy.

Now write the Doob decomposition of the supermartingale Z as $Z = \bar{M} - \bar{A}$, where $\bar{M}$ is a martingale and $\bar{A}$ a predictable increasing process. Also write $M_t = S_t^0 \bar{M}_t$ and $A_t = S_t^0 \bar{A}_t$.

Since the market is complete, we can attain the contingent claim M_T by a self-financing strategy θ (e.g., we could use the strategy constructed by means of the martingale representation in the proof of Proposition 4.2.1) and we may assume that θ is admissible. Thus $\bar{V}_T(\theta) = \bar{M}_T$, and as $\bar{V}(\theta)$ is a martingale under the EMM Q, $\bar{V}_t(\theta) = \bar{M}_t = Z_t + \bar{A}_t$ for all $t \in \mathbb{T}$. Hence also

$$Z_t S_t^0 = V_t(\theta) - A_t. \tag{5.28}$$

From the results of the previous section we know that on the set $C = \{(t, \omega) : 0 \le t < \tau^*(\omega)\}$ the Snell envelope Z is a martingale and $\bar{A}_t(\omega) = 0$ on this set. Hence:

$$V_t(\theta)(\omega) = \sup_{t \le \tau \le T} E_Q((1+r)^{-(\tau-t)} f_\tau | \mathcal{F}_t) \quad \forall (t, \omega) \in C. \tag{5.29}$$

Moreover, we saw that τ^* is the *smallest* optimal exercise time and that $\bar{A}_{\tau^*(\omega)}(\omega) = 0$. Hence (5.28) and (5.29) imply that

$$V_{\tau^*(\omega)}(\theta)(\omega) = Z_{\tau^*(\omega)}(\omega) S_{\tau^*(\omega)}^0(\omega) = f_{\tau^*(\omega)}(\omega). \tag{5.30}$$

Thus the hedge θ, with initial capital investment

$$V_0(\theta) = x = \sup_{\tau \in \mathcal{T}} E_Q((1+r)^{-\tau} f_\tau) \tag{5.31}$$

is minimal, and thus we have verified that this condition is *sufficient* for the existence of a minimal hedge for the option.

The Rational Price and Optimal Exercise

Since hedging requires the initial investment x to be at least $\sup_{\tau \in \mathcal{T}} E_Q((1+r)^{-\tau} f_\tau)$, and the supremum is attained at the optimal time τ^* it follows that x is the minimum initial investment for which a hedging strategy can be constructed. Thus (5.31) provides a natural choice for the 'fair' or *rational* price of the American option.

The optimal exercise time need not be uniquely defined, however; any optimal stopping times (under Q) for the payoff function f_t will be an optimal exercise time. In fact, the holder of the option (the buyer) has no incentive to exercise the option while $Z_t S_t^0 > f_t$, since using the option price as initial investment he could create a portfolio yielding greater payoff than the option at time τ, by using the hedging strategy θ. Thus the buyer would wait for a stopping time σ for which $\bar{Z}_\sigma = \bar{f}_\sigma$, that is, until the optimality criterion (i) in Proposition 5.4.5 is satisfied. However, he would also choose $\sigma < \nu$, where ν is the largest optimal stopping time defined in 5.4.7, since otherwise the strategy θ would, at times greater than $t > \nu$, yield value $V_t(\theta) > Z_t S_t^0$ by (5.28). Thus for any optimal exercise time σ we need to have $Z_{t\vee\sigma} = \bar{V}_{t\vee\sigma}$, so that Z^σ is a martingale, which means that Condition (ii) in Proposition 5.4.5 holds, so that σ is optimal for the stopping problem solved by the Snell envelope. (Note that the same considerations apply to the option writer: if the buyer exercises at a non-optimal time τ, the strategy θ provides an arbitrage opportunity for the option writer, since either $A_\tau > 0$ or $Z_\tau > \bar{f}_\tau$, so that $V_\tau(\theta) - f_\tau = Z_\tau S_\tau^0 + A_\tau - f_\tau > 0$.)

We have proved:

Theorem 5.5.1. *A stopping time $\hat{\tau} \in T$ is an optimal exercise time for the American option $(f_t)_{t\in T}$ if and only if*

$$E_Q((1+r)^{-\hat{\tau}} f_{\hat{\tau}}) = \sup_{\tau \in T} E_Q((1+r)^{-\tau} f_\tau). \tag{5.32}$$

Remark 5.5.2. We showed by an arbitrage argument in Chapter 1 that American options are more valuable than their European counterparts in general, but that for a simple call option there is no advantage in early exercise, so that the American and European call options have the same value. Using the theory of optimal stopping, we can recover these results from the martingale properties of the Snell envelope: if $f_t = (S_t^1 - K)^+$ is an American call option with strike K on $\mathbb{T}$, then its discounted value process is given by the Q-supermartingale (Z_t) as in (5.26). Now if $\bar{C}_t$ is the discounted time t value of the European option $C_T = (S_T^1 - K)^+$, then $C_T = f_T$, so that

$$Z_t \geq E_Q(Z_T|\mathcal{F}_t) = E_Q(\bar{f}_T|\mathcal{F}_t) = E_Q(\bar{C}_T|\mathcal{F}_t) = \bar{C}_t. \tag{5.33}$$

This shows that the value process of the American call option dominates that of the European call option.

On the other hand, for these call options $C_t \geq f_t = (S_t^1 - K)^+$, as we saw in (1.17), hence the Q-martingale $(\bar{C}_t)$ dominates $(\bar{f}_t)$. It is therefore a supermartingale dominating $(\bar{f}_t)$ and as by definition of the Snell envelope (Z_t) is the *smallest* supermartingale with this property, we conclude that $\bar{C}_t \geq Z_t$ for all $t \in \mathbb{T}$. Hence $\bar{C}_t = Z_t$ and so the value processes of the two options coincide.

5.6   Consumption–Investment Strategies

Extended 'Self-Financing' Strategies

In the study of American options in Chapter 8, and especially in Chapter 10, we wish to extend the concept of 'self-financing' strategies by allowing for potential consumption. In the present discrete-time setting, the basic concepts appear more transparent, and we outline them briefly here, in preparation for the technically more demanding discussion in the later chapters.

Assume that we are given a price process $\{S_t^i : i = 0, 1, \ldots, d; t = 0, 1, \ldots, T\}$ on a stochastic basis $(\Omega, \mathcal{F}, P, \mathbb{T}, \mathbb{F})$. For any process X, the discounted version is denoted by $\bar{X}$, where $\bar{X}_t = \beta_t X_t$ as usual.

If $c = (c_t)_{t \in \mathbb{T}}$ denotes a 'consumption process' (which, if c_t is negative, equates to additional investment at time t), then the self-financing constraint for strategies (i.e., $(\Delta\theta_t) \cdot S_{t-1} = 0$) should be widened to:

$$(\Delta\theta_t) \cdot S_{t-1} + c_t = 0. \tag{5.34}$$

An investment–consumption strategy is a pair (θ, c) of *predictable* processes that satisfies (5.34) and their associated value or *wealth process* V is given by $V_t = \theta_t \cdot S_t$, as before. Also define the cumulative consumption process C by $C_t = \sum_{u=1}^{t} c_u$.

The constraint (5.34) is trivially equivalent to each of the following (for all $t > 0$).

(i) $\Delta V_t = \theta_t \cdot \Delta S_t - c_t$.

(ii) $V_t = V_0 + \sum_{u=1}^{t} \theta_u \cdot \Delta S_u - C_t$.

(iii)   (Discounted version) $\bar{V}_t = V_0 + \sum_{u=1}^{t} \theta_u \cdot \Delta \bar{S}_u - \bar{C}_t$.

Assume from now on that the market model $(\Omega, \mathcal{F}, P, \mathbb{T}, \mathbb{F}, S)$ is viable and complete, and that Q is the unique EMM for $\bar{S}$. Assume further that C is a pure consumption process; that is, $c_t \geq 0$ for all $t \in \mathbb{T}$. Then for a strategy (θ, c) as previously the discounted value process $\bar{V}$ satisfies, for $t \in \mathbb{T}$,

$$E_Q(\Delta\bar{V}_t | \mathcal{F}_{t-1}) = E_Q((\theta_t \cdot \Delta\bar{S}_t - \bar{c}_t) | \mathcal{F}_{t-1}) = -\bar{c}_t \leq 0$$

since $\bar{S}$ is a Q-martingale and $\bar{c}_t \geq 0$. We have proved:

Proposition 5.6.1. *For every consumption strategy (θ, c) satisfying (5.34) the discounted value process $\bar{V}$ is a Q supermartingale.*

Construction of Hedging Strategies

Suppose that $U = (U_t)$ is an adapted process whose discounted version $\bar{U}$ is a Q-supermartingale. Then we can use the increasing process in its

Doob decomposition to define a consumption process c and a self-financing strategy θ such that the pair (θ, c) satisfies (5.34) and has value process U.

To do this, write $\bar{U} = \bar{M} - \bar{A}$ for the Doob decomposition of $\bar{U}$, so that $\bar{A}_0 = 0$ and $\bar{M}$ is a Q-martingale. The market is complete, so the contingent claim $M_T = S_T^0 \bar{M}_T$ can be generated by a unique self-financing strategy θ, so that $\theta_T \cdot S_T = M_T$; that is, $\theta_T \cdot \bar{S}_T = \bar{M}_T$. As $\bar{M}$ is a martingale, we have $\bar{M}_t = E_Q(\theta_T \cdot \bar{S}_T | \mathcal{F}_t)$ for all $t \in \mathbb{T}$. Thus for all t

$$\bar{U}_t = E_Q(\theta_T \cdot \bar{S}_T | \mathcal{F}_t) - \bar{A}_t$$

so that

$$U_t = S_t^0 \bar{U}_t = S_t^0 E_Q(\theta_T \cdot \bar{S}_T | \mathcal{F}_t) - \bar{A}_t$$

while the process $A_t = S_t^0 \bar{A}_t$ is increasing and has $A_0 = 0$. Since θ is self-financing, the portfolio $\theta_T \cdot \bar{S}_T$ has the form $\theta_0 \cdot S_0 + \sum_{u=1}^{T} \theta_u \cdot \Delta \bar{S}_u$, so that

$$E_Q(\theta_T \cdot \bar{S}_T | \mathcal{F}_t) = \theta_0 \cdot S_0 + \sum_{u=1}^{t} \theta_u \cdot \bar{S}_u. \tag{5.35}$$

Choosing C so that $\bar{A}_t = \sum_{u=1}^{t} \bar{c}_u$ and $C_0 = 0 = \bar{A}_0$ we see that $c_u = S_{u-1}^0(\Delta \bar{A}_u)$ meets the requirement, and that C is predictable and non-negative (as A is increasing). Inductively, $\bar{A}_t = \sum_{u=1}^{t} \bar{c}_u$ yields

$$\bar{A}_{t+1} = A_t + \Delta \bar{A}_{t+1} = \sum_{u=1}^{t+1} \bar{c}_u$$

and by the preceding (iii) we obtain $\bar{V}_t = \bar{U}_t$; that is, $V_t = U_t$ for the value process associated with (θ, c).

Guided by our discussion of American options, we now call a consumption strategy (θ, c) a *hedge* for a given claim (i.e., an adapted process) $X = (X_t)$ if $V_t(\theta) \geq X_t$ for all $t \in \mathbb{T}$. Writing Z for the Snell envelope of $\bar{X}$, the supermartingale Z dominates $\bar{X}$, and can be used as the process $\bar{U}$ in the previous discussion. Thus we can find a hedging strategy (θ, c) for X, and obtain, with $t \in \mathbb{T}$.

$$V_t(\theta) = U_t = S_t^0 Z_t \geq X_t, \qquad V_T(\theta) = S_t^0 Z_T.$$

As Z is the smallest supermartingale dominating $\bar{X}$, it follows that *any* hedge (θ', c') for X must have a value process dominating $S^0 Z$.

Financing Consumption

Suppose an investor is given an initial endowment $x > 0$ and follows a consumption strategy $c = (c_t)_{t \in \mathbb{T}}$ (a non-negative predictable process). How can this consumption be *financed* by a self-financing investment strategy, utilising the endowment x?

It seems natural to say that c *can be financed* (or is budget-feasible) from the endowment x provided that there is a predictable process $\theta = (\theta^0, \theta^1, \dots, \theta^d)$ for which (θ, c) is a consumption strategy with $V_0(\theta) = x$ and $V_t(\theta) \geq 0$ for all $t \in \mathbb{T}$.

By the preceding (iii), we require

$$\bar{V}_t(\theta) = x + \sum_{u=1}^{t} \theta_u \cdot \Delta \bar{S}_u - \sum_{u=1}^{t} \bar{c} \geq 0 \qquad (5.36)$$

if such a strategy θ exists. But $\bar{S}$ is a Q-martingale, so, taking expectations, (5.36) becomes, with $C = \sum_{u=1}^{t} c_u$ as cumulative consumption;

$$E_Q(\bar{C}_t) = E_Q(\sum_{u=1}^{t} \bar{c}_u) \leq x. \qquad (5.37)$$

The budget constraint (5.37) is therefore necessary if the consumption C is to be financed by the endowment x. It is also sufficient as shown in the following.

Given a consumption process C with $c_t = \Delta C_t$, define the process $\bar{U}_t = x - \bar{C}_t$. Since C is predictable and $c_{t+1} \geq 0$

$$\bar{U}_{t+1} = E_Q(\bar{U}_{t+1} | \mathcal{F}_t) \leq \bar{U}_t$$

so that $\bar{U}$ is a supermartingale. By (5.37), $E_Q(\bar{U}_t) \geq 0$ for all $t \in \mathbb{T}$. But then we can find a hedging strategy θ for the claim $X = 0$ with $V_0(\theta) = x$ and $V_t(\theta) \geq 0$ for all t. We have proved:

Theorem 5.6.2. *The consumption process C can be financed by an initial endowment x if and only if the constraint (5.37) is satisfied.*

6
A Review of Continuous-Time Stochastic Calculus

6.1 Continuous-Time Processes

In this and the succeeding chapters the time parameter takes values in either a finite interval $[0, T]$ or the infinite intervals $[0, \infty)$, $[0, \infty]$. We denote the time parameter set by $\mathbb{T}$ in each case.

Filtrations and Stopping Times

Suppose $(\Omega, \mathcal{F}, P)$ is a probability space. As before, we use the concept of a filtration on $(\Omega, \mathcal{F}, P)$ to model the acquisition of information as time evolves. The definition of a filtration is as in Chapter 2 and now takes account of the change in the time set $\mathbb{T}$.

Definition 6.1.1. A *filtration* $\mathbb{F} = (\mathcal{F}_t, t \in \mathbb{T})$ is an increasing family of sub-sigma-fields $\mathcal{F}_t \subset \mathcal{F}$.

Increasing means that if $s \leq t$, then

$$\mathcal{F}_s \subset \mathcal{F}_t.$$

We assume that $\mathbb{F}$ satisfies the 'usual conditions'. This means the filtration $\mathbb{F}$ is:

a) *complete*; that is, every null set in $\mathcal{F}$ belongs to $\mathcal{F}_0$, and so to each $\mathcal{F}_t$, and

b) *right* continuous; that is, $\mathcal{F}_t = \bigcap_{s>t} \mathcal{F}_s$.

Remark 6.1.2. Just as in the discrete case, $\mathcal{F}_t$ represents the history of some process or processes up to time t. However, all possible histories must be allowed. If an event $A \in \mathcal{F}$ is $\mathcal{F}_t$-measurable then it only depends on what has happened to time t. Unlike the situation we discussed in Chapter 2, new information can arrive at any time $t \in [0, T]$ (or even $t \in [0, \infty)$), and the filtration consists of an uncountable collection of σ-fields. The right continuity assumption is specific to this situation.

Definition 6.1.3. Suppose the time parameter $\mathbb{T}$ is $[0, \infty]$ (or $[0, \infty)$, or $[0, T]$). A random variable τ taking values in $\mathbb{T}$ is a *stopping time* if for every $t \geq 0$,

$$\{\tau \leq t\} \in \mathcal{F}_t.$$

Remark 6.1.4. Consequently, the event $\{\tau \leq t\}$ depends only on the history up to time t. The first time a stock price reaches a certain level is a stopping time, as is, say, the first time the price reaches a certain higher level after dropping by a specified amount. However, the last time, before some given date, at which the stock price reaches a certain level is not a stopping time, because to say it is the 'last time' requires information about the future. Note that in the continuous-time setting it does not make sense to replace the condition $\{\tau \leq t\} \in \mathcal{F}_t$ by $\{\tau = t\} \in \mathcal{F}_t$. Many of the properties of stopping times carry over to this setting, however.

Just as in Chapter 5, a constant random variable, $T(\omega) = t$ for all $\omega \in \Omega$, is a stopping time. If T is a stopping time, then $T + s$ is a stopping time for $s \geq 0$.

We continue with some basic properties of stopping times.

Proposition 6.1.5. *If S and T are stopping times, then $S \wedge T$ and $S \vee T$ are stopping times. Consequently, if $\{T_n\}$, $n \in N$, is a sequence of stopping times, then $\wedge_n T_n = \inf_n T_n$ and $\vee_n T_n = \sup_n T_n$ are stopping times.*

Proof. The proof is identical to that given in Example 5.2.3(ii) for the discrete case, writing $S \wedge T$ for $\min\{S, T\}$, and so on.

$$\{S \wedge T \leq t\} = \{S \leq t\} \cup \{T \leq t\} \in \mathcal{F}_t,$$
$$\{S \vee T \leq t\} = \{S \leq t\} \cap \{T \leq t\} \in \mathcal{F}_t.$$

$\square$

Definition 6.1.6. Suppose T is a stopping time with respect to the filtration $\{\mathcal{F}_t\}$. Then the σ-field $\mathcal{F}_T$ of events occurring up to time T is those events $A \in \mathcal{F}$ satisfying

$$A \cap \{T \leq t\} \in \mathcal{F}_t.$$

Exercise 6.1.7. Prove that $\mathcal{F}_T$ is a σ-field.

One then can establish (again, compare with Exercise 5.2.6 for the discrete case)

Theorem 6.1.8. *Suppose S, T are stopping times.*

a) *If $S \leq T$, then $\mathcal{F}_S \subset \mathcal{F}_T$.*

b) *If $A \in \mathcal{F}_S$, then $A \cap \{S \leq T\} \in \mathcal{F}_T$.*

Proof. a) Suppose $B \in \mathcal{F}_S$. Then

$$B \cap \{T \leq t\} = B \cap \{S \leq t\} \cap \{T \leq t\} \in \mathcal{F}_t.$$

b) Suppose $A \in \mathcal{F}_S$. Then

$$A \cap \{S \leq T\} \cap \{T \leq t\} = (A \cap \{S \leq t\}) \cap \{T \leq t\} \cap \{S \wedge t \leq T \wedge t\}.$$

Each of the three sets on the right is in $\mathcal{F}_t$: the first because $A \in \mathcal{F}_S$, the second because T is a stopping time, and the third because $S \wedge t$ and $T \wedge t$ are $\mathcal{F}_t$-measurable random variables. □

Definition 6.1.9. A continuous-time *stochastic process* X taking values in a measurable space $(E, \mathcal{E})$ is a family of random variables $\{X_t\}$ defined on $(\Omega, \mathcal{F}, P)$, indexed by t, which take values in $(E, \mathcal{E})$.

That is, for each t we have a random variable $X_t(\cdot)$ with values in E.

Alternatively, for each ω (i.e., fixing ω and letting t vary), we have a sample path $X.(\omega)$ of the process.

Remark 6.1.10. $X.$ could represent the price of oil, or the price of a stock.

For some (future) time t, $X_t(\omega)$ is a random quantity, a random variable. Each ω represents a 'state of the world', corresponding to which there is a price $X_t(\omega)$. Conversely, fixing ω means one realization of the world, as time evolves, is considered. This gives a realization, or *path*, of the price $X.(\omega)$ as a function of time t.

Equivalence of Processes

A natural question is to ask when two mathematical stochastic processes model the same phenomenon. Several possible definitions are now discussed:

We consider stochastic processes defined on a probability space $(\Omega, \mathcal{F}, P)$ and taking values in the measurable space $(E, \mathcal{E})$.

The weakest notion of equivalence of processes reflects the fact that in practice one can only observe a stochastic process at *finitely* many instants. Assume for simplicity, that $E = \mathbb{R}$ and $\mathcal{E}$ is the Borel σ-field $\mathcal{B}$ on $\mathbb{R}$. Then we can form the family of *finite-dimensional distributions* of the process $X = (X_t)_{t \geq 0}$ by considering the probability that for $n \in \mathbb{N}$, $t_1, t_2, \ldots, t_n \in \mathbb{T}$ and a Borel set $A \subset \mathbb{R}^n$, the random vector $(X_{t_1}, X_{t_2}, \ldots, X_{t_n})$ takes values in A : set

$$\phi^X_{t_1, t_2, \ldots, t_n}(A) = P[\{\omega \in \Omega : (X_{t_1}(\omega), X_{t_2}(\omega), \ldots, X_{t_n}(\omega)) \in A\}].$$

For each family $\{t_1, t_2, \ldots, t_n\}$ this defines $\phi^X_{t_1,t_2,\ldots,t_n}$ as a measure on $\mathbb{R}^n$. We say that two processes X and Y are *equivalent* (or have the same *law*) if their families of finite-dimensional distributions coincide, and then we write $X \sim Y$.

Note that the preceeding does *not* require Y to be defined on the *same* probability space as X. This means that we can avoid complicated questions about the 'proper' probability space for a particular problem, since only the finite-dimensional distributions, and not the full realizations of the process (i.e., the various random 'paths' it traces out) are relevant for our description of the probabilities concerned. It turns out that if we consider the process as a map $X : \Omega \mapsto \mathbb{R}^T$ (i.e., $\omega \mapsto X(\cdot, \omega)$) and we stick to *Borel sets* A in $\mathbb{R}^T$, then the finite-dimensional distributions give us sufficient information to identify a canonical version of the process, up to equivalence. (This is the famous *Kolmogorov Extension Theorem*; see, e.g., Theorem 2.2 of Karatzas and Shreve [164]).

However, at least when $\mathbb{T}$ is uncountable, most of the interesting sets in $\mathbb{R}^T$ are not Borel sets, so that we need a somewhat stronger concept of 'equivalence' that 'fixes' the paths of our process X tightly enough. Two such definitions are now given; each of them requires the two processes concerned to be defined on the same probability space.

Definition 6.1.11. Suppose $\{X_t\}$, $\{Y_t\}$ $t \geq 0$, are two processes defined on the same probability space $(\Omega, \mathcal{F}, P)$ and taking values in $(E, \mathcal{E})$.

The process $\{Y_t\}$ is said to be a *modification* of $\{X_t\}$ if for every t

$$X_t = Y_t \text{ a.s.}$$

Definition 6.1.12. With $\{X_t\}$, $\{Y_t\}$ as in 6.1.11. the processes $\{X_t\}$ and $\{Y_t\}$ are said to be *indistinguishable* if for almost every $\omega \in \Omega$,

$$X_t(\omega) = Y_t(\omega) \quad \text{for all } t.$$

The difference between 6.1.11 and 6.1.12 is that in 6.1.11 the set of zero measure on which X_t and Y_t may differ may depend on t, whereas in 6.1.12 there is a single set of zero measure outside which

$$X_t(\omega) = Y_t(\omega) \quad \text{for all } t.$$

When the time index set is countable the two definitions are the same.

Exercise 6.1.13. A process X is *right-continuous* if for almost every ω the map $t \to X_t(\omega)$ is right-continuous.

Show that if the processes X and Y are right continuous and one is a modification of the other, then they are indistinguishable.

Definition 6.1.14. Suppose $A \subset [0, \infty] \times \Omega$ and that $I_A(t, \omega) = I_A$ is the indicator function of A; that is, $I_A(t, \omega) = 1$ if $(t, \omega) \in A$ and $I_A(t, \omega) = 0$ if $(t, \omega) \notin A$. Then A is *evanescent* if I_A is indistinguishable from the zero process.

Exercise 6.1.15. Show A is evanescent if the projection $A = \{\omega \in \Omega :$ $\exists t$ with $(t, \omega) \in A\}$, of A onto Ω, is a set of measure zero.

6.2 Martingales

Definition 6.2.1. Suppose $\{\mathcal{F}_t\}$, $t \geq 0$, is a filtration of the measurable space $(\Omega, \mathcal{F})$ and $\{X_t\}$ is a stochastic process defined on $(\Omega, \mathcal{F})$ with values in $(E, \mathcal{E})$. Then X is said to be *adapted* to $\{\mathcal{F}_t\}$ if X_t is $\mathcal{F}_t$-measurable for each t.

The random process that models the concept of randomness in the most fundamental way is a martingale; we now give the continuous-time definition for $t \in [0, \infty]$; the discrete-time analogue was discussed in Chapters 2 through 5.

Definition 6.2.2. Suppose $(\Omega, \mathcal{F}, P)$ is a probability space with a filtration $\{\mathcal{F}_t\}$, $t \in [0, \infty]$. A real-valued adapted stochastic process $\{M_t\}$ is said to be a *supermartingale* (resp., *submartingale*) with respect to the filtration $\{\mathcal{F}_t\}$ if

a) $E[|M_t|] < \infty$ for all t,

b) $E[M_t|\mathcal{F}_s] \leq X_s$ if $s \leq t$, (resp., $E[M_t|\mathcal{F}_s] \geq X_s$ if $s \leq t$).

If $E[M_t|\mathcal{F}_s] = X_s$ for $s \leq t$, then $\{M_t\}$ is said to be a *martingale*.

Remark 6.2.3. A martingale is a purely random process in the sense that, given the history of the process so far, the expected value of the process at some later time is just its present value. Martingales can be thought of as modelling the winnings in a fair game of chance.
  Note in particular that $E[M_t] = E[M_0]$ for all t.

Brownian Motion

The most important example of a continuous-time martingale is a Brownian motion. This process is named for Robert Brown, a Scottish botanist who was studying pollen grains in suspension in the early nineteenth century. He observed the pollen was performing a very random movement and thought this was because the pollen grains were alive. We now know this rapid movement is due to collisions at the molecular level.

Definition 6.2.4. A *standard Brownian motion* $\{B_t\}$, $t \geq 0$, is a real valued stochastic process that has continuous sample paths and stationary Gaussian, independent increments. This means:

a) $B_0 = 0$ a.s.,

b) the map $t \to B_t(\omega)$ is continuous for almost all $\omega \in \Omega$,

c) for $s \leq t$, $B_t - B_s$ is a Gaussian random variable that has mean 0, variance $t - s$, and is independent of $\mathcal{F}_s = \sigma\{B_u : u \leq s\}$.

We can then establish

Theorem 6.2.5. *Suppose* $\{B_t\}$ *is a standard Brownian motion with respect to the filtration* $\{\mathcal{F}_t\}$, $t \geq 0$. *Then*

a) $\{B_t\}$ *is an* $\mathcal{F}_t$-*martingale,*

b) $\{B_t^2 - t\}$ *is an* $\mathcal{F}_t$-*martingale, and*

c) $\{\exp(\sigma B_t - (\sigma^2/2)t)\}$ *is an* $\mathcal{F}_t$-*martingale.*

Proof. a) $E[B_t - B_s | \mathcal{F}_s] = E[B_t - B_s] = 0$ because $B_t - B_s$ is independent of $\mathcal{F}_s$. Consequently, $E[B_t | \mathcal{F}_s] = B_s$.

b) $E[B_t^2 - B_s^2 | \mathcal{F}_s] = E[(B_t - B_s)^2 + 2B_s(B_t - B_s) | \mathcal{F}_s] = E[(B_t - B_s)^2 | \mathcal{F}_s] + 2B_s E[(B_t - B_s) | \mathcal{F}_s]$. The second term is zero by part a). The independence implies

$$E[(B_t - B_s)^2 | \mathcal{F}_s] = E[(B_t - B_s)^2]$$
$$= t - s.$$

Therefore, $E[B_t^2 - t | \mathcal{F}_s] = B_s^2 - s$.

c) If Z is a standard normal random variable, with density $(1/\sqrt{2\pi})e^{-x^2/2}$, and $\lambda \in \mathbb{R}$ then $E[e^{\lambda Z}] = (1/\sqrt{2\pi}) \int_{-\infty}^{\infty} e^{\lambda x} e^{-x^2/2} dx = e^{\lambda^2/2}$.

Now for $s < t$

$$\begin{aligned}
E[e^{\sigma B_t - \sigma^2 t/2} | \mathcal{F}_s] &= e^{\sigma B_s - \sigma^2 t/2} E[e^{\sigma(B_t - B_s)} | \mathcal{F}_s] \\
&= e^{\sigma B_s - \sigma^2 t/2} E[e^{\sigma(B_t - B_s)}] \qquad \text{by independence of} \\
&\qquad\qquad\qquad\qquad\qquad\qquad\quad \text{increments} \\
&= e^{\sigma B_s - \sigma^2 t/2} E[e^{\sigma B_{t-s}}] \qquad \text{by stationarity.}
\end{aligned}$$

Now σB_{t-s} is $N(0, \sigma^2(t-s))$; that is, if Z is $N(0,1)$ as previously, σB_{t-s} has the same law as $\sigma\sqrt{t-s}\, Z$ and $E[e^{\sigma B_{t-s}}] = E[e^{\sigma\sqrt{t-s}\, Z}] = e^{\sigma^2(t-s)/2}$. Therefore,

$$E[e^{\sigma B_t - \sigma^2 t/2} | \mathcal{F}_s] = e^{\sigma B_s - \sigma^2 s/2}$$

and the result is proved. $\square$

Conversely, we prove in Theorem 6.4.15 that a continuous process which satisfies a) and b) is, in fact, a Brownian motion. (Indeed, property c) characterises a Brownian motion.)

We first recall the following definition:

Uniform Integrability and Limit Theorems

Definition 6.2.6. A set K of random variables contained in $L^1(\Omega, \mathcal{F}, P)$ is said to be *uniformly integrable* if

$$\int_{\{|X|\geq c\}} |X| dP$$

converges to zero uniformly in $X \in K$ as $c \to \infty$.

We then state

Definition 6.2.7. A martingale $\{M_t\}$, $t \in [0, \infty)$ (or $t \in [0, T]$) is said to be uniformly integrable if the set of random variables $\{M_t\}$ is uniformly integrable.

If $\{M_t\}$ is a uniformly integrable martingale on $[0, \infty)$, then $\lim M_t = M_\infty$ exists a.s. The proof of this result can be found in Corollary 4.9 of Elliott [87].

Remark 6.2.8. A consequence of $\{M_t\}$ being a uniformly integrable martingale on $[0, \infty)$ is that $M_\infty = \lim M_t$ in the $L^1(\Omega, \mathcal{F}, P)$ norm; that is, $\lim_t \|M_t - M_\infty\|_1 = 0$.

In this case $\{M_t\}$ is a martingale on $[0, \infty]$ and

$$M_t = E[M_\infty | \mathcal{F}_t] \text{ a.s.} \quad \forall t.$$

We also say that M is *closed* by the random variable M_∞.

Exercise 6.2.9. Show that if a set K is $L^1(\Omega, \mathcal{F}, P)$ and is L^p-bounded for some $p > 1$, then K is uniformly integrable.

Notation 6.2.10. Write $\mathcal{M}$ for the set of uniformly integrable martingales.

An important concept is that of 'localization'.

If $\mathcal{C}$ is a class of processes, then $\mathcal{C}_{\ell oc}$ is the set of processes defined as follows.

$X \in \mathcal{C}_{\ell oc}$ if there is an increasing sequence $\{T_n\}$ of stopping times

$$T_1 \leq T_2 \leq T_3 \leq \dots$$

such that $\lim T_n = +\infty$ a.s. and $X_{t \wedge T_n} \in \mathcal{C}$.

For example, $\mathcal{C}$ might be the bounded processes, or the processes of bounded variation.

Notation 6.2.11. $\mathcal{M}_{\ell oc}$ denotes the set of local martingales.

The defining relation for martingales, $E[M_t | \mathcal{F}_s] = M_s$, can again be extended to stopping times. This result is known as Doob's Optional Stopping Theorem and it says the martingale equality is preserved even if (non-anticipative) random stopping rules are allowed. A complete proof of this result can be found in [87], Theorem 4.12, Corollary 4.13. We discussed the discrete case in Chapter 5; the extension from bounded to more general stopping times required the martingale convergence theorem and conditions under which a supermartingale is closed by an L^1-function. Note this is also assumed in the following.

Theorem 6.2.12. *Suppose* $\{M_t\}$, $t \in [0, \infty]$, *is a right-continuous supermartingale (resp. submartingale) with respect to the filtration* $\{\mathcal{F}_t\}$. *If* S *and* T *are two* $\mathcal{F}_t$-*stopping times such that* $S \leq T$ *a.s., then*

$$E[M_T|\mathcal{F}_S] \leq M_S \text{ a.s.}$$
$$(resp., \quad E[M_T|\mathcal{F}_S] \geq M_S \text{ a.s.}).$$

Corollary 6.2.13. *In particular, if* $\{M_t\}$, $t \in [0, \infty]$ *is a right-continuous martingale and* S, T *are* $\mathcal{F}_t$-*stopping times with* $S \leq T$, *then*

$$E[M_T|\mathcal{F}_S] = M_S \quad \text{a.s.}$$

Remark 6.2.14. Note, if T is any $\{\mathcal{F}_t\}$ stopping time, then

$$E[M_T] = E[M_0].$$

The following is a consequence of the Optional Stopping Theorem. Note we write $x^+ = \max(x, 0)$ and $x^- = \max(-x, 0)$.

Lemma 6.2.15. *Suppose* X_t, $t \in [0, \infty]$, *is a supermartingale. Then for every* $\alpha \geq 0$,

$$\alpha P\{(\inf_t X_t) \leq -\alpha\} \leq \sup_t E[X_t^-].$$

Proof. Write

$$S(\omega) = \inf\{t : X_t(\omega) \leq -\alpha\}$$

and

$$S_t = S \wedge t.$$

Using the Optional Stopping Theorem 6.2.12,

$$E[X_{S_t}] \geq E[X_t].$$

Therefore,

$$E[X_t] \leq -\alpha P\{(\inf_{s \leq t} X_s) \leq -\alpha\} + \int_{\{\inf_{s \leq t} X_s > -\alpha\}} X_t dP;$$

that is,

$$\alpha P\{(\inf_{s \leq t} X_s) \leq -\alpha\} \leq E[-X_t] + \int_{\{\inf_{s \leq t} X_s > -\alpha\}} X_t dP$$

$$= \int_{\{\inf_{s \leq t} X_s \leq -\alpha\}} -X_t dP \leq E[X_t^-]. \quad (6.1)$$

Letting $t \to \infty$ the result follows. □

As a consequence we can deduce Doob's Maximal Theorem.

Theorem 6.2.16. *Suppose* $\{X_t\}$, $t \in [0, \infty]$, *is a martingale. Then for every* $\alpha \geq 0$,

$$\alpha P\{\sup_t |X_t| \geq \alpha\} \leq \sup_t \|X_t\|_1.$$

Proof. From Jensen's inequality (see Proposition 5.3.3), if X is a martingale, then

$$Y_t := -|X_t| \quad \text{is a (negative) supermartingale}$$
$$\text{and} \quad \|Y_t\|_1 = \|X_t\|_1 = E[Y_t^-].$$
$$\text{Also,} \quad \{\inf_t Y_t \leq -\alpha\} = \{\sup_t |X_t| \geq \alpha\}$$

so the result follows from Lemma 6.2.15. $\qquad\qquad\square$

Before proving Doob's L^p inequality we first establish the following result.

Theorem 6.2.17. *Suppose* X *and* Y *are two positive random variables defined on the probability space* $(\Omega, \mathcal{F}, P)$ *such that* $X \in L^p$ *for some* p, $1 < p < \infty$, *and for every* $\alpha > 0$,

$$\alpha P(\{Y \geq \alpha\}) \leq \int_{\{Y \geq \alpha\}} X dP.$$

Then

$$\|Y\|_p \leq q\|X\|_p,$$

where

$$\frac{1}{p} + \frac{1}{q} = 1.$$

Proof. Let $F(\lambda) = P(\{Y > \lambda\})$ be (1 minus) the distribution function of Y. Then, using integration by parts,

$$E[Y^p] = -\int_0^\infty \lambda^p dF(\lambda)$$
$$= \int_0^\infty F(\lambda) d(\lambda^p) - \lim_{h \to \infty} [\lambda^p F(\lambda)]_0^h$$

$$\leq \int_0^\infty F(\lambda)d(\lambda^p)$$

$$\leq \int_0^\infty \lambda^{-1} \Big(\int_{\{Y \geq \lambda\}} X dP \Big) d(\lambda^p) \qquad \text{by hypothesis}$$

$$= E[X \int_0^Y \lambda^{-1} d(\lambda^p)] \qquad \text{by Fubini's Theorem,}$$

$$= \Big(\frac{p}{p-1} \Big) E[XY^{p-1}]$$

$$\leq q\|X\|_p \|Y^{p-1}\|_q \qquad \text{by Hölder's inequality.}$$

That is, $E[Y^p] \leq q\|X\|_p (E[Y^{pq-q}])^{1/q}$.

If $\|Y\|_p$ is finite the result follows immediately, because $pq - q = p$. Otherwise, consider the random variable

$$Y_k = Y \wedge k, \quad k \in N.$$

Then $Y_k \in L^p$ and Y_k also satisfies the hypotheses. Therefore

$$\|Y_k\|_p \leq q\|X\|_p.$$

Letting $k \to \infty$ the result follows.   □

Theorem 6.2.18. *Suppose $\{X_t\}$, $t \in [0, \infty]$, is a right-continuous positive supermartingale.*
   Write $X^*(\omega) = \sup_t X_t(\omega)$. Then, for $1 < p \leq \infty$, $X^* \in L^p$ if and only if

$$\sup_t \|X_t\|_p < \infty.$$

Also, for $1 < p < \infty$ and $q^{-1} = 1 - p^{-1}$,

$$\|X^*\|_p \leq q \sup_t \|X_t\|_p.$$

Proof. When $p = \infty$ the first part of the theorem is immediate, because if $\sup_t \|X_t\|_\infty = B < \infty$ then $X_t \leq B$ a.s. for all $t \in [0, \infty]$. The right continuity is required to ensure there is a single set of measure zero outside which this inequality is satisfied for all t. Also, for $1 < p < \infty$, if $X^* \in L^p$ then

$$\sup_t \|X_t\|_p \leq \|X^*\|_p < \infty.$$

From Exercise 6.2.9, the random variables $\{X_t\}$ are uniformly integrable so from Corollaries 3.18 and 3.19 of Elliott [87]

$$\lim_{t \to \infty} X_t(\omega) = X_\infty(\omega) \quad \text{exists a.s.}$$

Using Fatou's lemma

$$E[\lim_t X_t^p] \leq \liminf_t E[X_t^p]$$
$$\leq \sup_t E[X_t^p] < \infty.$$

Therefore, $X_\infty \in L^p$ and $\|X_\infty\|_p \leq \sup_t \|X_t\|_p$.

Write $X_t^*(\omega) := \sup_{s \leq t} X_s(\omega)$. Then $\{-X_t\}$ is a supermartingale so from inequality (6.1) in Lemma 6.2.15, for any $\alpha > 0$,

$$\alpha P(\{\inf_{s \leq t}(-X_s) \leq -\alpha\}) = \alpha P(\{X_t^* \geq \alpha\})$$
$$\leq \int_{\{X_t^* \geq \alpha\}} X_t dP \leq \int_{\{X^* \geq \alpha\}} X_t dP.$$

Letting $t \to \infty$ we have for any $\alpha > 0$,

$$\alpha P(\{X^* \geq \alpha\}) \leq \int_{\{X^* \geq \alpha\}} X_\infty dP.$$

Therefore, Theorem 6.2.17 can be applied with $Y = X^*$ and $X = X_\infty$ to obtain

$$\|X^*\|_p \leq q\|X_\infty\|_p$$

and the result follows.   □

The following important special case arises when $p = q = 2$ and the time interval is taken as $[0, T]$.

Corollary 6.2.19 (Doob's Inequality). *Suppose* $\{M_t\}$, $t \geq 0$, *is a continuous martingale. Then*

$$E[\sup_{0 \leq t \leq T} |M_t|^2] \leq 4E[|M_T|^2].$$

6.3   Stochastic Integrals

In discrete time the discounted value of a portfolio process having initial value V_0 and generated by a self-financing strategy (H_k), $k \geq 0$, is given by

$$V_0 + \sum_{j=1}^{n} H_j(\overline{S}_j - \overline{S}_{j-1}).$$

Recall that under an equivalent measure the discounted price process $\overline{S}$ is a martingale. Consequently, the preceding value process is a martingale transform. The natural extension to continuous time of such a martingale transform is the stochastic integral $\int_0^t H_s d\overline{S}_s$. However, $d\overline{S} = \overline{S}\sigma dW_t$ where

W_t is a Brownian motion. Almost all sample paths $W.(\omega)$ of Brownian motion are known to be of unbounded variation. They are, therefore, certainly not differentiable. The integral $\int H d\overline{S}$ cannot be defined as $\int H(dS/dt) \cdot dt$, or even as a Stieltjes integral. It can, however, be defined as the limit of suitable approximating sums in $L^2(\Omega)$.

We work initially on the time interval $[0, T]$. Suppose $\{W_t\}$ is an $\mathcal{F}_t$ Brownian motion defined on $(\Omega, \mathcal{F}, P)$ for $t \in [0, T]$; that is, W is adapted to the filtration $\{\mathcal{F}_t\}$.

Definition 6.3.1. A real-valued *simple process* on $[0, T]$ is a function H for which

a) there is a partition $0 = t_0 < t_1 < \ldots t_n = T$;

b) $H(t_0) = H_0(\omega)$ and $H(t) = H_i(\omega)$ for $t \in]t_i, t_{i+1}]$ where $H_i(\cdot)$ is $\mathcal{F}_{t_i}$ measurable and square integrable. That is,

$$H_t = H_0(\omega) + \sum_{i=0}^{n-1} H_i(\omega) \mathbf{1}_{]t_i, t_{i+1}]}.$$

Definition 6.3.2. If H is a simple process the *stochastic integral* of H with respect to the Brownian motion $\{W_t\}$ is the process defined for $t \in]t_k, t_{k+1}]$ by

$$\int_0^t H_s dW_s = \sum_{0 \leq i \leq k-1} H_i(W_{t_{i+1}} - W_{t_i}) + H_k(W_t - W_{t_k}).$$

This can be written as a martingale transform:

$$\int_0^t H_s dW_s = \sum_{0 \leq i \leq n} H_i(W_{t_{i+1} \wedge t} - W_{t_i \wedge t}).$$

We write $\int_0^t H dW = \int_0^t H_s dW_s$.

Note that, because $W_0 = 0$, there is no contribution to the integral at $t = 0$.

Theorem 6.3.3. *Suppose H is a simple process.*

a) *Then $(\int_0^t H_s dW_s)$ is a continuous $\mathcal{F}_t$ martingale.*

b) $E[(\int_0^t H_s dW_s)^2] = E[\int_0^t H_s^2 ds]$.

c) $E[\sup_{0 \leq t \leq T} |\int_0^t H_s dW_s|^2] \leq 4E[\int_0^T H_s^2 ds]$.

Proof. a) For $t \in]t_k, t_{k+1}]$

$$\int_0^t H_s dW_s = \sum_{0 \leq i \leq k-1} H_i(W_{t_{i+1}} - W_{t_i}) + H_k(W_t - W_{t_k}).$$

Now $W_t(\cdot)$ is continuous a.s. in t; therefore, $\int_0^t H_s dW_s$ is continuous a.s. in t. Suppose $0 \leq s \leq t \leq T$. Recall

$$\int_0^t H_s dW_s = \sum_{0 \leq i \leq n} H_i (W_{t_{i+1} \wedge t} - W_{t_i \wedge t}),$$

where H_i is $\mathcal{F}_{t_i}$ measurable. Now if $s \leq t_i$,

$$
\begin{aligned}
E\big[H_i(W_{t_{i+1} \wedge t} - W_{t_i \wedge t})|\mathcal{F}_s\big] &= E\Big[E\big[H_i(W_{t_{i+1} \wedge t} - W_{t_i \wedge t})|\mathcal{F}_{t_i}\big]\mathcal{F}_s\Big] \\
&= E\Big[H_i E\big[W_{t_{i+1} \wedge t} - W_{t_i \wedge t}|\mathcal{F}_{t_i}\big]\mathcal{F}_s\Big] \\
&= 0 \quad = \quad H_i(W_{t_{i+1} \wedge s} - W_{t_i \wedge s})
\end{aligned}
$$

because $t_{i+1} \wedge s = t_i \wedge s = s$.

If $s \geq t_i$,

$$
\begin{aligned}
E\big[H_i(W_{t_{i+1} \wedge t} - W_{t_i \wedge t})|\mathcal{F}_s\big] &= H_i E\big[W_{t_{i+1} \wedge t} - W_{t_i}|\mathcal{F}_s\big] \\
&= H_i(W_{t_{i+1} \wedge s} - W_{t_i \wedge s}).
\end{aligned}
$$

Consequently, for $s \leq t$,

$$E[(\int_0^t H_s dW_s)|\mathcal{F}_s] = (\int_0^s H dW)_s$$

and $(\int_0^t H dW)_t$ is a continuous martingale.

b) Now suppose $i < j$ so that $i + 1 \leq j$. Then

$$
\begin{aligned}
&E\big[H_i H_j (W_{t_{i+1} \wedge t} - W_{t_i \wedge t})(W_{t_{j+1} \wedge t} - W_{t_j \wedge t})\big] \\
&= E\Big[E\big[H_i H_j (W_{t_{i+1} \wedge t} - W_{t_i \wedge t})(W_{t_{j+1} \wedge t} - W_{t_j \wedge t})|\mathcal{F}_{t_j}\big]\Big] \\
&= E\Big[H_i H_j (W_{t_{i+1} \wedge t} - W_{t_i \wedge t})E\big[W_{t_{j+1} \wedge t} - W_{t_j \wedge t}|\mathcal{F}_{t_j}\big]\Big] \\
&= 0.
\end{aligned}
$$

Also,

$$
\begin{aligned}
E\big[H_i^2 (W_{t_{i+1} \wedge t} - W_{t_i \wedge t})^2\big] &= E\Big[H_i^2 E\big[(W_{t_{i+1} \wedge t} - W_{t_i \wedge t})^2|\mathcal{F}_{t_i}\big]\Big] \\
&= E\big[H_i^2 (t_{i+1} \wedge t - t_i \wedge t)\big].
\end{aligned}
$$

Consequently,

$$
\begin{aligned}
E\big[(\int_0^t H dW)_t^2\big] &= \sum_{0 \leq i \leq n} E\big[H_i^2 (t_{i+1} \wedge t - t_i \wedge t)\big] \\
&= E\big[\int_0^t H_s^2 ds\big] = \int_0^t E[H_s^2] ds.
\end{aligned}
$$

c) For the final part apply Doob's maximal inequality, Corollary 6.2.19, to the martingale

$$\int_0^t H_s dW_s.$$

$\square$

Notation 6.3.4. We write $\mathcal{H}$ for the space of processes adapted to $\{\mathcal{F}_t\}$ that satisfy $E[\int_0^T H_s^2 ds] < \infty$.

Lemma 6.3.5. *Suppose* $\{H_s\} \in \mathcal{H}$. *Then there is a sequence* $\{H_s^n\}$ *of simple processes such that*

$$\lim_{n\to\infty} E[\int_0^T |H_s - H_s^n|^2 ds] = 0.$$

Outline of the Proof. Fix $f \in \mathcal{H}$, and define a sequence of simple functions converging to f by setting

$$f_n(t,\omega) = n \int_{(k-1)/n}^{k/n} f(s,\omega) ds \quad \text{if } t \in \left[\frac{k}{n}, \frac{k+1}{n}\right).$$

If the integral diverges, replace it by 0. By Fubini's theorem this only happens on a null set in Ω, since f is integrable on $\mathbb{T} \times \Omega$.

Note that, using progressive measurability, as a random variable the preceding integral is $\mathcal{F}_{k/n}$-measurable, so that f_n is a simple process as defined in 6.3.1. We show in the following that $\int_0^T |f_n(t,\omega) - f(t,\omega)|^2 dt$ converges to 0 whenever $f(\cdot,\omega) \in L^2[0,T]$, and also that for all such $\omega \in \Omega$, $\int_0^T |f_n(t,\omega)|^2 dt \le \int_0^T |f(t,\omega)|^2 dt$. Thus the dominated convergence theorem allows us to conclude that

$$E\left[\int_0^T |f_n - f| dt\right] \to 0 \quad \text{as} \quad n \to \infty.$$

Therefore the proof reduces to a problem in $L^2[0,T]$, namely to show that if $f \in L^2[0,T]$ is fixed, then as $h \downarrow 0$, the 'time averages' f_h defined for $t \in [kh, (k+1)h \wedge h^{-1})$ by $f_h(t) = (1/h) \int_{(k-1)h}^{kh} f(s) ds$ and 0 outside $[h, h^{-1})$, remain L^2-dominated by f and converge to f in L^2-norm. To prove this, first consider the following estimate (which is exact if $(T/h) \in \mathbb{N}$ or $T = \infty$),

$$\int_0^T f_h^2(t) dt \le \sum_{k=1}^{[T/h]} \left| \int_{(k-1)h}^{kh} f(s) ds \right|^2.$$

Now the Schwarz inequality, applied to $1 \cdot f$, shows that each term in the latter sum is bounded above by $h \cdot \int_{(k-1)h}^{kh} f^2(s) ds$; hence the sum is bounded by $h \cdot \int_0^{[T/h] \cdot h} f^2(s) ds \le h \cdot \int_0^T f^2(s) ds$, which proves domination. To prove the convergence, consider $\varepsilon > 0$ and note that if f is a step function, then f_h will converge to f as $h \downarrow 0$. Since the step functions are dense in $L^2[0, T]$, choose a step function f^ε such that (with $\|\cdot\|$ denoting the norm in $L^2[0, T]$) $\|f^\varepsilon - f\| < \varepsilon$. Note that since f_h is also a step function, $f_h - f_h^\varepsilon = (f - f^\varepsilon)_h$. Moreover, by definition of f_h, it is easy to verify that $\|f_h - f_h^\varepsilon\| \le \|f - f^\varepsilon\|$. Therefore we can write

$$\|f_h - f\| = \|f_h^\varepsilon - f^\varepsilon + (f - f^\varepsilon)_h - (f - f^\varepsilon)\| \le \|f_h^\varepsilon - f^\varepsilon\| + 2\|f - f^\varepsilon\|.$$

But the first term goes to 0 as $h \downarrow 0$ since f_h is a step function, while the second is less than 2ε. This proves the result. $\qquad\square$

Theorem 6.3.6. *Suppose $\{W_t\}$, $t \ge 0$, is a Brownian motion on the filtration $\{\mathcal{F}_t\}$. Then there is a unique linear map I from $\mathcal{H}$ into the space of continuous $\mathcal{F}_t$ martingales on $[0, T]$ such that*

a) *if H is a simple process in $\mathcal{H}$, then*

$$I(H)_t = \int_0^t H_s dW_s.$$

b) *If $t \le T$,*

$$E\left[\left(I(H)_t\right)^2\right] = E\left[\int_0^t H_s^2 ds\right].$$

Identity b) is called the isometry property *of the integral.*

Proof. For H a simple process one defines $I(H)_t = \int_0^t H_s dW_s$. Suppose $H \in \mathcal{H}$ and $\{H^n\}$ is a sequence of simple processes converging to H. Then

$$
\begin{aligned}
I(H^{n+p} - H^n)_t &= \int_0^t (H^{n+p} - H^n) dW_t \\
&= \int_0^t H^{n+p} dW - \int_0^t H^n dW
\end{aligned}
$$

and from Doob's inequality, Corollary 6.2.19,

$$E\left[\sup_{0 \le t \le T} |I(H^{n+p} - H^n)_t|^2\right] \le 4E\left[\int_0^T |H_s^{n+p} - H_s^n|^2 ds\right]. \qquad (6.2)$$

Consequently, there is a subsequence H^{k_n} such that

$$E\left[\sup_{t \le T} |I(H^{k_{n+1}})_t - I(H^{k_n})_t|^2\right] \le 2^{-n}.$$

Almost surely, the sequence of continuous functions $I(H^{k_n})_t$, $0 \le t \le T$ is uniformly convergent on $[0, T]$ to a function $I(H)_t$. Letting $p \to \infty$ in (6.2) we see that

$$E\left[\sup_{t \le T} |I(H)_t - I(H^n)_t|^2\right] \le 4E\left[\int_0^T |H_s - H_s^n|^2 ds\right].$$

This argument also implies that $I(H)$ is independent of the approximating sequence (H^n).

Now $E[I(H^n)_t|\mathcal{F}_s] = I(H^n)_s$ a.s. The random variables $\{I(H^n), I(H)\}$ belong to $L^2(\Omega, \mathcal{F}, P)$, so

$$
\begin{aligned}
\|E[I(H)_t|\mathcal{F}_s] - I(H)_s\|_2 \;\leq\; & \|E[I(H)_t|\mathcal{F}_s] - E[I(H^n)_t|\mathcal{F}_s]\|_2 \\
& + \|E[I(H^n)_t|\mathcal{F}_s] - I(H^n)_s\|_2 \\
& + \|I(H^n)_s - I(H)_s\|_2.
\end{aligned}
$$

The right side can be made arbitrarily small so $I(H)_t$ is an $\mathcal{F}_t$ martingale.

The remaining results follow by continuity, and from the density in $\mathcal{H}$ of simple processes. $\qquad\square$

Notation 6.3.7. We write $I(H)_t = \int_0^t H_s dW_s$ for $H \in \mathcal{H}$.

Lemma 6.3.8. *For $H \in \mathcal{H}$,*

a) $E\big[\sup_{0\leq t\leq T} |\int_0^t H_s dW_s|^2\big] \leq 4E\big[\int_0^T |H|_s^2 ds\big].$

b) *If τ is an $\mathcal{F}_t$-stopping time such that $\tau \leq T$,*

$$
\int_0^\tau H_s dW_s = \int_0^T I_{\{s\leq\tau\}} H_s dW_s.
$$

Proof. a) We know

$$
E\big[I(H^n)_T^2\big] = E\Big[\int_0^T |H_s^n|^2 ds\Big]
$$

so taking limits

$$
E\big[I(H)_T^2\big] = E\Big[\int_0^T |H_s|^2 ds\Big].
$$

Also

$$
E\big[\sup_{t\leq T} I(H^n)_t^2\big] \leq 4E\Big[\int_0^T |H_s^n|^2 ds\Big].
$$

Taking limits the result follows.

b) Suppose τ is a stopping time of the form

$$
\tau = \sum_{1\leq i\leq n} I_{A_i} t_i, \tag{6.3}
$$

where $A_i \cap A_j = \emptyset$ for $i \neq j$ and $A_i \in \mathcal{F}_{t_i}$.

Then

$$
\int_0^T I\{s > \tau\} H_s dW_s = \int_0^T \Big(\sum_{1\leq i\leq n} I_{A_i} I_{s>t_i}\Big) H_s dW_s.
$$

Now for each i the process $I_{s>t_i} I_A H_s$ is adapted and in $\mathcal{H}$; it is zero if $s \leq t_i$ and equals $I_A H_s$ otherwise. Therefore

$$\int_0^T \Big(\sum_{1 \leq i \leq n} I_{A_i} I_{s>t_i} \Big) H_s dW_s = \sum_{1 \leq i \leq n} I_{A_i} \int_{t_i}^T H_s dW_s = \int_\tau^T H_s dW_s.$$

Consequently, for τ of the form (6.3),

$$\int_0^T I\{s \leq \tau\} H_s dW_s = \int_0^\tau H_s dW_s.$$

Now an arbitrary stopping time τ can be approximated by a decreasing sequence of stopping times τ_n where

$$\tau_n = \sum_{0 \leq i \leq 2^n} \frac{(k+1)T}{2^n} I\Big\{ \frac{kT}{2^n} \leq \tau < \frac{(k+1)T}{2^n} \Big\},$$

so that $\lim \tau_n = \tau$ a.s.

Consequently, because $(H \cdot W)_t$ is almost surely continuous in t,

$$\lim_{n \to \infty} \int_0^{\tau_n} H_s dW_s = \int_0^\tau H_s dW_s \quad \text{a.s.}$$

Also,

$$E\Big[|\int_0^T I\{s \leq \tau\} H_s dW_s - \int_0^T I\{s \leq \tau_n\} H_s dW_s|^2 \Big]$$

$$= E\Big[\int_0^T I\{\tau < s \leq \tau_n\} H_s^2 ds \Big]$$

and this converges to zero by the dominated convergence theorem. Therefore,

$$\lim_{n \to \infty} \int_0^T I\{s \leq \tau_n\} H_s dW_s = \int_0^T I_{\{s \leq \tau\}} H_s dW_s$$

both a.s. and in $L^2(\Omega)$; the result follows.   □

Notation 6.3.9. Write

$$\widehat{\mathcal{H}} = \Big\{ \{H_s\} : H \text{ is } \mathcal{F}_t \text{ adapted and } \int_0^T H_s^2 ds < \infty \text{ a.s.} \Big\}.$$

The preceding definition and results for the stochastic integral can be extended from $\mathcal{H}$ to $\widehat{\mathcal{H}}$.

Theorem 6.3.10. *There is a unique linear map $\widehat{I}$ of $\widehat{\mathcal{H}}$ into the space of continuous processes defined on $[0,T]$ such that*

a) *if $\{H_t\}$, $0 \le t \le T$, is in $\mathcal{H}$, then for all $t \in [0,T]$ the processes $\widehat{I}(H)_t$ and $I(H)_t$ are indistinguishable.*

b) *If $\{H^n\}$, $n \ge 0$, is a sequence in $\widehat{\mathcal{H}}$ such that $\int_0^T (H_s^n)^2 ds$ converges to zero in probability, then*

$$\sup_{0 \le t \le T} |\widehat{I}(H^n)_t|$$

converges to zero in probability.

Notation 6.3.11. One writes $\widehat{I}(H)_t = \int_0^t H_s dW_s$.

Proof. a) From Theorem 6.3.6 we know that for $H \in \mathcal{H}$, $I(H)$ is defined. Suppose $H \in \widehat{\mathcal{H}}$. Define $T_n = \inf \{0 \le u \le T : \int_0^u H_s^2 ds \ge n\}$ ($T_n = T$ if this set is empty). Because H_s is adapted, $\int_0^t H_s^2 ds$ is adapted and T_n is an $\mathcal{F}_t$-stopping time.

Then write $H_s^n = I\{s < T_n\} H_s$. The processes H^n are, therefore, in $\mathcal{H}$ and

$$\int_0^t H_s^n dW_s = \int_0^t I_{s \le T_n} H_s^{n+1} dW_s$$
$$= \int_0^{T_n \wedge t} H_s^{n+1} dW_s.$$

Therefore, on the set $\{\int_0^T H_u^2 du < n\}$, for all $t \le T$,

$$I(H^n)_t = I(H^{n+1})_t.$$

Now $\bigcup_{n \ge 0} \{\int_0^T H_u^2 du < n\} = \{\int_0^T H_u^2 du < \infty\}$. Therefore, one can define $\widehat{I}(H)_t$ by putting $\widehat{I}(H)_t = I(H^n)_t$ on $\{\int_0^T H_s^2 ds < n\}$. Clearly $\widehat{I}(H)_t = I(H)_t$ and is continuous a.s.

b) Write $I = \int_0^T H_u^2 du$, $B = \{I \ge 1/N\}$ and $A = \{\omega : \sup_{0 \le t \le T} |\widehat{I}(H)_t| \ge \varepsilon\}$. Then $P(A) = P(A \cap B) + P(A \cap B^c) \le P(B) + P(A \cap B^c)$. Therefore, for any $\varepsilon > 0$,

$$P\left(\sup_{0 \le t \le T} |\widehat{I}(H)_t| \ge \varepsilon\right) \le P\left(\int_0^T H_u^2 du \ge \frac{1}{N}\right) \qquad (6.4)$$

$$+ P\left(\left\{\int_0^T H_u^2 du < \frac{1}{N}\right\} \cap \left\{\sup_{0 \le t \le T} |\widehat{I}(H)|_t \ge \varepsilon\right\}\right).$$

Write $\tau_N = \inf \{s \le T : \int_0^s H_u^2 du \ge 1/N\}$. (Note $\tau_N = T$ if this set is empty.) On the set $\{\int_0^T H_u^2 du < 1/N\}$

$$\int_0^t H_s dW_s = \int_0^t I(s \le \tau_N) H_s dW_s.$$

Therefore , with $G_s = H_s I\{s \leq \tau_N\}$, $G_s = H_s$ on B^c and from Doob's inequality

$$E\left[\sup_{0 \leq t \leq T} \left|\int_0^t G_s dW_s\right|^2\right] \leq 4E\left[\int_0^t (G_s)^2 ds\right] \leq \frac{4}{N} . \qquad (6.5)$$

Using Chebyschev's inequality

$$P(A \cap B^c) = P\left(\{B^c\} \cap \left\{\sup_{0 \leq t \leq T} |\widehat{I}(H)_t| \geq \varepsilon\right\}\right) \leq P\left(\sup_{0 \leq t \leq T} |\widehat{I}(G)_t| \geq \varepsilon\right)$$

$$\leq E\left[\sup_{0 \leq t \leq T} \left|\int_0^t G_s dW_s\right|^2\right]\Big/ \varepsilon^3 \leq 4/N\varepsilon^2 \quad \text{by (6.5)}.$$

Consequently, from (6.4),

$$P\left(\sup_{0 \leq t \leq T} |\widehat{I}(H)_t| \geq \varepsilon\right) \leq P\left(\int_0^T H_u^2 du \geq \frac{1}{N}\right) + 4/N\varepsilon^2.$$

We can, therefore, see that if $\{H^n\}$ is a sequence in $\widehat{\mathcal{H}}$ such that $\int_0^T (H_u^n)^2 du$ converges to zero in probability, then $\sup_{0 \leq t \leq T} |\widehat{I}(H)_t|$ converges to zero in probability. The continuity of the operator $\widehat{I}$ is, therefore, established.

$\square$

If $H \in \widehat{\mathcal{H}}$ then, with $H_s^n = I\{s < T_n\}H_s$ we see that $\int_0^T (H_s - H_s^n)^2 ds$ converges to zero in probability. Using the continuity property we see the map $\widehat{I}$ is uniquely defined.

Similarly, for H, $K \in \widehat{\mathcal{H}}$ suppose there are the approximating sequences H^n, $K^n \in \mathcal{H}$. Now $\int_0^T (H_s - H_s^n)^2 ds$ and $\int_0^T (K_s - K_s^n)^2 ds$ converge to zero in probability as $n \to \infty$. Furthermore, $I(\alpha H^n + \beta K^n)_t = \alpha I(H^n)_t + \beta I(K^n)_t$. Letting $n \to \infty$ we see that $\widehat{I}$ is a linear map.

6.4   The Itô Calculus

If $f(t)$ is a real-valued, differentiable function for $t \geq 0$ and $f(0) = 0$, then

$$f(t)^2 = 2\int_0^t f(s)\dot{f}(s)ds$$

$$= 2\int_0^t f(s)df(s).$$

However, if W is a Brownian motion we know $E[W_t^2] = t$. Consequently, W_t^2 cannot be equal to $2\int_0^t W_s dW_s$ because this integral is a (local) martingale and $E[2\int_0^t W_s dW_s] = 0$.

The Itô calculus is described for a class of processes known as Itô processes which we now define.

Definition 6.4.1. Suppose $(\Omega, \mathcal{F}, P)$ is a probability space with a filtration $\{\mathcal{F}_t\}$, $t \geq 0$, and $\{W_t\}$ is a standard $\mathcal{F}_t$-Brownian motion. A real-valued *Itô process* $\{X_t\}$ $t \geq 0$ is a process of the form

$$X_t = X_0 + \int_0^t K_s ds + \int_0^t H_s dW_s,$$

where

a) X_0 is $\mathcal{F}_0$ measurable,

b) K and H are adapted to $\mathcal{F}_t$, and

c) $\int_0^T |K_s| ds < \infty$ a.s. and $\int_0^T |H_s^2| ds < \infty$ a.s.

We can then obtain a uniqueness property that is a consequence of the following result.

Lemma 6.4.2. *Suppose the process $\int_0^t K_s\, ds = M_t$ is a continuous martingale, where $\int_0^T |K_s| ds < \infty$ a.s. Then for all $t \leq T$, $M_t = 0$ a.s. and there is a set $N \subset \Omega$ of measure zero such that for $\omega \notin N$, $K_s(\omega) = 0$ for almost all s.*

Proof. Suppose initially that $\int_0^T |K_s| ds \leq C < \infty$ a.s. Then, with $t_i^n = T/n$, $0 \leq i \leq n$,

$$\sum_{i=1}^n (M_{t_i^n} - M_{t_{i-1}^n})^2 \leq \sup_i |M_{t_i^n} - M_{t_{i-1}^n}| \sum_{i=1}^n |M_{t_i^n} - M_{t_{i-1}^n}|$$

$$= \sup_i |M_{t_i^n} - M_{t_{i-1}^n}| \sum_{i=1}^n \left| \int_{t_{i-1}^n}^{t_i^n} K_s ds \right|$$

$$\leq \sup_i |M_{t_i^n} - M_{t_{i-1}^n}| \sum_{i=1}^n \int_{t_{i-1}^n}^{t_i^n} |K_s| ds$$

$$\leq C \sup_i |M_{t_i^n} - M_{t_{i-1}^n}|.$$

Consequently, $\lim_{n \to \infty} \sum_{i=1}^n (M_{t_i^n} - M_{t_{i-1}^n})^2 = 0$ a.s., so by the Bounded Convergence Theorem

$$\lim_{n \to \infty} E\left[\sum_{i=1}^n \left(M_{t_i^n} - M_{t_{i-1}^n} \right)^2 \right] = 0.$$

However, because M is a martingale this equals

$$E[M_t^2 - M_0^2].$$

By definition $M_0 = 0$ a.s. Consequently, $M_t = 0$ a.s., and so $M_t = 0$ a.s., $t \leq T$. Now no longer suppose $\int_0^T |K_s| ds$ is bounded. Write

$T_n = \inf \{0 \le s \le T : \int_0^s |K_u| du \ge n\} \wedge T$ and take $\inf\{\emptyset\} = \infty$. Then T is a stopping time because K is adapted, and

$$\lim_{n \to \infty} T_n = T.$$

The preceding result shows that

$$M_{t \wedge T_n} = 0 \text{ a.s.}$$

and so $\lim_{n \to \infty} M_{t \wedge T_n} = 0 = M_t$ a.s.   □

Corollary 6.4.3. *Suppose M is a martingale of the form $\int_0^t H_s dW_s + \int_0^t K_s ds$ with $\int_0^t H_s^2 ds < \infty$ a.s. and $\int_0^t |K_s| ds < \infty$ a.s. Then $\int_0^t K_s ds$ is a martingale which is zero a.s. and there is a set $N \subset \Omega$ such that for $\omega \notin N$ $K_s(\omega) = 0$ for almost all s.*

Corollary 6.4.4. *Suppose the Itô process X has representations*

$$X_t = X_0 + \int_0^t K_s ds + \int_0^t H_s dW_s,$$

and

$$X_t = X_0' + \int_0^t K_s' ds + \int_0^t H_s' dW_s.$$

Then: $X_0 = X_0'$ a.s., $H_s = H_s'$ a.s. $ds \times dP$, and $K_s = K_s'$ a.s. $ds \times dP$. In particular, if X is a martingale, then $K = 0$.

Proof. Clearly $X_0 = X_0'$. Therefore

$$\int_0^t (K_s - K_s') ds = \int_0^t (H_s' - H_s) dW_s$$

and $\int_0^t (K_s - K_s') ds$ is a martingale. The result follows from Lemma 6.4.2.   □

Remark 6.4.5. Suppose $\{W_t\}$ is a Brownian motion for $t \ge 0$ and $\pi = \{0 = t_0 \le t_1 \le \cdots \le t_N = t\}$ is a partition of $[0, t]$. Write

$$|\pi| = \max_i (t_{i+1} - t_i).$$

Then

$$E\left(\sum_{i=0}^{N-1} (W_{t_{i+1}} - W_{t_i})^2 \right) = E\left(\sum_{i=0}^{N} (W_{t_{i+1}}^2 - W_{t_i}^2) \right)$$

$$= t. \tag{6.6}$$

In fact we can show that as $|\pi| \to 0$ $\sum_{i=0}^{N-1}(W_{t_{i+1}} - W_{t_i})^2$ converges to t almost surely.

Choose a sequence (π_n) of partitions with $|\pi_n| \to 0$ as $n \to \infty$. Write $Q_n = \sum_{\pi_n}(W_{t_{i+1}} - W_{t_i})^2$; then we have shown that $Q_n \to t$ in L^2-norm as $n \to \infty$. By Chebychev's inequality we have, for any $\varepsilon > 0$, that $P(|Q_n - t| > \varepsilon) \le (E((Q_n - t)^2))/\varepsilon^2$. Set $E((Q_n - t)^2) = q_n$, so that $q_n \to 0$ as $n \to \infty$. Choosing a subsequence we can assume that $q_n < 1/2^{2n}$. Letting $\varepsilon_n = 1/2^n$ and writing $A_n = \{|Q_n - t| > 1/2^n\}$, we obtain $P(A_n) \le 1/2^n$, so that $\sum_{n=1}^{\infty} P(A_n) < \infty$. By the first Borel–Cantelli lemma it follows that $P(\cap_{n \ge 1} A_n) = 0$, hence that $Q_n \to t$ a.s as $n \to \infty$.

For a general, continuous (local) martingale $\{M_t, t \ge 0\}$,

$$\lim_{|\pi| \to 0} \sum_{i=0}^{N} \left(M_{t_{i+1}} - M_{t_i}\right)^2$$

exists and is a predictable, continuous increasing process denoted by $\langle M \rangle_t$. From Jensen's inequality M^2 is a submartingale and it turns out that $\langle M \rangle$ is the unique (continuous) increasing process in the Doob–Meyer decomposition of M^2. This decomposition is entirely analogous to the Doob decomposition described in Section 5.3, but the technical complexities involved are substantially greater in continuous time. For details, see the development in Elliott [87], Chapter 10 or Kopp [169], Chapter 3. $\langle M \rangle$ is called the (predictable) quadratic variation of M. Consequently (6.6) states that for a Brownian motion W,

$$\langle W \rangle_t = t.$$

For $H \in \hat{\mathcal{H}}$ we have seen that $M_t = \int_0^t H_s dW_s$ is a local martingale. It is shown in Elliott [87] that in this case

$$\langle M \rangle_t = \int_0^t H_s^2 ds \text{ a.s.}$$

In some sense (6.6) indicates that, very formally, $(dW)^2 \simeq dt$, or $(dW) \simeq \sqrt{dt}$.

Suppose X is an Itô process on $0 \le t \le T$,

$$X_t = X_0 + \int_0^t K_s ds + \int_0^t H_s dW_s, \tag{6.7}$$

where $\int_0^T |K_s| ds < \infty$ a.s. and $\int_0^T |H_s|^2 ds < \infty$ a.s. Considering partitions $\pi = \{0 = t_0 \le t_1 \le \cdots \le t_N = t\}$ of $[0, t]$ it can be shown that

$$\lim_{|\pi| \to 0} \sum_{i=0}^{N} \left(X_{t_{i+1}} - X_{t_i}\right)^2$$

converges a.s. to

$$\int_0^t |H_s|^2 ds.$$

That is, $\langle X \rangle_t = \langle M \rangle_t$, where $M_t = \int_0^t H_s dW_s$ is the martingale term in the representation (6.7) of X.

Again, if X is a differentiable process, that is, if $H_s = 0$ in (6.7), then the usual chain rule states that, for a differentiable function f,

$$f(X_t) = f(X_0) + \int_0^t f'(X_s)dX_s.$$

However, if X is an Itô process, the differentiation rule has the following form.

Theorem 6.4.6. *Suppose $\{X_t, t \geq 0\}$ is an Itô process of the form*

$$X_t = X_0 + \int_0^t K_s ds + \int_0^t H_s dW_s.$$

Suppose f is twice differentiable. Then

$$f(X_t) = f(X_0) + \int_0^t f'(X_s)dX_s + \frac{1}{2}\int_0^t f''(X_s)d\langle X \rangle_s.$$

Here, by definition, $\langle X \rangle_t = \int_0^t H_s^2 ds$; that is, the (predictable) quadratic variation of X is the quadratic variation of its martingale component

$$\int_0^t H_s dW_s.$$

Also,

$$\int_0^t f'(X_s)dX_s = \int_0^t f'(X_s)K_s ds + \int_0^t f'(X_s)H_s dW_s.$$

For a proof see Elliott [87].

Extension 6.4.7. *If $F : [0, \infty) \times \mathbb{R} \to \mathbb{R}$ is continuously differentiable in the first component and twice continuously differentiable in the second, then*

$$\begin{aligned} F(t, X_t) &= F(0, X_0) + \int_0^t \frac{\partial F}{\partial s}(s, X_s)ds \\ &\quad + \int_0^t \frac{\partial F}{\partial x}(s, X_s)dX_s + \frac{1}{2}\int_0^t \frac{\partial^2 F}{\partial x^2}(s, X_s)d\langle X \rangle_s. \end{aligned}$$

Example 6.4.8. (i) Let us consider the case when $K_s = 0$, $H_s = 1$. Then

$$X_t = X_0 + W_t,$$

where W_t is standard Brownian motion.

Taking $f(x) = x^2$ we have $\langle X \rangle_t = \langle W \rangle_t = t$ so

$$X_t^2 = X_0^2 + 2\int_0^t W_s dW_s + \frac{1}{2}\int_0^t 2ds.$$

That is,

$$X_t^2 - X_0^2 - t = 2 \int_0^t W_s dW_s.$$

For any $T < \infty$ $E[\int_0^T W_s^2 ds] < \infty$, so from Theorem 6.3.6 $\int_0^t W_s dW_s$ is a martingale. If $X_0 = 0$, then $X_t = W_t$ and we see that $W_t^2 - t$ is a martingale.

(ii) An often-used model for a price process is the so-called 'log-normal' model. In this case it is supposed the price process S_t evolves according to the stochastic dynamics

$$\frac{dS_t}{S_t} = \mu dt + \sigma dW_t, \tag{6.8}$$

where μ and σ are real constants and $S_0 = X_0$.

This means that

$$S_t = X_0 + \int_0^t S_s \mu ds + \int_0^t S_s \sigma dW_s.$$

Assuming such a process S exists it is, therefore, an Itô process with

$$K_s = \mu S_s \quad \text{and} \quad H_s = \sigma S_s.$$

Then $\langle X \rangle_t = \int_0^t \sigma^2 S_s^2 ds$. Assuming $S_t > 0$ and applying Itô's formula with $f(x) = \log x$ (formally, because $\log x$ is not twice continuously differentiable everywhere),

$$
\begin{aligned}
\log S_t &= \log X_0 + \int_0^t \frac{dS_s}{S_s} + \frac{1}{2} \int_0^t -\frac{1}{S_s^2} \sigma^2 S_s^2 ds \\
&= \log X_0 + \int_0^t \left(\mu - \frac{\sigma^2}{2} \right) ds + \int_0^t \sigma dW_s \\
&= \log X_0 + \left(\mu - \frac{\sigma^2}{2} \right) t + \sigma W_t.
\end{aligned}
$$

Consequently,

$$S_t = X_0 \exp \left(\left(\mu - \frac{\sigma^2}{2} \right) t + \sigma W_t \right).$$

Exercise 6.4.9. Consider the function

$$F(t, x) = x_0 \exp \left(\left(\mu - \frac{\sigma^2}{2} \right) t + \sigma x \right).$$

Apply the Itô formula of 6.4.7 to $S_t = F(t, W_t)$ to show that S_t does satisfy the log-normal equation (6.8). This "justifies" our formal application of the Itô formula.

Definition 6.4.10. Suppose we have a probability space $(\Omega, \mathcal{F}, P)$ with a filtration $\{\mathcal{F}_t\}$, $t \geq 0$. An m-dimensional $\mathcal{F}_t$-Brownian motion is a process $W_t = (W_t^1, W_t^2, \ldots, W_t^m)$ whose components W_t^i are standard, independent $\mathcal{F}_t$-Brownian motions.

Multi-Dimensional Itô Processes

We can extend our definition of an Itô process to the situation where the (scalar) stochastic integral involves an m-dimensional Brownian motion.

Definition 6.4.11. $\{X_t\}$, $0 \leq t \leq T$, is an Itô process if

$$X_t = X_0 + \int_0^t K_s ds + \sum_{i=1}^m \int_0^t H_s^i dW_s^i,$$

where the K and H^i are adapted to $\{\mathcal{F}_t\}$, $\int_0^T |K_s| ds < \infty$ a.s. and for all i, $1 \leq i \leq m$,

$$\int_0^T |H_s^i|^2 ds < \infty \text{ a.s.}$$

An n-dimensional Itô process is then a process $X_t = (X_t^1, \ldots, X_t^n)$, each component of which is an Itô process in the sense of Definition 6.4.11.

The differentiation rule takes the form:

Theorem 6.4.12. *Suppose $X_t = (X_t^1, \ldots, X_t^n)$ is an n-dimensional Itô process with*

$$X_t^i = X_0^i + \int_0^t K_s^i ds + \sum_{j=1}^m \int_0^t H_s^{ij} dW_s^j,$$

and suppose $f : [0, T] \times \mathbb{R}^n \to \mathbb{R}$ is in $C^{1,2}$ (the space of functions once continuously differentiable in t and twice continuously differentiable in $x \in \mathbb{R}^n$).

Then

$$
\begin{aligned}
f(t, X_t^1, \ldots, X_t^n) = {}& f(0, X_0^1, \ldots, X_0^n) + \int_0^t \frac{\partial f}{\partial s}(s, X_s^1, \ldots, X_s^n) ds \\
& + \sum_{i=1}^n \int_0^t \frac{\partial f}{\partial x_i}(s, X_s^1, \ldots, X_s^n) dX_s^i \\
& + \frac{1}{2} \sum_{i,j=1}^n \int_0^t \frac{\partial^2 f}{\partial x_i \partial x_j}(s, X_s^1, \ldots, X_s^n) d\langle X^i, X^j \rangle_s.
\end{aligned}
$$

Here

$$dX_s^i = K_s^i ds + \sum_{j=1}^m H_s^{i,j} dW_s^j$$

and

$$d\langle X^i, X^j \rangle_s = \sum_{r=1}^m H_s^{i,r} H_s^{j,r} ds.$$

Remark 6.4.13. For components

$$X_t^p = X_0^p + \int_0^t K_s^p ds + \sum_{j=1}^m \int_0^t H_s^{pj} dW_s^j,$$

$$X_t^q = X_0^q + \int_0^t K_s^q ds + \sum_{j=1}^m \int_0^t H_s^{qj} dW_s^j,$$

it can be shown (see Meyer [193]) that for partitions $\pi = \{0 = t_0 \le t_1 \le \cdots \le t_N = t\}$,

$$\lim_{|\pi| \to 0} \sum_i \left(X_{t_{i+1}}^p - X_{t_i}^p \right) \left(X_{t_{i+1}}^q - X_{t_i}^q \right)$$

converges in probability to

$$\int_0^t \sum_{r=1}^m H_s^{pr} H_s^{qr} ds.$$

This process is the predictable covariation of X^p and X^q and is denoted by

$$\langle X^p, X^q \rangle_t = \sum_{r=1}^m \int_0^t H_s^{pr} H_s^{qr} ds. \tag{6.9}$$

We note that $\langle X^p, X^q \rangle$ is symmetric and bilinear as a function on Itô processes.

Taking

$$Y_t = Y_0 + \int_0^t K_s' ds$$

and

$$X_t = X_0 + \int_0^t K_s ds + \sum_{j=1}^m H_s^j dW_s^j$$

we see $\langle X, Y \rangle_t = 0$.

Furthermore, considering special cases, formula (6.9) gives

$$\langle \int_0^t H_s^{pi} dW_s^i, \int_0^t H_s^{qj} dW_s^j \rangle = 0 \quad \text{if} \quad i \ne j$$

and

$$\langle \int_0^t H_s^{pi} dW_s^i, \int_0^t H_s^{qi} dW_s^i \rangle = \int_0^t H_s^{pi} H_s^{qi} ds.$$

Remark 6.4.14. We noted in 6.4.5 that if $\{M_t\}$, $t \geq 0$, is a continuous local martingale, then $\langle M \rangle_t$ is the unique continuous increasing process in the Doob–Meyer decomposition of the submartingale M_t^2. If

$$X_t = X_0 + \int_0^t K_s ds + \int_0^t H_s dM_s,$$

where H and K are adapted, $\int_0^T |K_s| ds < \infty$ a.s., and $\int_0^T H_s^2 ds < \infty$ a.s., the differentiation formula has the form

$$
\begin{aligned}
f(X_t) &= f(X_0) + \int_0^t \frac{\partial f}{\partial x}(X_s) K_s ds \\
&+ \int_0^t \frac{\partial f}{\partial x}(X_s) H_s dM_s + \frac{1}{2}\int_0^t \frac{\partial^2 f}{\partial x^2}(X_s) H_s^2 d\langle M \rangle_s.
\end{aligned}
$$

Using without proof the analogue of the Itô rule (Theorem 6.4.6) for general square integrable martingales M (see [87], page 138) we can prove the converse of Theorem 6.2.5.

Theorem 6.4.15. *Suppose* $\{W_t\}$, $t \geq 0$, *is a continuous (scalar) local martingale on the filtered probability space* $(\Omega, \mathcal{F}, P, \mathcal{F}_t)$, *such that* $\{W_t^2 - t\}$, $t \geq 0$ *is a local martingale.*
Then $\{W_t\}$ *is a Brownian motion.*

Proof. We must show that for $0 \leq s \leq t$ the random variable $W_t - W_s$ is independent of $\mathcal{F}_s$ and is normally distributed with mean 0 and covariance $t - s$.

In terms of characteristic functions this means we must show that for any real u.

$$
\begin{aligned}
E\left[e^{iu(W_t - W_s)} | \mathcal{F}_s\right] &= E\left[e^{iu(W_t - W_s)}\right] \\
&= \exp\left(-\frac{u^2(t-s)}{2}\right).
\end{aligned}
$$

Consider the (complex-valued) function

$$f(x) = e^{iux}.$$

Applying the differentiation rule to the real and imaginary parts of $f(x)$ we have

$$f(W_t) = e^{iuW_t} = f(W_s) + \int_s^t iu e^{iuW_r} dW_r - \frac{1}{2}\int_s^t u^2 e^{iuW_r} dr \qquad (6.10)$$

because $d\langle W \rangle_r = dr$ by hypothesis. Furthermore, the real and imaginary parts of $iu \int_s^t e^{iuW_r} dW_r$ are in fact square integrable martingales because the integrands are bounded by 1. Consequently, $E[iu \int_s^t e^{iuW_r} dW_r | \mathcal{F}_s] =$

0 a.s. For any $A \in \mathcal{F}_s$ we may multiply (6.10) by $I_A e^{-iuW_s}$ and take expectations to deduce:

$$E\left[e^{iu(W_t - W_s)} I_A\right] = P(A) - \frac{1}{2} u^2 \int_0^t E\left[e^{iu(W_r - W_s)} I_A\right] dr.$$

Solving this equation we see

$$E\left[e^{iu(W_t - W_s)} I_A\right] = P(A) \exp\left(-\frac{u^2(t-s)}{2}\right)$$

and the result follows. $\qquad \square$

6.5 Stochastic Differential Equations

We first establish a useful result known as Gronwall's Lemma.

Lemma 6.5.1. *Suppose $\alpha(s), \beta(s)$ are integrable functions for $a \le s \le b$. If there is a constant H such that*

$$\alpha(t) \le \beta(t) + H \int_a^t \alpha(s) ds, \quad t \in [a, b], \tag{6.11}$$

then

$$\alpha(t) \le \beta(t) + H \int_a^t e^{H(t-s)} \beta(s) ds.$$

Note if $\beta(t) = B$, a constant, then

$$\alpha(t) \le B e^{H(t-a)}.$$

Proof. Write $A(t) = \int_a^t \alpha(s) ds$, $g(t) = A(t) e^{-Ht}$. Then

$$\begin{aligned} g'(t) &= \alpha(t) e^{-Ht} - HA(t) e^{-Ht} \\ &\le \beta(t) e^{-Ht} \quad \text{from (6.11).} \end{aligned}$$

Integrating, $g(t) - g(a) \le \int_a^t \beta(s) e^{-Hs} ds$. That is, $A(t) \le e^{Ht} \int_a^t \beta(s) e^{-Hs} ds$. Using (6.11) again

$$\alpha(t) \le \beta(t) + HA(t) = \beta(t) + H \int_a^t \beta(s) e^{H(t-s)} ds$$

and the result is proved. $\qquad \square$

Definition 6.5.2. Suppose $(\Omega, \mathcal{F}, P)$ is a probability space with a filtration $\{\mathcal{F}_t\}$, $0 \le t \le T$. Let $W_t = (W_t^1, \ldots, W_t^m)$ be an m-dimensional $\mathcal{F}_t$-Brownian motion and $f(x, t)$, $\sigma(x, t)$ be measurable functions of $x \in \mathbb{R}^n$ and $t \in [0, T]$ with values in $\mathbb{R}^n$ and $L(\mathbb{R}^m, \mathbb{R}^n)$, the space of $m \times n$ matrices, respectively. ξ is an $\mathbb{R}^n$-valued, $\mathcal{F}_0$-measurable random variable.

A process X_t, $0 \leq t \leq T$ is a *solution* of the stochastic differential equation
$$dX_t = f(X_t, t)dt + \sigma(X_t, t)dW_t$$
with initial condition $X_0 = \xi$ if for all t the integrals
$$\int_0^t f(X_s, s)ds \quad \text{and} \quad \int_0^t \sigma(X_s, s)dW_s$$
are well defined and
$$X_t = \xi + \int_0^t f(X_s, s)ds + \int_0^t \sigma(X_s, s)dW_s \text{ a.s.} \tag{6.12}$$

Theorem 6.5.3. *Suppose that, in addition to the assumptions of Definition 6.5.2, ξ, f, and σ satisfy*
$$|f(x,t) - f(x',t)| + |\sigma(x,t) - \sigma(x',t)| \leq K|x - x'| \tag{6.13}$$
$$|f(x,t)|^2 + |\sigma(x,t)|^2 \leq K_0^2(1 + |x|^2) \tag{6.14}$$
$$E[|\xi|^2] < \infty.$$

Then there is a solution X_t of (6.12) such that
$$E\Big[\sup_{0 \leq t \leq T} |X_t|^2\Big] < C(1 + E[|\xi|^2]).$$

Note, for the matrix σ, $|\sigma|^2 = \mathrm{Tr}\, \sigma\sigma^*$. This solution is unique in the sense that, if X_t' is also a solution, then they are indistinguishable, in the sense of Definition 6.1.12.

Proof. Uniqueness: suppose X and X' are solutions. Then for all $t \in [0, T]$,
$$X_t - X_t' = \int_0^t \big(f(X_s, s) - f(X_s', s)\big)ds$$
$$+ \int_0^t \big(\sigma(X_s, s) - \sigma(X_s', s)\big)dW_s.$$

Therefore,
$$|X_t - X_t'|^2 \leq 2\Big[\int_0^t \big(f(X_s, s) - f(X_s', s)\big)ds\Big]^2$$
$$+ 2\Big[\int_0^t \big(\sigma(X_s, s) - \sigma(X_s', s)\big)dW_s\Big]^2.$$

Taking expectations
$$E[|X_t - X_t'|^2] \leq 2t \int_0^t E\big[\big(f(X_s, s) - f(X_s', s)\big)^2\big]ds$$
$$+ 2 \int_0^t E[|\sigma(X_s, s) - \sigma(X_s', s)|^2]ds.$$

Write $\phi(t) = E[|X_t - X_t'|^2]$ and use the Lipschitz conditions (6.13) to deduce

$$\phi(t) \leq 2(T+1)K^2 \int_0^t \phi(s)ds.$$

Gronwall's inequality 6.5.1, therefore, implies that $\phi(t) = 0$ for all $t \in [0,T]$. Consequently,

$$|X_t - X_t'| = 0 \text{ a.s.}$$

The process $|X_t - X_t'|$ is continuous, so there is a set $N \in \mathcal{F}_0$ of measure zero such that if $\omega \notin N$, $X_t(\omega) = X_t'(\omega)$ for all $t \in [0,T]$. That is, X' is a modification of X.

Existence: Write $X_t^0 = \xi$ for $0 \leq t \leq T$.
Define a sequence of processes X_t^n by

$$X_t^n := \xi + \int_0^t f(X_s^{n-1}, s)ds + \int_0^t \sigma(X_s^{n-1}, s)dW_s. \qquad (6.15)$$

It can be shown that $\sigma(X_s^{n-1}, s) \in \mathcal{H}$, so the stochastic integrals are defined.

Using arguments similar to those in the uniqueness proof we can show

$$E[X_t^{n+1} - X_t^n|^2 \leq L \int_0^t E|X_s^n - X_s^{n-1}|^2 ds, \qquad (6.16)$$

where $L = 2(1+T)K^2$.

Iterating (6.14) we see that

$$E|X_t^{n+1} - X_t^n|^2 \leq L^n \int_0^t \frac{(t-s)^{n-1}}{(n-1)!} E|X_s^1 - \xi|^2 ds$$

and

$$E|X_s^1 - \xi|^2 \leq LTK^2(1 + E|\xi|^2).$$

Therefore,

$$E|X_t^{n+1} - X_t^n|^2 \leq C \frac{T^n}{n!}. \qquad (6.17)$$

Also,

$$\sup_{0 \leq t \leq T} |X_t^{n+1} - X_t^n| \leq \int_0^T |f(X_s^n, s) - f(X_s^{n-1}, s)|ds$$

$$+ \sup_{0 \leq t \leq T} \left| \int_0^t \left(\sigma(X_s^n, s) - \sigma(X_s^{n-1}, s) \right) dW_s \right|;$$

so, using the vector form of Doob's inequality 6.2.19:

$$E\left[\sup_{0\leq t\leq T}|X_t^{n+1}-X_t^n|^2\right] \leq 2TK^2\int_0^T E|X_s^n-X_s^{n-1}|^2ds$$

$$+CE\int_0^T|X_s^n-X_s^{n-1}|^2ds$$

$$\leq C_1\frac{T^{n-1}}{(n-1)!},$$

using (6.17).

Consequently,

$$\sum_{n=1}^{\infty}P\left\{\sup_{0\leq t\leq T}|X_t^{n+1}-X_t^n|>\frac{1}{n^2}\right\}\leq\sum_{n=1}^{\infty}n^4C_1\frac{T^{n-1}}{(n-1)!}.$$

The series on the right converges. Therefore, almost surely the series $\xi+\sum_{n=0}^{\infty}(X_t^{n+1}-X_t^n)$ converges uniformly in t, and so X_t^n converges to some X_t uniformly in t.

Each X^n is a continuous process, so X is a continuous process. Now

$$E|X_t^n|^2 \leq 3\left\{E[|\xi|^2]+K_0^2T\int_0^t(1+E|X_s^{n-1}|^2)ds\right.$$

$$\left.+K_0^2\int_0^t(1+E|X_s^{n-1}|^2)ds\right\}$$

so

$$E|X_t^n|^2 \leq C(1+E|\xi|^2)+C\int_0^t E|X_s^{n-1}|^2ds.$$

By recurrence, taking $C>1$,

$$E|X_t^n|^2 \leq (1+E|\xi|^2)\left(C+C^2t+\cdots+C^{n-1}\frac{t^n}{n!}\right)$$

$$\leq C(1+E|\xi|^2)e^{Ct}.$$

Using the bounded convergence theorem we can take the limit in (6.15) to deduce that

$$X_t=\xi+\int_0^t f(X_s,s)ds+\int_0^t\sigma(X_s,s)dW_s \text{ a.s.}$$

Therefore, X is the unique solution of the equation (6.12). □

6.6 The Markov Property of Solutions of SDEs

Definition 6.6.1. Consider a probability space $(\Omega,\mathcal{F},P)$ with a filtration $\{\mathcal{F}_t\}$, $t\geq 0$. An adapted process $\{X_t\}$ is said to be a *Markov process* with respect to the filtration $\{\mathcal{F}_t\}$ if for all s, and all $t \geq s$,

$$E[f(X_t)|\mathcal{F}_s] = E[f(X_t)|X_s] \text{ a.s.}$$

for every bounded real-valued Borel function f defined on $\mathbb{R}^d$.

Consider a stochastic differential equation as in (6.12) with coefficients satisfying the conditions of Theorem 6.5.3 so the solution exists. Consider a point $x \in \mathbb{R}^n$ and for $s \leq t$ write $X_s(x,t)$ for the solution process of the equation

$$X_s(x,t) = x + \int_s^t f\big(X_s(x,u),u\big)du + \int_s^t \sigma\big(X_s(x,u),u\big)dW_u. \qquad (6.18)$$

We quote the following results.

Theorem 6.6.2. $X_s(x,t)$ is a continuous function of its arguments, and if the coefficients f and σ are C^1 functions of their first argument, the solution $X_s(x,t)$ is C^1 in x.

Proof. For a proof see Kunita [172].   □

Write $X_s(x,t,\omega)$ for the solution of (6.18) so $X_s(x,t,\omega) : \mathbb{R}^d \times [s,T] \times \Omega \to \mathbb{R}^d$, and $\mathcal{F}_{s,t}^W$ for the completion of the σ-field generated by $W_{s+u} - W_s$, $0 \leq u \leq t - s$.

Theorem 6.6.3. For $t \in [s,T]$ the restriction of $X_s(x,u,\omega)$ to $\mathbb{R}^d \times [s,t] \times \Omega$ is $\mathcal{B}(\mathbb{R}^d) \times \mathcal{B}([s,t]) \times \mathcal{F}_{s,t}^W$-measurable.

Proof. For a proof see Lemma 14.23 of Elliott [87].   □

We next prove the 'flow' property of solutions of equation (6.18).

Lemma 6.6.4. If $X_s(x,t)$ is the solution of (6.18) and $X_r(x,t)$ is the solution of (6.18) starting at time r with $r \leq s \leq t$, then $X_r(x,t) = X_s\big(X_r(x,s),t\big)$, in the sense that one is a modification of the other.

Proof. By definition

$$\begin{aligned} X_r(x,t) &= x + \int_r^t f\big(X_r(x,u),u\big)du + \int_r^t \sigma\big(X_r(x,u),u\big)dW_u \\ &= X_r(x,s) + \int_s^t f\big(X_r(x,u),u\big)du \\ &\quad + \int_s^t \sigma\big(X_r(x,u),u\big)dW_u. \end{aligned} \qquad (6.19)$$

However, for any $y \in \mathbb{R}^n$,

$$X_s(y,t) = y + \int_s^t f\big(X_s(y,u),u\big)du + \int_s^t \sigma\big(X_s(y,u),u\big)dW_u.$$

Therefore, using the continuity of the solution,

$$X_s\big(X_r(x,s),t\big) = X_r(x,s) + \int_s^t f\big(X_s(X_r(x,s),u),u\big)du$$

$$+ \int_s^t \sigma\big(X_s(X_r(x,s),u),u\big)dW_u. \quad (6.20)$$

Using the uniqueness of the solution we see from (6.19) and (6.20) that $X_r(x,s)$ is a modification of $X_s\big(X_r(x,s),t\big)$. □

Before establishing a result on the Markov property of solutions of (6.18) we prove a general result on conditional expectations.

Lemma 6.6.5. *Consider a probability space* $(\Omega,\mathcal{G},P)$ *and measurable spaces* $(E,\mathcal{E})$, $(F,\mathcal{F})$. *Suppose*

$$X : \Omega \to E$$
$$Y : \Omega \to F$$

are random variables, and $\mathcal{A} \subset \mathcal{G}$.
  X is $\mathcal{A}$ *measurable and Y is independent of* $\mathcal{A}$.
  For any bounded real-valued Borel function Φ *defined on* $(E \times F,\ \mathcal{E} \times \mathcal{F})$ *consider the function* ϕ *defined for all* $x \in E$ *by*

$$\phi(x) = E[\Phi(x,Y)].$$

Then ϕ *is a Borel function on* $(E,\mathcal{E})$ *and*

$$E[\Phi(X,Y)|\mathcal{A}] = \phi(X) \text{ a.s.}$$

Proof. Write P_Y for the probability law of Y. Then

$$\phi(x) = \int_F \Phi(x,y)dP_Y(y).$$

The measurability of Φ follows from Fubini's theorem.
  Suppose Z is any $\mathcal{A}$-measurable random variable. Write $P_{X,Z}$ for the probability law of (X,Z). Then, because Y is independent of (X,Z),

$$\begin{aligned}
E[\Phi(X,Y)Z] &= \iint \Phi(x,y)z\,dP_{X,Z}(x,z)dP_Y(y)\\
&= \int \Big(\int \Phi(x,y)dP_Y(y)\Big)z\,dP_{X,Z}(x,z)\\
&= \int \phi(x)z\,dP_{X,Z}(x,y)\\
&= E[\phi(X)Z].
\end{aligned}$$

This identity is true for all such Z and the result follows. □

Lemma 6.6.6. *Suppose $X_s(x, t, \omega)$ is the solution of (6.18) and $g : \mathbb{R}^d \to \mathbb{R}$ is a bounded Borel-measurable function. Then*

$$f(x, \omega) = g\big(X_s(x, t, \omega)\big)$$

is $\mathcal{B}(\mathbb{R}^d) \times \mathcal{F}_{s,t}^W$-measurable.

Proof. Write $\mathcal{A}$ for the collection of sets $A \in \mathcal{B}(\mathbb{R}^d)$ for which the lemma is true with $g = I_A$.

If $f(x, \omega) = I_A\big(X_s(x, t, \omega)\big)$, then

$$\{(x, \omega) : I_A\big(X_s(x, t, \omega)\big) = 1\} = \{(x, \omega) : X_s(x, t, \omega) \in A\} \in \mathcal{B}(\mathbb{R}^d) \times \mathcal{F}_{s,t}^W.$$

The lemma is, therefore, true for all $A \in \mathcal{B}(\mathbb{R}^d)$ and the result follows for general g by approximation with simple functions.   □

We now show solutions of stochastic differential equations of the form (6.18) are Markov processes with respect to the complete right-continuous filtration $\{\mathcal{F}_t\}$ generated by the Brownian motion $\{W_t\}$, $t \geq 0$, and the initial value $x \in \mathbb{R}^d$.

Theorem 6.6.7. *Suppose $X_0(x, t)$ is the solution of (6.18) such that $X_0(x, 0) = x \in \mathbb{R}^d$. Then for any bounded real-valued Borel function g defined on $\mathbb{R}^d$ and $0 \leq s \leq t$,*

$$E[g(X_t)|\mathcal{F}_s] = E[g(X_t)|X_s].$$

More precisely, if

$$\phi(z) \quad = \quad E\big[g\big(X_s(z, t)\big)\big]$$

then

$$E[g(X_t)|\mathcal{F}_s] \quad = \quad \phi\big(X_0(x, s)\big) \text{ a.s.}$$

Proof. Suppose $g : \mathbb{R}^d \to \mathbb{R}$ is any bounded Borel-measurable function. As in Lemma 6.6.6 write $f(x, \omega) = g\big(X_s(x, t, \omega)\big)$. Then for each $x \in \mathbb{R}^d$, $f(x, \cdot)$ is $\mathcal{F}_{s,t}^W$-measurable, and so independent of $\mathcal{F}_s$.

Write, as in Lemma 6.6.5,

$$\phi(x) = E\big[g\big(X_s(x, t, \omega)\big)\big]$$

so, if Z is any $\mathcal{F}_s$-measurable random variable,

$$E\big[g\big(X_s(Z, t, \omega)\big)|\mathcal{F}_s\big] = \phi(Z). \tag{6.21}$$

From the flow property of the solutions, Lemma 6.6.4:

$$X_t = X_0(x, t) = X_s\big(X_0(x, s), t\big)$$

and $X_0(x, s)$ is $\mathcal{F}_s$-measurable.

Substituting $Z = X_0(x, s)$ in (6.21), therefore,

$$
\begin{aligned}
E\big[g\big(X_0(x,t)\big)|\mathcal{F}_s\big] &= E[g(X_t)|\mathcal{F}_s] \\
&= \phi\big(X_0(x,s)\big) = \phi(X_s).
\end{aligned}
$$

Consequently, $E[g(X_t)|\mathcal{F}_s] = E[g(X_t)|X_s]$ and the result follows.   □

Theorem 6.6.8. *Suppose* $X_0(x, s) = X_s \in \mathbb{R}^d$ *is the solution of* (6.18) *and consider the process* $\beta_s(1, t) = \beta_t := e^{-\int_s^t r(u, X_u)du}$, *where* $r(s, x)$ *is a positive measurable function. Then*

$$
d\beta_t = -r(t, X_t)\beta_t dt, \qquad \beta_s = 1
$$

and the augmented process $(\beta_t, X_t) \in \mathbb{R}^{d+1}$ *is given by an equation similar to* (6.18). *Consequently, the augmented process is Markov and, for any bounded, Borel function* $f : \mathbb{R}^d \to \mathbb{R}$,

$$
E\big[e^{-\int_s^t r(u, X_u)du} f(X_t)|\mathcal{F}_s\big] = \phi(X_s),
$$

where $\phi(x) = E\big[e^{-\int_s^t r(u, X_s(x,u))du} f\big(X_s(x, t)\big)\big]$.

7

European Options in Continuous Time

In this chapter we develop a continuous time theory which is the analogue of that in Chapters 1 to 3. The simple model consists of a riskless bond and a risky asset, which can be thought of as a stock. The dynamics of our model are described in Section 7.1. The following two sections present the fundamental results of Girsanov and martingale representation. These are then applied to discuss the hedging and pricing of European options. In particular, we establish the famous results of Black and Scholes, results which are applied widely in the industry in spite of the simplified nature of the model.

7.1 Dynamics

We describe the dynamics of the Black–Scholes option pricing model. Our processes are defined on a complete probability space $(\Omega, \mathcal{F}, P)$. The time parameter t takes values in the intervals $[0, \infty)$ or $[0, T]$. We suppose the market contains a riskless asset, or bond, whose price at time t is S_t^0, and a risky asset, or stock, whose price at time t is S_t^1.

Let r be a non-negative constant that represents the instantaneous interest rate on the bond. (This instantaneous interest rate should not be confused with the interest rate over a period of time in discrete models.) We then suppose that the evolution in the price of the bond S_t^0 is described by the ordinary differential equation

$$dS_t^0 = rS_t^0 dt. \tag{7.1}$$

If the initial value at time 0 of the bond is $S_0^0 = 1$, then (7.1) can be solved to give

$$S_t^0 = e^{rt}, \quad t \geq 0. \tag{7.2}$$

Let μ and $\sigma > 0$ be constants and (B_t), $t \geq 0$, be a standard Brownian motion on $(\Omega, \mathcal{F}, P)$. We suppose that the evolution in the price of the risky asset S_t^1 is described by the stochastic differential equation

$$dS_t^1 = S_t^1(\mu dt + \sigma dB_t). \tag{7.3}$$

If the initial price at time 0 of the risky asset is S_0^1, then (7.3) can be solved to give

$$S_t^1 = S_0^1 \exp(\mu t - \frac{\sigma^2}{2}t + \sigma B_t). \tag{7.4}$$

Taking logarithms,

$$\log S_t^1 = \log S_0^1 + (\mu - \frac{\sigma^2}{2})t + \sigma B_t, \tag{7.5}$$

and we see that $\log S_t^1$ evolves like a Brownian motion with drift $(\mu - (\sigma^2/2))t$ and volatility σ. In particular, $\log S_t^1$ is a normal random variable that is often expressed by saying S_t^1 is 'log-normal'. It is immediate from (7.4) and (7.5) that (S_t^1) has continuous trajectories, and $\log S_t^1$ has independent stationary increments (so $(S_t^1 - S_v^1)/S_v^1$ is independent of the σ-field $\sigma(S_u^1 : u \leq v)$ and $(S_t^1 - S_v^1)/S_v^1$ is identically distributed to $(S_{t-v}^1 - S_0^1)/S_0^1$).

7.2   Girsanov's Theorem

Girsanov's Theorem discusses how martingales, in particular Brownian motion, transform under a different probability measure. We first define certain spaces of martingales.

The set of martingales for which convergence results hold is the set of *uniformly integrable* martingales. Let us recall Definition 6.2.7 applied to a martingale: if $\{M_t\}$ is a martingale, for $0 \leq t < \infty$ or $0 \leq t \leq T$, $\{M_t\}$ is uniformly integrable if

$$\int_{\{|M_t(\omega)| \geq c\}} |M_t(\omega)| dP(\omega)$$

converges to 0 uniformly in t as $c \to +\infty$.

If $\{X_t\}$, $t \geq 0$ is any real measurable process we write

$$X_t^* = \sup_{s \leq t} |X_s|.$$

We write $\mathcal{M}$ for the space of right-continuous, uniformly integrable martingales. From Notation 6.2.11, $\mathcal{M}_{\ell oc}$ denotes the set of processes that are locally in $\mathcal{M}$.

$$M_t^{T_n} = M_{t \wedge T_n} \quad \text{is in } \mathcal{M}.$$

$\mathcal{M}_{\ell oc}$ is the space of local martingales. $\mathcal{L}$ is the subset of $\mathcal{M}_{\ell oc}$ consisting of those local martingales for which $M_0 = 0$ a.s.

For $M \in \mathcal{M}$ and $p \in [1, \infty]$ write

$$\|M\|_{\mathcal{H}^p} := \|M_\infty^*\|_p.$$

Here $\|\ \ \|_p$ denotes the norm on $L^p(\Omega, \mathcal{F}, P)$. Then $\mathcal{H}^p$ is the space of martingales in $\mathcal{M}$ such that

$$\|M\|_{\mathcal{H}^p} < \infty.$$

In particular, $\mathcal{H}^2$ is the space of square integrable martingales.

Remark 7.2.1. Suppose $(\Omega, \mathcal{F}, P)$ is a probability space with a filtration $\{\mathcal{F}_t\}$, $t \geq 0$.

Also suppose Q is a second probability measure on $(\Omega, \mathcal{F})$ that is absolutely continuous with respect to P. Write

$$M_\infty = \frac{dQ}{dP}$$

and M_t for the martingale $E[M_\infty | \mathcal{F}_t]$, $t \geq 0$.

In continuous time versions of martingales are considered that are right continuous and have left limits. There is a right-continuous version of M, which has left limits, if the filtration $\{\mathcal{F}_t\}$ satisfies the usual conditions (see Elliott [87], Theorem 4.11).

Lemma 7.2.2. $\{X_t M_t\}$ *is a local martingale under P if and only if $\{X_t\}$ is a local martingale under Q.*

Proof. We prove the result for martingales. The extension to local martingales can be found in Proposition 3.3.8 of Jacod and Shiryaev [140]. Suppose $s \leq t$ and $A \in \mathcal{F}_s$. Then

$$\int_A X_t \, dQ = \int_A X_t M_t \, dP = \int_A X_s M_s \, dP = \int_A X_s \, dQ,$$

and the result follows. $\qquad \qquad \Box$

Suppose $(\Omega, \mathcal{F}, P)$ is a probability space. Recall from Theorem 6.4.15 that a real process (B_t), $t \geq 0$, is a standard Brownian motion if

a) $t \to B_t(\omega)$ is continuous a.s.,

b) B is a (local) martingale, and

c) $\{B_t^2 - t, t \geq 0\}$ is a (local) martingale.

This characterization of Brownian motion using properties a), b), and c) is due to Lévy, and it is shown in 6.4.15 that these properties imply the other well-known properties of Brownian motion, including, for example, that B is a Gaussian process with independent increments.

Write $\mathcal{F}_t^0 = \sigma\{B_s : s \leq t\}$ for the σ-field on Ω generated by the history of the Brownian motion up to time t. Then $(\mathcal{F}_t)$, $t \geq 0$, will denote the right continuous complete filtration generated by the $\mathcal{F}_t^0$.

We now establish a result on how (B_t) behaves under a change of measure.

Theorem 7.2.3 (Girsanov). *Suppose (θ_t), $0 \leq t \leq T$, is an adapted measurable process such that $\int_0^T \theta_s^2 ds < \infty$ a.s. and also so that the process $\Lambda_t = \exp(-\int_0^t \theta_s dB_s - \frac{1}{2}\int_0^t \theta_s^2 ds)$ is an $(\mathcal{F}_t, P)$ martingale. Define a new measure Q_θ on $\mathcal{F}_T$ by putting*

$$\frac{dQ_\theta}{dP}\Big|_{\mathcal{F}_T} = \Lambda_T.$$

Then the process $W_t := B_t + \int_0^t \theta_s ds$ is a standard Brownian motion on $(\mathcal{F}_t, Q_\theta)$.

Remark 7.2.4. A sufficient condition, known as Novikov's condition, for Λ to be a martingale is that

$$E\Big[\exp(\frac{1}{2}\int_0^T \theta_s^2 ds)\Big] < \infty$$

(see Elliott [87]).

Proof. Using the Itô rule and definition of Λ we see, as in Example 6.4.8, that

$$\Lambda_t = 1 - \int_0^t \Lambda_s \theta_s dB_s. \tag{7.6}$$

Clearly $\Lambda_t > 0$ a.s. and as Λ is a martingale

$$E[\Lambda_t] = 1.$$

Now for $A \in \mathcal{F}_T$, $Q_\theta(A) = \int_A \Lambda_T dP \geq 0$ and $Q_\theta(\Omega) = \int_\Omega \Lambda_T dP = E[\Lambda_t] = 1$ so Q_θ is a probability measure.

To show (W_t) is a standard Brownian motion we verify it satisfies Conditions a), b), and c). By definition (W_t) is a continuous process a.s. (B_t is continuous a.s. and an indefinite integral is a continuous process.) For b) we must show (W_t) is a local $(\mathcal{F}_t)$-martingale under measure Q_θ. Equivalently, from Lemma 7.2.2 we must show that $\{\Lambda_t W_t\}$ is a local martingale under P. Applying the Itô rule to (7.6) and (W_t),

$$\Lambda_t W_t = W_0 + \int_0^t \Lambda_s dW_s + \int_0^t W_s d\Lambda_s + \int_0^t d\langle \Lambda, W \rangle_s$$

$$= W_0 + \int_0^t \Lambda_s dB_s + \int_0^t \Lambda_s \theta_s ds - \int_0^t W_s \Lambda_s \theta_s dB_s - \int_0^t \Lambda_s \theta_s ds$$

$$= W_0 + \int_0^t \Lambda_s (1 - W_s \theta_s) dB_s$$

and, as a stochastic integral with respect to B, $\{\Lambda_t W_t, t \geq 0\}$ is a (local) martingale under P.

Property c) is established similarly

$$W_t^2 = 2 \int_0^t W_s dW_s + \langle W \rangle_t = 2 \int_0^t W_s dW_s + t.$$

We must prove that $W_t^2 - t$ is a local $(\mathcal{F}_t, Q_\theta)$ martingale. However,

$$W_t^2 - t = 2 \int_0^t W_s dW_s$$

and we have established that W is a (local) martingale under Q_θ. Consequently, the stochastic integral is a (local) martingale under Q_θ and the result follows. □

We need the following results on hitting times of Brownian motion. Their proofs involve an exponential martingale M, of a form similar to Λ. Suppose $\{B_t\}$, $t \geq 0$, is a standard Brownian motion with $B_0 = 0$ adapted to the filtration $\{\mathcal{F}_t\}$. For $a \in \mathbb{R}$ write

$$T_a = \inf\{s \geq 0 : B_s = a\}.$$

As usual, we take $\inf\{\emptyset\} = +\infty$.

Theorem 7.2.5. T_a is a stopping time that is almost surely finite and for $\lambda \geq 0$,

$$E[e^{-\lambda T_a}] = e^{-\sqrt{2\lambda}\,|a|}.$$

Proof. Suppose $a \geq 0$. Because B is continuous, with $\mathbb{Q}^+$ the positive rationals,

$$\{T_a \leq t\} = \bigcap_{\varepsilon \in \mathbb{Q}^+} \{\sup_{r \leq t} B_r > a - \varepsilon\}$$

$$= \bigcap_{\varepsilon \in \mathbb{Q}^+} \bigcap_{\substack{r \in \mathbb{Q}^+ \\ r \leq t}} \{B_r > a - \varepsilon\} \in \mathcal{F}_t.$$

Consequently, T_a is a stopping time.

For any $\sigma \geq 0$ the process

$$M_t = \exp\left(\sigma B_t - \left(\frac{\sigma^2}{2}\right)t\right)$$

is an $\{\mathcal{F}_t\}$ martingale by Theorem 6.2.5.

For $n \in \mathbb{Z}^+$ consider the stopping time $T_a \wedge n$. Then from the optional stopping theorem 6.2.12,

$$E[M_{T_a \wedge n}] = E[M_0] = 1.$$

However,

$$M_{T_a \wedge n} = \exp\left(\sigma B_{T_a \wedge n} - \frac{\sigma^2}{2}(T_a \wedge n)\right)$$

$$\leq \exp \sigma a.$$

Now if $T_a < \infty$ $\lim_{n \to \infty} M_{T_a \wedge n} = M_{T_a}$. If $T_a = \infty$, then $B_t \leq a$ for all $t \geq 0$, so $\lim_{n \to \infty} M_{T_a \wedge n} = 0$.

Using Lebesgue's dominated convergence theorem we have

$$E[I\{T_a < \infty\}M_{T_a}] = 1.$$

Now $B_{T_a} = a$ if $T_a < \infty$. Therefore, $E[I\{T_a < \infty\}e^{\sigma a}e^{-(\sigma^2/2)T_a}] = 1$ so

$$E\left[I\{T_a < \infty\}e^{(\sigma^2/2)T_a}\right] = e^{-\sigma a}.$$

Letting $\sigma \to 0$ we see

$$E[I\{T_a < \infty\}] = P(T_a < \infty) = 1,$$

so almost every sample path of the Brownian motion reaches the value a, and

$$E\left[e^{(-\sigma^2/2)T_a}\right] = e^{-\sigma a}.$$

Now $\{-B_t\}$ is also an $\{\mathcal{F}_t\}$-Brownian motion so the case $a < 0$ can be deduced by noting that

$$T_a = \inf_{s \geq 0}\{s \geq 0 : -B_s = -a\}.$$

$\square$

An application of Girsanov's theorem enables us to deduce the following extension.

Corollary 7.2.6. *Suppose* $\mu, a \in \mathbb{R}$. *Write*

$$T_a(\mu) = \inf \{t \geq 0 : \mu t + B_t = a\}.$$

Then, for $\alpha > 0$, $E[e^{-\alpha T_a(\mu)}] = \exp(\mu a - |a|\sqrt{\mu^2 + 2\alpha})$.

Proof. Introduce the probability measure Q by setting

$$\frac{dQ}{dP}\bigg|_{\mathcal{F}_t} = \exp\left(\mu B_t - \frac{\mu^2}{2} t\right).$$

From Girsanov's theorem, under Q the process $\widetilde{B}$ is a standard Brownian motion where

$$\widetilde{B}_t = B_t - \mu t.$$

Clearly the hitting time $T_a(\mu)$ of $\widetilde{B}_t + \mu t$ is the same as the hitting time $T_a(0)$ of B_t. Therefore, for all $\alpha > 0$ and $t > 0$

$$E[\exp -\alpha(T_a(\mu) \wedge t)] = E\bigg[\exp -\alpha(T_a(0) \wedge t)$$

$$\times \exp\left(\mu B_{T_a(0) \wedge t} - \frac{\mu^2}{2}(T_a(0) \wedge t)\right)\bigg].$$

Now $\exp -\alpha(T_a(0) \wedge t) \leq e^{-\alpha t}$. Noting $T_a(0) = T_a$, we have for $t < T_a$ that $t < \infty$. Therefore,

$$\exp\left(\mu B_{T_a \wedge t} - \frac{\mu^2}{2}(T_a \wedge t)\right) I\{t < T_a\} \leq \exp\left(\mu B_t - \frac{\mu^2}{2} t\right),$$

which has expected value 1, and

$$E\left[\exp(-\alpha(T_a \wedge t)) \exp\left(\mu B_{T_a \wedge t} - \frac{\mu^2}{2}(T_a \wedge t)\right) I\{t < T_a\}\right] \leq e^{-\alpha t}.$$

Suppose initially that $a \geq 0$ and write

$$\widetilde{M}_t = \exp(-\alpha(T_a \wedge t)) \exp\left(\mu B_{T_a \wedge t} - \frac{\mu^2}{2}(T_a \wedge t)\right).$$

Then $\widetilde{M}_t \leq \exp \mu a$ and again by the dominated convergence theorem

$$E\left[\lim_{t \to \infty} \widetilde{M}_t\right] = E\left[I\{T_a < \infty\} e^{-\alpha T_a} e^{\mu B_{T_a} - (\mu^2/2) T_a}\right]$$

$$= e^{\mu a} E\left[I\{T_a < \infty\} e^{-(\alpha + (\mu^2/2)) T_a}\right]$$

and from the theorem this is

$$= e^{\mu a} e^{-\sqrt{2\alpha + \mu^2} |a|}.$$

Again the case when $a < 0$ can be discussed by considering $-B$.

We have, therefore, established that

$$E\left[I\{T_a < \infty\}e^{-\alpha T_a}e^{\mu B_{T_a} - (\mu^2/2)T_a}\right] = \left[I\{T_a(\mu) < \infty\}e^{-\alpha T_a(\mu)}\right]$$
$$= e^{\mu a - \sqrt{2\alpha + \mu^2}\,|a|}.$$

Letting $\alpha \to 0$ we see that

$$P(T_a < \infty) = e^{\mu a - |\mu a|}$$

and this is 1 if μ and a have the same sign. Furthermore, as $e^{-\alpha T_a} = 0$ on $\{T_a = \infty\}$ we have

$$E\left[e^{-\alpha T_a(\mu)}\right] = e^{\mu a - \sqrt{2\alpha + \mu^2}\,|a|}.$$

$\square$

7.3   Martingale Representation

We first recall concepts related to martingales and stable subspaces of martingales.

Definition 7.3.1. Two local martingales M, $N \in \mathcal{M}_{\ell oc}$ are *orthogonal* if their product MN is in $\mathcal{L}$.

We then write $M \perp N$. Note orthogonality implies that $M_0 N_0 = 0$ a.s. We then have the following result.

Lemma 7.3.2. *Suppose M, $N \in \mathcal{H}^2$ are orthogonal. Then for every stopping time τ the random variables M_τ, N_τ are orthogonal in $L^2(\Omega, \mathcal{F}, P)$ and $MN \in \mathcal{H}^1$.*

Conversely, the random variables M_τ, N_τ are orthogonal in L^2 for every stopping time τ; then $M \perp N$.

Proof. Because M_∞^* and N_∞^* are in L^2 the product $M_\infty^* N_\infty^*$ is in L^1. Furthermore,

$$(MN)_\infty^* = \sup_t |M_t N_t| \leq M_\infty^* N_\infty^*$$

so $MN \in \mathcal{H}^1$ if $M \perp N$, and $M_0 N_0 = 0$ a.s. Consequently, $E[M_\tau N_\tau] = E[M_0 N_0] = 0$. Conversely, suppose for any stopping time τ, $M_\tau \in L^2$ and $N_\tau \in L^2$. Then $M_\tau N_\tau \in L^1$ so $E[|M_\tau N_\tau|] < \infty$ and $E[M_\tau N_\tau] = 0$.

From Lemma 4.18 of [87] this condition is sufficient for MN to be a uniformly integrable martingale, and the result follows. $\square$

Notation 7.3.3. If $X = \{X_t\}$, $t \geq 0$, is a process and τ is a stopping time, X^τ will denote the process X stopped at time τ. That is, $X_t^\tau = X_{t \wedge \tau}$.

Definition 7.3.4. A linear subspace $\mathcal{K} \subset \mathcal{H}^2$ is *stable* if

a) it is closed in the L^2 norm;

b) if $M \in \mathcal{K}$ and τ is a stopping time, then $M^\tau \in \mathcal{K}$;

c) if $M \in \mathcal{K}$ and $A \in \mathcal{F}_0$, then $I_A M \in \mathcal{K}$.

Theorem 7.3.5. *Suppose $\mathcal{K}$ is a stable subspace of $\mathcal{H}^2$. Write $\mathcal{K}^\perp$ for the set of martingales $N \in \mathcal{H}^2$ such that $E[M_\infty N_\infty] = 0$ for all $M \in \mathcal{K}$. Then $\mathcal{K}^\perp$ is a stable subspace, and if $M \in \mathcal{K}$, $N \in \mathcal{K}^\perp$, then $M \perp N$.*

Proof. Suppose $M \in \mathcal{K}$, $N \in \mathcal{K}^\perp$, and τ is a stopping time. Then $E[L_\infty N_\infty] = 0$ for all $L \in \mathcal{K}$. Now $M^\tau \in \mathcal{K}$ so $E[M^\tau_\infty N_\infty] = E[M_\tau N_\infty] = 0$. Therefore, $E[E[M_\tau N_\infty | \mathcal{F}_\tau]] = E[M_\tau E[N_\infty | \mathcal{F}_\tau]] = E[M_\tau N_\tau] = 0$. Taking $\tau = 0$, for any $A \in \mathcal{F}_0$, $\quad I_A M \in \mathcal{K}$ so $E[I_A M_0 N_0] = 0$.

Therefore, $M_0 N_0 = 0$ a.s. and M and N are orthogonal. Also: $E[(I_A M_\tau) N_\tau] = E[M_\infty (I_A N^\tau)_\infty] = 0$ so $I_A N^\tau \in \mathcal{K}^\perp$ for any $N \in \mathcal{K}^\perp$, any stopping time τ, and any $A \in \mathcal{F}_0$. Consequently, $\mathcal{K}^\perp$ is a stable subspace. $\qquad \square$

Corollary 7.3.6. *Suppose $\mathcal{K} \subset \mathcal{H}^2$ is a stable subspace. Then every element $M \in \mathcal{H}^2$ has a unique decomposition*

$$M = N + N^1,$$

where $N \in \mathcal{K}$ and $N^1 \in \mathcal{K}^\perp$.

Proof. Suppose $\mathcal{K}_\infty$ is the closed subspace of $L^2(\Omega, \mathcal{F}_\infty)$ generated by the random variables M_∞, for $M \in \mathcal{K}$. $\mathcal{K}_\infty^\perp$ is defined analogously. Then $\mathcal{K}_\infty$ and $\mathcal{K}_\infty^\perp$ give an orthogonal decomposition of $L^2(\Omega, \mathcal{F}_\infty)$ and, for any $M \in \mathcal{H}^2$, M_∞ has a unique decomposition

$$M_\infty = N_\infty + N^1_\infty,$$

where $N_\infty \in \mathcal{K}_\infty$ and $N^1_\infty \in \mathcal{K}_\infty^\perp$. Then define N (resp., N^1) to be the right-continuous version, with left limits, of the martingale

$$N_t := E[N_\infty | \mathcal{F}_t] \quad (\text{resp.}, \ N^1_t = E[N^1_\infty | \mathcal{F}_t]).$$

$\square$

Remark 7.3.7. From the isometry properties of the stochastic integral it can be shown that the stable subspace generated by $M \in \mathcal{H}^2$ is the set of all stochastic integrals with respect to M. See page 140 of Kopp [169].

A basic result of stochastic analysis is now given; the proof is adapted from Elliott [87].

(B_t), $t \geq 0$, denotes a Brownian motion on the probability space $(\Omega, \mathcal{F}, P)$. $\mathcal{F}_t^0 = \sigma\{B_s : s \leq t\}$ and $\mathcal{F}_t$ is the completion of $\mathcal{F}_t^0$, so that $(\mathcal{F}_t)$, $t \geq 0$, is the filtration generated by B which satisfies the 'usual conditions' of right continuity and completeness. We have seen that if (H_t), $0 \leq t \leq T$, is a measurable adapted process on $[0, T]$ such that $E[\int_0^T H_s^2 ds] < \infty$, then $\int_0^t H_s dB_s$ is a square integrable martingale. The representation result tells us that all square integrable martingales on $(\mathcal{F}_t)$, $0 \leq t \leq T$, are of this form.

Theorem 7.3.8. *Suppose (M_t), $0 \leq t \leq T$, is a square integrable martingale on $(\mathcal{F}_t)$, where $\mathcal{F}_t$ is the completion of $\sigma\{B_s : s \leq t\}$. Then there is a measurable adapted process (H_t), $0 \leq t \leq T$, such that $E(\int_0^T H_s^2 ds) < \infty$ and for all $t \in [0, T]$,*

$$M_t = M_0 + \int_0^t H_s dB_s \quad a.s. \tag{7.7}$$

Proof. First note that by subtracting $M_0 = E[M_t]$ from each side of (7.7) we can assume $M_0 = 0$. Second, M_T is $\mathcal{F}_T$-measurable and square integrable so all we have to establish is that any square integrable, $\mathcal{F}_T$-measurable, zero mean random variable M_T has a representation

$$M_T = \int_0^T H_s dB_s \text{a.s.}$$

Write $\mathcal{H}_T^2$ for the space of square integrable $(\mathcal{F}_t)$ martingales on $[0, T]$. We can consider the stable subspace of $\mathcal{H}_T^2$ generated by stochastic integrals with respect to (B_t); this is closed in the norm of $L^2(\Omega, \mathcal{F}_T)$. Consequently the martingale (M_t) has a projection on this stable subspace which we denote by (Y_t), $0 \leq t \leq T$. From Remark 7.3.7 (Y_t) is a stochastic integral with respect to (B_t), so there is a measurable adapted integrand (H_t), $0 \leq t \leq T$, such that

$$Y_t = \int_0^t H_s dB_s \quad \text{a.s.} \quad \text{for } t \in [0, T].$$

By construction $M_t - Y_t$ is orthogonal to the stable subspace $H_T^2(B)$ of H_T^2 generated by stochastic integrals with respect to B.

We can, therefore, suppose that the martingale (M_t) is orthogonal to $H_T^2(B)$ and show that this implies $M_T = 0$ a.s.

Suppose this is the case. Write

$$\sigma_n = \inf \{t : |M_t| \geq n\}$$

and

$$M_t^n = \frac{1}{2n} M_{t \wedge \sigma_n}.$$

Then $|M_t^n| \leq \frac{1}{2}$ and (M_t) is orthogonal to both (B_t) and $(B_t^2 - t) = (2 \int_0^t B_s dB_s)$.

With $\Lambda = 1 + M_T^n$ a new probability measure Q can be defined on $\mathcal{F}_T$ by putting $(dQ/dP) = \Lambda$. Now (B_t) and $(B_t^2 - t)$ are continuous martingales on $(\Omega, \mathcal{F}, Q)$. Consequently, (B_t) is a Brownian motion under Q as well as P, so P and Q coincide on $\mathcal{F}_T$. This implies that $M_T^n = 0$ a.s. Letting $n \to \infty$ we see $M_T = 0$ a.s. and the result is proved.   □

We now extend Theorem 7.3.8 to the situation where the filtration is generated by the weak solution of a stochastic differential equation.

Suppose we have a probability space $(\Omega, \mathcal{F}, P)$ and a process $\{x_t\}$, $0 \leq t \leq T$, $x_t \in \mathbb{R}^n$. $\{\mathcal{F}_t\}$ is the filtration generated by $\{x_t\}$ and $\{B_t\}$ is an $\{\mathcal{F}_t\}$ Brownian motion, $x_0 \in \mathbb{R}^n$ such that under P,

$$x_t = x_0 + \int_0^t f(s, x_s) ds + \int_0^t \sigma(s, x_s) dB_s \text{ a.s.}$$

Here, f and σ satisfy measurability and growth conditions, as in Theorem 6.5.3.

The predictable σ-field on $\Omega \times [0, T]$ is the σ-field generated by the left continuous processes. A process is called 'predictable' if it is measurable with respect to this σ-field.

Theorem 7.3.9. *Suppose $\{N_t\}$, $N_0 = 0$, is a square integrable P martingale with respect to the filtration $\{\mathcal{F}_t\}$. Here $0 \leq t \leq T$. Then there is an $\mathcal{F}_t$-predictable process $\{\gamma_t\}$ such that*

$$\int_0^t E|\gamma_s|^2 ds < \infty$$

and

$$N_t = \int_0^t \gamma_s dB_s \text{ a.s.}$$

Proof. For $n \in \mathbb{Z}^+$ define

$$T_n = \min \left\{ T, \inf \left(t : \int_0^t |\sigma_s^{-1} f_s|^2 ds \geq n \right) \right\}.$$

Then T_n is an $\{\mathcal{F}_t\}$-stopping time and $\lim T_n = T$. Write

$$\Lambda_t^* = \exp \left(-\int_0^t \sigma_s^{-1} f_s dB_s - \frac{1}{2} \int_0^t |\sigma_s^{-1} f_s|^2 ds \right)$$

and define a new measure P_n^* by setting

$$\frac{dP_n^*}{dP} \Big|_{\mathcal{F}_t} = \Lambda_{t \wedge T_n}^*.$$

P_n^* is a probability measure for each n and from Girsanov's theorem 7.2.3 the process

$$z_t^n := B_t + \int_0^{t \wedge T_n} \sigma_s^{-1} f_s ds$$

is a Brownian motion under P_n^*. Write

$$\mathcal{Z}_t^n = \sigma\{z_s^n : 0 \le s \le t\}.$$

From Theorem 7.3.8, if $\{\tilde{N}_t\}$ is a square integrable, zero mean martingale under P_n^* with respect to the filtration $\{\mathcal{Z}_t^n\}$, then there is a process $\{\phi_t^n\}$, adapted to $\{\mathcal{Z}_t^n\}$, such that $\tilde{N}_t = \int_0^t \phi_s^n dz_s^n$ a.s. Now for $t < T_n$:

$$z_t^n = \int_0^t \sigma_s^{-1}(\sigma_s dB_s + f_s ds)$$

$$= \int_0^t \sigma_s^{-1} dx_s,$$

so $\{\mathcal{Z}_t^n\} = \{\mathcal{F}_{t \wedge T_n}\}$. Therefore, we have shown that if $\{\tilde{N}_t\}$ is a square integrable, zero mean P_n^* martingale with respect to the filtration $\{\mathcal{Z}_t^n\}$, then

$$\tilde{N}_{t \wedge T_n} = \int_0^{t \wedge T_n} \phi_s^n \sigma_s^{-1} dx_s \text{ a.s.} \tag{7.8}$$

Now from Lemma 7.3.2, if $\{N_t\}$ is a square integrable P martingale with respect to the filtration $\{\mathcal{F}_t\}$, then $\{\tilde{N}_t\}$ is a square integrable martingale with respect to the filtration $\{\mathcal{F}_{t \wedge T_n}\}$, where

$$\tilde{N}_t = (\Lambda_{t \wedge T_n}^*)^{-1} N_{t \wedge T_n}.$$

In this situation certainly $\tilde{N}_t = \tilde{N}_{t \wedge T_n}$, so from (7.7),

$$\tilde{N}_t = \int_0^{t \wedge T_n} \phi_s^n \sigma_s^{-1} dx_s$$

$$= \int_0^{t \wedge T_n} \phi_s^n dB_s + \int_0^{t \wedge T_n} \phi_s^n \sigma_s^{-1} f_s ds.$$

Now $\Lambda_t^* = \exp\left(-\int_0^t \sigma_s^{-1} f_s dB_s - \frac{1}{2}\int_0^t |\sigma_s^{-1} f_s|^2 ds\right)$ so $\Lambda_{t\wedge T_n}^* = 1 - \int_0^{t\wedge T_n} \Lambda_s^* \sigma_s^{-1} f_s dB_s$. Therefore, using the Itô rule

$$
\begin{aligned}
N_{t\wedge T_n} &= \widetilde{N}_t \Lambda_{t\wedge T_n}^* \\
&= \int_0^{t\wedge T_n} \widetilde{N}_s d\Lambda_s^* + \int_0^{t\wedge T_n} \Lambda_s^* d\widetilde{N}_s + \langle \widetilde{N}, \Lambda^* \rangle_{t\wedge T_n} \\
&= -\int_0^{t\wedge T_n} \widetilde{N}_s \Lambda_s^* \sigma_s^{-1} f_s dB_s + \int_0^{t\wedge T_n} \Lambda_s^* \phi_s^n \sigma_s^{-1} dx_s \\
&\quad - \int_0^t \Lambda_s^* \phi_s^n \sigma_s^{-1} ds \\
&= \int_0^{t\wedge T_n} \gamma_s^n dB_s,
\end{aligned}
$$

where $\gamma_s^n = \Lambda_s(\phi_s^n - \widetilde{N}_s \sigma_s^{-1} f_s)$. Furthermore,

$$
\begin{aligned}
E[N_{t\wedge T_n}^2] &= \int_0^t E[(I(0 \leq s \leq T_n)\gamma_s^n)^2] ds \\
&\leq E[N_T^2] < \infty.
\end{aligned}
$$

The representation is unique, so that if $m \geq n$

$$\gamma_s^n = \gamma_s^m \qquad \text{for } s \leq T_n.$$

Define γ_s to be the process such that for $0 \leq s \leq T_n$

$$\gamma_s := \gamma_s^n.$$

Then

$$N_{t\wedge T_n} = \int_0^{t\wedge T_n} \gamma_s dB_s$$

and

$$N_t = \int_0^t \gamma_s dB_s \quad \text{for } t < T_n.$$

However, $\lim T_n = T$ a.s. so $\int_0^1 E_s[|\gamma_s|^2]ds < \infty$ and the result follows. $\square$

Corollary 7.3.10. *Suppose B is a Brownian motion under probability P and $(\mathcal{F}_t, t \geq 0)$ is the complete filtration generated by B. Furthermore, suppose $(\theta_t, t \geq 0)$ is a predictable process such that if Λ is given by*

$$d\Lambda_t = \Lambda_t \theta_t dB_t, \qquad \Lambda_0 = 1,$$

Λ is a (positive) martingale. Define a probability measure Q by

$$\left.\frac{dQ}{dP}\right|_{\mathcal{F}_t} = \Lambda_t,$$

so by Girsanov's theorem W is a Brownian motion under Q, where $dW_t = dB_t - \theta_t dt$. Then, if M is an $(\mathcal{F}_t, Q)$ martingale there is a predictable process ψ such that

$$M_t = M_0 + \int_0^t \psi_s dW_s.$$

Corollary 7.3.11. *By considering stopping times and pasting, the representation result applies to locally square integrable martingales.*

Remark 7.3.12. In the Markov case, when the coefficients are sufficiently differentiable, the form of the integrand in the martingale representation can be made more explicit.

Suppose again that $B = (B^1, \ldots, B^m)$ is an m-dimensional Brownian motion defined for $t \geq 0$ on $(\Omega, \mathcal{F}, P)$. Consider the stochastic differential equation

$$dx_t = f(t, x_t)dt + \sigma(t, x_t)dB_t \tag{7.9}$$

for $t \geq 0$, where $f : [0, \infty) \times \mathbb{R}^n \to \mathbb{R}^n$ and $\sigma : [0, \infty) \times \mathbb{R}^n \to \mathbb{R}^n \times \mathbb{R}^n$ are measurable functions that are three times differentiable in x, and which, together with their derivatives, have linear growth in x.

Write $\xi_{s,t}(x)$ for the solution of (7.9) for $t \geq s$ which has initial condition

$$\xi_{s,s}(x) = x \in \mathbb{R}^n.$$

From results of Bismut [16], or Kunita [172], we know there is a set $N \subset \Omega$ of measure zero such that for $\omega \notin N$ there is a version of $\xi_{s,t}(x)$ which is twice differentiable in x and continuous in t and s. Write

$$D_{s,t}(k) = \frac{\partial \xi_{s,t}(x)}{\partial x}$$

for the Jacobian of the map $x \to \xi_{s,t}(x)$. Then D is the solution of the linearized equation

$$dD_{s,t}(x) = f_x(t, x_t)D_{s,t}dt + \sigma_x(t, x_t)D_{s,t}dB_t$$

with initial condition $D_{s,s}(x) = I$, the $n \times n$ identity matrix.

It is known that the inverse $D_{s,t}^{-1}(x)$ exists; see [16], [172].

Suppose $g : [0, \infty) \times \mathbb{R}^n \to \mathbb{R}^m$ satisfies conditions similar to those of f and define the exponential $M_{s,t}(x)$ by

$$M_{s,t}(x) = 1 + \int_0^t M_{s,r}(x)g(r, \xi_{s,r}(x))dB_r.$$

Write $\{\mathcal{F}_t\}$ for the right-continuous complete family of σ-fields generated by B. As g satisfies a linear growth condition a new probability measure $\overline{P}$ can be defined by putting

$$\frac{d\overline{P}}{dP}\bigg|_{\mathcal{F}_t} = M_{0,t}(x_0).$$

From Girsanov's theorem, W is an $\{\mathcal{F}_t\}$ Brownian motion under $\overline{P}$ if

$$dW_t := dB_t - g(t, \xi_{0,t}(x_0))dt. \tag{7.10}$$

Suppose $c : \mathbb{R}^n \to \mathbb{R}$ is a C^2 function, which, together with its derivatives has linear growth, and for $0 \leq t \leq T$ consider the $\overline{P}$ martingale

$$N_t = \overline{E}[c(\xi_{0,T}(x_0))|\mathcal{F}_t].$$

Then from Theorem 7.3.9, N_t has a representation for $0 \leq t \leq T$ as

$$N_t = N_0 + \int_0^t \gamma_s dW_s, \tag{7.11}$$

where $\int_0^T E[|\gamma_s|^2]ds < \infty$.

We can now describe γ.

Theorem 7.3.13.

$$\gamma_t = \tilde{E}\Big[\int_t^T dW_r^* g_\xi \big(r, \xi_{0,r}(x_0)\big) D_{0,r}(x_0) c\big(\xi_{0,T}(x_0)\big)$$

$$+ c_\xi \big(\xi_{0,T}(x_0)\big) D_{0,T}(x_0) |\mathcal{F}_t \Big] D_{0,t}^{-1}(x_0) \sigma \big(t, \xi_{0,t}(x_0)\big).$$

Proof. For $0 \leq t \leq T$ write $x = \xi_{0,t}(x_0)$. From the semigroup property of the solution of stochastic differential equations, Lemma 6.6.4,

$$\xi_{0,T}(x_0) = \xi_{t,T}\big(\xi_{0,t}(x_0)\big) = \xi_{t,T}(x). \tag{7.12}$$

Differentiating (7.12) we have

$$D_{0,T}(x_0) = D_{t,T}(x) D_{0,t}(x_0).$$

Furthermore, the exponential M satisfies

$$M_{0,T}(x_0) = M_{0,t}(x_0) M_{t,T}(x).$$

For $y \in \mathbb{R}^n$ define

$$V(t, y) = E[M_{t,T}(y) c(\xi_{t,T}(y))]$$

and consider the martingale

$$\begin{aligned}
N_t &= \overline{E}[c(\xi_{0,T}(x_0))|\mathcal{F}_t] \\
&= \frac{E[M_{0,T}(x_0) c(\xi_{0,T}(x_0))|\mathcal{F}_t]}{E[M_{0,T}(x_0)|\mathcal{F}_t]} \\
&= E[M_{t,T}(x) c(\xi_{t,T}(x))|\mathcal{F}_t] \\
&= E[M_{t,T}(x) c(\xi_{t,T}(x))] \quad \text{by the Markov property} \\
&= V(t, x) \quad \text{by Theorem 6.6.7.}
\end{aligned}$$

The differentiability of $\xi_{t,T}(x)$ in x and t is established by Kunita [172].

Under $\overline{P}$,

$$\xi_{0,t}(x_0) = x_0 + \int_0^t (f(x,\xi_{0,s}(x_0)) + \sigma g(s,\xi_{0,s}(x_0)))ds$$
$$+ \int_0^t \sigma(s,\xi_{0,s}(x_0))dW_s.$$

Expand $V(t,x) = V(t,\xi_{0,t}(x_0))$ by the Itô rule to get

$$V(t,\xi_{0,t}(x_0)) = N_t = V(0,x_0) + \int_0^t \left(\frac{\partial V}{\partial t} + LV\right)(s,\xi_{0,s}(x_0))ds$$
$$+ \int_0^t \frac{\partial V}{\partial x}(s,\xi_{0,s}(x_0))\sigma(s,\xi_{0,s}(x_0))dW_s, \qquad (7.13)$$

where

$$L = \sum_{i=1}^n \left(f^i + \sum_{j=1}^m \sigma_{ij}g^j\right)\frac{\partial}{\partial x_i} + \frac{1}{2}\sum_{i,j=1}^n a_{ij}\frac{\partial^2}{\partial x_i \partial x_j}$$

and (a_{ij}) is the matrix $\sigma\sigma^*$.

A special semimartingale is a semimartingale that is the sum of a (local) martingale and a predictable process of (locally) integrable variation. Semimartingales have a unique decomposition of this form (see Elliott [87], Theorem 12.38).

Now N is a special semimartingale, so the decompositions (7.11) and (7.13) must be the same.

As there is no bounded variation term in (7.11) we must have

$$\frac{\partial V}{\partial t} + LV = 0 \qquad \text{with } V(T,x) = c(x).$$

Also:

$$\gamma_s = \frac{\partial V}{\partial x}(x,\xi_{0,s}(x_0))\sigma(s,\xi_{0,s}(x_0)).$$

However, $\xi_{t,T}(x) = \xi_{0,T}(x_0)$ so, from the differentiability and linear growth of g,

$$\frac{\partial V(t,x)}{\partial x} = E\left[\frac{\partial M_{t,T}(x)}{\partial x}c(\xi_{0,T}(x_0)) + M_{t,T}(x)\frac{\partial c}{\partial x}(\xi_{t,T}(x))\right].$$

Now using the existence of solutions of stochastic differential equations that are differentiable in their initial conditions we have

$$\frac{\partial M_{t,T}(x)}{\partial x} = \int_t^T g(r,\xi_{t,r}(x))\frac{\partial M_{t,r}(x)}{\partial x}dB_r$$
$$+ \int_t^T dB_r g_\xi(r,\xi_{t,r}(x))\frac{\partial \xi_{t,r}(x)}{\partial x}M_{t,r}(x). \qquad (7.14)$$

Now (7.14) can be solved by variation of constants to obtain

$$\frac{\partial M_{t,T}(x)}{\partial x} = M_{t,T}(x) \int_t^T dW_r^* g(r, \xi_{t,r}(x)) D_{t,r}(x).$$

Therefore, with $x = \xi_{0,t}(x_0)$,

$$\frac{\partial V(t,x)}{\partial x} = E\Big[M_{t,T}(x) \Big\{ \int_t^T dW_r^* g_\xi\big(r, \xi_{t,r}(x)\big) D_{t,r}(x) c(\xi_{0,T}(x_0))$$
$$+ c_\xi(\xi_{t,T}(x)) D_{t,T}(x) \Big\} \Big]$$
$$= \overline{E}\Big[\int_t^T dW_r^* g_\xi\big(r, \xi_{0,r}(x_0)\big) D_{0,r}(x_0) c\big(\xi_{0,T}(x_0)\big)$$
$$+ c_\xi\big(\xi_{0,T}(x_0)\big) D_{0,T}(x_0) \big| \mathcal{F}_t \Big] D_{0,t}^{-1}(x_0)$$

and the result follows.   □

7.4   Self-Financing Strategies

A hedging strategy is a measurable process $(\phi_t) = \big((H_t^0, H_t^1) \big)$ with values in $\mathbb{R}^2$ that is adapted to the filtration $(\mathcal{F}_t)$, $t \geq 0$, where $\mathcal{F}_t = \sigma\{B_u : u \leq t\} = \sigma\{S_u^1 : u \leq t\}$. H_t^0 (resp., H_t^1) denotes the amount of the bond S_t^0 (resp., the risky asset S_t^1) that is held at time t. Consequently, the value, or wealth, of the portfolio at time t is

$$V_t(\phi) = H_t^0 S_t^0 + H_t^1 S_t^1. \tag{7.15}$$

In discrete time we have established that a self-financing strategy should satisfy the identity

$$V_{n+1}(\phi) - V_n(\phi) = \phi_{n+1}(S_{n+1} - S_n)$$
$$= H_{n+1}^0 (S_{n+1}^0 - S_n^0) + H_{n+1}^1 (S_{n+1}^1 - S_n^1).$$

The continuous-time analogue of this condition, therefore, appears to be

$$dV_t(\phi) = H_t^0 dS_t^0 + H_t^1 dS_t^1. \tag{7.16}$$

Indeed, if H^0 and H^1 are of bounded variation, then

$$dV_t(\phi) = H_t^0 dS_t^0 + H_t^1 dS_t^1 + S_t^0 dH_t^0 + S_t^1 dH_t^1$$

and (7.16) is equivalent to saying

$$S_t^0 dH_t^0 + S_t^1 dH_t^1 = 0. \tag{7.17}$$

The intuitive meaning of (7.17) is that changes in the holdings of the bond $S_t^0 dH_t^0$ can only take place due to corresponding changes in the holding of the stock $S_t^1 dH_t^1$; that is, there is no net inflow or outflow of capital (see (2.6)).

We consider European options with an expiration time T and $\mathcal{F}_T$-measurable contingent claims. Consequently, for (7.16) to make sense we require

$$\int_0^T |H_t^0| dt < \infty \text{a.s.} \quad \text{and} \quad \int_0^T (H_t^1)^2 dt < \infty \quad \text{a.s.} \tag{7.18}$$

Therefore

$$\int_0^T H_t^0 dS_t^0 = \int_0^T H_t^0 r e^{rt} dt$$

and

$$\int_0^T H_t^1 dS_t^1 = \int_0^T (H_t^1 S_t^1 \mu) dt + \int_0^T (H_t^1 S_t^1 \sigma) dB_t.$$

We can, therefore, give the following definition.

Definition 7.4.1. A *self-financing strategy* $\phi = (\phi_t)$, $0 \le t \le T$, is given by two measurable adapted processes (H_t^0), (H_t^1) satisfying (7.16) and

$$\int_0^T |H_t^0| dt < \infty \text{a.s.} \quad \text{and} \quad \int_0^T (H_t^1)^2 dt < \infty \quad \text{a.s.} \tag{7.19}$$

The corresponding wealth process is given by

$$V_t(\phi) = H_t^0 S_t^0 + H_t^1 S_t^1 \tag{7.20}$$

$$= H_0^0 S_0^0 + H_0^1 S_0^1 + \int_0^t H_u^0 dS_u^0 + \int_0^t H_u^1 dS_u^1 \quad \text{a.s} \tag{7.21}$$

for all $t \in [0, T]$.

Notation 7.4.2. $\widetilde{S}_t^1 = e^{-rt} S_t^1$ is the discounted price of the risky asset and $\widetilde{V}_t(\phi) = e^{-rt} V_t(\phi)$ is the discounted wealth process.

We can then establish the following result.

Theorem 7.4.3. *Suppose $\phi = (\phi_t) = \big((H_t^0, H_t^1)\big)$, $0 \le t \le T$, is a pair of measurable adapted processes that satisfy (7.19). Then ϕ is a self-financing strategy if and only if*

$$\widetilde{V}_t(\phi) = V_0(\phi) + \int_0^t H_u^1 d\widetilde{S}_u^1 \quad \text{a.s.} \tag{7.22}$$

for all $t \in [0, T]$.

Proof. Suppose $\phi = ((H_t^0, H_t^1))$ is self-financing, so (7.16) holds. Then

$$
\begin{aligned}
d\widetilde{V}_t(\phi) &= d\left(e^{-rt}V_t(\phi)\right) \\
&= -r\widetilde{V}_t(\phi)dt + e^{-rt}dV_t(\phi) \\
&= -re^{-rt}(H_t^0 e^{rt} + H_t^1 S_t^1)dt + e^{-rt}H_t^0 d(e^{rt}) + e^{-rt}H_t^1 dS_t^1 \\
&= H_t^1(-re^{-rt}S_t^1 dt + e^{-rt}dS_t^1) \\
&= H_t^1 d\widetilde{S}_t
\end{aligned}
$$

and (7.22) follows.

The converse follows by considering $V_t(\phi) = e^{rt}\widetilde{V}_t(\phi)$, reversing the steps in the preceeding argument and using (7.22). $\qquad\square$

Remark 7.4.4. Although the concept of predictability can be defined in continuous time (see Elliott [87]) we have only required the trading strategies $\phi = ((H_t^0, H_t^1))$ to be measurable and adapted. Because the filtration $(\mathcal{F}_t)$, $t \geq 0$, is generated by the continuous Brownian motion (B_t) (or, equivalently, by the continuous process (S_t^1)), there is little significant difference between the two classes of processes.

Let us write SF for the set of self-financing strategies $\phi = (\phi_t)$, $0 \leq t \leq T$, so that $\phi_t = (H_t^0, H_t^1)$, where H^0 and H^1 satisfy (7.17). If there are no contributions or withdrawals, the corresponding wealth process is given in (7.15) as

$$
V_t(\phi) = H_t^0 S_t^0 + H_t^1 S_t^1.
$$

Suppose now there are contributions to the wealth process (say, from dividends), or withdrawals (consumption). Let these be modelled by the adapted right-continuous, increasing processes

$$
D_t \quad \text{(for contributions),}
$$

and

$$
C_t \quad \text{(for consumption).}
$$

(Here C_t is the accumulated consumption.) Then

$$
\begin{aligned}
V_t(\phi) &= H_t^0 S_t^0 + H_t^1 S_t^1 + D_t - C_t \\
&= V_0(\phi) + \int_0^t H_u^0 dS_u^0 + \int_0^t H_u^1 dS_u^1 + D_t - C_t.
\end{aligned}
$$

The self-financing condition (7.16) now becomes

$$
S_t^0 dH_t^0 + S_t^1 dH_t^1 = dD_t - dC_t.
$$

7.5   An Equivalent Martingale Measure

Consider the situation of Section 7.1 where the bond is described by a price process (S_t^0) satisfying

$$dS_t^0 = rS_t^0 dt \qquad (7.23)$$

and the risky asset has a price process (S_t^1) satisfying

$$dS_t^1 = S_t^1(\mu dt + \sigma dB_t). \qquad (7.24)$$

The discounted price of the risky asset is

$$\widetilde{S}_t = e^{-rt}S_t^1 \quad \text{with dynamics}$$
$$d\widetilde{S}_t = -re^{-rt}S_t^1 dt + e^{-rt}dS_t^1$$
$$= \widetilde{S}_t\big((\mu - r)dt + \sigma dB_t\big).$$

If we apply Girsanov's Theorem 7.2.3 with $\theta_t = (\mu/\sigma)$ we see there is a probability measure P^μ, defined on $\mathcal{F}_T$ by putting

$$\frac{dP^\mu}{dP} = \Lambda_T = \exp\left(-\int_0^t \theta_s dB_s - \frac{1}{2}\int_0^t \theta_s^2 ds\right),$$

such that under P^μ (W_t^μ), $0 \le t \le T$, is a standard Brownian motion where

$$W_t^\mu = \left(\frac{\mu - r}{\sigma}\right)t + B_t. \qquad (7.25)$$

Then, under P^μ we have

$$d\widetilde{S}_t = \widetilde{S}_t \sigma dW_t^\mu$$

and

$$\widetilde{S}_t = S_0 \exp\left(\sigma W_t^\mu - \frac{\sigma^2 t}{2}\right).$$

Definition 7.5.1. A strategy $\phi = (H_t^0, H_t^1)$, $0 \le t \le T$, is *admissible* if it is self-financing and the discounted value process

$$\widetilde{V}_t(\phi) = H_t^0 + H_t^1 \widetilde{S}_t$$

is non-negative and square integrable under $\widetilde{P}$.

Definition 7.5.2. A *European contingent claim* is a positive $\mathcal{F}_T$-measurable random variable h.

If $h = f(S_T)$ and $f(S_T) = (S_T - K)^+$ (resp., $f(S_T) = (K - S_T)^+$), then the option is a European call option (resp., European put option).

An option is replicable if its value at time T (the exercise time) is equal to the value $V_T(\phi) = H_T^0 S_T^0 + H_T^1 S_T^1$ of an admissible strategy ϕ.

Suppose $\phi \in SF$ is a self-financing strategy $\phi_t = (H_t^0, H_t^1)$. The corresponding wealth process is

$$V_t(\phi) = H_t^0 S_t^0 + H_t^1 S_t^1$$

$$= V_0(\phi) + \int_0^t H_u^0 dS_u^0 + \int_0^t H_u^1 dS_u^1.$$

From (7.23) and (7.24) this is

$$= V_0(\phi) + \int_0^t rH_u^0 S_u^0 du + \int_0^t H_u^1 S_u^1 (\mu\, du + \sigma dB_u)$$

$$= V_0(\phi) + \int_0^t rV_u(\phi_u) du + \int_0^t \sigma H_u^1 S_u^1 dW_u^\mu,$$

where W is defined in (7.25). Consider the discounted wealth

$$\widetilde{V}_t(\phi) = (S_t^0)^{-1} V_t(\phi).$$

From the differentiation rule

$$\widetilde{V}_t(\phi) = V_0(\phi_0) + \int_0^t \sigma H_u^1 (S_u^0)^{-1} (S_u^1) dW_u^\mu.$$

We have seen in Section 7.5 that under the measure P^μ the process W^μ is a standard Brownian motion. Consequently, under P^μ we see

$$M_t = \int_0^t \sigma H_u^1 (S_u^0)^{-1} S_u^1 dW_u^\mu$$

is a local martingale.

In fact consider the stopping times

$$T_n = \inf\left\{ t \geq 0 : \int_0^t (\sigma H_u^1 (S_u^0)^{-1} S_u^1)^2 du \geq n \right\}.$$

Then the T_n are increasing and $\lim_n T_n = T$. Furthermore, $M_{t \wedge T_n}$ is a uniformly integrable martingale under measure P^μ for each n. Consequently, $\widetilde{V}_t(\phi_t)$ is a local martingale under P^μ.

Suppose $\xi = \xi(\omega)$ is a non-negative $\mathcal{F}$-measurable random variable, with $E^\mu \xi < \infty$, where E^μ denotes expectation with respect to the measure P^μ. A strategy $\phi \in SF$ will belong to $SF(\xi)$ if for $t \geq 0$:

$$\widetilde{V}_t(\phi) \geq -E^\mu[\xi | \mathcal{F}_t] \text{ a.s.}$$

A strategy $\phi \in SF(\xi)$ will provide a hedge against a maximum loss of ξ. Under this condition Fatou's Lemma (Shiryayev [241], Chapter II, §6), can be applied and the local martingale $\widetilde{V}(\phi)$ is a supermartingale under measure P^μ.

Consequently, if τ_1 and τ_2 are two stopping times, with $\tau_i \leq T$ and $\tau_1 \leq \tau_2$ a.s., then

$$E^\mu[\widetilde{V}_{\tau_2}(\phi)|\mathcal{F}_{\tau_1}] \leq \widetilde{V}_{\tau_1}(\phi),$$

from the optimal stopping theorem.

In particular, if $V_0(\phi_0) = x \geq 0$ and $\phi \in SF(\xi)$, then

$$E^\mu[\widetilde{V}_\tau(\phi)] = E^\mu[e^{-rt}V_\tau(\phi)] \leq x. \tag{7.26}$$

We summarize the preceding observations in the following result.

Lemma 7.5.3.   a) *If $\phi \in SF$, then $\widetilde{V}(\phi)$ is a local martingale.*

b) *If $\phi \in SF(\xi)$, then $\widetilde{V}(\phi)$ is also a supermartingale.*

c) *If $\phi \in SF(0)$, then $\widetilde{V}(\phi)$ is also a non-negative supermartingale.*

Note that if $\phi \in SF(0)$ simultaneous borrowing from the bank and stocks is not permitted.

Definition 7.5.4. A strategy $\phi \in SF$ is said to provide an *arbitrage opportunity* if, with $V_0(\phi) = x \leq 0$ we have $V_T(\phi) \geq 0$ a.s. and

$$P\{\omega :\ V_T(\phi) > 0\} > 0.$$

We can then establish:

Lemma 7.5.5. *If ξ is a non-negative $\mathcal{F}$-measurable random variable with $E^\mu\xi < \infty$, then any $\phi \in SF(\xi)$ does not provide an arbitrage opportunity.*

Proof. Equation (7.26) rules out the possibility of ϕ providing an arbitrage opportunity.   □

Definition 7.5.6. Suppose $T > 0$ and f_T is an $\mathcal{F}_T$ measurable, non-negative random variable. A strategy $\phi \in SF$ is a *hedge* for the European claim f_T with initial investment x if

$$V_0(\phi) = x$$

and

$$V_T(\phi) \geq f_T \text{ a.s.}$$

We call $\phi \in SF$ an (x, f_T) hedge.

Although the next definition can be given for strategies in SF we restrict ourselves to strategies in $SF(0)$.

Definition 7.5.7. The investment price $C(T, f_T)$ for the European claim f_T at time $T > 0$ is the smallest initial investment with which the investor can attain an amount f_T at time T using strategies from $SF(0)$.

More precisely, write $\sum(T, x, f_T)$ for the set of (x, f_T) hedges that belong to $SF(0)$. Then

$$C(T, f_T) = \inf\{x \geq 0 : \textstyle\sum(T, x, f_T) \neq \emptyset\}.$$

For any European claim f_T we must, therefore,

a) determine the investment price $C(T, f_T)$ and

b) determine the (x, f_T) hedging strategy $\phi \in SF(0)$ for $x = C(T, f_T)$.

Remark 7.5.8. A European claim with exercise time $T > 0$ and payment f_T gives the right to the buyer of the contract of obtaining an amount f_T at time T.

Clearly, if the seller of the contract can start with an amount $x = C(T, f_T)$ and obtain $V_T(\phi_T) \geq f_T$ at time T, then $C(T, f_T)$ is the fair, or rational, price for the option from the seller's point of view. The discussion in Chapter 1 also applies here, in the continuous-time setting, and shows that (in a complete market, which is the case here) $C(T, f_T)$ is also the fair price from the buyer's standpoint.

Recall that the price of the European call option on S^1 with an exercise time T and a strike price K corresponds to taking:

$$f_T = (S_T^1 - K)^+.$$

Pricing

Suppose $\phi \in SF(0)$. Then, because $\widetilde{V}(\phi)$ is a supermartingale

$$x = V_0(\phi) \geq E^\mu\left[e^{-rT}V_T(\phi)\right].$$

If, furthermore, ϕ is an (x, f_T) hedge,

$$x \geq E^\mu\left[e^{-rT}f_T\right].$$

Consequently, the rational investment price $C(T, f_T)$ satisfies

$$C(T, f_T) \geq E^\mu\left[e^{-rT}f_T\right].$$

From (7.24),
$$dS_t^1 = S_t^1(\mu dt + \sigma dB_t),$$

where B is a standard Brownian motion under P. Write $S^1(\mu)$ for the solution of (7.24).

Then from (7.25), under measure P^μ the process $S^1(\mu)$ satisfies

$$dS_t^1 = S_t^1(r\, dt + \sigma\, dW_t^\mu),$$

where W^μ is a standard Brownian motion.

Let us write $S^1(r)$ for the solution of the equation:

$$dS_t^1(r) = S_t^1(r)(r\,dt + \sigma\,dB_t).$$

Then

$$\text{Law}\,(f_T(S^1(\mu))|P^\mu) = \text{Law}\,(f_T(S^1(r))|P)$$

and

$$\begin{aligned}
E^\mu[e^{-rT}f_T] &= E^\mu[e^{-rT}f_T(S^1(\mu))] \\
&= E[e^{-rT}f_T(S^1(r))].
\end{aligned} \tag{7.27}$$

This quantity has the unexpected property that it does not depend on μ.
  Suppose f_T is a non-negative $\mathcal{F}_T$-measurable random variable such that

$$E^\mu[f_T^2] < \infty. \tag{7.28}$$

Recall $E^\mu[f_T^2] = E[\Lambda_T f_T^2]$ where

$$\begin{aligned}
\Lambda_T &= \exp\left(-\int_0^T \theta dB_s - \frac{1}{2}\int_0^T \theta^2 ds\right), \\
&= \exp\left(-\theta B_T - \frac{1}{2}\theta^2 T\right) \\
\theta &= \frac{\mu - r}{\sigma}.
\end{aligned}$$

A sufficient condition for (7.28) is that $E[f_T^{2+\delta}] < \infty$ for some $\delta > 0$.
  Consider the square integrable $(P^\mu, \mathcal{F}_t)$ martingale

$$N_t := E^\mu[e^{-rT}f_T \mid \mathcal{F}_t], \quad 0 \le t \le T.$$

From the martingale representation result, Theorem 7.3.8, there is a pre-dictable process γ such that

$$E[\int_0^T \gamma_s^2 ds] < \infty \tag{7.29}$$

and

$$N_t = N_0 + \int_0^t \gamma_s dW_s^\mu \,\text{a.s.}$$

Here, $N_0 = E^\mu[e^{-rT}f_T]$.
  Now take

$$H_t^1 = \gamma_t e^{rt}\sigma^{-1}(S_t^1)^{-1}$$

and

$$H_t^0 = N_t - \sigma^{-1}\gamma_t;$$

consider the trading strategy $\phi_t^* = (H_t^0, H_t^1)$.

Lemma 7.5.9. *The strategy ϕ_t^* is*

a) *self-financing, and*

b) $N_t = \tilde{V}_t(\phi^*) = e^{-rt}V_t(\phi^*).$

Proof. By definition

$$V_t(\phi^*) = H_t^0 S_t^0 + H_t^1 S_t^1$$
$$= N_t S_t^0. \tag{7.30}$$

Therefore,

$$dV_t(\phi^*) = N_t dS_t^0 + S_t^0 dN_t$$
$$= rN_t S_t^0 dt + S_t^0 \gamma_t dW_t^\mu$$
$$= (N_t - \sigma^{-1}\gamma_t)dS_t^0 + \sigma^{-1}\gamma_t S_t^0(rdt + \sigma dW_t^\mu)$$
$$= H_t^0 dS_t^0 + H_t^1 dS_t^1.$$

Consequently, the strategy $\phi_t^* = (H_t^0, H_t^1)$ is self-financing. (The conditions (7.17) are satisfied because of (7.29) and the continuity of the paths of N.)

From (7.30) we see that

$$N_t = (S_t^0)^{-1}V_t(\phi^*);$$

that is, the P^μ martingale N is the discounted wealth process of the strategy ϕ_t^*. Also,

$$V_t(\phi^*) = N_t S_t^0$$
$$= E^\mu[S_t^0(S_T^0)^{-1}f_T \mid \mathcal{F}_t]$$
$$= E^\mu[e^{-r(T-t)}f_T \mid \mathcal{F}_t].$$

In particular,

$$V_0(\phi^*) = E^\mu[e^{-rT}f_T] \quad \text{and} \quad V_T(\phi^*) = f_T.$$

These equations mean that ϕ^* is an (x, f_T) hedge with initial capital

$$x = E^\mu[e^{-rT}f_T].$$

Clearly, if $\phi \in SF$ is any other hedge for f_T with initial capital x,

$$V_T(\phi) \geq V_T(\phi_T^*) = f_T.$$

Consequently, the rational price for the European option f_T is

$$C(T, f_T) = E^\mu[e^{-rT}f_T].$$

From (7.27) this is $E[e^{-rT}f_T(S^1(r))]$ so $C(T, f_T)$ does not depend on μ. $\square$

In conclusion, we have shown the following results hold

Theorem 7.5.10. *Suppose f_T represents a European claim, which can be exercised at time T. That is, f_T is an $\mathcal{F}_T$-measurable random variable and*

$$E^\mu[e^{-rT} f_T] < \infty.$$

Then the rational price for f_T is

$$C(T, f_T) = E^\mu[e^{-rT} f_T(S^1(\mu))]$$
$$= E[e^{-rT} f_T(S^1(r))].$$

There is a minimal hedge $\phi_t^* = (H_t^0, H_t^1)$ given by

$$H_t^1 = \sigma^{-1}\gamma_t e^{rt}(S_t^1)^{-1}$$
$$H_t^0 = N_t - e^{rt}S_t^1 H_t^1.$$

Here N is the martingale $E^\mu[e^{-rT} f_T|\mathcal{F}_t]$ and $(\gamma_t, t \le T)$ is the integrand in its martingale representation.

Definition 7.5.11. In the setting of a probability space $(\Omega, \mathcal{F}, P)$ an equivalent measure $\widetilde{P}$ is called a *martingale measure* if, under $\widetilde{P}$, all discounted asset prices are martingales. $\widetilde{P}$ is sometimes called a *risk-neutral measure*.

We have seen that, in the case of one risky asset, $\widetilde{P} = P^\mu$ is a martingale measure.

Suppose $B_t = (B_t^1, \dots, B_t^m), 0 \le t \le T$, is an m-dimensional Brownian motion on $(\Omega, \mathcal{F}, P)$ and let $\{\mathcal{F}_t\}$ be the filtration generated by B.

Suppose there is now a bond $S^0(t)$, or bank, whose instantaneous interest rate is $r(t)$ and n risky assets $S^1(t), \dots, S^n(t)$.

With $S^0(0) = 1$, we have $S^0(t) = \exp\{\int_0^t r(u)du\}$. The dynamics of the risky assets are described by the equations

$$dS^i(t) = \mu_i(t)S^i(t)dt + S^i(t)\left\{\sum_{j=1}^n \sigma_{ij}(t)dB^j(t)\right\}.$$

Here μ_i, σ_{ij}, are r are adapted processes. The prices $(S^1(t)/S^0(t)), \dots, (S^n(t)/S^0(t))$ are the discounted prices and the differentiation rule gives:

$$d\left(\frac{S^i(t)}{S^0(t)}\right) = (\mu_i(t) - r(t))\frac{S^i(t)}{S^0(t)}dt + \frac{S^i(t)}{S^0(t)}\sum_{j=1}^m \sigma_{ij}(t)dB^j(t). \tag{7.31}$$

Definition 7.5.12. $(\mu_i(t) - r(t))$ is called the *risk premium*.

Definition 7.5.13. If we can find processes $\theta_1(t), \ldots, \theta_n(t)$ so that for $1 \leq i \leq n$,

$$\mu_i(t) - r(t) = \sum_{j=1}^{m} \sigma_{ij}(t)\theta_j(t), \tag{7.32}$$

then the adapted process

$$\theta(t) := \big(\theta_1(t), \ldots, \theta_n(t)\big)$$

is called the *market price of risk*. Equation (7.31) then becomes

$$d\Big(\frac{S^i(t)}{S^0(t)}\Big) = \frac{S^i(t)}{S^0(t)} \Big(\sum_{j=1}^{m} \sigma_{ij}(t)[\theta_j(t)dt + dB^j(t)]\Big).$$

Consider the linear system (7.32). Three cases can arise:

a) it has a unique solution

$$\theta(t) = \big(\theta_1(t), \ldots, \theta_n(t)\big),$$

b) it has no solution; or

c) it has more than one solution.

In Cases a) and c) we have a solution process $\theta(t)$. Consider the process

$$\Lambda_t = \exp\Big(- \int_0^t \theta(u)dB(u) - \frac{1}{2} \int_0^t |\theta(u)|^2 du\Big)$$

and define a new measure P^θ by setting

$$\frac{dP^\theta}{dP}\Big|_{\mathcal{F}_T} = \Lambda_T.$$

The vector form of Girsanov's theorem states that, under P^θ, $W^\theta = (W^{\theta_1}, W^{\theta_2}, \ldots, W^{\theta_m})$ is an m-dimensional martingale, where

$$dW_t^\theta = \theta(t)dt + dB(t).$$

A hedging strategy is now a measurable adapted process $\phi_t = (H_t^0, H_t^1, \ldots, H_t^n)$, where H_t^i represents the number of units of asset i held at time t. Its corresponding wealth process is

$$V_t(\phi) = H_t^0 S_t^0 + H_t^1 S_t^1 + \cdots + H_t^n S_t^n.$$

ϕ is said to be self-financing if

$$dV_t(\phi) = \sum_{i=0}^{n} H_t^i dS_t^i;$$

so

$$V_t(\phi) = V_0(\phi) + \int_0^t \sum_{i=0}^n H_u^i dS_u^i$$

$$= V_0(\phi) + \int_0^t rH_u^0 S_u^0 du + \sum_{i=1}^n \int_0^t H_u^i S_u^i \left(\mu_i(u) + \sum_{j=1}^m \sigma_{ij}(u) dB^j(u) \right)$$

$$= V_0(\phi) + \int_0^t rV_u(\phi) du + \sum_{i=1}^n \sum_{j=1}^m \int_0^t H_u^i S_u^i \sigma_{ij} \left(\theta_j(u) du + dB^j(u) \right)$$

$$= V_0(\phi) + \int_0^t rV_u(\phi) du + \sum_{i=1}^n \sum_{j=1}^m \int_0^t H_u^i S_u^i \sigma_{ij}(u) dW_u^{\theta_j}.$$

Therefore, the discounted wealth

$$\widetilde{V}_t(\phi) = (S_t^0)^{-1} V_t(\phi)$$

$$= V_0(\phi) + \sum_{i=1}^n \sum_{j=1}^m \int_0^t H_u^i S_u^i \sigma_{ij}(u) dW_u^{\theta_j}$$

is a local martingale under P^θ. For $\phi \in SF(\xi)$ the proof of the first part of this section shows $V(\phi)$ is a supermartingale.

Consequently in Cases a) and c) there is no arbitrage.

In case a) when the solution is unique we must have $m = n$ and the matrix $\sigma = (\sigma_{ij}(t))$ is nonsingular.

If f_T is a European claim to be exercised at time T, we can consider the martingale

$$N_t = E^\theta[e^{-rT} f_T | \mathcal{F}_t].$$

By the martingale representation result this can be written

$$N_t = N_0 + \int_0^t \gamma_u dW_u^\theta,$$

where $\gamma_u = (\gamma_u^1, \gamma_u^2, \ldots, \gamma_u^n)$ is a measurable adapted process such that

$$E\left[\int_0^T |\gamma_u|^2 du \right] < \infty.$$

Write $\Delta(t)$ for the matrix diag $((S_t^1)^{-1}, \ldots, (S_t^n)^{-1})$ and $(H_t^1, H_t^2, \ldots, H_t^n) = S_t^0 \Delta(t) \sigma'(t)^{-1} \gamma_t,$

$$H_t^0 = N_t - \langle \sigma'(t)^{-1} \gamma_t, \mathbf{1} \rangle,$$

where $\mathbf{1} = (1, \ldots, 1)$. Then $(H_t^0, H_t^1, \ldots, H_t^n)$ is a self-financing strategy that hedges the claim f_T and the market is complete.

In Case c), although there are no arbitrage opportunities, there are claims that cannot be hedged and the market is incomplete.

In Case b), if (7.32) has no solution, there is no martingale measure and the market may allow arbitrage.

There is an extensive literature on the relationship between arbitrage and the existence of equivalent martingale measures. This has been discussed in the finite case in Chapter 3. Recall again that the fundamental theorems on asset pricing were given in two papers by Harrison and Pliska. In [121] it is shown that if a market has a martingale measure, there is no arbitrage opportunity. In [122] it is shown that the martingale measure is unique if and only if every claim can be hedged, that is, if and only if the market is complete. Recent contributions are due, among others, to Stricker [248] and Delbaen and Schachermayer [59].

7.6   The Black–Scholes Formula

In this section we suppose the European option has the form $f(S_T^1)$.

We require some integrability properties of f, so we suppose for some non-negative c, k_1, k_2,

$$f : (0, \infty) \to \mathbb{R}$$

and

$$f(s) \le c(1 + s^{k_1})s^{-k_2}. \tag{7.33}$$

From Theorem 7.5.10 the rational price for the option f is independent of μ and is given by

$$C(T, f) = E[e^{-rT} f(S_T^1(r))],$$

where S^1 is the solution of

$$dS_t^1 = S_t^1(r\,dt + \sigma\,dW_t). \tag{7.34}$$

Here W is a standard Brownian motion on $(\Omega, \mathcal{F}, P)$.

The wealth process of the corresponding minimal hedge is

$$V_t(\phi^*) = E[e^{-r(T-t)} f(S_T^1(r)) \,|\, \mathcal{F}_t].$$

Now from (7.34)

$$S_0^1 = S_0^1 \exp\left((r - \frac{\sigma^2}{2})t + \sigma W_t\right).$$

From the Markov property

$$
\begin{aligned}
V_t(\phi^*) &= E[e^{-r(T-t)} f(S_T^1(r)) \,|\, \mathcal{F}_t] \\
&= E[e^{-r(T-t)} f(S_T^1) \,|\, S_t^1] \\
&= e^{-r(T-t)} F(T - t, S_t^1). \tag{7.35}
\end{aligned}
$$

Here

$$F(T-t,s) = \frac{1}{\sqrt{2\pi}} \int_{-\infty}^{\infty} f\left(s\exp\left[\sigma y\sqrt{T-t} + \left(r - \frac{\sigma^2}{2}\right)(T-t)\right]\right) e^{-y^2/2} dy$$

$$= \frac{1}{s} \int_{-\infty}^{\infty} f(y) g\left(T-t, \frac{y}{s}, r - \frac{\sigma^2}{2}, \sigma\right) dy,$$

where

$$g(t,z,\alpha,\beta) = \frac{1}{\beta z\sqrt{2\pi} t} \exp\left[-\frac{(\log z - \alpha t)^2}{2\beta^2 t}\right].$$

From the integrability condition the function $F(T-t,s)$ is differentiable in t and s. Furthermore, $E[F(T-t,S_t^1)] < \infty$. Write $G(t,x) = F(T-t,e^{rt}x)$. Then from (7.35),

$$V_t(\phi^*)e^{-rt} = e^{-rT}G(t, e^{-rt}S_t^1).$$

Using the Itô differentiation rule

$$d\left(V_t(\phi^*)e^{-rt}\right) = e^{-rT} d\left(G(t, e^{-rt}S_t^1)\right)$$

$$= e^{-rT}\left[\frac{\partial G}{\partial x}(t, e^{-rt}S_t^1) d(e^{-rt}S_t^1)\right.$$

$$\left. + \left(\frac{\partial G}{\partial t} + \frac{1}{2}\frac{\partial^2 G}{\partial x^2} \sigma^2 (S_t^1)^2 e^{-2r}\right) dt\right].$$

That is,

$$V_t(\phi^*)e^{-rt} = N_t = E[e^{-rT}f(S_T^1(r)) \mid \mathcal{F}_t]$$

$$= e^{-rT}E[f(S_T^1(r))] + e^{-rT} \int_0^t \frac{\partial G}{\partial x} \cdot d(e^{-ru}S_u^1) \qquad (7.36)$$

$$+ e^{-rT} \int_0^t \left(\frac{\partial G}{\partial t} + \frac{1}{2}\frac{\partial^2 G}{\partial x^2} \cdot \sigma^2 (S_u^1)^2 e^{-2r}\right) du.$$

Now $d(e^{-ru}S_u^1) = \sigma e^{-ru}S_u^1 dW_u$. Consequently, the first integral in (7.36) is a local martingale. The left side of (7.36) is a martingale. Therefore, as in (7.13), the bounded variation process in (7.36) must be identically zero. This implies

$$\frac{\partial G}{\partial t} + \frac{1}{2}\frac{\partial^2 G}{\partial x^2} \sigma^2 (S_t^1)^2 e^{-2r} = 0$$

with $G(T,x) = f(e^{rT}x)$.

Noting that $\partial G/\partial x = e^{rt}(\partial Fx/\partial x)$ we have, therefore, proved the following theorem.

Theorem 7.6.1. *Consider a European option with exercise time $T > 0$ and payment function $f(S_T^1)$, where f satisfies the integrability condition (7.33).*

Then the rational price for the option is

$$C(T, f_T) = e^{-rT} F(T, S_0^1),$$

where

$$F(T, S_0^1) = \frac{1}{\sqrt{2\pi}} \int_{-\infty}^{\infty} f\left(S_0^1 \exp\left[(r - \frac{\sigma^2}{2})T + \sigma y \sqrt{T}\right]\right) e^{-y^2/2} dy.$$

The minimal hedge $\phi_t^* = (H_t^0, H_t^1)$ *is*

$$H_t^1 = e^{-r(T-t)} \frac{\partial F}{\partial s}(T - t, S_t^1),$$

$$H_t^0 = e^{-rT} \left[F(T - t, S_t^1) - S_t^1 \frac{\partial F}{\partial s}(T - t, S_t^1)\right].$$

The corresponding wealth process is

$$V_t(\phi^*) = e^{-r(T-t)} F(T - t, S_t^1).$$

This is also the rational price of the option at time t.

The Black–Scholes Formula

The standard European call option corresponds to taking $f(S_T^1) = (S_T^1 - K)^+$. Specializing the preceding results we have:

Theorem 7.6.2 (Black–Scholes). *The rational price of a standard European call option is*

$$C(T, (S_T^1 - K)^+) = S_0^1 \Phi(y_1) - K e^{-rT} \Phi(y_2).$$

Here $\Phi(y) = (1/\sqrt{2\pi}) \int_{-\infty}^{y} e^{-z^2/2} dz$ *is the standard normal cumulative distribution function*

$$y_1 = \frac{\log(S_0^1/K) + T(r + \sigma^2/2)}{\sigma \sqrt{T}},$$

$$y_2 = \frac{\log(S_0^1/K) + T(r - \sigma^2/2)}{\sigma \sqrt{T}} = y_1 - \sigma\sqrt{T}.$$

The minimal hedge, $\phi_t^* = (H_t^0, H_t^1)$ *is*

$$H_t^1 = \Phi\left(\frac{\log(S_t^1/K) + (T - t)(r + \sigma^2/2)}{\sigma \sqrt{T - t}}\right),$$

$$H_t^0 = -e^{-rT} K \Phi\left(\frac{\log(S_t^1/K) + (T - t)(r - \sigma^2/2)}{\sigma \sqrt{T - t}}\right).$$

The corresponding wealth process is

$$V_t(\phi^*) = H_t^0 S_t^0 + H_t^1 S_t^1.$$

Proof. With $f(s) = (s - K)^+$ we have from Theorem 7.6.1,

$$F(t, s) = \frac{1}{\sqrt{2\pi}} \int_{-\infty}^{\infty} f\left(s \exp\left[\sigma y \sqrt{t} + (r - \frac{\sigma^2}{2})t\right]\right) e^{-y^2/2} dy$$

$$= \frac{1}{\sqrt{2\pi}} \int_{y(t,s)}^{\infty} \left(s \exp\left[\sigma y \sqrt{t} + (r - \frac{\sigma^2}{2})t\right] - K\right) e^{-y^2/2} dy,$$

where $y(t, s)$ is the solution of

$$s \exp\left[\sigma y \sqrt{t} + (r - \frac{\sigma^2}{2})t\right] = K, \tag{7.37}$$

so $y(t, s) = \sigma^{-1} t^{-1/2}(\log(K/s) - (r - \sigma^2/2)t)$. Consequently,

$$F(t, s) = \frac{e^{rt}}{\sqrt{2\pi}} \int_{y(t,s)}^{\infty} s \exp[\sigma y \sqrt{y} - \sigma^2 t/2 - y^2/2] dy - K[1 - \Phi(y(t, s))]$$

$$= \frac{s e^{rt}}{\sqrt{2\pi}} \int_{y(t,s) - \sigma\sqrt{t}}^{\infty} e^{-x^2/2} dx - K[1 - \Phi(y(t, s))]$$

$$= s e^{rt}[1 - \Phi(y(t, s) - \sigma \sqrt{t})] - K[1 - \Phi(y(t, s))].$$

From Theorem 7.5.10 the rational price for the standard European call option is

$$C(T, (S_T - K)^+) = e^{-rT} F(T, S_0)$$

$$= S_0 \Phi(\sigma \sqrt{T} - y(T, S_0)) - K e^{-rT} \Phi(-y(T, S_0))$$

$$= S_0 \Phi(y_1) - K e^{-rT} \Phi(y_2).$$

Now from Theorem 7.6.1 the minimal hedge $H_t^1 = e^{-r(T-t)} (\partial F/\partial x) (T - t, S_t)$ so after some cancellations when performing the differentiation we obtain:

$$H_t^1 = \Phi(\sigma \sqrt{T-t} - y(T - t, S_t))$$

$$= \Phi\left(\sigma \sqrt{T-t} - \sigma^{-1}(T-t)^{-1/2}\left(\log(K/S_t) - (r - \frac{\sigma^2}{2})(T-t)\right)\right)$$

$$= \Phi\left(\frac{\log(S_t/K) + (T-t)(r + \sigma^2/2)}{\sigma \sqrt{T-t}}\right).$$

Now

$$V_t(\phi^*) = e^{-r(T-t)} F(T - t, S_t)$$

$$= S_t \Phi\left(\frac{\log(S_t/K) + (T-t)(r + \sigma^2/2)}{\sigma \sqrt{T-t}}\right)$$

$$- K e^{-r(T-t)} \Phi\left(\frac{\log(S_t/K) + (T-t)(r - \sigma^2/2)}{\sigma \sqrt{T-t}}\right).$$

Then

$$
\begin{aligned}
H_t^0 &= e^{-rt}V_t(\phi^*) - e^{-rt}H_t^1 S_t \\
&= -Ke^{-rT}\Phi\left[\frac{\log(S_t/K) + (r - \sigma^2/2)(T - t)}{\sigma\sqrt{T - t}}\right]
\end{aligned}
$$

and the result follows. $\square$

Call–Put Parity

This fundamental result was established in Chapter 1 by a basic no arbitrage argument. Recalling the definitions, the standard European put option gives the buyer the right (but not the obligation) to sell the stock at time $T > 0$ for the price $K > 0$.

It, therefore, has the value

$$
C(T, (K - S_T^1)^+) = E[e^{-rT}(K - S_T^1)^+].
$$

However, $(K - S)^+ = (S - K)^+ - S + K$ so

$$
\begin{aligned}
E[e^{-rT}(K - S_T^1)^+] &= E[e^{-rT}(S_T^1 - K)^+ - e^{-rT}S_T^1 + e^{-rT}K] \\
&= E[e^{-rT}(S_T^1 - K)^+] - E[e^{-rT}S_T^1] + E[e^{-rT}K] \\
&= C(T, (S_T^1 - K)^+) - S_0^1(r) + Ke^{-rT}.
\end{aligned}
$$

This formula relates the European put price P_T and European call price C_T by the formula

$$
P_T = C_T - S_0 + Ke^{-rT}.
$$

7.7   A Multi-Dimensional Situation

In Section 7.5 we considered a riskless bond $B_t = e^{rt}$ and a single risky asset S_t^1. Suppose now we have a vector of risky assets

$$
S_t = (S_t^1, \ldots, S_t^d)
$$

whose dynamics are described by stochastic differential equations of the form

$$
dS_t^i = S_t^i\left(\mu^i(t, S_t)dt + \sum_{j=1}^{d}\lambda_{ij}(t, S_t)dW_t^i\right), \quad 1 \le i \le d.
$$

When the μ^i and λ_{ij} are constant we have the familiar log-normal stock price. To ensure the claim is attainable the number of sources of noise, that is, the dimension of the Brownian motion w, is taken equal to the number of stocks. $\Lambda_t = \Lambda(t, S) = (\lambda_{ij}(t, S))$ is therefore a $d \times d$ matrix. We suppose

Λ is nonsingular, three times differentiable in S, and that $\Lambda^{-1}(t,S)$ and all derivatives of Λ are bounded. Writing $\mu(t,S) = (\mu^1(t,S), \ldots, \mu^d(t,S))'$ we also suppose μ is three times differentiable in S with all derivatives bounded.

Again suppose there is a bond B_t with a fixed interest rate r, so $B_t = e^{rt}$. The discounted stock price vector $\xi_t = (\xi_t^1, \ldots, \xi_t^d)'$ is then $\xi_t := e^{-rt}S_t$ so

$$d\xi_t^i = \xi_t^i\left((\mu^i(t, e^{rt}\xi_t) - r)dt + \sum_{j=1}^d \lambda_{ij}(t, e^{rt}\xi_t)dW_t^j\right). \tag{7.38}$$

Writing

$$\Delta_t = \Delta(t, \xi_t) = \begin{pmatrix} \xi_t^1 & & 0 \\ & \ddots & \\ 0 & & \xi_t^d \end{pmatrix}$$

and $\rho = (r, r, \ldots, r)'$ equation (7.38) can be written

$$d\xi_t = \Delta_t((\mu - \rho)dt + \Lambda_t dW). \tag{7.39}$$

As in Section 7.4, there is a flow of diffeomorphisms $x \to \xi_{s,t}(x)$ associated with this system, together with their nonsingular Jacobians $D_{s,t}$.

In the terminology of Harrison and Pliska [122], the return process $Y_t = (Y_t^1, \ldots, Y_t^d)$ is here given by

$$dY_t = (\mu - \rho)dt + \Lambda dW_t. \tag{7.40}$$

The drift term in (7.40) can be removed by applying the Girsanov change of measure. Write $\eta(t,S) = \Lambda(t,S)^{-1}(\mu(t,S) - \rho)$ and define the martingale M by

$$M_t = 1 - \int_0^t M_s\eta(s, S_s)'dW_s.$$

Then

$$M_t = \exp\left(-\int_0^t \eta_s'dW_s - \frac{1}{2}\int_0^t |\eta_s|^2 ds\right)$$

is the Radon–Nikodym derivative of a probability measure P^μ. Furthermore, under P^μ, $\widetilde{w}_t = w_t + \int_0^t \eta(s, S_s)'ds$ is a standard Brownian motion. Consequently, under P^μ,

$$dY_t = \Lambda_t d\widetilde{W}_t$$

and

$$d\xi_t = \Delta_t\Lambda_t d\widetilde{W}_t. \tag{7.41}$$

Therefore, the discounted stock price process ξ is a martingale under P^μ.

Consider a function $\overline{\psi} : \mathbb{R}^d \to \mathbb{R}$, where $\overline{\psi}$ is twice differentiable and $\overline{\psi}$ and $\overline{\psi}_x$ are of at most linear growth in x. For some future time $T > t$ we are interested in finding the current price (i.e., the current valuation at time t) of a contingent claim of the form $\overline{\psi}(S_T)$. It is convenient to work with the discounted claim as a function of the discounted stock price, so we consider equivalently the current value of

$$\psi(\xi_T) := e^{-rT}\overline{\psi}(e^{rT}\xi_T) = e^{-rT}\overline{\psi}(S_T).$$

ψ has linear growth, so we may define the square integrable P^μ martingale N by

$$N_t = E^\mu[\psi(\xi_T)|F_t], \quad 0 \le t \le T.$$

As in Section 7.5 the rational price for $\overline{\psi}$ is $E^\mu[\psi]$. Furthermore, if we can express N in the form

$$N_t = \widetilde{E}[\psi(\xi_T)] + \int_0^t \phi(s)'d\xi_s,$$

then the vector $H_t^1 = (\phi^1,\dots,\phi^d)'$ is a hedge portfolio that generates the contingent claim. Then $H_t^0 = N_t - H_t^1 \cdot e^{-rt}S_t$. We can apply Theorem 7.3.13 to derive immediately:

Theorem 7.7.1.

$$N_t = \widetilde{E}[\psi(\xi_T)] + \int_0^t \phi(s)'d\xi_s,$$

where

$$\phi(s) = E^\mu\Big[\int_s^T \eta_\xi(u, e^{ru}\xi_{0,x}(x_0))D_{0,u}(x_0)d\widetilde{W}_u \cdot \psi(\xi_{0,T}(x_0))$$
$$+ \psi_\xi(\xi_{0,T}(x_0))D_{0,T}(x_0)|\mathcal{F}_s\Big]D_{0,s}^{-1}(x_0).$$

Proof. From Theorem 7.3.13, under measure P^μ,

$$N_t = \widetilde{E}[\psi(\xi_T)] + \int_0^t \gamma_s d\widetilde{W}_s,$$

where

$$\gamma_s = E^\mu\Big[\int_s^T \eta_\xi D_{0,u}(x_0)d\widetilde{W}_u \cdot \psi(\xi_{0,T}(x_0))$$
$$+ \psi_\xi(\xi_{0,T}(x_0))D_{0,T}(x_0)|F_s\Big]D_{0,s}^{-1}(x_0)\Delta(\xi_{0,s}(x_0))\Lambda_s.$$

Because $d\xi_t = \Delta_t\Lambda_t d\widetilde{W}_t$, $\phi(s)$ has the stated form. $\square$

Remark 7.7.2. Note that if η is not a function of ξ (which is certainly the situation in the usual log-normal case where μ and Λ are constant), η_ξ is zero and the first term in ϕ vanishes.

The bond component H_t^0 in the portfolio is given by

$$H_t^0 = N_t - \sum_{i=1}^{d} \phi_t^i \xi_t^i, \quad 0 \le t \le T$$

and N_t is the price associated with the contingent claim at time t.

Examples

Stock price dynamics for which the hedging policy ϕ can be evaluated in closed form appear hard to find. However, if we consider a vector of log-normal stock prices we can rederive a vector form of the Black–Scholes results. Suppose, therefore, that the vector of stock prices $S = (S^1, \ldots, S^d)'$ evolves according to the equations

$$dS_t^i = S_t^i \left(\mu^i dt + \sum_{j=1}^{d} \lambda_{ij} dw_t^j \right), \tag{7.42}$$

where $\mu = (\mu^1, \ldots, \mu^d)$ and $\Lambda = (\lambda_{ij})$, are constant. The discounted stock price ξ is then given by (7.38).

Consider a contingent claim that consists of d European call options with expiry dates $T_1 \le T_2 \le \cdots \le T_d$ and exercise prices $c_1, \ldots, c_d$, respectively. Then

$$\psi(T_1, \ldots, T_d) = \sum_{k=1}^{d} \psi^k \big(\xi_{0,T_k}(x_0) \big) = \sum_{k=1}^{d} \big(\xi_{0,T_k}^k(x_0) - c_k e^{-rT_k} \big)^+.$$

From (7.42) we see that, with $a = (a_{ij})$ the matrix $\Lambda\Lambda'$, the Jacobian $D_{0,t}$ is just the diagonal matrix

$$D_{0,t} = \begin{bmatrix} \exp\left\{ \sum_{j=1}^{d} \lambda_{1j} \widetilde{w}_t^j - \frac{1}{2} a_{11} t \right\} & \cdots & 0 \\ & \vdots & \vdots \\ 0 & \cdots & \exp\left\{ \sum_{j=1}^{d} \lambda_{dj} \widetilde{w}_t^j - \frac{1}{2} a_{dd} t \right\} \end{bmatrix}$$

and its inverse is

$$D_{0,t}^{-1} = \begin{bmatrix} \exp\left\{ -\left(\sum_{j=1}^{d} \lambda_{1j} \widetilde{w}_t^j - \frac{1}{2} a_{11} t \right) \right\} & \cdots & 0 \\ & \vdots & \vdots \\ 0 & \exp\left\{ -\left(\sum_{j=1}^{d} \lambda_{dj} \widetilde{w}_t^j - \frac{1}{2} a_{dd} t \right) \right\} \end{bmatrix}.$$

(The explicit exponential form of the solution shows $D_{0,t}$ is independent of x_0.) Thus, the trading strategy ϕ_k that generates the contingent claim $\psi^k(\xi_{T_k})$ is

$$
\phi_k(s)' = E^\mu \left[\psi_\xi^k(\xi_{0,T_k}(x_0)) D_{0,T_k} \mid \mathcal{F}_s \right] D_{0,s}^{-1}
$$

$$
= \left(0, \ldots, 0, \widetilde{E}\left[I\left\{ \xi_{0,T_k} > c_k e^{-rT_k} \right\} \exp\left\{ \sum_{j=1}^d \lambda_{kj}(\widetilde{w}_{T_k}^j - \widetilde{w}_s^j) \right. \right. \right.
$$

$$
\left. \left. \left. - \frac{1}{2} a_{kk}(T_k - s) \right\} \mid \mathcal{F}_s \right], 0, \ldots, 0 \right),
$$

for $0 \le s \le T_k$. Note that $\phi_k(s) = 0$ for $s > T_k$; that is, $\phi_k(s)$ stops at T_k. However, from (7.42),

$$
\xi_{0,T_k}^k(x_0) = x_0^k \exp\left\{ \sum_{j=1}^d \lambda_{kj}\widetilde{w}_{T_k}^j - \frac{1}{2} a_{kk}T_k \right\} > c_k e^{-rT_k} \tag{7.43}
$$

iff

$$
\sum_{j=1}^d \lambda_{kj}\widetilde{w}_{T_k}^j > \log\left(\frac{c_k}{x_0^k} \right) + \left(\frac{1}{2} a_{kk} - r \right) T_k = \alpha_k,
$$

say; that is, iff

$$
\sum_{j=1}^d \lambda_{kj}(\widetilde{w}_{T_k}^j - \widetilde{w}_s^j) > \alpha_k - \sum_{j=1}^d \lambda_{kj}\widetilde{w}_s^j.
$$

Now, under $\widetilde{P}$, $\sum_{j=1}^d \lambda_{kj}(\widetilde{w}_{T_k}^j - \widetilde{w}_s^j)$ is normally distributed with mean zero, variance $a_{kk}(T_k - s)$, and is independent of $\mathcal{F}_s$. Therefore, the nonzero component of $\phi_k(s)$ is

$$
\int_{\alpha_k - \sum_{j=1}^d \lambda_{kj}\widetilde{w}_s^j}^{\infty} \exp\left\{ x - \frac{1}{2} a_{kk}(T_k - s) \right\}
$$

$$
\times \exp\left\{ \frac{-x^2}{2a_{kk}(T_k - s)} \right\} \frac{dx}{\sqrt{2\pi a_{kk}(T_k - s)}}
$$

$$
= \int_{\alpha_k - \sum_{j=1}^d \lambda_{kj}\widetilde{w}_s^j}^{\infty} \exp\left\{ \frac{-[x - a_{kk}(T_k - s)]^2}{2a_{kk}(T_k - s)} \right\} \frac{dx}{\sqrt{2\pi a_{kk}(T_k - s)}}
$$

$$
= \int_{\frac{\alpha_k - \sum \lambda_{kj}\widetilde{w}_s^j - a_{kk}(T_k - s)}{\sqrt{a_{kk}(T_k - s)}}}^{\infty} e^{-y^2/2} \frac{dy}{\sqrt{2\pi}}
$$

$$
= \Phi\left(\frac{-\alpha_k + \sum \lambda_{kj}\widetilde{w}_s^j - a_{kk}(T_k - s)}{\sqrt{a_{kk}(T_k - s)}} \right).
$$

Again from (7.43), $\sum_{j=1}^{d} \lambda_{kj}\tilde{w}_s^j = \log\left((\xi_{0,s}^k(x_0))/(x_0^k)\right) + \frac{1}{2}a_{kk}s$, which together with (7.43) gives

$$\phi_k(s) = \left(0,\ldots,0,\Phi\left(\frac{\log\left(\frac{\xi_{0,s}^k(x_0)}{c_k}\right) - \frac{1}{2}a_{kk}(T_k-s)+rT_k}{\sqrt{a_{kk}(T_k-s)}}\right),0,\ldots,0\right)',$$

or, in terms of the (nondiscounted) price S_s^k,

$$\phi_k(s) = \left(0,\ldots,0,\Phi\left(\frac{\log\left(\frac{S_s^k}{c_k}\right) - \frac{1}{2}(a_{kk}-r)(T_k-s)}{\sqrt{a_{kk}(T_k-s)}}\right),0,\ldots,0\right)',\quad (7.44)$$

$0 \le s \le T_k$. Therefore, the trading strategy ϕ generating $\psi(T_1,\ldots,T_k) = \sum_{k=1}^{d}\psi^k(\xi_{T_k})$ can be written, with a slight abuse of notation, as $\phi(s) = (\phi_1(s),\ldots,\phi_d(s))'$, where

$$\phi_k(s) = I_{\{s\le T_k\}}\Phi\left(\frac{\log\left(\frac{S_t^k}{c_k}\right) - (\frac{1}{2}a_{kk}-r)(T_k-s)}{\sqrt{a_{kk}(T_k-s)}}\right).\quad (7.45)$$

Finally, we calculate the price of the claim $E^\mu[\psi(T_1,\ldots,T_d)] = \sum_{k=1}^{d}E^\mu[\psi^k(\xi_{T_k})]$ similarly:

$$\sum_{k=1}^{d}E^\mu[\psi^k(\xi_{T_k})] = \sum_{k=1}^{d}E^\mu(\xi_{T_k}^k - c_k e^{-rT_k})^+$$

$$= \sum_{k=1}^{d}E^\mu\left[I\left\{\sum_{j=1}^{d}\lambda_{kj}\tilde{w}_{T_k}^j > \alpha_k\right\}\right.$$

$$\times\left.\left(Z_0\exp\left\{\sum_{j=1}^{d}\lambda_{kj}\tilde{w}_{T_k}^j - \frac{1}{2}a_{kk}T_k\right\} - c_k e^{-rT_k}\right)\right]$$

$$= \sum_{k=1}^{d}S_0^k\Phi\left(\frac{\log\left(\frac{S_0^k}{c_k}\right) + (\frac{1}{2}a_{kk}+r)T_k}{\sqrt{a_{kk}T_k}}\right)$$

$$- c_k e^{-rT_k}\Phi\left(\frac{\log\left(\frac{S_0^k}{c_k}\right) + (\frac{1}{2}a_{kk}+r)T_k}{\sqrt{a_{kk}T_k}} - \sqrt{a_{kk}T_k}\right)$$

(where we have used $\xi_0^k = S_0^k$, $k = 1,\ldots,d$). When $d = 1$ the preceding result reduces to the well-known Black–Scholes formula.

7.8 Barrier Options

Consider a standard Brownian motion $B(t)$ defined on $(\Omega,\mathcal{F},P)$, $t \ge 0$. The filtration $\{\mathcal{F}_t\}$ is that generated by B.

Write $\phi(x) = (2\pi)^{-1/2}e^{-x^2/2}$ for the standard normal density and

$$\Phi(x) = \int_{-\infty}^{x} \phi(y)dy$$

for the standard normal distribution function.

Recall $B(t)$ is normal and

$$P\Big(B(t) < x\Big) = \Phi\Big(\frac{x}{\sqrt{t}}\Big).$$

Therefore, $P(B(t) \geq x) = 1 - \Phi(x/\sqrt{t}) = \Phi(-x/\sqrt{t})$. If

$$X(t) := \mu t + \sigma B(t), \tag{7.46}$$

then $P(X(t) < x) = \Phi((x - \mu t)/(\sigma \sqrt{t}))$.

For a real-valued process X we write

$$M^X(t) := \max_{0 \leq s \leq t} X(s),$$

$$m^X(t) := \min_{0 \leq s \leq t} X(s).$$

If

$$X(t) = \mu t + \sigma B(t),$$
$$-X(t) = (-\mu)t + \sigma(-B(t)).$$

$-B(t)$ is also a standard Brownian motion, so $-X$ has the same form as X but with μ replaced by $-\mu$. Now $m^X(t) = -M^{-X}(t)$; therefore, we consider only $M^X(t)$.

Consider the event

$$\{B(T) < b, \ M^B(T) > c\}, \quad \text{for } T > 0.$$

Suppose $c > 0$ and $b \leq c$.

For each path that hits level c before time T and ends up below b at time T there is, by the 'reflexion principle,' an equally probable path that hits level c and ends up above $2c - b$ at time T.

Therefore,

$$P\{B(T) < b, \ M^B(T) > c\} = P\{B(T) > 2c - b\}$$
$$= \Phi\Big(\frac{b - 2c}{\sqrt{T}}\Big).$$

Let us calculate the joint distribution function of $B(T)$ and $M^B(T)$,

$$F^B(T, b, c) = P\big(B(T) < b, \ M^B(T) < c\big)$$
$$= P\big(B(T) < b\big) - P\big(B(T) < b, \ M^B(T) > c\big)$$
$$= \Phi\Big(\frac{b}{\sqrt{T}}\Big) - \Phi\Big(\frac{b - 2c}{\sqrt{T}}\Big).$$

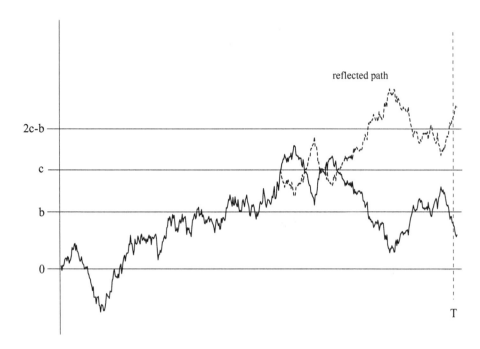

FIGURE 7.1. Reflexion principle

For $c < 0$ and $b \le 0$ $F^B(T, b, c) = 0$. For $c > 0$, $B \ge c$ $F^B(T, b, c) = \Phi(c/\sqrt{T}) - \Phi(-c/\sqrt{T})$.

Differentiating in (b, c) the random variable $(B(T), M^B(T))$, therefore, has a bivariate density

$$f^B(T, b, c) = \frac{2(2c - b)}{T\sqrt{T}}\, \phi\left(\frac{2c - b}{\sqrt{T}}\right). \qquad (7.47)$$

Consider now the process

$$X(t) := \mu t + B(t).$$

Introduce the exponential process

$$\Lambda_t := \exp\left(-\mu B(t) - \frac{1}{2}\mu^2 t\right)$$

and define a new measure P^μ by setting

$$\frac{dP^\mu}{dP}\Big|_{\mathcal{F}_t} = \Lambda_t.$$

Suppose $c > 0$ and $b \le c$. Then, from Girsanov's theorem, under P^μ $X(t)$ is a standard Brownian motion and $(X(T), M^X(T))$ has the same distribution under P^μ as $(B(T), M^B(T))$ has under P. Then, writing E^μ for expectation with respect to P^μ,

$$
\begin{aligned}
F^X(T, b, c) &= P(X(T) < b, M^X(T) < c) \\
&= E\big[I\big(X(T) < b,\ M^X(T) < c\big)\big] \\
&= E^\mu\big[\Lambda_T^{-1} I\big(X(T) < b,\ M^X(T) < c\big)\big] \\
&= E^\mu\Big[\exp\big(\mu X(T) - \tfrac{1}{2}\mu^2 T\big) I\big(X(T) < b,\ M^X(T) < c\big)\Big].
\end{aligned}
$$

Under P^μ the process X is a standard Brownian motion so this is:

$$
= \int_0^c \int_{-\infty}^b \exp\big(\mu z - \tfrac{1}{2}\mu^2 T\big) f(T, z, y)\, dz\, dy, \quad \text{where } f \text{ is given by (7.47)}
$$

$$
= \int_{-\infty}^b \exp\big(\mu z - \tfrac{1}{2}\mu^2 T\big) \frac{1}{\sqrt{T}}\Big(\phi(\tfrac{z}{\sqrt{T}}) - \phi(\tfrac{z - 2c}{\sqrt{T}})\Big) dz
$$

$$
= \int_{-\infty}^0 \exp\big(\mu(b + z) - \tfrac{1}{2}\mu^2 T\big) \frac{1}{\sqrt{T}}\Big(\phi(\tfrac{b + z}{\sqrt{T}}) - \phi(\tfrac{b + z - 2c}{\sqrt{T}})\Big) dz
$$

$$
= \exp\big(\mu b - \tfrac{1}{2}\mu^2 T\big) \cdot \big(\Psi(b) - \Psi(b - 2c)\big), \tag{7.48}
$$

where $\Psi(b) = (1/\sqrt{T}) \int_{-\infty}^0 \exp(\mu z) \cdot \phi((b + z)/\sqrt{T})\, dz$.

Now

$$
\Psi(b) = \frac{1}{\sqrt{2\pi T}} \int_{-\infty}^0 \exp\Big(\mu z - \big(\tfrac{b + z}{T}\big)^2\Big) dz.
$$

Completing the square in the exponential this is:

$$
= \exp\big(-\mu b + \tfrac{1}{2}\mu^2 T\big) \int_{-\infty}^0 \frac{1}{\sqrt{T}} \phi\Big(\frac{b + z - \mu T}{\sqrt{T}}\Big) dz
$$

$$
= \exp\big(-\mu b + \tfrac{1}{2}\mu^2 T\big) \Phi\Big(\frac{b - \mu T}{\sqrt{T}}\Big).
$$

Substituting in (7.48) we see that

$$
F^X(T, b, c) = \Phi\Big(\frac{b - \mu T}{\sqrt{T}}\Big) - e^{2\mu c}\Phi\Big(\frac{b - 2c - \mu T}{\sqrt{T}}\Big). \tag{7.49}
$$

Differentiating in b, c we find the random variable $(X(T), M^X(T))$ has bivariate density

$$
f^X(T, b, c) = \frac{2(2c - b)}{T\sqrt{T}} \phi\Big(\frac{2c - b}{\sqrt{T}}\Big) \cdot e^{\mu b - (1/2)\mu^2 T}.
$$

Finally consider the process

$$
Y(t) := \mu t + \sigma B(t), \quad \text{for } \sigma > 0.
$$

Note that the process $(\mu t - \sigma B(t), t \geq 0)$ has the same law as $(\mu t + \sigma B(t), t \geq 0)$, so we can take $\sigma > 0$.

Write $F^Y(T, b, c) = P(Y(T) < b, M^Y(T) < c)$. Consider

$$\widehat{X}(t) := \sigma^{-1} Y(t)$$
$$= (\mu/\sigma)t + B(t).$$

Then

$$P(Y(T) < b, M^Y(T) < c) = P(\widehat{X}(T) < (b/\sigma), M^{\widehat{X}}(T) < c/\sigma)$$

and from (7.49) this is

$$= \Phi\Big(\frac{b - \mu T}{\sigma\sqrt{T}}\Big) - e^{2\mu c \sigma^{-2}}\Phi\Big(\frac{b - 2c - \mu T}{\sigma\sqrt{T}}\Big). \tag{7.50}$$

Furthermore, $(Y(T), M^Y(T))$ has bivariate density

$$f^Y(T, b, c) = \frac{2(2c - b)}{\sigma T\sqrt{T}} \phi\Big(\frac{2c - b}{\sigma\sqrt{T}}\Big) \exp\Big((\mu b - \frac{1}{2}\mu^2 T)\sigma^{-2}\Big). \tag{7.51}$$

Remark 7.8.1. The preceding formulae enable us to derive the distribution of the first hitting time of level $y > 0$.

Write $\tau(y) = \inf_{t \geq 0}\{t : Y(t) \geq y\}$.

Lemma 7.8.2.

$$P(\tau(y) > T) = \Phi\Big(\frac{y - \mu T}{\sigma\sqrt{T}}\Big) - \exp\Big(\frac{2\mu y}{\sigma^2}\Big)\Phi\Big(\frac{-y - \mu T}{\sigma\sqrt{T}}\Big).$$

Proof. Clearly

$$\{\omega : \tau(y)(\omega) > t\} = \{\omega : M^Y(t)(\omega) < y\}$$

so

$$P(\tau(y) > t) = P\{\omega : M^Y(t)(\omega) < y\}$$
$$= P\{\omega : Y(t) < y, M^Y(t) < y\}$$
$$= F^Y(t, y, y)$$

and the result follows.   □

The Black–Scholes Model

Consider again the situation with two assets, the riskless bond

$$S_t^0 = e^{rt}$$

and a risky asset S^1 with dynamics

$$dS_t^1 = S_t^1 \big(\mu dt + \sigma dB(t) \big).$$

Here B is a standard Brownian motion on a probability space $(\Omega, \mathcal{F}, P)$. We consider the risk-neutral probability P^θ and the P^θ-Brownian motion W^θ given by

$$dW^\theta(t) = \theta dt + \sigma dB(t).$$

Here $\theta = (r - \mu)/\sigma$, and under P^θ,

$$dS_t^1 = S_t^1(rdt + \sigma dW^\theta(t))$$

so that

$$S_t^1 = S_0^1 \exp \big((r - \frac{\sigma^2}{2})t + \sigma W^\theta(t) \big)$$
$$= S_0^1 \exp Y(t),$$

where $Y(t) = (r - (\sigma^2/2))t + \sigma W^\theta(t)$. Write

$$\overline{S}^1(T) = \max [S_t^1 : 0 \le t \le T],$$
$$\underline{S}^1(T) = \min [S_t^1 : 0 \le t \le T].$$

Clearly, with

$$M^Y(T) = \max[Y(t) : 0 \le t \le T],$$
$$m^Y(T) = \min[Y(t) : 0 \le t \le T]$$

we have

$$\overline{S}^1(T) = S_0^1 \exp M^Y(T)$$
$$\underline{S}^1(T) = S_0^1 \exp m^Y(T).$$

Lemma 7.8.3. *Write*

$$d_1 = \Big(\log \Big(\frac{K}{S_0^1} \Big) - \Big(r - \frac{\sigma^2}{2} \Big) T \Big) / \sigma \sqrt{T},$$
$$d_2 = \Big(\log \Big(\frac{K S_0^1}{H^2} \Big) - \Big(r - \frac{\sigma^2}{2} \Big) T \Big) / \sigma \sqrt{T}.$$

Then

$$P^\theta \big(S_T^1 \le K, \overline{S}^1(T) \le H \big) = \Phi(d_1) - \Big(\frac{H}{S_0^1} \Big)^{(2r/\sigma^2)-1} \Phi(d_2).$$

Proof. $P^\theta(S_T^1 \leq K, \overline{S}^1(T) \leq H) = P^\theta(S_T^1 < K, \overline{S}^1(T) < H)$, by continuity,

$$= P^\theta\left(Y(T) \leq \log\left(\frac{K}{S_0^1}\right), M^Y(T) \leq \log\left(\frac{H}{S_0^1}\right)\right)$$

and the result follows from (7.50).   □

Remark 7.8.4. We assume $H > K$ because if $H \leq K$, then

$$P^\theta\left(S_T^1 \leq K, \overline{S}^1(T) \leq H\right) = P^\theta\left(S_T^1 \leq H, \overline{S}^1(T) \leq H\right),$$

which is a special case.

Furthermore, if $S_0^1 > H$ the probability is zero.

Lemma 7.8.5. *Write*

$$d_3 = \left(\log\left(\frac{S_0^1}{K}\right) + \left(r - \frac{\sigma^2}{2}\right)T\right)/\sigma\sqrt{T},$$

$$d_4 = \left(\log\left(\frac{H^2}{S_0^1 K}\right) + \left(r - \frac{\sigma^2}{2}\right)T\right)/\sigma\sqrt{T}.$$

Then

$$P^\theta\left(S_T^1 \geq K, \underline{S}^1(T) \geq H\right) = \Phi(d_3) - \left(\frac{H}{S_0^1}\right)^{(2r/\sigma^2)-1}\Phi(d_4).$$

Proof. $P^\theta(S_T^1 \geq K, \underline{S}^1(T) \geq H)$

$$= P^\theta\left(Y(T) \geq \log\left(\frac{K}{S_0^1}\right), m^Y(T) \geq \log\left(\frac{H}{S_0^1}\right)\right)$$

$$= P^\theta\left(-Y(T) \leq \log\left(\frac{S_0^1}{K}\right), M^{-Y}(T) \leq \log\left(\frac{S_0^1}{H}\right)\right).$$

Now $-Y(t) = (-r + (\sigma^2/2))t + \sigma(-B(t))$, and so has the same form as Y, because $-B$ is a standard Brownian motion. The result follows from (7.50).   □

Remark 7.8.6. Here $K > H$ and $S_0^1 > H$. If $K \leq H$ and $S_0^1 < H$ the same result is obtained with $K = H$ in (7.50). If $S_0^1 < H$, the probability is zero.

Lemma 7.8.7. *Write*

$$d_5 = \left(\log\left(\frac{K}{S_0^1}\right) - \left(r + \frac{\sigma^2}{2}\right)T\right)/\sigma\sqrt{T},$$

$$d_6 = \left(\log\left(\frac{K S_0^1}{H^2}\right) - \left(r + \frac{\sigma^2}{2}\right)T\right)/\sigma\sqrt{T}.$$

Then

$$E^\theta\left[S_T^1\left(I(S_T^1 \leq K, \overline{S}^1(T) \leq H)\right)\right]$$

$$= S_0^1\left(\exp rT\right)\left(\Phi(d_5) - \left(\frac{H}{S}\right)^{1+(2r/\sigma^2)}\Phi(d_6)\right).$$

Proof. Write

$$\Gamma(t) = \exp\left(\sigma W^\theta(t) - \frac{1}{2}\sigma^2 t\right)$$

and define a new probability P^θ by setting

$$\frac{dP^\sigma}{dP^\theta}\bigg|_{\mathcal{F}_T} = \Gamma(T).$$

Girsanov's theorem states that, under P^σ, W^σ is a standard Brownian motion, where

$$dW^\sigma = dW^\theta - \sigma\, dt.$$

Consequently, under P^σ,

$$Y(t) = \left(r + \frac{\sigma^2}{2}\right)t + \sigma W^\sigma(t).$$

Therefore

$$E^\theta\left[S_T^1 I(S_t^1 \le K, \overline{S}^1(T) \le H)\right]$$
$$= S_0^1 e^{rT} E^\theta\left[\Gamma(T)\, I\left(Y(T) \le \log\left(\frac{K}{S_0^1}\right),\, M^Y(T) \le \log\left(\frac{H}{S_0^1}\right)\right)\right]$$
$$= S_0^1 e^{rT} E^\theta\left[I\left(Y(T) \le \log\left(\frac{K}{S_0^1}\right),\, M^Y(T) \le \log\left(\frac{H}{S_0^1}\right)\right)\right]$$

and the result follows from Lemma 7.8.3. $\square$

Lemma 7.8.8. *Write*

$$d_7 = \left(\log\left(\frac{S_0^1}{K}\right) + \left(r + \frac{\sigma^2}{2}\right)T\right)/\sigma\sqrt{T},$$
$$d_8 = \left(\log\left(\frac{H^2}{KS_0^1}\right) + \left(r + \frac{\sigma^2}{2}\right)T\right)/\sigma\sqrt{T}.$$

Then

$$E^\theta\left[S_T^1 I(S_T^1 \ge K,\, \underline{S}^1(T) \ge H)\right]$$
$$= S_0^1 e^{rT}\left[\Phi(d_7) - \left(\frac{H}{S_0^1}\right)^{1+(2r/\sigma^2)}\Phi(d_8)\right].$$

Proof. The proof is similar to that of Lemma 7.8.7. $\square$

Remark 7.8.9. In the following we determine the expressions for prices $V(0)$ as functions $f(S,T)$ of the price $S = S_0^1$ at time 0 of the risky asset and the time T to expiration. The price at any time $t < T$ when the price is S_t^1 is then

$$V(t) = f(S_t^1, T - t).$$

Definition 7.8.10. A *down and out call option* with strike price K, expiration time T, and barrier H gives the holder the right (but not the obligation) to buy S^1 for price K at time T provided the price S^1 at no time fell below H (in which case the option ceases to exist).

Its price is sometimes denoted

$$C_{t,T}(K|H \downarrow O)$$

and it corresponds to a payoff $(S_T^1 - K)^+ I(\underline{S}(T) \geq H)$. The $\downarrow$ denotes "down" and the O "out." From our pricing formula

$$
\begin{aligned}
C_{0,T}(K|H \downarrow O) &= e^{-rT} E^\theta \left[(S_T^1 - K)^+ I\big(\underline{S}^1(T) \geq H\big) \right] \\
&= e^{-rT} E^\theta \left[S_T^1 I\big(S_T^1 \geq K, \, \underline{S}^1(T) \geq H\big) \right] \\
&\quad - e^{-rT} K E^\theta \left[I\big(S_T^1 \geq K, \, \underline{S}^1(T) \geq H\big) \right].
\end{aligned}
$$

The right side is then given by Lemmas 7.8.5 and 7.8.8 as

$$
S_0^1 \left[\Phi(d_7) - \left(\frac{H}{S_0^1} \right)^{1+(2r/\sigma^2)} \Phi(d_8) \right] - e^{-rT} K \left[\Phi(d_3) - \left(\frac{H}{S_0^1} \right)^{(2r/\sigma^2)-1} \Phi(d_4) \right].
$$

$$(7.52)$$

Definition 7.8.11. An *up and out call option* gives the holder the right to buy S^1 for strike price K at time T provided that the price S_t^1 does not rise above H (in which case the option ceases to exist).

Its price is denoted by $C_{t,T}(K|H \uparrow O)$ and corresponds to a payoff $(S_T^1 - K)^+ I(\overline{S}^1(T) \leq H)$.

$$
\begin{aligned}
C_{0,T}(K|H \uparrow O) &= e^{-rT} E^\theta \left[(S_T^1 - K) I\big(S_T^1 \geq K, \, \overline{S}^1(T) \leq H\big) \right] \\
&= e^{-rT} E^\theta \left[S_T^1 I\big(S_T^1 \geq K, \, \overline{S}^1(T) \leq H\big) \right] \\
&\quad - e^{-rT} K E^\theta \left[I\big(S_T^1 \geq K, \, \overline{S}^1(T) \leq H\big) \right].
\end{aligned}
$$

Now, with $p = 0$ or 1,

$$
\begin{aligned}
E^\theta \left[(S_T^1)^p I\big(S_T^1 \geq K, \, \overline{S}^1(T) \leq H\big) \right] &= E^\theta \left[(S_T^1)^p I\big(\overline{S}^1(T) \leq H\big) \right] \\
&\quad - E^\theta \left[(S_T^1)^p I\big(S_T^1 < K, \, \overline{S}^1(T) \leq H\big) \right]
\end{aligned}
$$

and

$$
E^\theta \left[(S_T^1)^p I\big(\overline{S}^1 \leq H\big) \right] = E^\theta \left[(S_T^1)^p I\big(S_T^1 \leq H, \, \overline{S}^1(T) \leq H\big) \right].
$$

The price $C_{0,T}(K|H \uparrow O)$ is, therefore, again given by the formula of Lemmas 7.8.5 and 7.8.7.

Definition 7.8.12. An *up and in call option* gives the holder the right to buy S^1 at time T for strike price K provided that at some time before T the price S^1_t becomes greater than H; otherwise the option does not yet exist.

Its price is denoted by $C_{t,T}(K|H \uparrow I)$. It corresponds to a payoff $(S^1_T - K)^+ I(\overline{S}^1(T) \geq H)$. Now

$$C_{t,T}(K|H \uparrow I) + C_{t,T}(K|H \uparrow O) = C_{t,T}(K),$$

where $C_{t,T}(K)$ is the usual European call option price at time t given by

$$C_{t,T}(K) = S^1_t \Phi(\delta_1(t)) - Ke^{-r(T-t)} \Phi(\delta_2(t)).$$

Here

$$\delta_1(t) = \left(\log\left(\frac{S^1_t}{K}\right) + \left(r + \frac{\sigma^2}{2}\right)(T-t) \right)/\sigma\sqrt{T-t},$$

$$\delta_2(t) = \left(\log\left(\frac{S^1_t}{K}\right) + \left(r - \frac{\sigma^2}{2}\right)(T-t) \right)/\sigma\sqrt{T-t}.$$

Definition 7.8.13. A *down and in call option* gives the holder the right to buy S^1 for a strike price K at time T provided that at some time $t \leq T$ the price S^1_t fell below H; otherwise the option does not yet exist.

Its price is denoted by $C_{t,T}(K|H \downarrow I)$. It corresponds to a payoff

$$(S^1_T - K)^+ I(\underline{S}^1(T) \leq H).$$

Again

$$C_{t,T}(K|H \downarrow I) + C_{t,T}(K|H \downarrow O) = C_{t,T}(K).$$

Remark 7.8.14. All the corresponding put options can be defined and prices similarly. To give one example, the down and out put has a price $P_{t,T}(K|H \downarrow O)$ and corresponds to a payoff

$$(K - S^1_T)^+ I(\underline{S}^1(T) \geq H).$$

Then

$$(K - S^1_T)^+ I(\underline{S}^1(T) \geq H) = (S^1_T - K)^+ I(\underline{S}^1(T) \geq H)$$
$$- (S^1_T - K)I(\underline{S}^1(T) \geq H)$$

so

$$P_{0,T}(K|H \downarrow O) = C_{0,T}(K|H \downarrow O) - e^{-rT} E^\theta\left[S^1_T I(\underline{S}^1(T) \geq H)\right]$$
$$+ Ke^{-rT} E^\theta\left[I(\underline{S}^1(T) \geq H)\right].$$

Then, with $p = 0$ or 1,

$$E^\theta\left[(S_T^1)^p I(\underline{S}^1(T) \geq H)\right]$$
$$= E^\theta\left[(S_T^1)^p I(S_T^1 \geq H, \underline{S}^1(T) \geq H)\right]$$

and the result follows from Lemmas 7.8.5 and 7.8.7.

Again we have the identity

$$P_{t,T}(K|H \downarrow O) + P_{t,T}(K|H \downarrow I) = P_{t,T}(K),$$

where $P_{t,T}(K)$ is the usual European put price given by the Black–Scholes formula. In fact, from the call–put parity

$$C_{t,T}(K) - P_{t,T}(K) = S_t^1 - e^{-r(T-t)}K.$$

Definition 7.8.15. A *lookback call option* corresponds to a payoff function

$$h_3(S^1) = S_T^1 - \underline{S}^1(T).$$

A *lookback put option* corresponds to a payoff function

$$h_4(S^1) = \overline{S}^1(T) - S_T^1.$$

The price of a lookback put at time 0 is therefore,

$$V_p(0) = e^{-rT} E^\theta[\overline{S}^1(T) - S_T^1]$$
$$= e^{-rT} S_0^1[E^\theta(\exp M^Y(T)) - e^{rT}],$$

where $Y(t) = (r - (\sigma^2/2))t + \sigma W^\theta(t)$. From (7.52) the density of the random variable $M^Y(T)$ is, with $\mu = r - \sigma^2/2$,

$$f^M(c) = \int_{-\infty}^{\infty} f^Y(T, b, c)db$$
$$= \Phi\left(\frac{c - \mu T}{\sigma\sqrt{T}}\right) - \frac{2\mu}{\sigma^2} \exp\left(\frac{2\mu c}{\sigma^2}\right)\Phi\left(\frac{-c - \mu T}{\sigma\sqrt{T}}\right)$$
$$+ \exp\left(\frac{2\mu c}{\sigma^2}\right)\Phi\left(\frac{c + \mu T}{\sigma\sqrt{T}}\right).$$

Therefore, the lookback put price at time 0 is:

$$V_p(0) = S_0^1\left\{e^{-rT}\int_{-\infty}^{\infty} f^M(c)dc - 1\right\}.$$

Completing the square and integrating we obtain, with $d = ((2r + \sigma^2)/2\sigma\sqrt{T})$,

$$V_p(0) = S_0^1\left\{\Phi(-d) + e^{-rT}\Phi(-d + \sigma\sqrt{T})\right.$$
$$\left. + \frac{\sigma^2}{2r} e^{-rT}\left[-\Phi\left(d - \frac{2r}{\sigma}\sqrt{T}\right) + e^{-rT}\Phi(d)\right]\right\}.$$

Similarly, it can be shown (see [36]) that the price of the lookback call option at time 0 is:

$$V_C(0) = S_0^1 \Big\{ \Phi(d) - e^{-rT}\Phi(-d + \sigma\sqrt{T}) $$
$$+ \frac{\sigma^2}{2r} e^{-rT}\Big[\Phi\Big(-d + \frac{2r}{\sigma}\sqrt{T}\Big) - e^{-rT}\Phi(-d)\Big]\Big\}.$$

Partial Differential Equations

In the Black–Scholes framework the riskless bond has a price $S_t^0 = e^{rT}$ and the risky asset has dynamics

$$dS_t^1 = S_t^1(r\,dt + \sigma\,dW^\theta)$$

under the risk-neutral measure P^θ. Consider a European claim with expiration time T of the form $h(S_T)$. Here h is C^2 and $|h(s)| \le K(1+|s|^\beta)$ for some $\beta > 0$.

We have shown that the price of this claim at time t is

$$V_{t,T}(S_t^1) = E^\theta[e^{-r(T-t)}h(S_T^1)|\mathcal{F}_t]$$
$$= E^\theta[e^{-r(T-t)}h(S_T^1)|S_t^1].$$

Consequently $e^{-rt}V_{t,T}(S_t^1) = E^\theta[e^{-rT}h(S_T^1)|\mathcal{F}_t]$ and so is an $(\mathcal{F}_t, P^\theta)$ martingale. (Indeed, every discounted price process is a martingale.) Now $S_T^1 = S_T^1 \exp\big((r - (\sigma^2/2))(T - t) + \sigma(W_T^\theta - W_t^\theta)\big)$ and h is C^2, so (by differentiating under the expectation) $V_{t,T}(x)$ is a $C^{1,2}$ function. Applying the Itô rule

$$e^{-rt}V_{t,T}(S_t^1) = V_{0,T}(S_0^1)$$
$$+ \int_0^t \Big(\frac{\partial V}{\partial u} + rS_u^1\frac{\partial V}{\partial S} + \frac{\sigma^2}{2}(S_u^1)^2\frac{\partial^2 V}{\partial S^2} - rV\Big)(u, S_u^1)e^{-ru}du$$
$$+ \int_0^t \sigma S_u^1 \frac{\partial V}{\partial S}(u, S_u^1)\,dW_u^\theta. \tag{7.53}$$

Note $e^{-rt}V_{t,T}(S_t^1)$ is a martingale; consequently the du-integral in (7.53) must be the identically zero process.

Consequently, the European option price $V_{t,T}(x)$ satisfies the partial differential equation

$$LV = \frac{\partial V}{\partial t} + rS\frac{\partial V}{\partial S} + \frac{\sigma^2}{2}S^2\frac{\partial^2 V}{\partial S^2} - rV = 0, \quad 0 \le t < T \tag{7.54}$$

with terminal condition $V_{T,T}(s) = h(s)$. This is often called the Black–Scholes equation.

The representation of the option price and

$$V_{t,T}(S) = E^\theta \left[e^{-r(T-t)} h(S_T^1) | S_t^1 = S \right]$$

corresponds to the famous Feynman–Kac formula (see [164]). As the solution (7.54), with the boundary condition $V_{T,T}(s) = h(s)$, is unique the partial differential equation approach to option pricing investigates numerical solutions to this equation. However, for the vanilla European option, with $h(S) = (S - K)^+$ for a call, or $(K - S)^+$ for a put, the exact solution is given by the Black–Scholes formula.

We note from (7.53), or Theorem 7.6.1, that the amount H_t^1 invested in the risky asset is $(\partial/\partial x)V_{t,T}(S_t^1)$, which is the partial derivative of the option with respect to the price of the underlying asset evaluated at the price of the asset. It is called the *Delta* of the option

$$\Delta := \frac{\partial V}{\partial S}.$$

If one considered a portfolio consisting of shorting an option and holding an amount of stock S^1, investing $\Delta = \partial V/\partial S$ in S^1 at each time t would make the portfolio riskless. This method of investing is known as delta hedging. However, as the portfolio is then only instantaneously riskless it can be kept riskless only by continuous adjustment. This is a mathematical idealization and, furthermore, ignores such frictions as transaction costs which are present in the real world.

Other important quantities are the other derivatives of the option price:

$$\text{Gamma} \quad \Gamma = \frac{\partial^2 V}{\partial S^2},$$

$$\text{Theta} \quad \Theta = \frac{\partial V}{\partial t},$$

$$\text{Rho} \quad \rho = \frac{\partial V}{\partial r},$$

$$\text{Vega} \quad \frac{\partial V}{\partial \sigma}.$$

Collectively these derivatives are known as the 'Greeks' (although there is no Greek letter 'vega' that is the term used).

The preceding derivation was made under the assumption that h is C^2. Approximating by C^2 functions establishes the result for payoff functions h that are not necessarily C^2 in S. In particular, the European call option $C_{t,T}(K)(S)$ is a solution of (7.54) with terminal condition

$$C_{T,T}(K)(S) = (S - K)^+.$$

Now if $V(t, S)$ satisfies $LV = 0$ it can be checked that $L(S^{2-(2r/\sigma^2)}V(t, \frac{C}{S})) = 0$ for any constant $C > 0$.

The partial differential equation methods can also be applied to barrier options. From formula (7.52) we see the price of the down and out option is, in fact,

$$C_{t,T}(K|H \downarrow O)(S) = C_{t,T}(K)(S) - \left(\frac{H}{S}\right)^{-1+(2r/\sigma^2)} C_{t,T}(K)\left(\frac{H^2}{S}\right).$$

Consequently, $C_{t,T}(K|H \downarrow O)(S)$ is a solution of (7.54) satisfying appropriate boundary conditions.

There are analogous representations for the other barrier options.

8

The American Option

8.1 Extended Trading Strategies

As in Chapter 7, we suppose there is an underlying probability space $(\Omega, \mathcal{F}, Q)$. The time parameter t takes values in $[0, T]$. There is a filtration $\mathbb{F} = \{\mathcal{F}_t\}$ that satisfies the 'usual conditions' (see Chapter 6, page 99).

We assume as before that the market is *frictionless*; that is, there are no transaction costs or taxes, restrictions on short sales and trading can take place at any t in $[0, T]$.

We suppose there is a savings account S^0 with constant interest rate r, such that

$$dS_t^0 = rS_t^0 dt. \tag{8.1}$$

As usual, we take $S_0^0 = 1$.

In addition we suppose there is a risky asset S^1 whose dynamics are given by the usual log-normal equation:

$$dS_t^1 = S_t^1(\mu dt + \sigma dW_t). \tag{8.2}$$

Here, W is a standard Brownian motion on $(\Omega, \mathcal{F}, Q)$. μ is the appreciation rate and σ is the volatility of S_t^1.

Recall (see Elliott [87], Definition 2.30) that a process $(t, \omega) \rightarrow \phi_t(\omega)$ from $([0, T] \times \Omega, \mathcal{B}([0, T] \times \mathcal{F}))$ to a measurable space $(E, \mathcal{E})$ is said to be *progressively measurable*, or progressive, if for every $t \in [0, T]$ the map $(s, \omega) \rightarrow \phi_s(\omega)$ of $[0, t] \times \Omega$ to E is measurable with respect to the σ-field $\mathcal{B}([0, t]) \times \mathcal{F}_t$.

A trading strategy is a process $\pi_t = (\pi_t^0, \pi_t^1)$ that is adapted and which satisfies

$$\int_0^T (\pi_u^i)^2 (S_u^i)^2 du < \infty \text{ a.s.}$$

The amount (π^i) is the amount held, or shorted, in units of the savings account $(i = 0)$, or stock $(i = 1)$. A short position in the savings account is a loan.

A consumption process is a progressive, continuous nondecreasing process C.

What investment and consumption processes are admissible? Such a triple of processes (π^0, π^1, C) is admissible if the corresponding wealth process is self-financing. The wealth process is

$$V_t(\pi) = \pi_t^0 S_t^0 + \pi_t^1 S_t^1.$$

We saw in Section 7.4 that this is self-financing if

$$\pi_t^0 S_t^0 + \pi_t^1 S_t^1 = \pi_0^0 + \pi_0^1 S_0^1 + \int_0^t \pi_u^0 dS_u^0 + \int_0^t \pi_u^1 dS_u^1 - C_t \qquad (8.3)$$

for $t \in [0, T]$, with $C_0 = 0$ a.s.

We note that equation (8.3) states that all changes in total wealth come from changes in the stock price, plus interest on the savings account less the amount consumed, C_t.

It can be shown (see, e.g., Delbaen and Schachermayer [59]) that there are essentially no arbitrage opportunities in the model if and only if there is an equivalent probability measure $\widetilde{Q}$ (a martingale measure) such that S_t^1 / S_t^0 is a martingale under $\widetilde{Q}$. We assume the existence of $\widetilde{Q}$ throughout this chapter without further comment. For the dynamics (8.1), (8.2) the martingale measure $\widetilde{Q}$ is defined by setting

$$\frac{d\widetilde{Q}}{dQ} \bigg|_{\mathcal{F}_t} = \Lambda_t,$$

where $\Lambda_t = \exp\left(((r - \mu)/\sigma) W_t - \frac{1}{2} (((r - \mu)/\sigma))^2 t\right)$. Under $\widetilde{Q}$, $\widetilde{W}_t$ is a standard Brownian motion, where

$$\widetilde{W}_t = W_t - \left(\frac{r - \mu}{\sigma}\right) t \qquad \text{and} \qquad dS_t^1 = S_t^1 (r dt + \sigma d\widetilde{W}_t). \qquad (8.4)$$

In the remainder of this chapter we work under the probability $\widetilde{Q}$, so the stock price has dynamics (8.4) and the wealth process $V_t(\pi)$ satisfies

$$V_t(\pi) = V_0(\pi) + \int_0^t r V_u(\pi) du + \int_0^t \sigma \pi_u^1 S_u^1 d\widetilde{W}_u - C_t \quad \text{a.s.} \qquad (8.5)$$

Definition 8.1.1. A *reward function* ψ is a continuous non-negative function on $\mathbb{R}^+ \times [0,T]$. We suppose ψ is in $C^{1,0}$ and piecewise in $C^{2,1}$. The latter condition means there is a partition of $\mathbb{R}^+$ into intervals in the interior of which ψ is $C^{2,1}$ in x. We require that, where defined, all the functions ψ, $\partial\psi/\partial x$, $\partial^2\psi/\partial x^2$, $\partial\psi/\partial t$ have polynomial growth as $x \to +\infty$.

Definition 8.1.2. An *American option* with reward ψ is a security that pays the amount $\psi(S_t, t)$ when exercised at time t.

If one sells such a claim one accepts the obligation to pay $\psi(S_t, t)$ to the buyer at any time $t \in [0,T]$. The final time T is the expiry date.

Recall, as in Chapter 1, that examples are the

American call option: $\qquad\qquad \psi(S_t, t) = (S_t - K)^+,$

American put option: $\qquad\qquad \psi(S_t, t) = (K - S_t)^+,$

American straddle (bottom version): $\quad \psi(S_t, t) = |S_t - K|.$

Having introduced this new financial instrument, the American option, into the market it is expedient to extend the notion of trading strategy. Recall $P(x,t) = P(x) = P_t = P$ denotes the value process of the American option.

Definition 8.1.3. For any stopping time $\tau \in \mathcal{T}_{0,T}$ a *buy-and-hold strategy* in the option P is a pair (π^2, τ), where π^2 is the process

$$\pi^2(t) := kI_{[0,\tau]}(t), \quad t \in [0,T].$$

The associated position in P is then $\pi^2(t)P(x,t)$. This means that k units of the American option security are purchased (or shorted if $k < 0$) at time 0 and held until time τ. Π^+ (resp., Π^-) is the set of buy-and-hold strategies in P for which $k \geq 0$ (resp., $k < 0$).

Write $\widehat{\pi}$ for a triple (π^0, π^1, π^2).

An *extended admissible trading strategy* in (S^0, S^1, P) is then a collection $(\pi^0, \pi^1, \pi^2, \tau)$ such that (π^0, π^1) is an admissible trading strategy in S^0, S^1, (π^2, τ) is a buy-and-hold strategy in P, and on the interval $(\tau, T]$:

$$\pi_t^0 = \pi_\tau^0 + \pi_\tau^1 S_\tau^1/S_\tau^0 + \pi_\tau^2 \psi(S_\tau, \tau)/S_\tau^0,$$
$$\pi_t^1 = 0, \qquad \pi_t^2 = 0.$$

This means that, using the extended strategy $\widehat{\pi} = (\pi^0, \pi^1, \pi^2)$, at time τ we liquidate the stock and option accounts and invest everything in the riskless bond (savings account). $(\widehat{\pi}, \tau)$ is now self-financing if with a consumption process C_t,

$$\pi_t^0 S_t^0 + \pi_t^1 S_t^1 = \pi_0^0 + \pi_0^1 S_0^1 + \int_0^t \pi_u^0 dS_u^0 + \int_0^t \pi_u^1 dS_u^1 - C_t \quad \text{a.s.} \quad \text{for } t \in [0,\tau]$$

and

$$\int_\tau^t dC_u = 0 \quad \text{a.s.} \quad \text{for } t \in [0,\tau].$$

That is, C is constant on $(\tau, T]$.

Notation 8.1.4. The set of extended admissible trading strategies in (S^0, S^1, P) is denoted by $\mathcal{A}$.

Definition 8.1.5. There is said to be *arbitrage* in the market if either

$$\exists\, (\pi^2, \tau) \in \Pi^+ \quad \text{with} \quad (\pi^0, \pi^1, C)$$

such that

$$\begin{aligned}
(\pi, \tau) \in \mathcal{A} \quad &\text{and} \quad \pi_0^0 + \pi_0^1 S_0^1 + \pi_0^2 V_0 < 0 \\
&\text{and} \quad \pi_T^0 S_T^0 \geq 0 \quad \text{a.s.,}
\end{aligned} \tag{8.6}$$

or $\exists\, (\pi^2, \tau) \in \Pi^-$ with (π^0, π^1, C) such that

$$\begin{aligned}
(\pi, \tau) \in \mathcal{A} \quad &\text{and} \quad \pi_0^0 + \pi_0^1 S_0^1 + \pi_0^2 V_0 < 0 \\
&\text{and} \quad \pi_T^0 S_T^0 \geq 0 \quad \text{a.s.}
\end{aligned} \tag{8.7}$$

Statement (8.6) means it is possible to hold an American option and find an exercise policy that gives riskless profits.

Conversely, statement (8.7) means it is possible to sell the American option and be able to make riskless profits for every exercise policy option of the buyer.

Statements (8.6) and (8.7) define arbitrage opportunities for the buyer or seller, respectively, of an American option. Our assumption is that arbitrage is not possible and the fundamental question is: what price should be paid today (time t) for such an option?

Our discussion concentrates on the American put option.

(We showed in Chapter 1, using simple arbitrage arguments, that the price of an American call on a stock that does not pay dividends is equal to the price of the European call (cf. Merton [190]).)

8.2   Analysis of American Put Options

Notation 8.2.1. $\mathcal{T}_{t_1 t_2}$ denotes the set of all stopping times that take values in $[t_1, t_2]$.

Lemma 8.2.2. *Consider the process*

$$X_t = \operatorname{ess.sup}_{\tau \in \mathcal{T}_{t,T}} \widetilde{E}[e^{-r(\tau - t)}(K - S_\tau)^+ | \mathcal{F}_t] \tag{8.8}$$

defined for $t \in [0, T]$. (That is, X_t is the supremum of the random variables $\widetilde{E}[e^{-r(\tau-t)}(K - S_\tau)^+ | \mathcal{F}_t]$ for $\tau \in \mathcal{T}_{t,T}$, in the complete lattice $L^1(\Omega, \mathcal{F}_t, \widetilde{Q})$.)

*Then there are admissible strategies π^0, π^1 and a consumption process C
such that with $V_t(\pi)$ given by (8.5),*

$$X_t = V_t(\pi).$$

Proof (Karatzas [153]). Define

$$J_t = \text{ess.sup}_{\tau \in T_{t,T}} \ \widetilde{E}[e^{-r\tau}(K - S_\tau)^+ | \mathcal{F}_t] \quad \text{a.s.}$$

Then J is a supermartingale, and, in fact, J is the smallest supermartingale
that majorizes the discounted reward $e^{-r\tau}(K - S_\tau)^+$. J is called the *Snell
envelope* (cf. Chapter 5 for the discrete case). $\qquad\square$

Recall (see Elliott [87], Chapter 8) that a right-continuous supermartingale X is said to be of class D if the set of random variables X_τ is uniformly
integrable, where τ is any stopping time.

Furthermore, J is right continuous, has left limits, is regular, and is of
class D (in fact J is bounded). Consequently (see Elliott [87]), J has a
Doob–Meyer decomposition as the difference of a (right-continuous) martingale M and a predictable increasing process A

$$J_t = M_t - A_t. \tag{8.9}$$

Here M is a $(\widetilde{Q}, \mathcal{F}_t)$ martingale and A is a unique, predictable continuous
non-decreasing process with $A_0 = 0$. From the martingale representation
theorem we can write

$$M_t = J_0 + \int_0^t \eta_u d\widetilde{W}_u$$

for some progressively measurable process η with

$$\int_0^T \eta_u^2 du < \infty \text{ a.s.}$$

Consequently,

$$X_t = e^{rt} J_t$$

and

$$dX_t = re^{rt} J_t dt + e^{rt} \eta_t d\widetilde{W}_t - e^{rt} dA_t.$$

Therefore, $X_t = V_t(\pi)$ if we take

$$\pi_t^0 = e^{rt} J_t - e^{rt} \sigma^{-1} \eta_t, \quad \pi_t^1 = e^{rt} \eta_t \sigma^{-1} (S_t^1)^{-1}$$

and

$$dC_t = e^{rt} dA_t. \tag{8.10}$$

Remark 8.2.3. Note that $X_t \geq (K - S_t)^+$ a.s. for $t \in [0, T]$, and

$$X_T = (K - S_T)^+ \text{ a.s.} \tag{8.11}$$

Also, τ^* is said to be an *optimal stopping time* if $J_t = \widetilde{E}[e^{-r\tau^*}(K - S_{\tau^*})^+ | \mathcal{F}_t]$.

We can now establish the following result.

Notation 8.2.4. Write

$$\rho_t = \inf \{ u \in [t, T] : J_u = e^{-ru}(K - S_u)^+ \}.$$

That is, ρ_t is the first time in $[t, T]$ that J falls to the level of the discounted reward.

From the work of El Karoui [77] we know that (analogously to the results in Chapter 5):

1) ρ_t is an optimal stopping time on $[t, T]$;

2) A, in the decomposition (8.9), is constant on the interval $[t, \rho_t]$;

3) the stopped process $(J_{s \wedge \rho_t}, t \leq s \leq T)$ is a martingale on $[t, T]$.

Theorem 8.2.5. *Taking the price of the American put option at time $t = 0$ to be X_0 is necessary and sufficient for there to be no arbitrage.*

Proof. Suppose the market price of the American put option were $Y_0 > X_0$.

Consider the trading strategies π^0, π^1, and C given by (8.7). For any stopping time $\tau \in \mathcal{T}_{0,T}$, and with $k = -1$, consider the buy-and-hold strategy

$$\pi_t^2 = -I_{[0,\tau]}(t).$$

Construct the extended trading strategy: $\widehat{\pi}_t = (\widehat{\pi}_t^0, \widehat{\pi}_t^1, \widehat{\pi}_t^2)$ by setting:

$$\widehat{\pi}_t^0 = \pi_t^0 \qquad\qquad t \in [0, \tau]$$
$$\pi_\tau^0 + \pi_\tau^1 e^{-r\tau} S_\tau^1 - (K - S_\tau)^+ e^{-r\tau} \quad t \in (\tau, T]$$
$$\widehat{\pi}_t^1 = \pi_t^1 I_{[0,\tau]}(t)$$
$$\widehat{\pi}_t^2 = \pi_t^2 = -I_{[0,\tau]}(t),$$

with a consumption process

$$\widehat{C}_t = C_{t \wedge \tau}.$$

From the hedging property (8.10)

$$X_\tau = \pi_\tau^0 e^{r\tau} + \pi_\tau^1 S_\tau^1 \geq (K - S_\tau)^+ \text{ a.s.}$$

we see that

$$e^{rT}\widehat{\pi}_T^0 \geq 0 \text{ a.s.}$$

However, by definition

$$\widehat{\pi}_0^0 + \widehat{\pi}_0^1 S_0 + \widehat{\pi}_0^2 Y_0 = X_0 - Y_0 < 0.$$

We would, therefore, have an arbitrage opportunity.

Now suppose $Y_0 < X_0$. Take π^0, π^1, and C as in (8.9), and use the optimal stopping time ρ_0 of Notation 8.2.4. Construct the following extended trading strategy

$$\widehat{\pi}_t^0 = -\pi_t^0 \qquad\qquad t \in [0, \rho_0]$$
$$\quad -\pi_{\rho_0}^0 - \pi_{\rho_0}^1 e^{-r\rho_0} S_{\rho_0}^1 + (K - S_{\rho_0})^+ e^{-r\rho_0}, \quad t \in (\rho_0, T].$$
$$\widehat{\pi}_t^1 = -\pi_t^1 I_{[0,\rho_0]}(t)$$
$$\widehat{\pi}_t^2 = I_{[0,\rho_0]}(t)$$

with the consumption process

$$\widehat{C}_t = -C_{t \wedge \rho_0}.$$

However, we know $C = \widehat{C} \equiv 0$ on $[0, \rho_0]$ (see the remarks after Notation 8.2.4), and from the definition of ρ_0,

$$\pi_{\rho_0}^0 e^{r\rho_0} + \pi_{\rho_0}^1 S_{\rho_0}^1 = (K - S_{\rho_0})^+.$$

Therefore, $\widehat{\pi}_T^0 S_T^0 = 0$ but

$$\widehat{\pi}_0^0 + \widehat{\pi}_0^1 S_0^0 + \widehat{\pi}_0^2 Y_0 = Y_0 - X_0 < 0.$$

Again there is arbitrage.

Furthermore, from Lemma 8.2.2, $X_t = V_t(\pi)$ is a martingale under $\widetilde{Q}$ up to time ρ_0 so X_0 is the fair price at time 0 for the American put option. □

Definition 8.2.6. For $t \in [0,T]$ and $x \in \mathbb{R}^+$ define

$$P(x,t) = \sup_{\tau \in \mathcal{T}_{t,T}} \widetilde{E}[e^{-r(\tau-t)}(K - S_\tau)^+ | S_t = x]. \qquad (8.12)$$

Then $P(x,t)$ is the value function and represents the fair, or arbitrage-free, price of the American put at time t.

From Theorem 3.1.10 of Krylov [171] we can state the following:

Theorem 8.2.7. *The first optimal stopping time after time t is*

$$\rho_t = \inf\{u \in [t,T] : P(S_u, u) = (K - S_u)^+\}.$$

It is important to represent (8.12) using analytical methods.

Lemma 8.2.8. *The American put value $P(x,t)$ is convex and nonincreasing in $x > 0$ for every $t \in [0,T]$. The function $P(x,t)$ is nonincreasing in t for every $x \in \mathbb{R}^+$. The function $P(x,t)$ is continuous on $\mathbb{R}^+ \times [0,T]$.*

Proof. The convexity of $P(\cdot, t)$ follows from the supremum operation, and the nonincreasing properties of $P(\cdot, t)$ and $P(x, \cdot)$ are immediate from the definition.

For $(t_i, x_i) \in \mathbb{R}^+ \times [0,T]$, $i = 1, 2$ we have

$$
\begin{aligned}
P(x_2, t_2) - P(x_1, t_1) &= \sup_{\tau \in \mathcal{T}_{t_2,T}} \widetilde{E}[e^{-r(\tau-t_2)}(K - S_\tau)^+ | S_{t_2} = x_2] \\
&\quad - \sup_{\tau \in \mathcal{T}_{t_2,T}} \widetilde{E}[e^{-r(\tau-t_1)}(K - S_\tau)^+ | S_{t_1} = x_1] \\
&\quad + \sup_{\tau \in \mathcal{T}_{t_2,T}} \widetilde{E}[e^{-r(\tau-t_1)}(K - S_\tau)^+ | S_{t_1} = x_1] \\
&\quad - \sup_{\tau \in \mathcal{T}_{t_1,T}} \widetilde{E}[e^{-r(\tau-t_1)}(K - S_\tau)^+ | S_{t_1} = x_1].
\end{aligned}
$$

Therefore,

$$
\begin{aligned}
|P(x_2, t_2) - P(x_1, t_1)| \\
&\leq \widetilde{E}\left[\sup_{t_2 \leq s \leq T} \left| e^{-r(s-t_2)}(K - S_s^{t_2,x_2}) - e^{-r(s-t_1)}(K - S_s^{t_1,x_2})^+ \right| \right] \\
&\quad + \widetilde{E}\left[\sup_{t_1 \leq s \leq t_2} \left| e^{-r(s-t_1)}(K - S_s^{t_1,x_1})^+ - e^{-r(t_2-t_1)}(K - S_s^{t_1,x_2})^+ \right| \right]
\end{aligned}
$$

and the result follows from the continuity properties of the flow. □

Definition 8.2.9. Consider the two sets

$$
\begin{aligned}
\mathcal{C} &= \{(x,t) \in \mathbb{R}^+ \times [0,T) | P(x,t) > (K - x)^+\}, \\
\mathcal{S} &= \{(x,t) \in \mathbb{R}^+ \times [0,T) | P(x,t) = (K - x)^+\}.
\end{aligned}
$$

$\mathcal{C}$ is called the *continuation region* and $\mathcal{S}$ is the *stopping region*.

Then $\rho_t = \inf\{u \in [t,T] : S_t \notin \mathcal{C}\}$. We now establish some properties of P and $\mathcal{C}$.

Lemma 8.2.10. $P(x,t) > 0$ *for all $x \geq 0$, $t \in [0,T]$.*

Proof. Note $(K - x)^+ > 0$ for $x < K$.

Let t be fixed and consider the solution of $dS_u^1 = S_u^1(\mu dt + \sigma dW_u)$ such that $S_t^1 = x$.

Write $\tau_{K/2} = \inf\{u \geq t : S_u^1 \leq K/2\} \wedge T$. Then if $x \geq K$, from (8.12),

$$
\begin{aligned}
P(x,t) &\geq (K/2)E[e^{-\tau_{K/2}} I(\tau_{K/2} < T)] \\
&> 0.
\end{aligned}
$$

□

The following two results are adapted from Jacka [136].

Lemma 8.2.11. *For each $t > 0$ the t-section of $\mathcal{C}$, $\mathcal{C}_t$, is defined as*

$$
\begin{aligned}
\mathcal{C}_t :&= \{x : (x,t) \in \mathcal{C}\} \\
&= \{x : (x,t) \in \mathbb{R}^+ \times [0,T),\ P(x,t) > (K-x)^+\} \\
&= (S_t^*, \infty),
\end{aligned}
$$

for some S_t^* such that $0 < S_t^* < K$.

Proof. Clearly $0 \notin \mathcal{C}_t$.

We show that if $x < y$ and $x \in \mathcal{C}_t$, then $y \in \mathcal{C}_t$.

Write $\tau = \inf\{s \geq 0 : (S_s(x), s) \notin \mathcal{C}\}$, so τ is the optimal stopping time for $S(x)$. Now τ is also a stopping time for $S(y)$ so

$$
\begin{aligned}
P(y,t) - P(x,t) &= P(y,t) - E[e^{-r\tau}(K - S_\tau(x))^+] \\
&\geq E[e^{-r\tau}\{(K - S_\tau(y))^+ - (K - S_\tau(x))^+\}] \\
&= E[e^{-r\tau}\{(K - S_\tau(y)) - (K - S_\tau(x))\}] \\
&\quad + E[e^{-r\tau}\{(K - S_\tau(y))^- - (K - S_\tau(x))^-\}]. \quad (8.13)
\end{aligned}
$$

Now $S_\tau(y) = y\,\exp\left((r - (\sigma^2/2))\tau + \sigma\widetilde{W}_\tau\right)$ and similarly for $S_\tau(x)$; therefore, the second expectation in (8.13) is non-negative and

$$
\begin{aligned}
P(y,t) - P(x,t) &\geq E\left[e^{-r\tau}(S_\tau(x) - S_\tau(y))\right] \\
&= (x-y)E\left[\exp\left(-\frac{\sigma^2}{2}\tau + \sigma\widetilde{W}_\tau\right)\right] \\
&= (x-y). \quad (8.14)
\end{aligned}
$$

Therefore,

$$
\begin{aligned}
P(y,t) &\geq (x-y) + P(x,t) \\
&> (x-y) + (K-x)^+ \\
&\geq K - y
\end{aligned}
$$

because $x \in \mathcal{C}_t$ (implying $P(x,t) > (K-x)^+$). Now $P(y,t) > 0$ so $P(y,t) > (K-y)^+$ and $y \in \mathcal{C}_t$.

Clearly $S_t^* \leq K$ for all $t > 0$ because if $x > K$, $(K-x)^+ = 0$ although $P(x,t) > 0$. □

Corollary 8.2.12. *From (8.14) we see that for $x, y \in \mathcal{C}_t$, $((\partial P(x,t))/\partial x) \geq -1$.*

Proposition 8.2.13. *The boundary (or critical price) S^* is increasing in t and is bounded above by K.*

Proof. Clearly for $0 \leq s \leq t \leq T$, $P(x,s) \geq P(x,t)$. Therefore, for $t > 0$, $s \geq 0$, $\varepsilon > 0$,

$$(K - S^*_{t+s} - \varepsilon)^+ < P(S^*_{t+s} + \varepsilon, t+s) \leq P(S^*_{t+s} + \varepsilon, t)$$

so for $\varepsilon > 0$, $s > 0$, $S^*_{t+s} + \varepsilon \in C_t$, and $S^*_t \leq S^*_{t+s}$.

Now $(K - x)^+$ is zero for $x \geq K$. However, $P(x,t) > 0$ from Lemma 8.2.10, so $S^*_t < K$.   □

8.3   The Perpetual Put Option

We now discuss the limiting behaviour of S^* by introducing the 'perpetual' American put option; this is the situation when $T = \infty$. The mathematics involves deeper results from analysis and optimal stopping, particularly when we discuss free boundaries and smooth pasting. Perpetual put options are a mathematical idealisation: no such options are traded in real markets.

Theorem 8.3.1. *Consider the function*

$$P(x) = \sup_{\tau \in \mathcal{T}_{0,\infty}} \widetilde{E}_x[e^{-r\tau}(K - S_\tau)^+ I_{\tau < \infty}].$$

Then $P(x) = K - x$ for $x \leq S^*$ and

$$P(x) = (K - S^*)\left(\frac{x}{S^*}\right)^{-\gamma} \quad \text{for } x > S^*,$$

where $S^* = (K\gamma/(1+\gamma))$ and $\gamma = 2r/\sigma^2$.

Proof. From the definition it is immediate that $P(x)$ is convex, decreasing on $[0, \infty)$, and satisfies $P(x) > (K - x)^+$. Furthermore, for any $T > 0$,

$$P(x) \geq E[e^{-rT}(K - S_T)^+].$$

This implies $P(x) > 0$ for all $x \geq 0$. Write $S^* = \sup\{x \geq 0 : P(x) = K - x\}$. Then clearly

$$\begin{aligned} \text{for } x \leq S^* \qquad & P(x) = K - x \\ \text{and for } x > S^* \qquad & P(x) > (K - x)^+. \end{aligned} \qquad (8.15)$$

However, from the results for the Snell envelope (see El Karoui [77]), we know that

$$P(x) = E[(Ke^{-r\rho_x} - S_{\rho_x})^+ I_{\{\rho_x < \infty\}}].$$

Here

$$\rho_x = \rho_0(x) = \inf\{t \geq 0 : P(S_t) = (K - S_t)^+\},$$

with $\inf\{\emptyset\} = +\infty$.

Recall

$$S_t = x \, \exp((r - \frac{\sigma^2}{2})t + \sigma B_t).$$

We have seen that ρ_x is an optimal stopping time. Now from the inequalities (8.15) ρ_x is also given by

$$\rho_x = \inf\{t \geq 0 : S_t \leq S^*\}$$

$$= \inf\{t \geq 0 : (r - \frac{\sigma^2}{2})t + \sigma B_t \leq \log S^*/x\}.$$

For any $z \in \mathbb{R}^+$ define the stopping time

$$\tau_{x,z} = \inf\{t \geq 0 : S_t \leq z\}.$$

Then $\rho_x = \tau_{x,S^*}$. For any fixed $x \in \mathbb{R}^+$ consider the function

$$u(z) := E\left[e^{-r\tau_{x,z}} I_{\{\tau_{x,z} < \infty\}} \left(K - S_{\tau_{x,z}}\right)^+\right].$$

As τ_{x,S^*} is an optimal stopping time the function u is maximized when $z = S^*$.

Now if $z > x$, clearly $\tau_{x,z} = 0$ and $u(z) = (K - x)^+$.

If $z \leq x$, then $\tau_{x,z} = \inf\{t \geq 0 : S_t = z\}$ as the trajectories of S are continuous. Therefore,

$$u(z) = (K - z)^+ E\left[e^{-r\tau_{x,z}} I_{\{\tau_{x,z} < \infty\}}\right]$$

$$= (K - z)^+ E\left[e^{-r\tau_{x,z}}\right]$$

(as $e^{-r\infty} = 0$). Now

$$\tau_{x,z} = \inf\left\{t \geq 0 : \left(r - \frac{\sigma^2}{2}\right)t + \sigma B_t = \log \frac{z}{x}\right\}$$

$$= \inf\left\{t \geq 0 : \gamma t + B_t = \frac{1}{\sigma} \log \frac{z}{x}\right\},$$

where $\gamma = \sigma^{-1}(r - (\sigma^2/2))$.

For any $b \in \mathbb{R}$ write, as in Corollary 7.2.6,

$$T(b) = \inf\{t \geq 0 : \gamma t + B_t = b\}.$$

Then

$$u(z) = \begin{cases} (K - x)^+ & \text{if } z > x \\ (K - z)E[e^{-rT(\log(z/x)/\sigma)}] & \text{if } z \in [0, x] \cap [0, K] \\ 0 & \text{if } z \in [0, x] \cap [K, \infty). \end{cases}$$

The maximum value of u is, therefore, attained in the interval $[0, x] \cap [0, K]$.

Now from Corollary 7.2.6

$$E[e^{-\alpha T(b)}] = \exp\left(\gamma b - |b| \sqrt{\gamma^2 + 2\alpha}\right).$$

Therefore, for all $z \in [0, x] \cap [0, K]$

$$u(z) = (K - z) \left(\frac{z}{x}\right)^\lambda,$$

where $\lambda = 2r/\sigma^2$.

This function has derivative

$$u'(z) = \frac{z^{\lambda-1}}{x^\lambda} (\lambda K - (\lambda + 1)z).$$

Therefore, it follows that if $x \leq \lambda K/(\lambda + 1)$, then $\max_z u(z) = u(x) = K - x$, and if $x > (\lambda K/(\lambda + 1))$, then $\max_z u(z) = u((\lambda K/(\lambda + 1)))$. The stated results are then established. $\qquad\square$

Remark 8.3.2. Consider the free boundary problem:

$$-ru + Sr\, u' + \frac{1}{2} \sigma^2 S^2\, u'' = 0, \tag{8.16}$$

$$u(\infty) = 0,$$

with free "boundary" S^* given by

$$u(S^*) = (K - S^*)^+,$$

$$u'\big|_{S=S^*} = -1.$$

It is known (see Bensoussan [13]) that the American put price $P(S)$ and the critical price S^* of Theorem 8.3.1 give the solution of this boundary value problem.

In fact any solution of the homogeneous equation (8.16) is of the form

$$a_1 S^{\gamma_1} + a_2 S^{\gamma_2},$$

where γ_1, γ_2 are the roots of the quadratic equation

$$\frac{1}{2} \sigma^2 \gamma(\gamma - 1) + r\gamma - r = 0.$$

Therefore,

$$\gamma = \frac{-r + \frac{\sigma^2}{2} \pm \sqrt{r^2 + \frac{\sigma^4}{4} - r\sigma^2 + 4r\frac{\sigma^2}{2}}}{\sigma^2}.$$

Discarding the positive root, because of the condition at $S = \infty$, we see the solution is of the form

$$u(S) = a_1 S^{-2r/\sigma^2}.$$

The conditions $u(S^*) = (K - S^*)^+$

$$\frac{\partial u}{\partial S}\Big|_{S=S^*} = -1$$

give

$$S^* = \frac{2rK}{2r + \sigma^2}$$

and

$$a_1 = (K - S^*)(S^*)^{2r/\sigma^2},$$

agreeing with the result of Theorem 8.3.1.

8.4 Early Exercise Premium

Let us return to the general case.

Theorem 8.4.1. *The Snell envelope J has the decomposition for $t \in [0, T]$,*

$$J_t = \widetilde{E}[e^{-rT}(K - S_T)^+|\mathcal{F}_t] + \widetilde{E}\left[\int_t^T e^{-ru} rK I_{\{S_u < S_u^*\}} du|\mathcal{F}_t\right] \quad a.s.$$

Proof. Suppose $\rho_t = \inf\{u \in [t, T] : S_u \leq S_u^*\} \wedge T$. Then ρ_t is an optimal stopping time in $[0, T]$ and

$$J_t = \widetilde{E}[e^{-r\rho_t}(K - S_{\rho_t})^+|\mathcal{F}_t].$$

Write

$$J_t = \widetilde{E}[e^{-rT}(K - S_T)^+|\mathcal{F}_t] + \widetilde{E}[e^{-r\rho_t}(K - S_{\rho_t})^+ - e^{-rT}(K - S_T)^+|\mathcal{F}_t].$$

The first term is the value of the associated European option with exercise time T. The second term is the early exercise premium, representing the advantage the American option has over the European. Using the generalized Itô rule for convex functions (see Karatzas and Shreve [164]), it can be represented as

$$\widetilde{E}\left[\int_{\rho_t}^T e^{-ru} rK I_{\{S_u < K\}} du - \int_{\rho_t}^T e^{-ru} dL_u^K(S)|\mathcal{F}_t\right].$$

Here $L_u^K(S)$ is the local time of S at level K in the interval $[0, u]$.

Consider the anticipating right continuous process of finite variation

$$D_t := \int_{\rho_0}^{\rho_t} e^{-ru} rK I_{\{S_u < K\}} du - \int_{\rho_0}^{\rho_t} e^{-ru} dL_u^K(S).$$

From Elliott [87] we know there is a unique predictable process D^p, the dual predictable projection of D, such that

$$\tilde{E}[D_T - D_t | \mathcal{F}_t] = \tilde{E}[D^p_T - D^p_t | \mathcal{F}_t].$$

Consequently,

$$\begin{aligned} J_t &= \tilde{E}[e^{-rT}(K - S_T)^+ | \mathcal{F}_t] + \tilde{E}[D_T - D_t | \mathcal{F}_t] \\ &= \tilde{E}[e^{-rT}(K - S_T)^+ | \mathcal{F}_t] + \tilde{E}[D^p_T - D^p_t | \mathcal{F}_t] \\ &= \tilde{E}[e^{-rT}(K - S_T)^+ + D^p_T | \mathcal{F}_t] - D^p_t. \end{aligned}$$

This expresses the supermartingale J as the difference of a martingale and a predictable process. From the uniqueness of the decomposition of the special semimartingale J we see that $D^p = A$, so D^p is nondecreasing.

Write $D_t = A_t + B_t$, where

$$A_t := \int_{\rho_0}^{\rho_t} e^{-ru} rK I_{\{S_u < K\}} I_{\{S_u \leq S^*_u\}} du - \int_{\rho_0}^{\rho_t} e^{-ru} I_{\{S_u \leq S^*_u\}} dL^K_u(S),$$

$$B_t := \int_{\rho_0}^{\rho_t} e^{-ru} rK I_{\{S_u < K\}} I_{\{S_u > S^*_u\}} du - \int_{\rho_0}^{\rho_t} e^{-ru} I_{\{S_u > S^*_u\}} dL^K_u(S).$$

Now $S^*_t < K$ for $t \in [0, T)$ and dL^K does not charge $\{S < K\}$; that is, the dL^K measure of $\{S < K\}$ is zero. Therefore,

$$\begin{aligned} A_t &= \int_{\rho_0}^{\rho_t} e^{-ru} rK I_{\{S_u \leq S^*_u\}} du \quad \text{a.s.} \\ &= \int_0^t e^{-ru} rK I_{\{S_u < S^*_u\}} du \quad \text{a.s.} \end{aligned}$$

so A is predictable and nondecreasing. Consequently, $A^p = A$.

The dual predictable projection of B is more difficult to determine. Although not necessary (see van Moerbeke [254]); we assume the critical price boundary S^*_t is continuous. Write

$$\chi(\omega) := \{t \in [\rho_0(\omega), T) : S_t(\omega) > S^*_t\}$$

for the excursion intervals of the stock process into the continuation region.

From the continuity of S^* and the continuity (a.s) of S the random set χ is a countable union of open sets.

Choose $\varepsilon > 0$ and note that, for every choice, the number of excursions (N^ε) in χ, whose duration is greater than ε, is finite. Label these intervals (a_n, b_n) with $a_n < b_n < a_{n+1} < b_{n+1}$ and put $N^\varepsilon_t := \sup\{1 \leq n \leq N^\varepsilon | a_n \leq t\}$. Consider the approximate process

$$B^\varepsilon_t := \sum_{n=1}^{N^\varepsilon_t} \left[\int_{a_n+\varepsilon}^{b_n} e^{-ru} rK I_{\{S_u < K\}} du - \int_{a_n+\varepsilon}^{b_n} e^{-ru} dL^K_u(S) \right].$$

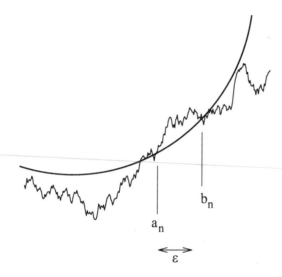

FIGURE 8.1. Excursion intervals

Using dominated convergence B_t^ε converges to B_t as $\varepsilon \to 0$ for almost every ω and also in L^1.

However, B^ε is constant off $\{t \in [0, T) | S_t \geq S_t^*\}$ so its dual predictable projection $(B^\varepsilon)^p$ is also constant off this set. Now in [82] it is shown that because $(J_{u \wedge \rho_t})$, $t \leq u \leq T$, is a martingale $(B^\varepsilon)^p$ is *nonincreasing*. The limit process B^p inherits both these properties. Now $D^p = A^p + B^p$ is *nondecreasing*, so we must have $B^p \equiv 0$. Consequently,

$$\widetilde{E}[D_T^p - D_t^p | \mathcal{F}_t] = \widetilde{E}\left[\int_t^T e^{-ru} rK I_{\{S_u < S_u^*\}} du \Big| \mathcal{F}_t \right] \text{ a.s.}$$

and the result follows. □

Remark 8.4.2. The supermartingale property of the Snell envelope requires B^p to be a process with nondecreasing sample paths. On the other hand, the minimal property of the Snell envelope implies B^p should have nonincreasing sample paths. Consequently, we must have $B^p \equiv 0$.

D^p can be thought of as the (predictable) hedging process that covers the nonadapted process D. Also $D_t^p = \int_0^t rK I_{\{S_u < S_u^*\}} du$ a.s., so D^p is absolutely continuous, nondecreasing, and constant off $\{t \in [0, T) | S_t < S_t^*\}$.

Recall $P(x, t) = X_t$, as defined in (8.8). The following result is immediate.

Corollary 8.4.3. *The value $P(x, t)$ of the American put has the following decomposition on $\mathbb{R}^+ \times [0, T]$.*

$$P(x, t) = p(x, t) + e(x, t),$$

where

$$p(x,t) = \widetilde{E}_x[e^{-r(T-t)}(K - S_T)^+]$$

and

$$e(x,t) = \widetilde{E}_x[\int_t^T e^{-r(u-t)}rKI_{\{S_u < S_u^*\}}du],$$

with $S_t = x$, where S_T is the terminal value of the solution of $dS_u = S_u(rdu + \sigma dW_u)$.

Here $p(x,t)$ is the value of the European put with exercise date T. The early exercise premium is $e(x,t)$; it measures the advantage of being able to stop at any time between t and T.

Indeed, $e^{-r\Delta}rK$ represents the discounted gain of exercising compared with continuing when the stock price belongs to the stopping region S over the time $[u, u + \Delta]$.

From the preceding representation we can deduce the following result.

Lemma 8.4.4. *For each $t \in [0,T)$,*

$$P(\cdot,t) \in C^1(\mathbb{R}^+).$$

Remark 8.4.5. We can also write

$$\begin{aligned}
J_t &= e^{-rt}(K - S_t)^+ + \widetilde{E}[e^{-r\rho_t}(K - S_{\rho_t})^+ - e^{-rt}(K - S_t)^+|\mathcal{F}_t] \\
&= e^{-rt}(K - S_t)^+ \\
&\quad + \widetilde{E}\Big[-\int_t^{\rho_t} e^{-ru}KrI_{\{S_u < K\}}du + \int_t^{\rho_t} e^{-ru}dL_u^K(S)|\mathcal{F}_t\Big].
\end{aligned}$$

Paralleling the computations of Theorem 8.4.1, we obtain the representation of $P(x,t)$ in terms of the delayed exercise value:

$$\begin{aligned}
P(x,t) = (K - x)^+ + \widetilde{E}_x\Big[\int_t^T e^{-r(u-t)}dL_u^K(S) \\
- \int_t^T e^{-r(u-t)}rKI_{\{S_u^* < S_u < K\}}du\Big].
\end{aligned}$$

The delayed exercise value describes the gain relative to stopping now; the early exercise premium describes the gain relative to stopping at the final expiration time T.

8.5 Relation to Free Boundary Problems

McKean [184] and van Moerbeke [254] established the following representation for P. It relates the value function P of the American option to the solution of a free boundary problem. Such a problem consists of a partial differential equation, its Dirichlet conditions, and a Neumann condition that determines an unknown stopping boundary, or 'free boundary,' S_t^*. Write

$$L = \frac{\sigma^2}{2} x^2 \frac{\partial^2}{\partial x^2} + rx \frac{\partial}{\partial x} + \frac{\partial}{\partial t}.$$

From the martingale property of $J_{u \wedge \rho_t}$ and the smoothness of P on the continuation region $\mathcal{C}$ it can be shown that

$$L(e^{-rt} P(x,t)) = 0.$$

For a proof see van Moerbeke [254], Lemma 5.

There are also the Dirichlet and optimality conditions for P given in the next result.

Theorem 8.5.1. *The American put $P(x,t)$ and the boundary S_t^* satisfy*

$$\lim_{x \downarrow S_t^*} P(x,t) = K - S_t^* \qquad t \in [0,T),$$

$$\lim_{t \to T} P(x,t) = (K-x)^+ \qquad x \geq 0,$$

$$\lim_{x \to +\infty} P(x,t) = 0 \qquad t \in [0,T),$$

$$P(x,t) \geq (K-x)^+, \quad (x,t) \in [0,\infty) \times [0,T).$$

Proof. The first result follows from the optimality of S^*. The second is a consequence of the continuity of P.

Write $S_t(x)$ for the solution of (8.2) with $S_0(x) = x$ and $\tau_K = \inf \{t : S_t(x) \leq K\}$. Now $\tau_K \to \infty$ a.s. as $x \to \infty$ and, for $x > K$,

$$0 < P(x,t) \leq KP(\tau_K \leq t).$$

Therefore, $\lim_{x \to \infty} P(x,t) = 0$.

The final condition restates the hedging property.   □

These conditions do not determine the 'free boundary,' or 'critical price' S^*. An additional 'smooth pasting' condition is required.

Proposition 8.5.2. *The derivative $(\partial P(x,t))/\partial x$ is continuous across the free boundary S^*. That is,*

$$\lim_{x \downarrow S_t^*} \frac{\partial P(x,t)}{\partial x} = -1 = \lim_{S \uparrow S_t^*} \frac{\partial (K-S)^+}{\partial S} \bigg|_{S=S_t^*}.$$

Proof. We adapt McKean's argument. Lemma 8.5.6 shows that, in the sense of distributions,

$$L(e^{-rt} P(x,t)) \leq 0 \quad \text{for } (x,t) \in \mathbb{R}^+ \times [0,T). \tag{8.17}$$

Introduce the change of variable

$$\xi = \log x$$

and write

$$\widehat{P}(\xi, t) = P(e^\xi, t).$$

Then (8.17) implies that

$$\frac{\sigma^2}{2} \widehat{P}_{\xi\xi} \le \left(\frac{\sigma^2}{2} - r\right)\widehat{P}_\xi - \widehat{P}_t + r\widehat{P}. \tag{8.18}$$

In the new variable ξ the free boundary S^* becomes $\xi_t^* = \log(S_t^*)$.

Integrate (8.18) over a region $\mathcal{R}$ in (ξ, t) space where $\mathcal{R}$ has width ε either side of ξ_t and is over the interval $[t_1, t_2]$. Consequently,

$$\frac{\sigma^2}{2} \int_{t_1}^{t_2} \left(\widehat{P}_\xi(\xi_t^* + \varepsilon, t) - \widehat{P}_\xi(\xi_t^* - \varepsilon, t)\right) dt$$

$$\le \left(\frac{\sigma^2}{2} - r\right) \int_{t_1}^{t_2} \left(\widehat{P}(\xi_t^* + \varepsilon, t) - \widehat{P}(\xi_{t_1}^* - \varepsilon, t)\right) dt$$

$$+ \int_R (r\widehat{P} - \widehat{P}_t) d\xi\, dt.$$

For a fixed ξ consider the horizontal line in $\mathcal{R}$ that goes from time $t^-(\xi)$ to time $t^+(\xi)$. There is an interval $\mathcal{R}_\xi$ of ξ-space such that the final integral can be written

$$\int_R r\widehat{P}d\xi\, dt - \int_{R_\xi} \left(\widehat{P}(\xi, t^*(\xi)) - \widehat{P}(\xi, t^-(\xi))\right) d\xi.$$

On the (transformed) stopping region $\mathcal{S}$, $\widehat{P}_\xi = \varepsilon^{-\xi}$. Therefore, from the dominated convergence theorem, using the continuity of $\widehat{P}$, as $\varepsilon \downarrow 0$ we have

$$\int_{t_1}^{t_2} \left(\lim_{\xi \downarrow \xi^*} \widehat{P}_\xi + e^{\xi^*}\right) dt \le 0. \tag{8.19}$$

From Corollary 8.2.12 we know that in $\mathcal{C}$, $(\partial P(x, t))/\partial x) \ge -1$. Therefore, in the variable $\xi = \log x$,

$$\frac{\partial P}{\partial x} = \frac{\partial \widehat{P}}{\partial \xi} \cdot \frac{\partial \xi}{\partial x}$$

so $\widehat{P}_\xi \ge -e^{-\xi}$.

Consequently, from (8.19) we must have $\lim_{\xi \downarrow \xi^*} \widehat{P}_\xi + e^{\xi^*} = 0$ and the slope exhibits the smooth pasting condition across ξ^*.   □

The results of Theorem 8.5.1 and Proposition 8.5.2 suggest the American put value $P(x, t)$ can be expressed as the solution of a free boundary problem. McKean was the first to discuss the problem and provide this formulation.

Using the regularity we have now established for $P(x, t)$ the following result can be proved.

Theorem 8.5.3. $P = p + e$, *where* p *is the European put function and* e *is the early exercise premium as in Corollary 8.4.3. The critical price* S^* *is determined by the equation*

$$P(S_t^*, t) = K - S_t^* \quad for\ t \in [0, T)$$

together with $S_T^* = K$.

Proof. The function $P(x, t)$ is in $C^{1,0}$ and piecewise in $C^{2,1}$ on $\mathbb{R}^+ \times [0, T)$. Regularity of the boundary S_t^* implies the derivative P_t is continuous across S^* and so, in fact, in all $\mathbb{R}^+ \times [0, T)$. An extension of the Itô differentiation rule due to Krylov ([171], Theorem 2.10.1) implies that for $t \in [0, T]$,

$$e^{-r(T-t)} P(S_T, T) = P(S_t, t) + \int_t^t e^{-r(u-t)} \sigma S_u P_x(S_u, u) d\widetilde{W}_u$$

$$+ \int_t^T L(e^{-r(u-t)} P)(S_u, u) du. \tag{8.20}$$

We have already noted that $L(e^{-r(u-t)} P)(x, u) = 0$ when $(x, u) \in \mathcal{C}$. When $(x, u) \in \mathcal{S}$,

$$P(x, u) = (K - x)$$

and

$$L(e^{-r(u-t)}(K - x)) = -e^{-r(u-t)} rK.$$

Substituting in (8.20), for $t \in [0, T]$,

$$e^{-r(T-t)} P(S_T, T) = P(S_t, t) + \int_t^T e^{-r(u-t)} \sigma S_u P_x(S_u, u) d\widetilde{W}_u$$

$$- \int_t^T e^{-r(u-t)} rK I_{\{S_u < S_u^*\}} du.$$

The derivative P_x is bounded, so the stochastic integral is a martingale. With $S_t = x$ and $P(x, T) = (K - x)^+$ we have

$$P(x, t) = \widetilde{E}_x[e^{-r(T-t)}(K - S_T)^+]$$

$$+ \widetilde{E}_x \left[\int_t^T e^{-r(T-t)} rK I_{\{S_u < S_u^*\}} du \right].$$

The equation for S^* follows from the first statement of Theorem 8.5.1. $\quad\square$

Definition 8.5.4. A function $g(x, t) \in C^{3,1}(\mathbb{R} \times [0, T))$ has Tychonov growth if g, g_t, g_x, g_{xx}, and g_{xxx} have growth at most $\exp(o(x^2))$ uniformly on compact sets, as $|x|$ goes to infinity.

If we assume the equation for S^* has a C^1 solution the following uniqueness result is a consequence of Theorem 8.5.1; its proof can be found in van Moerbeke [254].

Theorem 8.5.5. *Suppose $\mathcal{D} \subset \mathbb{R}^+ \times [0, T)$ is an open domain with a continuously differentiable boundary c.*

Furthermore, suppose $f \in C^{3,1}$, that $g(x, t) = f(e^x, t)$ has Tychonov growth, and $L[e^{-rt} f(x, t)] = 0$ on $\mathcal{D}$,

$$f(x, T) = (K - x)^+, \qquad x \in \mathbb{R}^+$$
$$f(x, t) > (K - x)^+ \qquad on\ \mathcal{D}$$
$$f(x, t) = (K - x)^+ \qquad on\ \mathbb{R}^+ \times [0, T) \cap \mathcal{D}^c$$
$$\lim_{x \downarrow c(t)} f_x(x, t) = -1, \qquad t \in [0, T).$$

Then $f(x, t) = P(x, t)$, the American put function, $\mathcal{D} = \mathcal{C}$, the continuation region, and $c(t) = S_t^*$, the optimal stopping boundary.

We require the following extension of the harmonic property of P on $\mathcal{C}$.

Lemma 8.5.6. *On $\mathbb{R}^+ \times [0, T]$,*

$$L[e^{-rt} P(x, t)] \leq 0$$

is the sense of Schwartz distributions. This states the American put value function P is 'r-excessive.'

Proof. Choose $\varepsilon > 0$.

Consider the set of stopping times

$$V_\varepsilon = \{\tau : t \leq \tau \leq T,\ \tilde{E}[e^{-r(\tau - t)} (K - S_\tau)^+ | S_t] \geq P(S_t, t) - \varepsilon\}.$$

This set is not empty for all $t \in [0, T)$. Choose $\tau_\varepsilon \in V_\varepsilon$ and write $\tilde{E}_x$ for the $\tilde{Q}$ expectation given $S_0 = x$. Then

$$\tilde{E}_x\left[e^{-r\tau_\varepsilon}(K - S_{\tau_\varepsilon})^+\right] = \tilde{E}_x\left[e^{-rt} \tilde{E}\left[e^{-r(\tau_\varepsilon - t)}\left(K - S_{\tau_\varepsilon}\right)^+ \Big| S_t\right]\right]$$
$$\geq \tilde{E}_x\left[e^{-rt} P(S_t, t)\right] - \varepsilon e^{-rt}.$$

However, by definition

$$P(S_0, 0) = P(x, 0) \leq \tilde{E}_x[e^{-r\tau_\varepsilon}(K - S_{\tau_\varepsilon})^+]$$
$$\geq \tilde{E}_x[e^{-rt} P(S_t, t)] - \varepsilon e^{-rt}.$$

Letting $\varepsilon \downarrow 0$ gives

$$P(x, 0) \geq \tilde{E}_x[e^{-rt} P(S_t, t)].$$

This inequality implies the result, as any excessive function is the limit of an increasing sequence of infinitely differentiable excessive functions (see Port and Stone [207]). $\square$

Lemma 8.5.7. *The American put function $P(x, t)$ satisfies the following equation on $\mathbb{R}^+ \times [0, T]$.*

$$[L[e^{-rt}P(x, t)]]((K - x)^+ - P(x, t)) = 0.$$

Proof. In the continuation region we know $L[e^{-rt}P(x, t)] = 0$. In the stopping region $P(x, t) = (K - x)^+$. □

Definition 8.5.8. For any $m \in \mathbb{Z}^+$ and $\lambda > 0$ write $H^{m,\lambda}$ for the space of measurable real-valued functions f on $\mathbb{R}$ whose derivatives, in the sense of distributions, up to and including the mth order, belong to $L^2(\mathbb{R}, e^{-\lambda|x|}dx)$. Write

$$\|f\| = \left(\sum_{i=0}^{m} \int_R |\partial^i f(x)|^2 e^{-\lambda|x|} dx \right)^{1/2}.$$

The space $L^2([0, T], H^{m,\lambda})$ is the set of measurable functions $g : [0, T] \to H^{m,\lambda}$ such that

$$\int_{[0,T]} \|g(t)\|^2 dt < \infty.$$

In [141], Jaillet, Lamberton, and Lapeyre extend the work of Bensoussan and Lions [15] to show the American put value function is characterized by a variational inequality. Their result is as follows.

Theorem 8.5.9. *Consider a continuous function $f(x, t)$ defined on $\mathbb{R}^+ \times [0, T]$ that satisfies*

$$f(e^x, t) \in L^2([0, T], H^{2,\lambda})$$
$$f_t(e^x, t) \in L^2([0, T], H^{0,\lambda})$$
$$L[e^{-rt}f(x, t)] \leq 0$$
$$f(x, t) \geq (K - x)^+$$
$$f(x, T) = (K - x)^+$$
$$(L[e^{-rt}f(x, t)])(f(x, t) - (K - x)^+) = 0.$$

Then $f(x, t)$ is unique and equals the American put value function $P(x, t)$.

Remark 8.5.10. This application of variational inequalities to the American option is due to Jaillet, Lamberton, and Lapeyre [141]. It gives rise to a numerical algorithm. In fact the early numerical work of Brennan and Schwartz [25] for the American put was justified, using variational inequalities, by Jaillet, Lamberton, and Lapeyre [141].

The most widely used numerical technique for calculating the American option value is dynamic programming. The risky asset price S is modelled as evolving on a binomial tree in discrete time. The Bellman equation is then solved recursively by evaluating.

$$P_i = \max \left\{ (K - S_i)^+, e^{-r\Delta} \widetilde{E}[P_{i+1} | \mathcal{F}_i] \right\}$$

with

$$P_T = (K - S_T)^+.$$

8.6 An Approximate Solution

We have seen that the American put function $P(x,t)$ can be written

$$P(x,t) = p(x,t) + e(x,t),$$

where $p(x,t) = \widetilde{E}_x[e^{-r(T-t)}(K - S_T)^+]$ is the European put value, and

$$e(x,t) = \widetilde{E}_x\left[\int_t^T e^{-r(u-t)}rKI_{\{S_u < S_u^*\}}du\right]$$

is the 'early exercise' premium.

The early exercise premium involves the critical price, or free boundary S^*, and is consequently difficult to evaluate.

In [2] Allegretto, Barone-Adesi, and Elliott proposed an approximation for $e(x,t)$ of the form

$$\varepsilon(x,t) = A(t)\left(\frac{x}{S_t^*}\right)^{q(t)},$$

where A and q are functions of t that are to be determined.

Now we know that in the continuation region $\mathcal{C}$:

$$L[e^{rt}P(x,t)] = 0$$

and

$$L[e^{-rt}p(x,t)] = 0. \tag{8.21}$$

Also, at the critical price

$$P(S_t^*, t) = (K - S_t^*)^+$$

and

$$\left.\frac{\partial P}{\partial x}\right|_{x=S_t^*} = -1. \tag{8.22}$$

Now $LP(x,t) = 0$ in $\mathcal{C}$ and $Lp(x,t) = 0$ in $\mathcal{C}$ so

$$L[e^{-rt}e(x,t)] = 0 \quad \text{in } \mathcal{C}. \tag{8.23}$$

Substituting $P = p + A(t)\left(S/S_t^*\right)^{q(t)}$ in (8.22) we have

$$p(S_t^*, t) + A(t) = K - S_t^*$$

and

$$\frac{A(t)q(t)}{S_t^*} - e^{-(\mu-r)(T-t)}\Phi(-d_1(S_t^*, t)) = -1, \qquad (8.24)$$

where Φ is the standard normal distribution and

$$d_1(x, t) = \frac{\log(\frac{x}{S_t^*}) + (\mu + \frac{\sigma^2}{2})(T - t)}{\sigma\sqrt{T - t}}.$$

However, we also would like $L[e^{-rt}\varepsilon(x, t)] = 0$. This is the case if

$$\frac{1}{2}\sigma^2 q(t)(q(t) - 1)A(t)\left(\frac{x}{S_t^*}\right)^{q(t)} - rA(t)\left(\frac{x}{S_t^*}\right)^{q(t)} + A(t)\mu q(t)\left(\frac{x}{S_t^*}\right)^{q(t)}$$

$$+ \frac{\partial}{\partial t}\left[A(t)\left(\frac{x}{S_t^*}\right)^{q(t)}\right] = 0. \qquad (8.25)$$

Now

$$\frac{\partial}{\partial t}\left[A(t)\left(\frac{x}{S_t^*}\right)^{q(t)}\right] = \frac{dA(t)}{dt}\left(\frac{x}{S_t^*}\right)^{q(t)}$$

$$- \frac{dS_t^*}{dt}\left(\frac{A(t)q(t)}{x}\right)\left(\frac{x}{S_t^*}\right)^{q(t)+1}$$

$$+ \frac{dq(t)}{dt}A(t)\left(\frac{x}{S_t^*}\right)^{q(t)}\log\left(\frac{x}{S_t^*}\right).$$

Substituting into (8.25) and dividing by $A(t)(x/S_t^*)^{q(t)}$ implies

$$\frac{1}{2}\sigma^2 q(t)(q(t) - 1) - r + \mu q(t) + \left[\frac{1}{A(t)}\frac{dA(t)}{dt} - \frac{q(t)}{S_t^*}\frac{dS_t^*}{dt}\right]$$

$$+ \log\left(\frac{x}{S_t^*}\right)\frac{dq(t)}{dt} = 0. \qquad (8.26)$$

However, this equation indicates q is not independent of x, and so $e(x, t)$ is not of the form given by $\varepsilon(x, t)$. Nonetheless, a useful approximation is obtained by neglecting the last term of (8.26). That is, we suppose $q(t)$ is a solution of

$$\frac{1}{2}\sigma^2 q(t)(q(t) - 1) - r + \mu q(t)$$

$$+ \left[\frac{1}{A(t)}\frac{dA(t)}{dt} - \frac{q(t)}{S_t^*}\frac{dS_t^*}{dt}\right] = 0. \qquad (8.27)$$

This approximation is reasonable when $\log(x/S_t^*) \cdot ((dq(t))/dt)$ is small. This is the case when x is in a neighbourhood of S_t^* or when $((dq(t))/dt)$ is small (at long maturities).

From equation (8.24) we have

$$\frac{dA(t)}{dt} = \left[e^{(\mu-r)(T-t)} N\left(-d_1(S_t^*, t) \right) - 1 \right] \frac{dS_t^*}{dt} - \frac{\partial p(x,t)}{\partial t}.$$

From the second equation of (8.24)

$$\frac{1}{A(t)} \frac{dA(t)}{dt} - \frac{q(t)}{S_t^*} \frac{dS_t^*}{dt} = -\frac{1}{A(t)} \cdot \frac{\partial p(S_t^*, t)}{\partial t}.$$

Writing $g(t) = (1/A(t)) ((\partial p(S_t^*, t))/\partial t)$, $M = 2r/\sigma^2$, $N = 2b/\sigma^2$, $G(t) = (2q(t))/\sigma^2$, equation (8.27) becomes

$$q(t)^2 + (N-1)q(t) - (M - G(t)) = 0.$$

To satisfy the boundary condition of zero at $x = +\infty$ we consider only the root

$$q(t) = \frac{1}{2} \left(1 - N - \sqrt{(1-N)^2 + 4(M + G(t))} \right).$$

With this value of $q(t)$ an approximation for the early exercise premium is

$$\varepsilon(x,t) = A(t) \left(\frac{x}{S_t^*} \right)^{q(t)}.$$

To summarize, we have the following system of three equations in three unknowns $A(t)$, $q(t)$, and S_t^*.

$$S_t^* = \frac{(K - p(S_t^*, t))q(t)}{-1 + q(t) + e^{(\mu-r)(T-t)} N(-d_1(S_t^*, t))}, \qquad (8.28)$$

$$A(t) = -p(S_t^*, t) - S_t^* + K \qquad (8.29)$$

$$q(t)^2 + (N-1)q(t) - M + G(t) = 0. \qquad (8.30)$$

For a fixed value of t these equations can be solved using the iterative procedure:

i) give a trial value of S_t^*;

ii) calculate $A(t)$ from (8.29);

iii) calculate $q(t)$ from (8.30);

iv) calculate a new value of S_t^* from (8.28).

Using the new value for S_t^* the steps (ii), (iii), and (iv) are repeated.

This algorithm was investigated in the paper of Allegretto, Barone-Adesi, and Elliott [2] and shown to give satisfactory results.

9

Bonds and Term Structure

9.1 Market Dynamics

Suppose $(\Omega, \mathcal{F}, P)$ is a probability space and B_t, $0 \le t \le T$, is a Brownian motion. $\{\mathcal{F}_t\}$ denotes the (complete, right-continuous) filtration generated by B. We first review the martingale pricing results of Chapter 7.

Consider again the case of a bond S^0 and a single risky asset S^1. We suppose

$$S^0(t) = \exp \int_0^t r(u)du$$

and

$$S^1(t) = S^1(0) + \int_0^t \mu(u)S^1(u)du + \int_0^t \sigma(u)S^1(u)dB(u).$$

Here r, μ, and σ are adapted (random) processes. (In particular, r is now a stochastic interest rate in general.) Consider a self-financing trading strategy (H^0, H^1). The corresponding wealth process is

$$X(t) = H_t^0 S_t^0 + H_t^1 S_t^1$$

and

$$\begin{aligned}
dX(t) &= r H_t^0 S_t^0 dt + H_t^1 dS_t^1 \\
&= r\big(X(t) - H_t^1 S_t^1\big)dt + H_t^1 dS_t^1.
\end{aligned}$$

With $\theta(t) = (\mu(t) - r(t))/(\sigma(t))$ (which requires $\sigma(t) \ne 0$) under the measure P^θ the process W^θ is a Brownian motion, where

$$dW_t^\theta = \theta(t)dt + dB_t.$$

Consequently, under P^θ the discounted wealth process is $(X(t))/(S^0(t))$ and

$$d\left(\frac{X(t)}{S^0(t)}\right) = H_t^1 \sigma(t) \frac{S^1(t)}{S^0(t)} \, dW_t^\theta.$$

That is, for any self-financing strategy the discounted wealth process $(X(t))/(S^0(t))$ is a martingale under the martingale measure P^θ.

Consider a contingent claim $h \in L^2(\Omega, \mathcal{F}_T)$. Then,

$$M_t := E^\theta\left[\frac{h}{S_T^0} \mid \mathcal{F}_t\right]$$

is a martingale and, using the martingale representation result (Theorem 7.3.9),

$$M_t = M_0 + \int_0^t \phi_u dW_u^\theta.$$

If we take $H_t^1 = (S^0(t)\phi_t)/(\sigma(t)S^1(t))$, $X(0) = M_0 = E^\theta[h/S_T^0]$ and write

$$M_t = \frac{X(t)}{S^0(t)} = X(0) + \int_0^t H_u^1 \sigma(t) \frac{S^1(u)}{S^0(u)} \, dW_u^\theta,$$

then with

$$H_t^0 = \frac{X(t)}{S^0(t)} - H_t^1 \frac{S^1(t)}{S^0(t)}$$

(H^0, H^1) is a self-financing strategy that hedges the claim h. That is,

$$X(T) = H_T^0 S_T^0 + H_T^1 S_T^1 = h.$$

The natural price for the claim at time 0 is $E^\theta[h/S_T^0]$; the price at time $t \in [0,T]$ is $X_h(t) = X(t)$ and this equals $S_t^0 E^\theta[h/S_T^0 \mid \mathcal{F}_t] = S_t^0 E^\theta[X(T)/S_T^0 \mid \mathcal{F}_t]$ because $X(t)/S^0(t)$ is a martingale under P^θ.

Suppose we have a market with several risky assets $S_t^0, S_t^1, \ldots, S_t^n$ that have dynamics

$$dS_t^0 = r(t)S_t^0 dt, \qquad S_0^0 = 1,$$

$$dS_t^i = S_t^i\left(\mu_i(t)dt + \sum_{j=1}^m \sigma_{ij}(t)dW_j(t)\right),$$

$$S_0^i = s_i.$$

Here $W(t) = (W_1(t), \ldots, W_m(t))$ is an m-dimensional Brownian motion on $(\Omega, \mathcal{F}, P)$; the risk-neutral pricing formula holds as long as there is a unique risk-neutral measure P^θ, as introduced in Chapter 7.

Then in such an example the price at time $t \le T$ of a claim $h \in L^2(\mathcal{F}_T)$ is

$$X(t) = S_t^0 E^\theta[h \cdot (S_T^0)^{-1} \mid \mathcal{F}_t].$$

Notation 9.1.1. From now on in this chapter we assume we are working in a market where there is a unique risk-neutral measure P^θ. The superscript θ is dropped. For simplicity we suppose there is a single risky asset that has dynamics (under $P^\theta = P$)

$$dS^1(t) = r(t)S^1(t)dt + \sigma(t)S^1(t)dW(t).$$

Furthermore, we suppose the martingale representation result holds, so that every $(\mathcal{F}_t, P)$ martingale has a representation as a stochastic integral with respect to W (see, e.g., page 32 of Revuz and Yor [208]).

Definition 9.1.2. A *zero coupon bond* maturing at time T is a claim that pays 1 at time T.

From the pricing formula, its value at time $t \in [0, T]$ is

$$B(t, T) = S_t^0 E\left[\frac{1}{S_T^0} \Big| \mathcal{F}_t\right].$$

As $S_t^0 = \exp \int_0^t r(u)du$ this is

$$B(t, T) = E\left[\exp\left(-\int_t^T r(u)du\right) \Big| \mathcal{F}_t\right].$$

Consequently, given $B(t, T)$ dollars at time t one can construct a self-financing hedging strategy (H_t^0, H_t^1) such that the corresponding wealth process $X(t) = H_t^0 S_t^0 + H_t^1 S_t^1$ has value 1 at time T.

If the instantaneous rate $r(t)$ is deterministic $B(t, T) = \exp\{-\int_t^T r(u)du\}$ and $dB(t, T) = r(t)B(t, T)dt$ so H_t^1 is identically 0.

Definition 9.1.3. The *T-forward price* $F(t, T)$ for the risky asset S^1 is a price agreed at time $t \le T$ (and so $\mathcal{F}_t$-measurable), which will be paid for S^1 at time T.

Such a price $F(t, T)$ is characterized by requiring that the claim $S_T^1 - F(t, T)$ has (discounted) value 0 under the risk-neutral (martingale) measure P. Therefore,

$$E\left[(S_T^0)^{-1}(S_T^1 - F(t, T)) \Big| \mathcal{F}_t\right] = 0$$

$$= E\left[\frac{S_T^1}{S_T^0} \Big| \mathcal{F}_t\right] - \frac{F(t, T)}{S_t^0} E\left[\frac{S_t^0}{S_T^0} \Big| \mathcal{F}_t\right]$$

$$= \frac{S_t^1}{S_t^0} - \frac{F(t, T)}{S_t^0} B(t, T),$$

because the discounted price S^1/S^0 is a martingale under the measure P. Therefore, $F(t, T) = S_t^1/B(t, T)$.

Remark 9.1.4. The forward price can be defined for other claims. Indeed, suppose $h \in L^2(\Omega, \mathcal{F}_T)$ is a contingent claim with exercise date T. The *T-forward price* for h, denoted by $F(h, t, T)$, is the $\mathcal{F}_t$-measurable random variable which has the property that

$$E\left[(S_T^0)^{-1}(h - F(h, t, T)) \big| \mathcal{F}_t\right] = 0.$$

Consequently,

$$F(h, t, T) = \frac{S_t^0 E[(S_T^0)^{-1} h | \mathcal{F}_t]}{B(t, T)}$$

$$= \frac{X_h(t)}{B(t, T)},$$

where $X_h(t)$ is, from the pricing discussion, the natural price for h at time t.

In particular, h could be a zero coupon bond of maturity $T^* \geq T$. Then

$$F\left(B(T, T^*), t, T\right) = \frac{B(t, T^*)}{B(t, T)}.$$

Definition 9.1.5. Define a new probability measure Q_T, equivalent to P, on $(\Omega, \mathcal{F}_T)$ by setting

$$\frac{dQ_T}{dP}\Big|_{\mathcal{F}_T} = \frac{(S_T^0)^{-1}}{E[(S_T^0)^{-1}]}$$

$$= \frac{1}{S_T^0 B(0, T)}.$$

The measure Q_T is called the *forward measure* for the settlement date T. It was introduced in [112] and [142]. Define:

$$\Gamma_t := E\left[\frac{dQ_T}{dP} \big| \mathcal{F}_t\right]$$

$$= E\left[\frac{1}{S_T^0 B(0, T)} \big| \mathcal{F}_t\right] = \frac{B(t, T)}{S_t^0 B(0, T)}.$$

The process Γ is a $(P, \mathcal{F}_t)$ martingale so there is an integrand $\gamma(s, T)$ such that

$$\Gamma_t = 1 + \int_0^t \gamma(s, T) dW_s.$$

Now $\Gamma_s > 0$ a.s. for all s; define

$$\beta(s, T) = \Gamma_s^{-1} \gamma(s, T).$$

Then

$$\Gamma_t = 1 + \int_0^t \Gamma_s \beta(s, T) dW_s$$

and so
$$\Gamma_t = \exp\left(\int_0^T \beta(s,T)dW_s - \frac{1}{2}\int_0^T \beta(s,T)^2 ds\right).$$

The next lemma shows how the forward price can be expressed in terms of the forward measure.

Lemma 9.1.6. *Suppose* $h \in L^2(\Omega, \mathcal{F}_T)$ *is a contingent claim with exercise time T. Then*
$$F(h,t,T) = E_{Q_T}[h|\,\mathcal{F}_t].$$

Consequently, the forward price of h is a Q_T martingale.

Proof. Using Bayes' rule
$$E_Q[h\,|\mathcal{F}_t] = \frac{E[\Gamma_T h | \mathcal{F}_t]}{E[\Gamma_T | \mathcal{F}_t]}$$
$$= E[\Gamma_t^{-1}\Gamma_T h\,|\mathcal{F}_t].$$

Substituting the expressions for Γ the result follows. $\square$

Remark 9.1.7. Consider the T-forward price for the contingent claim $h \in L^2(\Omega, \mathcal{F}_T)$ at time 0.
$$F(h,0,T) = \frac{X_h(0)}{B(0,T)}.$$

By definition $F(h,0,T)$ is the price, agreed at time 0, that one will pay at time T for the claim h. The related claim $V = h - F(h,0,T)$ has price 0 at time 0. However, at later times $t \in [0,T]$ this claim V does not have value 0. Indeed, using the pricing formula, at time t it has value
$$V(t) = S_t^0 E\big[(S_T^0)^{-1}\big(h - F(h,0,T)\big)|\mathcal{F}_t\big]$$
$$= X_h(t) - F(h,0,T)/B(t,T).$$

One can hedge this claim as follows. At time 0 one shorts $F(h,0,T)$ zero coupon bonds with maturity T. This provides an amount $F(h,0,T)/B(0,T) = (X_h(0))/(B(0,T)) \cdot B(0,T) = X_h(0)$ where $X_h(0)$ is the price of the claim h at time 0. Consequently, this amount $X_h(0)$ can be used at time 0 to buy the claim h. This strategy requires no initial investment. If this position is held until time T it is then worth
$$X_h(T) - F(h,0,T)/B(T,T) = h - F(h,0,T).$$

9.2 Future Price and Futures Contracts

Suppose a contingent claim h has a price \$h at time T. (By abuse of notation we write h for the claim and its price at time T.)

Clearly at time T one need not pay anything for the right to buy the claim for $h. Therefore, at time T the price of the claim is $G(h, T, T) = h$. (Note this assumes there are no transaction costs and we are not discussing problems of delivering the claim itself—we are thinking of a cash settlement.)

Suppose initially there are only a finite number of trading times $t_0, \ldots, t_n$ with

$$0 = t_0 < t_1 < \cdots < t_n = T.$$

Furthermore, suppose that $r(u)$ is constant on each interval $[t_i, t_{i+1})$. Then

$$S^0_{t_{j+1}} = \exp \int_0^{t_{j+1}} r(u)du$$

$$= \exp \left(\sum_{i=0}^n r(t_i)(t_{i+1} - t_i) \right),$$

and $S^0_{t_{j+1}}$ is $\mathcal{F}_{t_j}$-measurable.

Consider the time t_{n-1} and suppose the price agreed at time t_{n-1} for the claim (to be delivered at time $t_n = T$) is

$$G(h, t_{n-1}, T).$$

Then the difference in the price agreed at time t_{n-1} and the price at $t_n = T$ is

$$G(h, t_n, T) - G(h, t_{n-1}, T).$$

At time t_{n-1} one estimates $G(h, t_{n-1}, T)$, given the information $\mathcal{F}_{t_{n-1}}$, so that this difference, discounted and conditioned on $\mathcal{F}_{t_{n-1}}$, is zero. That is, so that the claim $G(h, t_n, T) - G(h, t_{n-1}, T)$ has value zero at time t_{n-1}; that is,

$$S^0_{t_{n-1}} E\left[(S^0_{t_n})^{-1} (G(h, t_n, T) - G(h, t_{n-1}, T)) | \mathcal{F}_{t_{n-1}} \right] = 0.$$

Similarly, at time t_{n-2} one estimates $G(h, t_{n-2}, T)$ so that

$$S^0_{t_{n-2}} E\left[(S^0_{t_{n-1}})^{-1} (G(h, t_{n-1}, T) - G(h, t_{n-2}, T)) | \mathcal{F}_{t_{n-2}} \right] = 0.$$

Here $G(h, t_{n-2}, T)$ is the estimate at time t_{n-2} of the price of the claim h at time T.

Consequently, the value at time $t = t_k$ of the sum of future adjustments is

$$S^0_{t_k} E\left[\sum_{j=k}^{n-1} S^0_{t_{j+1}} (G(h, t_{j+1}, T) - G(h, t_j, T)) | \mathcal{F}_{t_k} \right] = 0.$$

The continuous-time version of this condition gives, for $0 \le t \le T$,

$$S^0_t E\left[\int_t^T (S^0_u)^{-1} dG(h, u, T) | \mathcal{F}_t \right] = 0. \tag{9.1}$$

Write
$$M_t := \int_0^t (S_u^0)^{-1} dG(h, u, T).$$

Then (9.1) implies that for $0 \le s \le t \le T$,
$$E[M_t | \mathcal{F}_s] = M_s.$$

That is, M is an $(\mathcal{F}_t, P)$ martingale. Consequently,
$$\int_0^t S_u^0 dM_u = G(h, t, T) - G(h, 0, T)$$

is an $(\mathcal{F}_t, P)$ martingale. Therefore, as $G(h, T, T) = h$,
$$G(h, t, T) = E[h | \mathcal{F}_t]$$

is the "future price" at time t for the claim h. This motivates the following definition.

Definition 9.2.1. The T-*future price* G at time t of the $\mathcal{F}_T$-measurable contingent claim h is:
$$G(h, t, T) = E[h | \mathcal{F}_t].$$

By definition $G(h, t, T)$ is a martingale under P.

Lemma 9.2.2.   a) $(S_T^0)^{-1}$ and h are (conditionally) uncorrelated if and only if $F(h, t, T) = G(h, t, T)$.

b) If $(S_T^0)^{-1}$ and h are positively correlated conditional on $\mathcal{F}_t$, then
$$G(h, t, T) \le F(h, t, T).$$

Proof. The T-future price is
$$G(h, t, T) = E[h | \mathcal{F}_t].$$

The T-forward price is
$$F(h, t, T) = \frac{X_h(t)}{B(t, T)} = E_Q[h | \mathcal{F}_t]$$
$$= \frac{E[(S_T^0)^{-1} h | \mathcal{F}_t]}{E[(S_T^0)^{-1} | \mathcal{F}_t]}.$$

Part a) is immediate. Part b) states that
$$E\left[\left((S_T^0)^{-1} - E[(S_T^0)^{-1} | \mathcal{F}_t] \right) \left(X - E[X | \mathcal{F}_t] \right) | \mathcal{F}_t \right] \ge 0$$

and the result follows.   □

Remark 9.2.3. The hypothesis of Part b) of the lemma arises when the stock price tends to rise with a fall in the interest rate, and conversely. Holding a futures contract is not advantageous if there is positive correlation between $(S_T^0)^{-1}$ and h.

Therefore, a buyer of a futures contract is compensated by the lower future price compared with the forward price.

Futures Contracts

We have noticed that forward contracts possibly have nonzero value. In contrast, a futures contract is constructed so that the risk of default inherent in a forward contract is eliminated.

The value at time 0 of a forward contract, entered into at time 0, is 0. However, at later times $t \in [0, T]$ it has value

$$V(t) = X_h(t) - F(h, 0, T)/B(t, T).$$

In contrast to a forward contract, the value of a future contract is maintained at zero at all times. Consequently, either party to the contract can close his or her position at any time. This is done by 'marking to market.'

To describe this process suppose again that trading takes place only at the finite number of times $t_0, \ldots, t_n$ with

$$0 = t_0 < t_1 \cdots < t_n = T,$$

and that $r(u)$ is constant on each interval $[t_i, t_{i+1})$.

At time t_k the future price of the claim h is $G(h, t_k, T) = E[h|\mathcal{F}_{t_k}]$. Suppose we buy a future contract at this price. At the time t_{k+1} the future price of h is $G(h, t_{k+1}, T)$.

If $G(h, t_{k+1}, T) > G(h, t_k, T)$, the buyer of the future contract receives a payment of $G(h, t_{k+1}, T) - G(h, t_k, T)$.

If $G(h, t_{k+1}, T) < G(h, t_k, T)$ the buyer of the future contract makes a payment of

$$G(h, t_k, T) - G(h, t_{k+1}, T).$$

To make or receive these payments a 'margin account' is held by the broker.

At the final time $T = t_n$ the buyer of the future contract will have received payments

$$G(h, t_{k+1}, T) - G(h, t_k, T), \ G(h, t_{k+2}, T) - G(h, t_{k+1}, T)$$
$$\cdots \ G(h, t_n, T) - G(h, t_{n-1}, T)$$

at times $t_{k+1}, \ldots, t_n = T$. The value at time $t = t_k$ of this sequence of payments is:

$$(S_t^0) E\left[\sum_{i=k}^{n-1} (S_{t_{i+1}}^0)^{-1} \left(G(h, t_{i+1}, T) - G(h, t_i, T) \right) \Big| \mathcal{F}_t \right].$$

The future price $G(h, t, T)$ is such that the cost of entering a future contract at any time is zero. Consequently, the value of this sequence of payments at time t must be 0.

With a continuum of trading times the preceding sum becomes a stochastic integral and the condition is

$$(S_t^0) E\left[\int_t^T (S_u^0)^{-1} dG(h, u, T) \Big| \mathcal{F}_t \right] = 0.$$

Now by definition $G(h, t, T) = E[h|\mathcal{F}_t]$ is a martingale. This integral is, therefore, a stochastic integral with respect to a martingale and so, under standard conditions, has conditional expectation zero.

With a T-forward contract the only payment is at time T; the buyer agrees at time 0 to pay $F(h, 0, T)$ for the claim h at time T.

With a T-future contract the buyer receives a (positive or negative) cash flow from time 0 to time T. If she still holds the contract at time T she pays an amount h at time T for the claim, which has value h. Between time 0 and time T the buyer has received an amount

$$\int_0^T dG(h, u, T) = G(h, T, T) - G(h, 0, T)$$

$$= h - G(h, 0, T).$$

Therefore, at time T she has *paid* an amount $-(h - G(h, 0, T)) + h = G(h, 0, T)$ for the claim that has value h at time T.

9.3 Changing Numéraire

Consider again the situation described in Notation 9.1.1 where, under a risk-neutral measure P, there is a risky asset S^1 with dynamics

$$dS^1(t) = r(t)S^1(t)dt + \sigma(t)S^1(t)dW(t).$$

Here W is a Brownian motion on a probability space $(\Omega, \mathcal{F}, P)$ with a filtration $\{\mathcal{F}_t\}$, $0 \le t \le T^*$. In general, $\{\mathcal{F}_t\}$ may be larger than the filtration generated by W. The short-term rate r and volatility σ are adapted (random) processes. The value of a dollar in the money market is, as before, $S^0(t) = \exp \int_0^t r(u)du$. We note that

$$d\left(\frac{S^1(t)}{S^0(t)}\right) = \frac{S^1(t)}{S^0(t)} \sigma(t)dW(t)$$

so the discounted asset price is a martingale.

When we consider the discounted price $(S^1(t))/(S^0(t))$ we are saying that, at time t, one unit of stock is worth $(S^1(t))/(S^0(t))$ units of the money market account. Similarly, from the expression after Definition 9.1.2 at time t, with $T \le T^*$, the T-maturity bond is worth $(B(t, T))/(S^0(t))$ units of the money market account; again this discounted price is $E[S^0(T)^{-1}|\mathcal{F}_t]$ and so is a martingale.

Now any strictly positive price process could play the role of $S^0(t)$ and other assets can be expressed in terms of this process.

Definition 9.3.1. Such a strictly positive process is said to be the *numéraire*.

For example, the T-maturity bond price $B(t,T)$ could be taken as the numéraire for $t \leq T$. In terms of $B(t,T)$, at time t, the risky asset is worth

$$\frac{S^1(t)}{B(t,T)} = F(t,T) \text{units of } B(t,T),$$

where $B(t,T)$ is the forward price of Definition 9.1.3. Of course, the price of the bond itself in terms of the numéraire $B(t,T)$ is just $(B(t,T))(B(t,T)) = 1$ unit.

We could also, for example, take $S^1(t)$ to be the numéraire. Then the price at time t of a T-maturity bond in units of $S^1(t)$ is

$$\frac{B(t,T)}{S^1(t)} = \frac{1}{F(t,T)}.$$

Definition 9.3.2. Suppose $Z(t)$ is a strictly positive process so $Z(t)$ can be taken as a numéraire. A probability measure P_Z on $(\Omega, \mathcal{F}, P)$ is said to be *risk neutral* for Z if the price of any asset divided by Z (i.e., expressed in units of Z) is a martingale under P_Z.

We assumed in Notation 9.1 that the original measure P was risk neutral for the numéraire $S^0(t)$.

Theorem 9.3.3. *Suppose Z is a numéraire, so it is the strictly positive price process of some asset.*

Define a new probability measure P_Z on $(\Omega, \mathcal{F}, P)$ by putting for any $A \in \mathcal{F}_{T^*}$,

$$P_Z(A) = Z(0)^{-1} \int_A \frac{Z(T)}{S^0(T)} dP.$$

Then P_Z is equivalent to P and is a risk-neutral measure for the numéraire Z.

Proof. Note for $A \in \mathcal{F}_{T^*}$,

$$P(A) = Z(0) \int_A S^0(T) Z(T)^{-1} dP_Z$$

so P and P_Z have the same null sets.

From the definition of P, Z/S^0 is a martingale under P. Consequently,

$$\begin{aligned}
P_Z(\Omega) &= Z(0)^{-1} \int_\Omega \frac{Z(T)}{S^0(T)} dP \\
&= Z(0)^{-1} E\left[\frac{Z(T)}{S^0(T)}\right] \\
&= Z(0)^{-1} \frac{Z(0)}{S^0(0)} = 1
\end{aligned}$$

because Z/S^0 is a P martingale. Consequently, P_Z is a probability measure.

Now suppose X is the price process of some asset, so X/S^0 is a P martingale. We show X/Z is then a P_Z martingale. Write

$$M_T := Z(0)^{-1} \frac{Z(t)}{S^0(t)}$$

$$= Z(0)^{-1} E\left[\frac{Z(T^*)}{S^0(T^*)} \mid \mathcal{F}_t\right]$$

(because Z/S^0 is a P martingale). From Lemma 7.2.2, X/Z is a P_Z martingale if and only if $X/Z, M = Z(0)^{-1} (X/Z) \cdot (Z/S^0)$ is a P martingale and the result follows. $\square$

Remark 9.3.4. Note that, if we take the numéraire Z to be the bond price $B(t,T)$ for $0 < T \leq T^*$, then the risk-neutral measure P_B for this bond $Z(t) = B(t,T)$ has a density

$$B(0,T)^{-1} \frac{B(T,T)}{S^0(T)} = B(0,T)^{-1} \cdot \frac{1}{S^0(T)}.$$

Consequently, the risk-neutral measure for the bond B is just the forward-measure given in Definition 9.1.5. Note that, as the bond is not defined after time T, the measure change is defined only on $\mathcal{F}_T$, that is, only up to time T.

With the T-maturity bond as numéraire we have seen that the price of the risky asset S^1 is given by its forward price

$$F(t,T) = \frac{S^1(t)}{B(t,T)} \qquad \text{for } 0 \leq t \leq T.$$

Now $F(t,T)$ must be a martingale under the risk-neutral measure $P_{B(t,T)}$ for B and consequently the differential $dF(t,T)$ must be of the form

$$dF(t,T) = \sigma_F(t,T)F(t,T)dW_B(t), \quad 0 \leq t \leq T. \qquad (9.2)$$

We note this is a differential without any bounded variation dt terms and $W_B(t)$, $0 \leq t \leq T$, is a process that is a standard Brownian motion under the measure P_B. As usual, $\sigma_F(t,T)$ can be taken to be nonnegative.

Suppose now the price S^1 of the risky asset is taken as the numéraire. Of course, in terms of S^1 the price of the risky asset S^1 is always 1 unit. The risk-neutral measure for the numéraire S^1 is defined by

$$P_S(A) = \frac{1}{S^1(0)} \int_A \frac{S^1(T^*)}{S^0(T^*)} \, dP \qquad \text{for } A \in \mathcal{F}_{T^*}.$$

In terms of units of S^1 the value of a T-maturity bond is just

$$\frac{B(t,T)}{S^1(t)} = \frac{1}{F(t,T)}, \quad 0 \leq t \leq T \leq T^*.$$

However, this is to be a martingale under P_S so it has a differential

$$d\left(\frac{1}{F(t,T)}\right) = \sigma_{F^{-1}}(t,T)\left(\frac{1}{F(t,T)}\right)dW_S(t), \quad 0 \le t \le T \le T^*. \quad (9.3)$$

Again there will be no dt terms in the differential and $W_S(t)$, $0 \le t \le T$, is a standard Brownian motion under P_S. Again, $\sigma_{F^{-1}}(t,T)$ can be taken non-negative.

Theorem 9.3.5. $\sigma_F(t,T) = \sigma_{F^{-1}}(t,T)$.

Proof. Applying the Itô rule to (9.3):

$$\begin{aligned}
d\left(\frac{1}{F(t,T)}\right) &= -\frac{1}{F(t,T)^2}\,\sigma_F(t,T)F(t,T)dW_B(t) \\
&\quad + \frac{1}{F(t,T)^3}\,\sigma_F(t,T)^2 F(t,T)^2 dt \\
&= \sigma_F(t,T)\left(\frac{1}{F(t,T)}\right)\left[-dW_B(t) + \sigma_F(t,T)dt\right]. \quad (9.4)
\end{aligned}$$

We know that $W_B(t)$ is a standard Brownian motion under $P_{B(t,T)}$, as is $-W_B(t)$. Therefore, under $P_{B(t,T)}$ the process $1/(F(t,T))$ has volatility $\sigma_F(t,T)$ and mean rate of return $\sigma_F(t,T)^2$. Changing the measure from $P_{B(t,T)}$ to P_S transforms $1/(F(t,T))$ into a $P_S$martingale. Consequently, under P_S the mean rate of return of $1/(F(t,T))$ is zero, but the volatility is not changed. In fact, from (9.4),

$$d\left(\frac{1}{F(t,T)}\right) = \sigma_{F^{-1}}(t,T)\frac{1}{F(t,T)}\,dW_S(t), \quad 0 \le t \le T \le T^*. \quad (9.5)$$

Comparing (9.4) and (9.5) we see

$$\sigma_F(t,T) = \sigma_{F^{-1}}(t,T)$$

and

$$W_S(t) = -W_B(t) + \int_0^t \sigma_F(s,T)ds.$$

$\square$

9.4   A General Option Pricing Formula

Following El Karoui, Geman and Rochet [80] the risk-neutral measures for the numéraires S^1 and B can be used to express the price of a European call option:

$$
\begin{aligned}
V(0) &= E\big[S^0(T)^{-1}\big(S^1(T) - K\big)^+\big] \\
&= E\big[S^0(T)^{-1}S^1(T)I_{S^1(T)>K}\big] - KE\big[S^0(T)^{-1}I_{S^1(T)>K}\big] \\
&= S^1(0)\int_{\{S^1(T)>K\}} \frac{S^1(T)}{S^1(0)S^0(T)}\,dP - KB(0,T) \\
&\quad \times \int_{\{S^1(T)>K\}} \frac{1}{B(0,T)S^0(T)}\,dP \\
&= S^1(0)P_S\{S^1(T) > K\} - KB(0,T)P_B\{S^1(T) > K\} \\
&= S^1(0)P_S\{F(T,T) > K\} - KB(0,T)P_B\{F(T,T) > K\} \\
&= S^1(0)P_S\Big\{\frac{1}{F(T,T)} < \frac{1}{K}\Big\} - KB(0,T)P_B\{F(T,T) > K\}.
\end{aligned}
$$

Let us suppose that $\sigma_F(t,T)$ is a constant σ_F. Then from (9.3), recalling $\sigma_F = \sigma_{F-1}$,

$$
\frac{1}{F(T,T)} = \frac{B(0,T)}{S^1(0)}\,\exp\Big(\sigma_F W_S(T) - \frac{1}{2}\sigma_F^2 T\Big),
$$

where W_S is a standard Brownian motion under P_S. Consequently,

$$
\begin{aligned}
P_S\Big\{\frac{1}{F(T,T)} < \frac{1}{K}\Big\} &= P_S\Big\{\sigma_F W_S(T) - \frac{1}{2}\sigma_F^2 T < \log\frac{S^1(0)}{KB(0,T)}\Big\} \\
&= P_S\Big\{\frac{W_S(T)}{\sqrt{T}} < \frac{1}{\sigma_F\sqrt{T}}\log\frac{S^1(0)}{KB(0,T)} + \frac{1}{2}\sigma_F\sqrt{T}\Big\}.
\end{aligned}
$$

Now $(W_S(T))/\sqrt{T}$ is a standard normal random variable.

Writing, as in Theorem 7.6.2, $\Phi(y)$ for the standard normal distribution, this is equal to

$$
\Phi(h_1),
$$

where

$$
h_1 = \frac{1}{\sigma_F\sqrt{T}}\Big[\log\frac{S^1(0)}{KB(0,T)} + \frac{1}{2}\sigma_F^2 T\Big].
$$

From (9.2) we also have that

$$
F(T,T) = \frac{S^1(0)}{B(0,T)}\,\exp\Big(\sigma_F W_B(T) - \frac{1}{2}\sigma_F^2 T\Big),
$$

where W_B is a standard Brownian motion under P_B. Therefore,

$$
\begin{aligned}
P_B\{F(T,T) > K\} &= P_B\Big\{\sigma_F W_B(T) - \frac{1}{2}\sigma_F^2 T > \log\frac{KB(0,T)}{S^1(0)}\Big\} \\
&= P_B\Big\{\frac{W_B(T)}{\sqrt{T}} < \frac{1}{\sigma_F\sqrt{T}}\Big[\log\frac{KB(0,T)}{S^1(0)} + \frac{1}{2}\sigma_F^2 T\Big]\Big\} \\
&= P_B\Big\{-\frac{W_B(T)}{\sqrt{T}} < \frac{1}{\sigma_F\sqrt{T}}\Big[\log\frac{S^1(0)}{KB(0,T)} - \frac{1}{2}\sigma_F^2 T\Big]\Big\}.
\end{aligned}
$$

Again, $(W_B(T))/\sqrt{T}$ is a standard normal random variable so this is equal to

$$\Phi(h_2),$$

where

$$h_2 = \frac{1}{\sigma_F \sqrt{T}} \left[\log \frac{S^1(0)}{KB(0,T)} - \frac{1}{2} \sigma_F^2 T \right].$$

Consequently, the price of the European call is

$$V(0) = S^1(0)\Phi(h_1) - KB(0,T)\Phi(h_2).$$

If r is constant, then $B(0,T) = e^{-rT}$ and this formula reduces to the Black–Scholes formula of Theorem 7.6.2.

A modification of this argument shows that for any intermediate time t, $0 \le t \le T$, the value of the European call, with strike price K and expiration time T, is

$$V(t) = S^1(t)\Phi(h_1(t)) - KB(t,T)\Phi(h_2(t)), \tag{9.6}$$

where now, recalling $F(t,T) = (S^1(t))/(B(t,T))$,

$$h_1(t) = \frac{1}{\sigma_F \sqrt{T-t}} \left[\log \frac{F(t,T)}{K} + \frac{1}{2} \sigma_F^2 (T - t) \right]$$

and

$$h_2(t) = \frac{1}{\sigma_F \sqrt{T-t}} \left[\log \frac{F(t,T)}{K} - \frac{1}{2} \sigma_F^2 (T - t) \right].$$

Formula (9.6) suggests the European call can be hedged by, at each time t, holding $\Phi(h_1(t))$ units of S^1 and shorting $K\Phi(h_2(t))$ bonds.

We establish that this is a self-financing strategy. However, first we show that a change of numéraire does not change a trading strategy.

Lemma 9.4.1. *Suppose $S^1, S^2, \ldots, S^d$ are the price processes of d assets. Consider a self-financing strategy $(\theta^1, \theta^2, \ldots, \theta^d)$, where $\theta^i(t)$ represents the number of units of asset i held at time t. Suppose Z is a numéraire and $\widehat{S}^i = S^i Z^{-1}$, $1 \le i \le d$, is the price of asset i in units of Z. Then θ^i represents the number of units of $\widehat{S}^i$ in the portfolio, 'evaluated' in terms of the new numéraire (there are no other riskless assets).*

Proof. The wealth process is

$$X(t) = \sum_{i=1}^{d} \theta^i(t) S^i(t).$$

As the strategy is self financing

$$dX(t) = \sum_{i=1}^{d} \theta^i(t) dS^i(t).$$

Write $\widehat{X}(t) = X(t) \cdot Z(t)^{-1}$ for the wealth process expressed in terms of the numéraire Z. Then

$$d\widehat{X} = dX \cdot Z^{-1} + X d(Z^{-1}) + d\langle X, Z^{-1} \rangle$$

$$= \left(\sum_{i=1}^{d} \theta^i dS^i \right) Z^{-1} + \left(\sum_{i=1}^{d} \theta^i S^i \right) d(Z^{-1}) + \sum_{i=1}^{d} \theta^i d\langle S^i, Z^{-1} \rangle$$

$$= \sum_{i=1}^{d} \theta^i d\widehat{S}^i.$$

$\square$

Corollary 9.4.2. *In Lemma 9.4.1 the strategy $(\theta^1, \theta^2, \ldots, \theta^d)$ determined the wealth process X. Suppose now that components $\theta^1, \theta^2, \ldots, \theta^{d-1}$ are given, together with the wealth process X. Then*

$$\theta^d(t) = \left(X(t) - \sum_{i=1}^{d-1} \theta^i(t) S^i(t) \right) S^d(t)^{-1}$$

and

$$dX(t) = \sum_{i=1}^{d} \theta^i(t) dS^i(t)$$

$$= \sum_{i=1}^{d-1} \theta^i(t) dS^i(t) + \left(X(t) - \sum_{i=1}^{d-1} \theta^i(t) S^i(t) \right) \frac{dS^d(t)}{S^d(t)}.$$

In terms of the numéraire Z we still have

$$\theta^d(t) = \frac{\left(X(t) - \sum_{i=1}^{d-1} \theta^i(t) S^i(t) \right)}{S^d(t)}$$

$$= \frac{\left(\widehat{X}(t) - \sum_{i=1}^{d-1} \theta^i(t) \widehat{S}^i(t) \right)}{\widehat{S}^d(t)}$$

and

$$d\widehat{X}(t) = \sum_{i=1}^{d-1} \theta^i(t) d\widehat{S}^i(t) + \left(\widehat{X}(t) - \sum_{i=1}^{d-1} \theta^i(t) \widehat{S}^i(t) \right) \frac{d\widehat{S}^d(t)}{\widehat{S}^d(t)}.$$

Let us return to the price (9.6) at time t for a European call option.

Theorem 9.4.3. *Holding at each time t, $0 \le t \le T$, $\Phi(h_1(t))$ units of S^1 and shorting $K\Phi(h_2(t))$ bonds is a self-financing strategy for the European call option with strike price K and expiration time T.*

Proof. This result could be established using Lemma 9.4.1. Alternatively, suppose we start with an initial investment of $V(0)$ and hold $\Phi(h_1(t))$ units of S^1 at each time t. To maintain this position we short as many bonds as necessary.

If we can show the number of bonds we must short at time t is $K\Phi(h_2(t))$ then the value of our portfolio is indeed

$$\Phi(h_1(t))S^1(t) - KB(t,T)\Phi(h_2(t))$$

which equals $V(t)$, the price of the call option at time t, $0 \le t \le T$, and we have a hedge.

Let us write $\theta^1(t) = \Phi(h_1(t))$ so that at time t we hold $\theta^1(t)$ units of S^1.

Suppose $X(t)$ is the value of our portfolio at time t; then we invest $X(t) - \theta^1(t)S^1(t)$ in the bond and the number of bonds in the portfolio is

$$\theta^2(t) := \frac{(X(t) - \theta^1(t)S^1(t))}{B(t,T)}.$$

Then

$$dX(t) = \theta^1(t)dS^1(t) + \theta^2(t)dB(t,T)$$

$$= \theta^1(t)dS^1(t) + \frac{(X(t) - \theta^1(t)S^1(t))}{B(t,T)} dB(t,T).$$

We must show that, if $X(0) = V(0)$, then

$$X(t) = V(t) \qquad \text{for } 0 \le t \le T.$$

To establish this it is easier to work with $B(t,T)$ as numéraire. In terms of this zero coupon bond the asset values become:

$$S^1: \quad \widehat{S}^1(t) = \frac{S^1(t)}{B(t,T)} = F(t,T) \quad \text{the forward price}$$

$$B: \widehat{B}(t,T) = \frac{B(t,T)}{B(t,T)} = 1, \qquad \text{constant,}$$

$$X: \quad \widehat{X}(t) = \Phi(h_1(t))F(t,T) + (\widehat{X}(t) - \theta^1(t)S^1(t)),$$

and $d\widehat{X}(t) = \Phi(h_1(t))dF(t,T)$.

The option value is

$$V(t) = \Phi(h_1(t))S^1(t) - KB(t,T)\Phi(h_2(t))$$

and in terms of the numéraire $B(t,T)$ becomes

$$\widehat{V}(t) = \Phi(h_1(t))F(t,T) - K\Phi(h_2(t)).$$

Consequently,

$$d\widehat{V}(t) = \Phi\big(h_1(t)\big)dF(t,T) + F(t,T)d\Phi\big(h_1(t)\big)$$
$$- Kd\Phi\big(h_2(t)\big) + d\langle\Phi\big(h_1(t)\big), F(t,T)\rangle.$$

Recall the dynamics (9.2),

$$dF(t,T) = \sigma_F F(t,T)dW_B(t).$$

Recall $\phi(x) = (1/\sqrt{2\pi})\,e^{-x^2/2}$ and $\Phi(y) = \int_{-\infty}^{y}\phi(x)dx$, so with

$$h_1(t) = \frac{1}{\sigma_F\sqrt{T-t}}, \left[\log\frac{F(t,T)}{K} + \frac{1}{2}\sigma_F^2(T-t)\right],$$

the Itô rule gives, after some cancellation,

$$d\Phi\big(h_1(t)\big) = \phi(h_1)\cdot\frac{1}{\sigma_F\sqrt{T-t}}\cdot\frac{1}{F}\,dF - \phi(h_1)\frac{\sigma_F}{2\sqrt{T-t}}\,dt.$$

Also, $F\phi(h_1) = K\phi(h_2)$ and some elementary but tedious calculations confirm that

$$Fd\Phi(h_1) - Kd\Phi(h_2) + d\langle N(h_1), F\rangle = 0.$$

The result follows. $\qquad\qquad\qquad\qquad\qquad\qquad\qquad\qquad\qquad\square$

9.5   Term Structure Models

Again suppose W is a standard Brownian motion on $(\Omega, \mathcal{F}, P)$ and $\{\mathcal{F}_t\}$, $0 \le t \le T$, is the filtration generated by W.

The instantaneous interest rate $r(t)$ is an adapted measurable process and the numéraire asset S_t^0 has value

$$S_t^0 = \exp\left(\int_0^t r(u)du\right), \quad 0 \le t \le T.$$

We have seen that the price at time $t \in [0,T]$ of a zero coupon bond maturing at time T is

$$B(t,T) = S_t^0 E[(S_T^0)^{-1}\,|\mathcal{F}_t].$$

If r is nonrandom this is

$$= \exp\left(-\int_t^T r(u)du\right).$$

Zero coupon bonds are traded in the market and their prices can be used to calibrate the model. They are known as 'zeros.'

Definition 9.5.1. A *term structure model* is a mathematical model for the prices $B(t,T)$, for all t,T with $0 \leq t \leq T \leq T_2$.

The *yield* $R(t,T) = -((\log B(t,T))/(T-t))$ provides a *yield curve* for each fixed time t, as the graph of $R(t,T)$ against T, which displays the average return of bonds after elimination of the distorting effects of maturity. We expect different yields at different maturities, reflecting market beliefs about future changes in interest rates. While the greater uncertainty about interest rates in the distant future will tend to lead to increases in yield with maturity, high current rates (which may be expected to fall) can produce "inverted" yield curves, in which long bonds will have lower yields than short ones. A satisfactory term structure model should be able to handle both situations.

Remark 9.5.2. Recall we are working under a martingale, or risk-neutral, measure P and that

$$B(t,T) = S_t^0 E[(S_T^0)^{-1} | \mathcal{F}_t].$$

That is,

$$\frac{B(t,T)}{S_t^0} = E[(S_T^0)^{-1} | \mathcal{F}_t]$$

and so is a martingale under P.

If the market measure P does not have the property that all processes $(B(t,T))/S_t^0$ are martingales, then the term structure model is free of arbitrage only if there is an equivalent measure $\widetilde{P}$ such that, under $\widetilde{P}$, all processes $(B(t,T)/S_t^0)$ are martingales, for all maturity times T.

$B(t,T)$ is a positive process for all T so that, using the martingale representation theorem, the dynamics for $B(t,T)$ can be expressed in a lognormal form

$$dB(t,T) = \mu(t,T)B(t,T)dt + \sigma(t,T)B(t,T)dW(t), \quad 0 \leq t \leq T.$$

Consequently,

$$d\left(\frac{B(t,T)}{S_t^0}\right) = (\mu(t,T) - r(t))\frac{B(t,T)}{S_t^0} dt + \sigma(t,T)\frac{B(t,T)}{S_t^0} dW(t)$$

and $(B(t,T))/S_t^0$ is a martingale under P if and only if $\mu(t,T) = r(t)$.

The statement that

$$B(t,T) = E\left[\exp - \int_t^T r(u)du \, | \mathcal{F}_t \right]$$

is sometimes called the *Local Expectations Hypothesis*.

The assumption that holding a discount bond to maturity gives the same return as rolling over a series of single period bonds is called the *Return to*

Maturity Expectations Hypothesis. In continuous time it would state that, under some probability P',

$$B(t,T)^{-1} = E_{P'}\left[\exp\left(\int_t^T r(u)du\right)\bigg|\mathcal{F}_t\right].$$

The *Yield to Maturity Expectations Hypothesis* states that the yield from holding a bond equals the yield from rolling over a series of single-period bonds. In continuous time this would imply

$$B(t,T) = \exp\left[-E_{P'}\left(\int_t^T r(u)du\right)\bigg|\mathcal{F}_t\right]$$

for some probability P'. A discussion of these concepts can be found in the papers of Frachot and Lesne, [109], [110], [177].

9.6 Diffusion Models for the Short-Term Rate Process

Vasicek's Model

In [255] Vasicek proposed a mean-reverting version of the Ornstein–Uhlenbeck process for the short term rate r. Specifically, under the risk-neutral measure P, r is given by

$$dr_t = a(b - r_t)dt + \sigma dW_t, \quad \text{for} \quad r_0 > 0, \quad a > 0, \quad b > 0, \quad \text{and} \sigma > 0.$$

Then

$$r_t = e^{-at}\left(r_0 + b(e^{at} - 1) + \sigma\int_0^t e^{au}dW_u\right).$$

Consequently, r_t is a normal random variable with mean

$$E[r_t] = e^{-at}\left(r_0 + b(e^{at} - 1)\right)$$

and variance

$$\text{Var}\,(r_t) = \sigma^2\left(\frac{1 - e^{-2at}}{2a}\right).$$

However, a normal random variable can be negative with positive probability so this model for r is not too realistic (unless the probability of being negative is small). Nonetheless, its simplicity validates its discussion.

As $t \to +\infty$ we see that r_t converges in law to a Gaussian random variable with mean b and variance $\sigma^2/2a$.

The price of a zero coupon bond in the Vasicek model is, therefore,

$$B(t,T) = E\left[\exp\left(-\int_t^T r(u)du\right)\bigg|\mathcal{F}_t\right]$$

$$= e^{-b(T-t)}E\left[\exp\left(-\int_t^T X(u)du\right)\bigg|\mathcal{F}_t\right],$$

where $X(u) = r(u) - b$. Now $X(u)$ is the solution of the classical Ornstein–Uhlenbeck equation

$$dX(t) = -aX(t)dt + \sigma \, dW_t, \tag{9.7}$$

with $X(0) = r(0) - b$. Write

$$\Phi(t, x) = E\left[\exp\left(-\int_0^t X(u, x)du\right)\right], \tag{9.8}$$

where $X(u, x)$ is the solution of (9.2) with $X(0, x) = x$. Now

$$X(u, x) = e^{-au}\left(x + \int_0^u \sigma e^{as}dW_s\right)$$

so $X(u, x)$ is a Gaussian process with continuous sample paths. Consequently, $\int_0^t X(u, x)du$ is a Gaussian process; this can be established by considering moment-generating functions $\exp(u_1 X(t_1) + \cdots + u_n X(t_n))$.

If ϕ is a Gaussian random variable with $E[\phi] = m$ and $\mathrm{Var}\,\phi = \gamma^2$ we know that

$$E[e^{-\phi}] = e^{-m+(1/2)\gamma^2}.$$

Now $E[X(u, x)] = xe^{-au}$ so $E[\int_0^t X(u, x)du] = (x/a)(1 - e^{-at})$; and

$$\mathrm{Cov}\,[X(t, x), X(u, x)] = \sigma^2 e^{-a(u+t)} E\left[\int_0^t e^{as}dW_s \int_0^u e^{as}dW_s\right]$$

$$= \sigma^2 e^{-a(u+t)} \int_0^{u\wedge t} e^{2as}ds$$

$$= \frac{\sigma^2}{2a} e^{-a(u+t)}\left(e^{2a(u\wedge t)} - 1\right). \tag{9.9}$$

Therefore,

$$\mathrm{Var}\left[\int_0^t X(u, x)du\right] = \mathrm{Cov}\left[\int_0^t X(u, x)du, \int_0^t X(s, x)ds\right]$$

$$= \int_0^t \int_0^t \mathrm{Cov}[X(u, x), X(s, x)]du\,ds$$

$$= \int_0^t \int_0^t \frac{\sigma^2}{2a} e^{-a(u+s)}\left(e^{2a(u\wedge s)} - 1\right)du\,ds$$

$$= \frac{\sigma^2}{2a^3}\left(2at - 3 + 4e^{-at} - e^{-2at}\right).$$

Consequently,

$$\Phi(t, x) = E\left[\exp\left(-\int_0^t X(u, x)du\right)\right]$$

$$= \exp\left(-\frac{x}{a}(1 - e^{-at}) + \frac{1}{4}\frac{\sigma^2}{a^3}\left(2at - 3 + 4e^{-at} - e^{-2at}\right)\right).$$

Using the time homogeneity of the X process,

$$B(t, T) = e^{-b(T-t)}\Phi(T - t, r(t) - b).$$

This can be written as

$$B(t, T) = \exp\left[-(T - t)R(T - t, r(t))\right]$$

where $R(T - t, r(t))$ can be thought of as the interest rate between times t and T. With $R_\infty = b - (\sigma^2/2a^2)$ we can write

$$R(t, r) = R_\infty - \frac{1}{at}\left[(R_\infty - r)(1 - e^{-at}) - \frac{\sigma^2}{4a^2}(1 - e^{-at})^2\right].$$

Note $R_\infty = \lim_{t\to\infty} R(t, r)$, so R_∞ can be thought of as the long-term interest rate. However, R_∞ does not depend on the instantaneous rate $r(t)$. Practitioners consider this to be a weakness of the Vasicek model.

The Hull–White Model

In its simplest form this model is a generalization of the Vasicek model using deterministic, time-varying coefficients. It is popular with practitioners. Its more general form includes a term r_t^β in the volatility, in which case it generalizes the Cox–Ingersoll–Ross model discussed in the next section.

In this model the short rate process is supposed given by the stochastic differential equation

$$dr_t = \left(\alpha(t) - \beta, (t)r_t\right)dt + \sigma(t)dW_t \tag{9.10}$$

for $r_0 > 0$. Here, α, β, and σ are deterministic functions of t.

Write $b(t) := \int_0^t \beta(u)du$, so b is also nonrandom. Then we can solve (9.10) by variation of constants to obtain

$$r_t = e^{-b(t)}\left(r_0 + \int_0^t e^{b(u)}\alpha(u)du + \int_0^t e^{b(u)}\sigma(u)dW_u\right).$$

Again, r_t is a deterministic quantity plus the stochastic integral of a deterministic function.

Consequently, r is a Gaussian Markov process with mean

$$E[r_t] = m(t) = e^{-b(t)}\left[r_0 + \int_0^t e^{b(u)}\alpha(u)du\right]$$

and covariance

$$\text{Cov}(r_t, r_s) = e^{-b(s)-b(t)}\int_0^{s\wedge t} e^{2b(u)}\sigma^2(u)du.$$

Again we can argue $\int_0^T r_t dt$ is normal. Its mean is

$$E\Big[\int_0^T r_t dt\Big] = \int_0^T e^{-b(t)}\Big[r_0 + \int_0^t e^{b(u)}\alpha(u)du\Big]dt$$

and its variance is

$$\text{Var}\Big[\int_0^T r_t dt\Big] = \int_0^T e^{2b(u)}\sigma^2(u)\Big(\int_u^T e^{-b(s)}ds\Big)^2 du.$$

The price of a zero coupon bond for this model is

$$B(0,T) = E\Big[\exp\Big(-\int_0^T r_t dt\Big)\Big].$$

The quantity in the exponential is Gaussian, so this is

$$= \exp\Big[-E\Big[\int_0^T r_t dt\Big] + \frac{1}{2}\text{Var}\Big[\int_0^T r_t dt\Big]\Big]$$

$$= \exp\Big[-r_0\int_0^T e^{-b(t)}dt - \int_0^T\int_0^t e^{-b(t)+b(u)}\alpha(u)dudt$$

$$+ \frac{1}{2}\int_0^T e^{2b(u)}\sigma^2(u)\Big(\int_u^T e^{-b(s)}ds\Big)^2 du\Big]$$

$$= \exp[-r_0 C(0,T) - A(0,T)],$$

where

$$C(0,T) = \int_0^T e^{-b(t)}dt$$

and

$$A(0,T) = \int_0^T\int_0^t e^{-b(t)+b(u)}\alpha(u)du\,dt$$

$$- \frac{1}{2}\int_0^T e^{2b(u)}\sigma^2(u)\Big(\int_u^T e^{-b(s)}ds\Big)^2 du.$$

Note the first term in A can be written, using Fubini's theorem,

$$\int_0^T\int_u^T e^{-b(t)+b(u)}\alpha(u)dudt$$

$$= \int_0^T e^{b(u)}\alpha(u)\Big(\int_u^T e^{-b(s)}ds\Big)du.$$

Therefore,

$$A(0,T) = \int_0^T\Big[e^{b(u)}\alpha(u)\gamma(u) - \frac{1}{2}e^{2b(u)}\sigma^2(u)\gamma^2(u)\Big]du,$$

where

$$\gamma(u) = \int_u^T e^{-b(s)} ds.$$

The price at time t of a zero coupon bond is

$$B(t,T) = E\Big[\exp\Big(-\int_t^T r_u du\Big)\Big|\mathcal{F}_t\Big].$$

Because r is Markov this should equal

$$= E\Big[\exp\Big(-\int_t^T r_u du\Big)\Big|r_t\Big].$$

Write

$$C(t,T) = e^{b(t)} \int_t^T e^{-b(u)} du = e^{b(t)}\gamma(t)$$

and

$$A(t,T) = \int_t^T \Big[e^{b(u)}\alpha(u)\gamma(u) - \frac{1}{2} e^{2b(u)}\sigma^2(u)\gamma^2(u)\Big] du.$$

Then it can be shown that

$$B(t,T) = \exp\big(-r_t C(t,T) - A(t,T)\big). \tag{9.11}$$

Now α, β, and γ are deterministic functions of time t; consequently $C(t,T)$ and $A(t,T)$ are also functions only of t. Write $C_t(t,T)$ and $A_t(t,T)$ for their derivatives in t. From (9.11) we have

$$\begin{aligned} dB(t,T) = B(t,T)[&-C(t,T)\big(\alpha(t) - \beta(t)r_t\big)dt \\ &- C(t,T)\sigma(t)dW_t - \frac{1}{2} C^2(t,T)\sigma^2(t)dt \\ &- r(t)C_t(t,T)dt - A_t(t,T)dt]. \end{aligned} \tag{9.12}$$

We are working under the risk-neutral measure, so

$$dB(t,T) = r(t)B(t,T)dt + \Delta(t)dW_t, \tag{9.13}$$

where Δ is some coefficient function. Comparing (9.12) and (9.13) we see that we must have

$$\begin{aligned} r_t = &-C(t,t)\big(\alpha(t) - \beta(t)r_t\big) \\ &- \frac{1}{2} C^2(t,T)\sigma^2(t) - r_t C_t(t,T) - A_t(t,T). \end{aligned} \tag{9.14}$$

Consequently,

$$dB(t,T) = r_t B(t,T)dt - B(t,T)\sigma(t)C(t,T)dW_t.$$

The volatility of the zero coupon bond is $\sigma(t)C(t,T)$.

Some Normal Densities

Consider times $0 \leq t \leq T_1 < T_2$. In the Hull–White framework we have seen that $r(T_1)$ is Gaussian with

$$E[r(T_1)] = m_1 = e^{-b(T_1)}\left[r_0 + \int_0^{T_1} e^{b(u)}\alpha(u)du\right],$$

$$\text{Var } r(T_1) = \sigma_1^2 = e^{-2b(T_1)}\left[\int_0^{T_1} e^{2b(u)}\sigma^2(u)du\right].$$

Also, $\int_0^{T_1} r(u)du$ is Gaussian with

$$E\left[\int_0^{T_1} r(u)du\right] = m_2 = \int_0^{T_1} e^{-b(v)}\left[r_0 + \int_0^v e^{b(u)}\alpha(u)du\right]dv,$$

$$\text{Var } \int_0^{T_1} r(u)du = \sigma_2^2 = \int_0^{T_1} e^{2b(u)}\sigma^2(u)\left(\int_u^{T_1} e^{-b(s)}ds\right)^2 du.$$

The covariance of $r(T_1)$ and $\int_0^{T_1} r(u)du$ is

$$E\left[\left(\int_0^{T_1} (r(u) - Er(u))du\right)\left(r(T_1) - E(r(T_1))\right)\right]du$$

$$= \int_0^{T_1} E\left[(r(u) - E(r(u)))(r(T_1) - E(r(T_1)))\right]du$$

$$= \int_0^{T_1} \text{Cov}\left(r(u), r(T_1)\right)du$$

$$= \int_0^{T} \left(e^{-b(u)-b(T_1)}\int_0^{T} e^{2b(s)}\sigma^2(s)ds\right)du$$

$$= \rho\sigma_1\sigma_2,$$

say.

Bond Options

Consider a European call option on the zero coupon bond that has strike price K and expiration time T_1. The bond matures at time $T_2 > T_1$.

The preceding calculations imply that $(r(T_1), \int_0^{T_1} r(u)du)$ is Gaussian with a density

$$f(x, y) = \frac{1}{2\pi\sigma_1\sigma_2\sqrt{1-\rho^2}}$$

$$\times \exp\left[-\frac{1}{2(1-\rho^2)}\right.$$

$$\left.\times \left(\frac{(x-m_1)^2}{\sigma_1^2} - \frac{2\rho(x-m_1)(y-m_2)}{\sigma_1\sigma_2} + \frac{(y-m_2)^2}{\sigma_2^2}\right)\right].$$

The price of the European option on B with expiration time T_1 and strike K at time 0 is

$$
\begin{aligned}
V(0) &= E\left[e^{-\int_0^{T_1} r(u)du}\left(B(T_1,T_2)-K\right)^+\right] \\
&= E\left[e^{-\int_0^{T_1} r(u)du}\left(\exp\{-r(T_1)C(T_1,T_2)-A(T_1,T_2)\}-K\right)^+\right] \\
&= \int_{-\infty}^{\infty}\int_{-\infty}^{\infty} e^{-y}\left(\exp\{-xC(T_1,T_2)-A(T_1,T_2)\}-K\right)^+ f(x,y)dxdy.
\end{aligned}
$$

To determine the price of the bond option at time $t \le T_1 < T_2$ we note the random variable $\left(r(T_1), \int_t^{T_1} r(u)du\right)$ is Gaussian with a density similar to $f(x,y)$, except that $m_1, m_2,\ \sigma_1,\sigma_2$, and ρ are replaced by

$$
\begin{aligned}
m_1(t) &= E[r(t_1)|r(t)] \\
&= e^{-b(T_1)}\left(e^{b(t)}r(t)+\int_t^{T_1} e^{b(u)}\alpha(u)du\right),
\end{aligned}
$$

$$
\begin{aligned}
\sigma_1^2(t) &= E\left[\left(r(T_1)-m_1(t)\right)^2\big|r(t)\right] \\
&= e^{-2b(T_1)}\int_t^{T_1} e^{2b(u)}\sigma^2(u)du,
\end{aligned}
$$

$$
\begin{aligned}
m_2(t) &= E\left[\int_t^{T_1} r(u)du\big|r(t)\right] \\
&= \int_t^{T_1}\left\{r(t)e^{-b(v)+b(t)}+e^{-b(v)}\int_t^v e^{b(u)}\alpha(u)du\right\}dv,
\end{aligned}
$$

$$
\begin{aligned}
\sigma_2^2(t) &= E\left[\left(\int_t^{T_1} r(u)du-m_2(r)\right)^2\big|r(t)\right] \\
&= \int_t^{T_1} e^{2b(v)}\sigma^2(v)\left(\int_v^{T_1} e^{-b(s)}ds\right)^2 dv,
\end{aligned}
$$

$$
\begin{aligned}
\rho(t)\sigma_1(t)\sigma_2(t) &= E\left[\left(\int_t^{T_1} r(u)du-m_2(t)\right)\left(r(T_1)-m_1(t)\right)\big|r(t)\right] \\
&= \int_t^{T_1} e^{-b(u)-b(T_1)}\int_t^u e^{2b(s)}\sigma^2(s)dsdu.
\end{aligned}
$$

These quantities now depend on $r(t)$ and so are stochastic as, therefore, is the corresponding option price:

$$E\left[e^{-\int_t^{T_1} r(u)du}\left(B(T_1,T_2) - K\right)^+|\mathcal{F}_t\right]$$
$$= E\left[e^{-\int_t^{T_1} r(u)du}\left(\exp\left\{-r(T_1)C(T_1,T_2) - A(T_1,T_2)\right\} - K\right)^+|r(t)\right].$$

This price can be expressed in terms of an integration with respect to a density analogous to $f_t(x,y)$ in which $m_1, \sigma_1, m_2, \sigma_2, \rho$ are replaced by $m_1(t), \sigma_1(t), m_2(t), \sigma_2(t), \rho(t)$, respectively.

The Hull–White model leads to a closed form expression for the option on the bond. Also, the parameters of the model can be estimated so the initial yield curve is matched exactly. However, it is a 'one factor' model and

$$B(t,T) = \exp\left\{-r(t)C(t,T) - A(t,T)\right\}$$

so all bond prices for all T are perfectly correlated. Furthermore, the short rate $r(t)$ is normally distributed. This means it can take negative values with positive probability, and the bond price can exceed 1.

The Cox–Ingersoll–Ross Model

We have noted that in the Vasicek and Hull–White models for $r(t)$, because $r(t)$ is Gaussian, there is a positive probability that $r(t) < 0$.

The Cox–Ingersoll–Ross model for $r(t)$ provides a stochastic differential equation for $r(t)$, the solution of which is always nonnegative. To describe this process recall the Ornstein–Uhlenbeck equation (9.7),

$$dX(t) = -aX(t)dt + \sigma dW_t \qquad (9.15)$$

with solution

$$X(t,x) = e^{-at}\left(x + \int_0^t \sigma e^{as}dW_s\right).$$

Here W is a standard Brownian motion on a probability space $(\Omega, \mathcal{F}, P)$.

In fact suppose we have n independent Brownian motions $W_1(t), \ldots, W_n(t)$ on $(\Omega, \mathcal{F}, P)$ and n Ornstein–Uhlenbeck processes $X_1(t), \ldots, X_n(t)$ given by equations

$$dX_i(t) = -\frac{1}{2}\alpha X_i(t)dt + \frac{1}{2}\sigma dW_i(t)$$

so that

$$X_i(t) = e^{-(1/2)\alpha t}\left(X_i(0) + (1/2)\sigma\int_0^t e^{(1/2)\alpha s}dW_i(s)\right).$$

Consider the process

$$r(t) := X_1^2(t) + X_2^2(t) + \cdots + X_n^2(t).$$

From Itô's differential rule

$$dr(t) = \sum_{i=1}^{n} 2X_i(t)\left(-\frac{1}{2}\alpha X_i(t)dt + \frac{1}{2}\sigma dW_i(t)\right)$$

$$+ \sum_{i=1}^{n} \frac{1}{4}\sigma^2 dt$$

$$= -\alpha r(t)dt + \sigma\left(\sum_{i=1}^{n} X_i(t)dW_i(t)\right) + \frac{n\sigma^2}{4}dt$$

$$= \left(\frac{n\sigma^2}{4} - \alpha r(t)\right)dt + \sigma\sqrt{r(t)}\sum_{i=1}^{n} \frac{X_i(t)dW_i(t)}{\sqrt{r(t)}}.$$

Consider the process

$$W(t) := \sum_{i=1}^{n} \int_0^t \frac{X_i(u)dW_i(u)}{\sqrt{r(u)}}.$$

Then W is a continuous martingale and

$$W^2(t) = 2\int_0^t W(u)dW(u) + \sum_{i=1}^{n} \int_0^t \frac{X_i^2(u)du}{r(u)}$$

$$= 2\int_0^t W(u)dW(u) + t,$$

so $(W^2(t) - t, t \geq 0)$ is a martingale. From Lévy's characterization, therefore, W is a standard Brownian motion and we can write

$$dr(t) = \left(\frac{n\sigma^2}{4} - \alpha r(t)\right)dt + \sigma\sqrt{r(t)}\,dW(t).$$

It is known (see Revuz and Yor [208], e.g.) that when $n = 1$, $P(r(t) > 0) = 1$ but $P\{$there are infinitely many times $t > 0$ for which $r(t) = 0\} = 1$.
However, if $n \geq 2$ $P\{$there is at least one time $t > 0$ for which $r(t) = 0\} = 0$.

Definition 9.6.1. A *Cox–Ingersoll–Ross (CIR) process* is the process defined by an equation of the form

$$dr(t) = \big(a - br(t)\big)dt + \sigma\sqrt{r(t)}\,dW(t), \tag{9.16}$$

where $a > 0$, $b > 0$, and $\sigma > 0$ are constant. With $n = 4a/\sigma^2$ we can interpret $r(t)$ as $\sum_{i=1}^{n} X_i^2(t)$ for Ornstein–Uhlenbeck processes X_i as previously. However equation (9.16) makes sense whether or not n is an integer.

Remark 9.6.2. Geman and Yor [114] explore the relationship between the Vasicek and CIR model and show in particular that the CIR process is a Bessel process.

Similarly to the results for integer n we quote the following ([204]). If $a < \sigma^2/2$, so $n < 2$, then

$$P\left\{\text{there are infinitely many times } t > 0 \text{ for which } r(t) = 0\right\} = 1.$$

Consequently, this range for a is not too useful.

If $a \geq \sigma^2/2$, so $n \geq 2$, then

$$P\left\{\text{there is at least one time } t > 0 \text{ for which } r(t) = 0\right\} = 0.$$

Write $r_{0,t}(x)$ for the solution of (9.16) for which $r(0) = x$.

The following result describes the law of the pair of random variables $\left(r_{0,t}(x), \int_0^t r_{0,u}(x)du\right)$. Note ϕ and ψ are functions of t only, reminiscent of the A and C functions in the Hull–White model.

Theorem 9.6.3. *For any $\lambda > 0$, $\mu > 0$,*

$$E\left[e^{-\lambda r_{0,t}(x)} e^{-\mu \int_0^t r_{0,u}(x)du}\right] = e^{-a\phi_{\lambda,\mu}(t)} e^{-x\psi_{\lambda,\mu}(t)},$$

where

$$\phi_{\lambda,u}(t) = -\frac{2}{\sigma^2}\log\left(\frac{2\gamma e^{t(b+\gamma)/2}}{\sigma^2\lambda(e^{\gamma t}-1)+\gamma-b+e^{\gamma t}(\gamma+b)}\right)$$

$$\psi_{\lambda,u}(t) = \frac{\lambda(\gamma+b)+e^{\gamma t}(\gamma-b)+2\mu(e^{\gamma t}-1)}{\sigma^2\lambda(e^{\gamma t}-1)+\gamma-b+e^{\gamma t}(\gamma+b)}$$

and

$$\gamma = \sqrt{b^2+2\sigma^2\mu}\,.$$

Proof. Suppose $0 \leq t \leq T$. From the uniqueness of solutions of (9.16) we have the following 'flow' property,

$$r_{0,T}(x) = r_{t,T}\left(r_{0,t}(x)\right).$$

Consider the expectation

$$E\left[e^{-\lambda r_{t,T}(r_{0,t}(x))} e^{-\mu \int_t^T r_{0,u}(x)d\mu}\Big|\mathcal{F}_t\right].$$

From the Markov property this is the same as conditioning on $r_{0,t}(x)$, so write

$$V\left(t, r_{0,t}(x)\right) = E\left[e^{-\lambda r_{0,T}(x)} e^{-\mu \int_t^T r_{0,u}(x)du}\Big|r_{0,t}(x)\right].$$

Now

$$e^{-\mu \int_0^t r_{0,u}(x)du} V\left(t, r_{0,t}(x)\right) = E\left[e^{-\lambda r_{0,T}(x)} e^{-\mu \int_0^T r_{0,u}(x)du}\Big|\mathcal{F}_t\right]$$

and so is a martingale. However, applying the Itô differentiation rule:

$$e^{-\mu \int_0^t r_{0,u}du} V(t, r_{0,t}(x))$$

$$= V(0, x) + \int_0^t \left[\frac{\partial V}{\partial u} (u, r_{0,u}(x)) - \mu r_{0,u}(x) V(u, r_{0,u}(x)) \right.$$

$$+ \frac{\partial V}{\partial \xi} (u, r_{0,u}(x))(a - br_{0,u}(x))$$

$$\left. + \frac{1}{2} \frac{\partial^2 V}{\partial \xi^2} (u, r_{0,u}(x)) \sigma^2 r_{0,u}(x) \right] e^{-\mu \int_0^u r_{0,s}(x)ds} du$$

$$+ \int_0^t e^{-\mu \int_0^u r_{0,s}(x)ds} \frac{\partial V}{\partial \xi} (u, r_{0,u}(x)) \sigma \sqrt{r_{0,u}(x)} \, dW(u).$$

As the left side is a martingale and the right side is an Itô process the du integral must be the zero process. Consequently,

$$\frac{\partial V}{\partial t} (t, y) - \mu y V(t, y) + \frac{\partial V}{\partial y} (t, y)(a - by) + \frac{1}{2} \frac{\partial^2 V}{\partial y^2} (t, y)\sigma^2 y = 0$$

with

$$V(t, y) = E\left[e^{-\lambda r_{t,T}(y)} e^{-\mu \int_t^T r_{t,u}(y)du} \right].$$

Because the coefficients of (9.16) are independent of t the solution of (9.16) is stationary and we can write

$$V(t, y) = E\left[e^{-\lambda r_{0,T-t}(y)} e^{-\mu \int_0^{T-t} r_{0,u}(y)du} \right].$$

Define

$$F(t, y) = E\left[e^{-\lambda r_{0,t}(y)} e^{-\mu \int_0^t r_{0,u}(y)du} \right]$$

so that $V(t, y) = F(T - t, y)$ and F satisfies

$$\frac{\partial F}{\partial t} = \frac{\partial F}{\partial y} (a - by) - \mu y F + \frac{1}{2} \sigma^2 y \frac{\partial^2 F}{\partial y^2} \qquad (9.17)$$

with $F(0, y) = e^{-\lambda y}$.

Motivated by the formula of the Hull–White model we look for a solution of (9.17) in the form

$$F(t, y) = e^{-a\phi(t) - x\psi(t)}.$$

This is the case if $\phi(0) = 0$ and $\psi(0) = \lambda$ with

$$\phi'(t) = \psi(t)$$

and

$$-\psi'(t) = \frac{\sigma^2}{2} \psi^2(t) + b\psi(t) - \mu.$$

Solving these equations gives the expressions for ϕ and ψ. □

Remark 9.6.4. Taking $\mu = 0$ we obtain the Laplace transform of $r_t(x)$.

$$E[e^{\lambda r_t(x)}] = (2\lambda K + 1)^{-2a/\sigma^2} \exp\left(\frac{-\lambda K z}{2\lambda K + 1}\right),$$

where

$$K = \frac{\sigma^2}{4b}(1 - e^{-bt})$$

and

$$z = \frac{4bx}{\sigma^2(e^{bt} - 1)}.$$

Consequently, the Laplace transform of $r_t(x)/K$ is given by $g_{4a/\sigma^2, z}$, where

$$g_{\delta, z} = \frac{1}{(2\lambda + 1)^{\delta/2}} \exp\left(-\frac{\lambda z}{2\lambda + 1}\right).$$

However, consider the chi-square density $f_{\delta, z}$, having δ degrees of freedom and decentral parameter z, given by

$$f_{\delta, z}(x) = \frac{e^{-z/2}}{2z^{(\delta/4)-(1/2)}} e^{-x/2} x^{\delta/4-(1/2)} I_{\delta/2-1}(\sqrt{xz}) \quad \text{for} \quad x > 0.$$

Here I_ν is the modified Bessel function of order ν, given by

$$I_\nu(x) = \left(\frac{x}{2}\right)^\nu \sum_{n=0}^{\infty} \frac{\left(\frac{x}{2}\right)^{2n}}{n!\Gamma(\nu + n + 1)}.$$

Then it can be shown that $g_{\delta, z}$ is the Laplace transform of the law of a random variable having density $f_{\delta, z}(x)$.

Consequently, $r_t(x)/K$ is a random variable having a chi-square density with δ degrees of freedom.

Recall we are working under the risk-neutral probability P. The price of a zero coupon bond at time 0 is

$$B(0, T) = E\left[\exp - \int_0^T r_u(x) du\right]$$

$$= e^{-a\phi_{0,1}(0,T) - r_0(x)\psi_{0,1}(0,T)}.$$

Here

$$\phi_{0,1}(T) = -\frac{2}{\sigma^2} \log\left(\frac{2\gamma e^{T(\gamma+b)/2}}{\gamma - b + e^{\gamma T}(\gamma + b)}\right)$$

$$\psi_{0,1}(T) = \frac{2(e^{\gamma T} - 1)}{\gamma - b + e^{\gamma T}(\gamma + b)}$$

with

$$\gamma = \sqrt{b^2 + 2\sigma^2}.$$

The price of a zero coupon bond at time t is, similarly, because of stationarity:

$$B(t,T) = e^{-a\phi_{0,1}(T-t)-r_t(x)\psi_{0,1}(T-t)}.$$

Suppose $0 \le T \le T^*$. Consider a European call option with expiration time T and strike price K on the zero coupon bond $B(t, T^*)$. At time 0 this has a price

$$V(0) = E\left[e^{-\int_0^T r_u(x)du}\left(B(T,T^*) - K\right)^+\right]$$

$$= E\left[E\left[e^{-\int_0^T r_u(x)du}\left(B(T,T^*) - K\right)^+ \big| \mathcal{F}_T\right]\right]$$

$$= E\left[e^{-\int_0^T r_u(x)du}\left(e^{-a\phi_{0,1}(T^*-T)-r_T(x)\psi_{0,1}(T^*-T)} - K\right)^+\right].$$

Write

$$r^* = \frac{-a\phi_{0,1}(T^* - T) + \log K}{\psi_{0,1}(T^* - T)}.$$

Then

$$V(0) = E\left[e^{-\int_0^T r_u(x)du}B(T,T^*)I_{r_T(x)<r^*}\right] - KE\left[e^{-\int_0^T r_u(x)du}I_{r_T(x)<r^*}\right].$$

Now

$$E\left[e^{-\int_0^T r_u(x)du}B(T,T^*)\right] = B(0,T^*)$$

$$\text{and}\quad E\left[e^{-\int_0^T r_u(x)du}\right] = B(0,T).$$

Define two new probability measures P_1 and P_2 by setting

$$\frac{dP_1}{dP}\Big|_{\mathcal{F}_T} = \frac{e^{-\int_0^T r_u(x)du}B(T,T^*)}{B(0,T^*)},$$

$$\frac{dP_2}{dP}\Big|_{\mathcal{F}_T} = \frac{e^{-\int_0^T r_u(x)du}}{B(0,T)}.$$

Then

$$V(0) = B(0,T^*)P_1\left(r_T(x) < r^*\right) - KB(0,T)P_2\left(r_T(x) < r^*\right).$$

Write

$$K_1 = \frac{\delta^2}{2}\cdot\frac{(e^{\gamma T} - 1)}{\gamma(e^{\gamma T} + 1) + \left(\sigma^2\psi_{0,1}(T^* - T) + b\right)(e^{\gamma T} - 1)},$$

$$K_2 = \frac{\sigma^2}{2}\cdot\frac{(e^{\gamma T} - 1)}{\gamma(e^{\gamma T} + 1) + b(e^{\gamma T} - 1)}.$$

Then it can be shown that the law of $(r_T(x))/(K_1)$ under P_1 (resp., the law of $(r_T(x))/K_2$ under P_2) is a decentral chi-square with $4a/\sigma^2$ degrees of freedom and decentral parameter ξ_1 (resp., ξ_2), where

$$\xi_1 = \frac{8r_0(x)\gamma^2 e^{\gamma T}}{\sigma^2(e^{\gamma T}-1)\big(\gamma(e^{\gamma T}+1)\big) + \big(\sigma^2\psi_{0,1}(T^*-T)+b\big)(e^{\gamma T}-1)},$$

$$\xi_2 = \frac{8r_0(x)\gamma^2 e^{\gamma T}}{\sigma^2(e^{\gamma T}-1)\big(\gamma(e^{\gamma T}+1)+b(e^{\gamma T}-1)\big)}.$$

Consequently, if $F_{\delta,z}$ is the probability distribution function for a chi-square random variable with δ degrees of freedom and decentral parameter z, then:

$$V(0) = B(0,T^*)F_{4a/\sigma^2,\xi_1}\left(\frac{r^*}{K_1}\right) - KB(0,T)F_{4a/\sigma^2,\xi_2}\left(\frac{r^*}{K_2}\right).$$

9.7   The Heath–Jarrow–Morton Model

Forward Rate Agreement

Suppose $0 \le t \le T < T + \varepsilon \le T^*$. 'Today' is time t. We wish to enter a contract to borrow \$1 at the future time T and repay it (with interest) at the time $T + \varepsilon$. The rate of interest to be paid between T and $T + \varepsilon$ is to be agreed today, and so must be $\mathcal{F}_t$-measurable.

We could approximate this transaction by buying today a T-maturity zero for $B(t,T)$ and shorting an amount $(B(t,T))/(B(t,T+\varepsilon))$ of $(T+\varepsilon)$-maturity zeros.

The cost of this portfolio at time t is

$$B(t,T) - \frac{B(t,T)}{B(t,T+\varepsilon)} \cdot B(t,T+\varepsilon) = 0.$$

Now at the future time T we receive \$1 for the T-maturity zero. Then at the time $(T+\varepsilon)$ we must pay $(B(t,T))/(B(t,T+\varepsilon))$ for the $(T+\varepsilon)$-maturity zeros.

In effect, we are looking at borrowing \$1 at the future time T and paying $\$(B(t,T))/(B(t,T+\varepsilon))$ at time $T + \varepsilon$.

Consequently, the interest rate we are paying on the dollar received at time T is $R(t,T,T+\varepsilon)$, where

$$\frac{B(t,T)}{B(t,T+\varepsilon)} = \exp\big(\varepsilon R(t,T,T+\varepsilon)\big)$$

so

$$R(t,T,T+\varepsilon) = -\frac{1}{\varepsilon}\left[\log B(t,T+\varepsilon) - \log B(t,T)\right].$$

Definition 9.7.1. The instantaneous interest rate for money borrowed at time T, agreed upon at time $t \leq T$, is the *forward rate* $f(t,T)$.

In fact

$$f(t,T) = \lim_{\varepsilon \downarrow 0} R(t,T,T+\varepsilon)$$

$$= \frac{-\partial}{\partial T} \log B(t,T).$$

Then

$$\log B(t,T) = \int_t^T \frac{\partial}{\partial T} \log B(t,u)du \quad (\text{as} \quad B(t,t) = 1)$$

$$= - \int_t^T f(t,u)du.$$

Therefore, $B(t,T) = \exp\left(- \int_t^T f(t,u)du\right)$.

We note this is an alternative representation for $B(t,T)$ in contrast to its expression in terms of the short rate process r :

$$B(t,T) = E\left[\exp\left(- \int_t^T r(u)du\right)\Big|\mathcal{F}_t\right].$$

Agreeing at time t on the forward rate $f(t,u)$ means one agrees, at time t, that the instantaneous interest rate at time $u \in [t,T]$ will be $f(t,u)$.

Consequently, one agrees that investing \$ 1 at time t will give \$ $\exp \int_t^T f(t,u)du$ at time T; investing $\$B(t,T)$ at time t will give

$$\$B(t,T) \cdot \exp\left(\int_t^T f(t,u)du\right) = \$1$$

at time T.

Lemma 9.7.2. $r(t) = f(t,t)$.

Proof. We have two representations

$$B(t,T) = E\left[\exp\left(- \int_t^T r(u)du\right)\Big|\mathcal{F}_t\right] \tag{9.18}$$

and

$$B(t,T) = \exp\left(- \int_t^T f(r,u)du\right). \tag{9.19}$$

From (9.18), $(\partial B(t,T))/\partial T = E[-r(T)\exp(- \int_t^T r(u)du)|\mathcal{F}_t]$. Evaluating at $T = t$.

$$\frac{\partial B(t,T)}{\partial T}\Big|_{T=t} = -r(t).$$

From (9.19), $(\partial B(t,T))/\partial T = -f(t,T)\exp(- \int_t^T f(t,u)du)$ and $(\partial B(t,T))/\partial T|_{T=t} = -f(t,t)$. $\qquad\square$

The Heath–Jarrow–Morton Model

The Heath–Jarrow–Morton (HJM) model for term structure considers stochastic differential equations for the evolution of the forward rate $f(t, T)$. For each $T \in (0, T^*]$ suppose the dynamics of f are given by

$$df(t, T) = \alpha(t, T)dt + \sigma(t, T)dW(t). \tag{9.20}$$

Here the coefficients $\alpha(u, T)$ and $\sigma(u, T)$, for $0 \le u \le T$, are measurable (in (u, ω)) and adapted. The integral form of (9.20) is

$$f(t, T) = f(0, T) + \int_0^t \alpha(u, T)du + \int_0^t \sigma(u, T)dW(u). \tag{9.21}$$

Note we have two time parameters and recall

$$B(t, T) = \exp\left(-\int_t^T f(t, u)du\right).$$

With d denoting a differential in the t variable:

$$
\begin{aligned}
d\left(-\int_t^T f(t, u)du\right) &= f(t, t)dt - \int_t^T \left(df(t, u)\right)du \\
&= r(t)dt - \int_t^T [\alpha(t, u)dt + \sigma(t, u)dW(t)]du \\
&= r(t)dt - \alpha^*(t, T)dt - \sigma^*(t, T)dW(t), \tag{9.22}
\end{aligned}
$$

where

$$\alpha^*(t, T) = \int_t^T \alpha(t, u)du$$

$$\sigma^*(t, T) = \int_t^T \sigma(t, u)du.$$

Recall, by definition, $f(t, u)$ is an $\mathcal{F}_t$-adapted process. Therefore,

$$X(t) := -\int_t^T f(t, u)du$$

is an $\mathcal{F}_t$-adapted process. In fact it is an Itô process with, as in (9.22),

$$dX(t) = \left(r(t) - \alpha^*(t, T)\right)dt - \sigma^*(t, T)dW(t).$$

Also, $B(t, T) = e^{X(t)}$ so

$$
\begin{aligned}
dB(t, T) &= e^{X(t)}[r(t) - \alpha^*(t, T) + \frac{1}{2}\sigma^*(t, T)^2]dt - e^{X(t)}\sigma^*(t, T)dW(t) \\
&= B(t, T)\left[\left(r(t) - \alpha^*(t, T) + \frac{1}{2}\sigma^*(t, T)^2\right)dt - \sigma^*(t, T)dW(t)\right].
\end{aligned}
$$

Now, the discounted $B(t,T)$ will be a martingale under P (so P is a risk-neutral measure), if for $0 \le t \le T \le T$,*

$$\alpha^*(t,T) = \frac{1}{2}\left(\sigma^*(t,T)\right)^2.$$

From the definitions of α^* and σ^* this means

$$\int_t^T \alpha(t,u)du = \frac{1}{2}\left(\int_t^T \sigma(t,u)du\right)^2.$$

This is equivalent to

$$\alpha(t,T) = \sigma(t,T)\int_t^T \sigma(t,u)du.$$

If P itself is not a risk-neutral measure there may be a probability P^θ under which $B(t,T)/S_t^0$ is a martingale. This is the content of the following result due to Heath, Jarrow, and Morton [125].

Theorem 9.7.3. *For each $T \in (0,T^*]$ suppose $\alpha(u,T)$ and $\sigma(u,T)$ are adapted processes. We assume $\sigma(u,T) > 0$ for all u,T, and $f(0,T)$ is a deterministic function of T. The instantaneous forward rate $f(t,T)$ is defined by*

$$f(t,T) = f(0,T) + \int_0^t \alpha(u,T)du + \int_0^t \sigma(u,t)dW(u).$$

Then the term structure model determined by the processes $f(t,T)$ does not allow arbitrage if and only if there is an adapted process $\theta(t)$ such that

$$\alpha(t,T) = \sigma(t,T)\int_t^T \sigma(t,u)du + \sigma(t,T)\theta(t)$$

$$\text{for all } \ 0 \le t \le T \le T^*,$$

and the process

$$\Lambda^\theta(t) := \exp\left\{-\int_0^t \theta(u)dW(u) - \frac{1}{2}\int_0^t \theta(u)^2 du\right\}$$

is an $(\mathcal{F}_t, P)$ martingale.

Proof. Suppose θ is an adapted process such that $\Lambda^\theta(t)$ is an $(\mathcal{F}_t, P)$ martingale and define a new probability measure P^θ by setting

$$\frac{dP^\theta}{dP}\bigg|_{\mathcal{F}_{T^*}} = \Lambda^\theta(T^*).$$

By Girsanov's theorem W^θ is a Brownian motion under P^θ where

$$W^\theta(t) = \int_0^t \theta(u)du + W(t),$$

and

$$dB(t,T) = B(t,T)\left[\left(r(t) - \alpha^*(t,T) + \frac{1}{2}\sigma^*(t,T)^2\right.\right.$$
$$\left.\left. + \sigma^*(t,T)\theta(t)\right)dt - \sigma^*(t,T)dW^\theta(t)\right],$$

where, as before, $\alpha^*(t,T) = \int_t^T \alpha(t,u)du$ and $\sigma^*(t,T) = \int_t^T \sigma(t,u)du$. For $B(t,T)$ to have rate of return $r(t)$ under P^θ, θ must satisfy

$$\alpha^*(t,T) = \frac{1}{2}\sigma^*(t,T)^2 + \sigma^*(t,T)\theta(t).$$

This must hold for all maturities T. Differentiating with respect to T, that is

$$\alpha(t,T) = \sigma(t,T)\sigma^*(t,T) + \sigma(t,T)\theta(t),$$
$$\text{for} \quad 0 \le t \le T \le T^*.$$

$\square$

Remark 9.7.4. The point to note is that, if there is such a process $\theta(t)$, it is independent of the time T maturity of the bond $B(t,T)$, and

$$\theta(t) = -\left[\frac{-\alpha^*(t,T) + \frac{1}{2}\sigma^*(t,T)^2}{\sigma^*(t,T)}\right].$$

Now under the 'market' probability P the rate of return of the bond is

$$r(t) - \alpha^*(t,T) + \frac{1}{2}\sigma^*(t,T)^2.$$

The rate of return above the interest rate $r(t)$ is, therefore,

$$-\alpha^*(t,T) + \frac{1}{2}\sigma^*(t,T)^2$$

and the market price of risk is just

$$\frac{-\alpha^*(t,T) + \frac{1}{2}\sigma^*(t,T)^2}{\sigma^*(t,T)} = -\theta(t).$$

The requirement of the theorem, therefore, is that the market price of risk is independent of the maturity times T. Substituting for θ we have that, under P^θ,

$$dB(t,T) = B(t,T)[r(t)dt - \sigma^*(t,T)dW^\theta(t)]$$

and

$$df(t,T) = \sigma(t,T)\sigma^*(t,T)dt + \sigma(t,T)dW^\theta(t).$$

9.8   A Markov Chain Model

In a recent paper ([95]) by Elliott, Hunter, and Jamieson an alternative self-calibrating model for the short-term rate is introduced. It is supposed the short-term rate $r(t)$ is a finite state space Markov chain defined on a probability space $(\Omega, \mathcal{F}, P)$ taking (positive) values $r_1, \ldots, r_N$. Each of these values can be identified with one of the canonical unit vectors e_i in $\mathbb{R}^N$, $e_i = (0, \ldots, 0, 1, 0, \ldots, 0)$. (In effect we are considering an indicator function $I_{r_i}(r)$ on the set $\{r_1, \ldots, r_N\}$). Without loss of generality we can take the state space of our Markov chain X_t, $t \geq 0$, to be the set $S = \{e_1, e_2, \ldots, e_N\}$. Writing $r = (r_1, \ldots, r_N) \in \mathbb{R}^N$ we then have

$$r(t) = \langle r, X_t \rangle = r(X_t),$$

where the pointed bracket denotes the scalar product in $\mathbb{R}^N$. Considering the Markov chain to have state space S simplifies the notation.

The unconditional distribution of X_t is the vector $E[X_t] = p_t = (p_t^1, \ldots, p_t^N)$, where

$$p_t^i = P(X_t = e_i) = E[\langle e_i, X_t \rangle] = P(r(t) = r_i).$$

Suppose this distribution evolves according to the Kolmogorov equation

$$\frac{dp_t}{dt} = Ap_t.$$

Here A is a 'Q-matrix', that is, if $A = (a_{ji})$, $1 \leq i, j \leq N$, $\sum_{j=1}^N a_{ij} = 0$, and $a_{ji} \geq 0$ if $i \neq j$. The components a_{ji} could be taken to be time varying, although this would complicate their estimation.

The price of a zero coupon bond at time t, with maturity T, in this model is

$$B(t, T) = E\left[\exp\left(-\int_t^T r(X_s)ds \right) \Big| \mathcal{F}_t \right],$$

where $\{\mathcal{F}_t\}$ is the filtration generated by X (or, equivalently, by r).

Because of the Markov property this is

$$E\left[\exp\left(-\int_t^T r(X_s)ds \right) \Big| X_t \right] = B(t, T, X_t),$$

say, and so is a function of $X_t \in S$. Any (real) function of $X_t \in S$ is given as the scalar product of some function $\phi_t = (\phi_t^1, \phi_t^2, \ldots, \phi_t^N)' \in \mathbb{R}^N$ with X_t. That is, we can write

$$B(t, T, X_t) = \langle \phi_t, X_t \rangle,$$

where $\phi_t^i = B(t, T, e_i)$.

Now

$$\exp\left(-\int_0^t r(X_s)ds\right)B(t,T,X_t) = \exp\left(-\int_0^t r(X_s)ds\right)\langle\phi_t, X_t\rangle$$

$$= E\left[\exp\left(-\int_0^T r(X_s)ds\right)\Big|\mathcal{F}_t\right]$$

and so is a martingale.

Lemma 9.8.1. *Define the $\mathbb{R}^N$-valued process M by*

$$M_t = X_t - X_0 - \int_0^t AX_s ds.$$

Then M is an $(\mathcal{F}_t, P)$ martingale.

Proof. Consider the matrix exponential $e^{A(t-s)}$. Then, because of the Markov property,

$$E[X_t|X_s] = e^{A(t-s)}X_s$$

for $t \geq s$. (In effect, one solves the Kolmogorov equation with initial condition X_s.) Now for $t \geq s$

$$E[M_t - M_s|\mathcal{F}_s] = E[X_t - X_s|\mathcal{F}_s] - E\left[\int_s^t AX_u du\Big|\mathcal{F}_s\right]$$

$$= e^{A(t-s)}X_s - X_s - \int_s^t Ae^{A(u-s)}X_s du$$

$$= \left[e^{A(t-s)} - I - \int_s^t Ae^{A(u-s)}du\right]X_s,$$

where I is the $N \times N$ identity matrix,

$$= \left[e^{A(t-s)} - I - [e^{A(u-s)}]_s^t\right]X_s = 0.$$

$\square$

Corollary 9.8.2. *The semimartingale representation of X is, therefore,*

$$X_t = X_0 + \int_0^t AX_s ds + M_t.$$

Theorem 9.8.3. *The process $\phi_t \in \mathbb{R}^N$ has dynamics*

$$\frac{d\phi_t}{dt} = (\text{diag } r - A^*)\phi_t$$

with terminal condition $\phi_T = \mathbf{1} = (1, 1, \ldots, 1)' \in \mathbb{R}^N$.

Proof. We have seen that

$$\exp\left(-\int_0^t r(X_s)ds\right)B(t,T,X_t) = \exp\left(-\int_0^t r(X_s)ds\right)\langle\phi_t, X_t\rangle$$

is an $(\mathcal{F}_t, P)$-martingale. Consequently, the dt term in its Itô process (or semimartingale) representation must be identically zero. Now

$$\exp\left(-\int_0^t r(X_s)ds\right)\langle\phi_t, X_t\rangle$$

$$= B(0,T,X_0) + \int_0^t \left(-r(X_s)\exp\left(-\int_0^s r(X_u)du\right)\right)\langle\phi_s, X_s\rangle ds$$

$$+ \int_0^t \exp\left(-\int_0^s r(X_u)du\right)\left[\langle\frac{d\phi_s}{ds}, X_s\rangle + \langle\phi_s, AX_s\rangle\right]ds$$

$$+ \int_0^t \exp\left(-\int_0^s r(X_u)du\right)\langle\phi_s, dM_s\rangle.$$

Consequently,

$$\exp\left(-\int_0^s r(X_u)du\right)\left[-r(X_s)\langle\phi_s, X_s\rangle + \langle\frac{d\phi_s}{ds}, X_s\rangle + \langle\phi_s, AX_s\rangle\right] = 0.$$

Now $r(X_s) = \langle r, X_s\rangle$, where $r = (r_1, r_s, \ldots, r_s)'$, and $r(X_s)\langle\phi_s, X_s\rangle = \langle$ diag $r \cdot \phi_s, X_s\rangle$, where diag r is the matrix with r on its diagonal. Therefore

$$\langle\frac{d\phi_s}{ds}, X_s\rangle + \langle A^*\phi_s, X_s\rangle - \langle\text{diag}r \cdot \phi_s, X_s\rangle = 0 \qquad \text{for all } X_s.$$

Consequently, ϕ is given by the vector equation

$$\frac{d\phi_t}{dt} = (\text{diag}r - A^*)\phi_t$$

with terminal condition $\phi_T = (1, \ldots, 1)' = \mathbf{1}$.   □

Corollary 9.8.4. *Write $B = \text{diag}r - A^*$. Then $\phi_t = e^{-B(T-t)}\mathbf{1}$ and the price at time t of a zero coupon bond is*

$$B(t,T,X_t) = \langle\phi_t, X_t\rangle$$
$$= \langle e^{-B(T-t)}, X_t\rangle\mathbf{1}.$$

The yield for such a bond is

$$y_{t,T} = -\frac{1}{T-t}\log B(t,T,X_t).$$

Yield values are quoted in the market.

In [95] it is supposed that yield values give noisy information about such a Markov chain term structure model. The techniques of filtering from Hidden Markov models (see [88]), are then applied to estimate the state of X and the model parameters.

10

Consumption-Investment Strategies

10.1 Utility Functions

The results of this chapter are a presentation of the comprehensive, fundamental, and elegant contributions of Karatzas, Lehoczky, Sethi, and Shreve.
See, for example, the papers [157] through [161].

We first review in the multi-asset situation concepts relating to trading
strategies, consumption processes, and utility functions.

On a probability space $(\Omega, \mathcal{F}, P)$ consider a market that includes a bond
$S^0(t)$ and n risky assets $S^1(t), \ldots, S^n(t)$, $0 \le t < \infty$. Their dynamics are
given by the equations

$$dS^0(t) = S^0(t)r(t)dt, \qquad S^0(0) = 1 \tag{10.1}$$

$$dS^i(t) = S^i(t)[\mu_i(t)dt + \sum_{j=1}^{n} \sigma_{ij}(t)dW_j(t)], \tag{10.2}$$

$$S^i(0) = s_i, \quad 1 \le i \le n, 0 \le t < \infty.$$

Here $W(t) = (W_1(t), \ldots, W_n(t))$ is an n-dimensional Brownian motion
defined on $(\Omega, \mathcal{F}, P)$ and $\{\mathcal{F}_t\}$ denotes the completion of the filtration

$$\sigma\{W(u) : 0 \le u \le t\}.$$

The interest rate $r(t)$, mean rate of return $\mu(t) = (\mu_1(t), \ldots, \mu_n(t))'$ and
the volatility $\sigma(t) = (\sigma_{ij}(t))$, $1 \le i, j \le d$, are taken to be measurable,
adapted, and bounded processes.

Note we have taken the dimension n of the Brownian motion equal to the number of risky assets.

Write $a(t) = \sigma(t)\sigma^*(t)$. We assume there is an $\varepsilon > 0$ such that

$$\xi^* a(t)\xi \geq \varepsilon\|\xi\|^2 \quad \text{for all} \xi \in \mathbb{R}^n \text{and} (t, w) \in [0, \infty) \times \Omega.$$

Consequently, the inverses of σ and σ^* exist and are bounded

$$\|\sigma(t, w)^{-1}\xi\| \leq \varepsilon^{-1/2}\|\xi\| \tag{10.3}$$
$$\|\sigma^*(t, w)^{-1}\xi\| \leq \varepsilon^{-1/2}\|\xi\|, \quad \forall\, \xi \in \mathbb{R}^n.$$

$\{\mathcal{F}_t, t \geq 0\}$ is then equivalently given as the completion of the filtration generated by the prices S.

In this situation, therefore, the market price of risk defined by equation (7.32) has a unique solution:

$$\theta(t) = \sigma(t)^{-1}\big(b(t) - r(t)\mathbf{1}\big);$$

furthermore, θ is bounded and progressively measurable.

As in Chapter 8, introduce

$$\Lambda(t) = \exp\left(-\int_0^t \theta'(s)dW(s) - \frac{1}{2}\int_0^t \|\theta'(s)\|^2 ds\right)$$

and define a new probability measure P^θ by setting

$$\frac{dP^\theta}{dP}\bigg|_{\mathcal{F}_t} = \Lambda(t).$$

We know from Girsanov's theorem that $W^\theta(t)$ is a Brownian motion under P^θ, where

$$W^\theta(t) := W(t) + \int_0^t \theta(s)ds.$$

Furthermore, under P^θ,

$$dS^i(t) = S^i(t)\left[r(t)dt + \sum_{j=1}^n \sigma_{ij}(t)dW_j^\theta(t)\right]$$

$$1 \leq i \leq n.$$

That is, in this situation, P^θ is the unique risk-neutral or martingale measure.

Definition 10.1.1. A utility function $U : [0, \infty) \times (0, \infty) \to \mathbb{R}$ is a $C^{0,1}$ function such that

a) $U(t, \cdot)$ is strictly increasing and strictly concave;

b) the derivative $U'(t,c) = (\partial/\partial c)U(t,c)$ is such that, for every $t > 0$,

$$\lim_{c \to \infty} U'(t,c) = 0$$

and

$$\lim_{c \downarrow 0} U'(t,c) = U'(t,0+) = \infty.$$

These conditions have natural economic interpretations. The increasing property of U represents the fact that the investor prefers higher levels of consumption or wealth. The strict concavity of $U(t,c)$ in c implies $U'(t,c)$ is decreasing in c; this models the concept that the investor is risk averse. The condition that $U'(t,0+) = \infty$ is not strictly necessary, but it simplifies some of the proofs.

$U'(t,c)$ is strictly decreasing in c; therefore, there is an inverse map $I(t,c)$ so that

$$I\big(t,U'(t,c)\big) = c = U'\big(t,I(t,c)\big),$$

for $c \in (0,\infty)$.

The concavity of U implies that

$$U\big(t,I(t,y)\big) \geq U(t,c) + y\big(I(t,y) - c\big), \quad \forall\, c,y. \tag{10.4}$$

For some later results we require that $U(t,c)$ is C^2 in $c \in (0,\infty)$ for all $t \in [0,T]$, and $U''(t,c) = \partial^2 U/\partial c^2$ is nondecreasing in c for all $t \in [0,T]$. These two conditions imply that $I(t,c)$ is convex and of class C^1 in $c \in (0,\infty)$, and

$$\frac{\partial}{\partial y} U\big(t,I(t,y)\big) = y \,\frac{\partial}{\partial y} I(t,y).$$

10.2 Admissible Strategies

We recall that a portfolio process or trading strategy $H(t) = \big(H^1(t),\ldots,H^n(t)\big)'$ is a measurable $\mathbb{R}^n$-valued process that is adapted $\{\mathcal{F}_t\}$ and which is such that

$$\int_0^T |H(s)|^2 ds < \infty \quad \text{a.s.}$$

A consumption process $c(t)$, $0 \leq t \leq T$, is a nonnegative, measurable, adapted process (with respect to $\{\mathcal{F}_t\}$) such that

$$\int_0^T c(t)dt < \infty \quad \text{a.s.}$$

The adapted condition means the investor cannot anticipate the future, so 'insider trading' is not allowed.

The wealth of the investor at time t is then

$$X(t) = \sum_{i=0}^{n} H^i(t)S^i(t) - \int_0^t c(s)ds.$$

Here $H^i(t)S^i(t)$ represents the amount invested in asset i, $0 \leq i \leq n$, and $\int_0^t c(s)ds$ represents the total amount consumed up to time t.

If the strategy H is self-financing, changes in the wealth derive only from changes in the asset prices, interest on the bond, and from consumption, and then:

$$dX(t) = \sum_{i=1}^{d} H^i(t)dS^i(t) + \left(1 - \sum_{i=1}^{n} H^i(t)\right)dS^0(t) - c(t)dt.$$

From (10.1) and (10.2) this is

$$\left(r(t)X(t) - c(t)\right)dt + H(t)'\left(\mu(t) - r(t)\mathbf{1}\right)dt + H(t)'\sigma(t)dW(t)$$
$$= \left(r(t)X(t) - c(t)\right)dt + H(t)'\sigma(t)dW^\theta(t).$$

Writing $\beta(t) = S^0(t)^{-1} = \exp\left(-\int_0^t r(s)ds\right)$ we see

$$\beta(t)X(t) = x - \int_0^t \beta(s)c(s)ds + \int_0^t \beta(s)H(s)'\sigma(s)dW^\theta(s), \qquad (10.5)$$

where $x = X(0)$ is the initial wealth of the investor.

Consequently,

$$D(t) = \beta(t)X(t) + \int_0^t \beta(s)c(s)ds = x + \int_0^t \beta(s)H(s)'\sigma(s)dW^\theta(s),$$

which is the present discounted wealth plus the total discounted consumption so far, is a continuous local martingale under P^θ.

Definition 10.2.1. The *deflator* for the market is the process ξ defined by

$$\xi(t) = \beta(t)\Lambda(t).$$

This equals the discount factor β modified by the Girsanov density Λ, to take account of the financial market.

Now

$$\Lambda(t)D(t) = \Lambda(t)\left(\beta(t)X(t) + \int_0^t \beta(s)c(s)ds\right)$$
$$= \Lambda(t)\left(x + \int_0^t \beta(s)H(s)'\sigma(s)dW^\theta(s)\right)$$
$$= \xi(t)X(t) + \int_0^t \xi(s)c(s)ds - \int_0^t C(s)\Lambda(s)\theta(s)'dW(s),$$

where $C(s) = \int_0^s \beta(u)c(u)du$. For any $\mathcal{F}$-measurable P^θ-integrable random variable Φ a version of Bayes' rule (see [88]), states that

$$E^\theta[\Phi|\mathcal{F}_s] = \frac{E[\Lambda(t)\Phi|\mathcal{F}_s]}{\Lambda(s)}.$$

Therefore, $\Lambda(t)D(t)$ is a continuous local martingale under P, as is $\int_0^t C(s)\Lambda(s)\theta(s)'dW(s)$. Consequently,

$$N(t) := \xi(t)X(t) + \int_0^t \xi(s)c(s)ds \tag{10.6}$$

is a continuous local martingale under P. Furthermore, from the Bayes' rule, we see that $N(t)$ is a P-supermartingale if and only if $D(t)$ is a P^θ-supermartingale.

Definition 10.2.2. Similarly to the set of trading strategies $SF(\xi)$ of Chapter 8 we introduce the set $SF(K, x)$. A portfolio process $H = \left(H^1(t), \ldots, H^n(t)\right)'$ and a consumption process c belong to $SF(K, x)$ if, for initial capital $x \geq 0$, and some nonnegative, P-integrable random variable $K = K(H, c)$, the corresponding wealth process satisfies

$$X(T) \geq 0 \quad \text{a.s.}$$

and

$$\xi(t)X(t) \geq -K(\omega), \quad \forall\, 0 \leq t \leq T.$$

Here $\xi(t)$ is the deflator process of Definition 10.2.1.

Consequently, for every $(H, c) \in SF(K, x)$ the P-local martingale N of (10.6) is bounded from below. Using Fatou's Lemma as in Chapter 8 we deduce that N is a P supermartingale; therefore, D is a P^θ supermartingale.

Write $\mathcal{T}_{u,v}$ for the set of stopping times with values in $[u, v]$. Using the Optional Stopping Theorem on N (or D), for any $\tau \in \mathcal{T}_{0,T}$, for $(H, c) \in SF(K, x)$,

$$E\left[\xi(\tau)X(\tau) + \int_0^\tau \xi(s)c(s)ds\right] \leq x$$

or equivalently

$$E^\theta\left[\beta(\tau)X(\tau) + \int_0^\tau \beta(s)c(s)ds\right] \leq x. \tag{10.7}$$

These inequalities state that the expected value of current wealth at any time τ, and consumption up to time τ, deflated to time 0, should not exceed the initial capital x.

Definition 10.2.3. We now introduce consumption rate processes and final claims whose (deflated) expected value is bounded by the initial investment $x \geq 0$.

a) Write $\mathcal{C}(x)$ for the consumption rate processes c that satisfy

$$E^\theta \left[\int_0^T c(s) e^{-\int_0^s r(u)du} ds \right] \leq x.$$

b) Write $\mathcal{L}(x)$ for the nonnegative $\mathcal{F}_T$-measurable random variables B that satisfy

$$E^\theta \left[Be^{-\int_0^T r(u)du} \right] \leq x.$$

From the inequality (10.6) we see that $(H, c) \in SF(0, x)$ implies $c \in \mathcal{C}(x)$ and $X(T) \in \mathcal{L}(x)$.

We now investigate to what extent we can deduce the opposite implications.

Theorem 10.2.4. *For every $c \in \mathcal{C}(x)$ there is a portfolio H such that $(H, c) \in SF(0, x)$.*

Furthermore, if c belongs to the class

$$\mathcal{D}(x) := \left\{ c \in \mathcal{C}(x) : \ E^\theta \left[\int_0^T \beta(s)c(s)ds \right] = x \right\},$$

then the corresponding wealth process X satisfies $X(T) = 0$ and the process M is a martingale.

Proof. For $c \in \mathcal{C}(x)$ write

$$C = C(T) = \int_0^T \beta(s)c(s)ds$$

and define the martingale

$$m_t = E^\theta[C|\mathcal{F}_t] - E^\theta[C].$$

Then, from the martingale representation result, m can be expressed as

$$m_t = \int_0^t \phi'(s)dW^\theta(s), \quad 0 \leq t \leq T$$

for some $\{\mathcal{F}_t\}$-adapted, measurable $\mathbb{R}^d$-valued process ϕ, with $\int_0^T \|\phi_s\|^2 ds < \infty$ a.s.

Now the process

$$X(t) := \left[E^\theta \left[\int_0^T e^{-\int_0^s r(u)du} c(s)ds | \mathcal{F}_t \right] + (x - E^\theta[C]) \right] \beta(t)^{-1} \quad (10.8)$$

is non-negative because $c \in \mathcal{C}(x)$, and recalling $\beta(t) = (S_t^0)^{-1} =$
$\exp - \int_0^t r(u)du$,

$$X(t)\beta(t) = x + m_t - \int_0^t \beta(s)c(s)ds$$

$$= x + \int_0^t \phi'(s)dW^\theta(s) - \int_0^t \beta(s)c(s)ds.$$

Write $H(t) = (H'(t), \ldots, H^n(t)) := e^{\int_0^t r(u)du} (\sigma'(t))^{-1}\phi(t)$. From (10.3)
this is a portfolio process, so

$$X(t)\beta(t) = x + \int_0^t \beta(s)H'(s)\sigma(s)dW^\theta(s) - \int_0^t \beta(s)c(s)ds$$

and we see from (10.4) that $X(t)$ is a wealth process corresponding to
$(H, c) \in SF(0, x)$.

Now if, furthermore, $c \in \mathcal{D}(x)$, then $X(T) = 0$ from (10.8), so $D(T) =$
$\int_0^T \beta(s)c(s)ds$. We have seen that the process D is a P^θ-supermartingale
and, in this situation, it has a constant expectation

$$x = E[D(T)] = E\left[\int_0^T \xi(s)c(s)ds\right]$$

$$= E[D(0)].$$

Therefore, D is a P-martingale.   □

The next result describes the levels of terminal wealth attainable from
an initial endowment x.

Theorem 10.2.5.   a) *If $B \in \mathcal{L}(x)$, there is a pair $(H, c) \in SF(0, x)$
such that the corresponding wealth process X satisfies $X(T) = B$ a.s.*

b) *Write $\mathcal{M}(x) = \{B \in \mathcal{L}(x) : E^\theta[\beta(T)B] = x\}$.
Then if $B \in \mathcal{M}(x)$ we can take $c \equiv 0$ and the process*

$$(X(t)\beta(t), 0 \le t \le T)$$

is a P^θ martingale.

Proof. For $B \in \mathcal{L}(x)$ we define the nonnegative process Y_t by

$$Y_t\beta(t) := E^\theta[\overline{B}|\mathcal{F}_t] + (x - E^\theta[\overline{B}])(1 - \frac{t}{T})$$

$$= x + v(t) - \rho t,$$

where

$$\overline{B} := \beta(T)B$$
$$\rho := T^{-1}(x - E^\theta[\overline{B}])$$
$$v(t) := E^\theta[\overline{B}|\mathcal{F}_t] - E^\theta[\overline{B}].$$

Take the consumption rate process to be

$$c(t) = \rho\beta(t)^{-1}$$

and represent $v(t)$ as

$$\int_0^t \psi'(s)dW^\theta(s) = \int_0^t \beta(s)\widehat{H}'(s)\sigma(s)dW^\theta(s),$$

where $\widehat{H}'(s) = e^{\int_0^s r(u)du}(\sigma'(s))^{-1}\psi(s)$. The result follows as in Theorem 10.2.4.   □

Remark 10.2.6. Minor modifications show that Theorem 10.2.5 still holds when T is replaced by a stopping time $\tau \in \mathcal{T}_{0,T}$.

10.3   Utility Maximization from Consumption

We consider an investor with initial wealth $x > 0$. The problem discussed in this section is how the investor should choose his trading strategy $H_1(t)$ and consumption rate $c_1(t)$ in order to remain solvent and also to maximize his utility over $[0, T]$, with $(H_1, c_1) \in SF(0, x)$.

As previously, prices are discounted by $\beta(t) = (S_t^0)^{-1} = \exp\left(-\int_0^t r(u)du\right)$. Consider a utility function U_1.

The problem, then, is to maximize the expected discounted utility from consumption

$$J_1(x, H_1, c_1) := E\left[\int_0^T U_1(c_1(s))ds\right]$$

over all strategies $(H_1, c_1) \in SF(0, x)$ that satisfy

$$E\left[\int_0^T U_1^-(c_1(s))ds\right] < \infty.$$

Write $SF_B(x)$ for the set of such strategies. Following Definition 10.2.3 we have seen that $(H_1, c_1) \in SF(0, x)$ implies $c_1 \in \mathcal{C}(x)$. Therefore,

$$E^\theta\left[\int_0^T \beta(s)c_1(s)ds\right] \le x,$$

In this situation utility is coming only from consumption, so it is easily seen that one should increase consumption up to the limit imposed by the bound. Consequently, we should consider only consumption rate processes for which

$$E^\theta \Big[\int_0^T \beta(s)c_1(s)ds \Big] = E \Big[\int_0^T \Lambda_s \beta(s)c_1(s)ds \Big] = x.$$

That is, we consider $c_1 \in \mathcal{D}(x)$. In other words, if we define the value function

$$V_1(x) := \sup_{(H_1,c_1)\in SF_B(x)} J_1(x, H_1, c_1)$$

then

$$V_1(x) = \sup_{\substack{(H_1,c_1)\in SF_B(x) \\ c_1\in \mathcal{D}(x)}} J_1(x, H_1, c_1). \qquad (10.9)$$

For this constrained maximization problem we consider the Lagrangian

$$\Gamma(c_1, y) = E \Big[\int_0^T U_1\big(c_1(s)\big)ds \Big] - y\Big[E\Big[\int_0^T \Lambda_s \beta(s)c_1(s)ds \Big] - x \Big].$$

The first order conditions imply the optimal consumption rate $c_1^*(s)$ should satisfy

$$U_1'\big(c_1^*(s)\big) = y\Lambda_s \beta(s)$$

and

$$E \int_0^T \Lambda_s \beta(s)c_1^*(s)ds = x. \qquad (10.10)$$

With I_1 the inverse function of the strictly decreasing map U_1', therefore,

$$c_1^*(s) = I_1(s, y\Lambda_s \beta(s)),$$

and y is determined by the condition (10.10).

In fact, write

$$L_1(y) = E \Big[\int_0^T \Lambda_s \beta(s)I_1\big(s, y\Lambda_s \beta(s)\big)ds \Big],$$

$$\text{for} \quad 0 < y < \infty.$$

Assume that $L_1(y) < \infty$ for $0 < y < \infty$. Then, from the corresponding properties of I_1, L_1 is continuous and strictly decreasing,

$$L_1(0+) = \infty \quad \text{and} \quad L_1(\infty) = 0.$$

Consequently, there is an inverse map for L_1, which we denote by G_1, so that

$$L_1\big(G_1(y)\big) = y.$$

That is, for any $x > 0$ there is a unique y such that

$$y = G_1(x).$$

Differentiating we also see that $L_1'(G_1(y))G_1'(y) = 1$. The corresponding optimal consumption process is, therefore,

$$c_1^*(s) = I\big(s, G_1(x)\Lambda_s\beta(s)\big), \quad 0 \le t \le T. \tag{10.11}$$

By construction $c_1^* \in \mathcal{D}(x)$. From Theorem 10.2.4 there is a unique portfolio process H_1^* (up to equivalence) such that $(H_1^*, c_1^*) \in SF(0, x)$. The corresponding wealth process is then X_1, where

$$\beta(t)X_1(t) = E^\theta\left[\int_t^T \beta(s)c^*(s)ds\Big|\mathcal{F}_t\right]$$

$$= x - \int_0^t \beta(s)c^*(s)ds + \int_0^t \beta(s)H^*(s)'\sigma(s)dW^\theta(s).$$

Note that $X_1(t) > 0$ on $[0, T)$ and $X_1(T) = 0$ a.s.

Theorem 10.3.1. *Assume $L_1(y) < \infty$ for $0 < y < \infty$. Then for any $x > 0$, with c_1^* given by (10.11), the pair (H_1^*, c_1^*) belongs to $SF_B(x)$ and is optimal for the problem (10.9). That is,*

$$V_1(x) = J_1(x, H_1^*, c_1^*).$$

Proof. Consider any other $c \in \mathcal{C}(x)$. From the concavity of U_1 inequality (10.4) implies that

$$U_1\big(t, c_1^*(t)\big) \ge U_1\big(t, c(t)\big) + G_1(x)\Lambda_t\beta(t)\big[I(t, G_1(x)\Lambda_t\beta(t)) - c(t)\big]. \tag{10.12}$$

Write $\widehat{c}(t) = x\big[E\int_0^T \Lambda_u\beta(u)du\big]^{-1}$. Then $\widehat{c}$ is a constant rate of consumption and

$$E^\theta\left[\int_0^T \beta(u)\widehat{c}(u)du\right] = E\left[\Lambda_T\int_0^T \beta(u)\widehat{c}(u)du\right] = x,$$

so

$$\widehat{c} \in \mathcal{D}(x).$$

Also, substituting $\widehat{c}$ in the right side of (10.12) and integrating we obtain

$$E\left[\int_0^T U_1\big(t, \widehat{c}(t)\big)dt\right] + G_1(x)\big(L_1(G_1(x)) - x\big) = E\left[\int_0^T U_1\big(t, \widehat{c}(t)\big)dt\right].$$

Therefore, integrating both sides of (10.12) we see that $E\big[\int_0^T U_1^-(c^*(s))ds\big] < \infty$. Finally, consider $c \in \mathcal{C}(x)$. Integrating both sides of (10.12) we have

$$E\Big[\int_0^T U_1(t, c_1^*(t))dt\Big] \geq E\Big[\int_0^T U_1(t, c(t))dt\Big]$$
$$+ \quad G_1(x)\Big[x - E\big[\int_0^T \Lambda_t \beta(t)c(t)dt\big]\Big].$$

The final bracket equals $E[\Lambda_T \int_0^T \beta(t)c(t)dt] = E^\theta[\int_0^T \beta(t)c(t)dt]$ and so is non-negative. Therefore, c_1^* is optimal. $\qquad\square$

Remark 10.3.2. From the optimality conditions we have seen that the optimal consumption rate $c_1^*(t)$ is of the form

$$c_1^*(t) = I_1\big(t, y\xi(t)\big), \quad \text{for some} \quad y > 0.$$

Here $\xi(t) = \beta(t)\Lambda_t$ is the market deflator of Definition 10.2.1. Let us consider the expected utility function associated with a consumption rate process of this form:

$$K_1(y) := E\Big[\int_0^T U_1\big(t, I_1(t, y\xi(t))\big)dt\Big], \qquad (10.13)$$

for $0 < y < \infty$.
We require

$$E\Big[\int_0^T |U_1\big(t, I(t, y\xi(t))\big)|dt\Big] < \infty, \qquad (10.14)$$

for all $y \in (0, \infty)$.
Then K_1 is continuous and strictly decreasing in y. We have proved in Theorem 10.3.1 that

$$V_1(x) = K_1\big(G_1(x)\big).$$

Under, for example, the assumption that $U_1(t, y)$ is C^2 in y, $0 < y < \infty$, and $(\partial^2 U_1(t, y))/\partial y^2$ is nondecreasing in y for all $t \in [0, T]$, we can perform the differentiations of $L_1(y)$ and $K_1(y)$ to obtain

$$L_1'(y) = E\Big[\int_0^T \xi^2(t)\frac{\partial}{\partial z}I_1\big(t, y\xi(t)\big)dt\Big].$$

Recalling

$$\frac{\partial U_1}{\partial z}\big(t, I_1(t, z)\big) = z\frac{\partial}{\partial z}I_1(t, z)$$

we have, with $z = y\xi(t)$, that

$$K_1'(y) = E\left[\int_0^T \xi(t)\frac{\partial U_1}{\partial z}\left(t, I_1(t, y\xi(t))\right)dt\right]$$

$$= E\left[\int_0^T y\xi^2(t)\frac{\partial}{\partial z}\,I_1\left(t, y\xi(t)\right)dt\right]$$

$$= yL_1'(y).$$

We can, therefore, state the following result.

Theorem 10.3.3. *Under the integrability conditions, that $L_1(y) < \infty$ and (10.4) holds, the value function is given by*

$$V_1(x) = K_1\big(G_1(x)\big). \tag{10.15}$$

Also, if the utility function $U_1(t, y)$ is C^2 in y and $(\partial^2 U/\partial y^2)(t, y)$ is non-decreasing in y, then the strictly decreasing functions L_1 and K_1 are continuously differentiable and

$$K_1'(y) = yL_1'(y).$$

Furthermore, from (10.15),

$$V_1'(x) = K_1'\big(G_1(x)\big)G_1'(x) = G_1(x)L_1'\big(G_1(x)\big)G_1'(x)$$
$$= G_1(x).$$

In addition, note that V_1 is strictly increasing and concave.

Example 10.3.4. Suppose $U_1(t, c) = \exp\{-\int_0^t \rho(u)du\}\log c$, where $\rho : [0, T] \to \mathbb{R}$ is measurable and bounded. Then

$$U_1'(t, c) = \exp\left\{-\int_0^t \rho(u)du\right\}c^{-1}$$

and

$$I_1(t, c) = \exp\left\{-\int_0^t \rho(u)du\right\}c^{-1}$$

$$L_1(y) = \frac{a_1}{y}, \quad K_1(y) = -a_1\log y + b_1$$

so

$$V_1(x) = a_1\log\left(\frac{x}{a_1}\right) + b_1,$$

where

$$a_1 = \int_0^T \exp\left(-\int_0^t \rho(u)du\right)dt$$

and

$$b_1 = E\left[\int_0^T \exp\left(-\int_0^t \rho(u)du\right)\left\{\int_0^t \left(r(u) + \frac{1}{2}\,\|\theta(u)\|^2 - \rho(u)\right)du\right\}dt\right].$$

Example 10.3.5. Suppose $U_1(t,c) = -\exp\left(-\int_0^t \rho(u)du\right)c^{-1}$. Then

$$L_1(y) = d_1 y^{-1/2}, \qquad G_1(y) = -d_1 y^{1/2}$$

so

$$V_1(x) = -d_1^2/x,$$

where

$$d_1 = E\left[\int_0^T \exp\left(-\frac{1}{2}\int_0^t (\rho(u) + r(u))du \,\Lambda_t^{1/2} dt\right)\right].$$

Note that conditions $L_1(y) < \infty$ and (10.14) are both satisfied in these examples.

10.4 Maximization of Terminal Utility

The previous section discussed maximization of consumption. This section considers the dual problem of maximization of terminal wealth. That is, for any $(H_2, c_2) \in SF(0,x)$ we consider

$$J_2(x, H_2, c_2) = E\left[U_2\big(X(T)\big)\right]$$

for a utility function U_2.

We restrict ourselves to the subset $SF_C(0,x)$ consisting of those (H,c) such that

$$E\left[U_2^-\big(X(T)\big)\right] < \infty.$$

Define the value function

$$V_2(x) := \sup_{(H_2, c_2) \in SF_C(0,x)} J_2(x, H_2, c_2). \qquad (10.16)$$

The expected terminal wealth discounted to time 0 should not exceed the initial investment x; that is,

$$E^\theta[\beta(T)X(T)] = E[\xi(t)X(T)] \le x.$$

The methods are similar to those of Theorem 10.3.1, so we sketch the ideas and proofs. Define

$$L_2(y) := E\left[\xi(T)I_2\big(T, y\xi(T)\big)\right], \quad 0 < y < \infty.$$

We assume $L_2(y) < \infty$ for $y \in (0, \infty)$. Again L_2 is continuous and strictly decreasing with $L_2(0+) = \infty$, $L_2(\infty) = 0$.

Write G_2 for the inverse function of L_2. For an initial capital x_2 consider

$$X_2(T) := I_2\big(T, G_2(x_2)\xi(T)\big). \qquad (10.17)$$

This belongs to the class $\mathcal{M}(x_2)$ of Theorem 10.2.5 because

$$E^\theta[X_2(T)\beta(T)] = E[\xi(T)X_2(T)]$$
$$= E\big[\xi(T)I_2\big(T, G_2(x_2)\xi(T)\big)\big] = x_2.$$

Therefore, from Theorem 10.3.1 we know there is a trading strategy $(H_2, c_2) \in SF(0, x_2)$ that attains the terminal wealth $X_2(T)$. This strategy is unique up to equivalence, and for this pair $c_2 \equiv 0$. Consequently, the corresponding wealth process is given by

$$\beta(t)X_2(t) = E^\theta[\beta(T)X_2(T)|\mathcal{F}_t]$$
$$= x_2 + \int_0^t \beta(s)H_2'(s)\sigma(s)dW^\theta(s), \quad 0 \le t \le T. \tag{10.18}$$

Using again the inequality (10.4) for utility functions we can parallel the proof of Theorem 10.3.1 to show that $X_2(T)$, defined by (10.17), satisfies

$$E\big[U_2^-\big(X_2(T)\big)\big] < \infty$$

and

$$E\big[U_2\big(X_2(T)\big)\big] \ge E\big[U_2\big(X(T)\big)\big], \tag{10.19}$$

where $X(T)$ is any other random variable satisfying (10.19).

Consequently, we have proved the following result.

Theorem 10.4.1. *If $L_2(y) < \infty$ for all $y \in (0, \infty)$, consider any $x_2 > 0$ and the random variable*

$$X_2(T) = I_2\big(T, G_2(x_2)\xi(T)\big).$$

Then the trading strategy $(H_2, 0)$ belongs to $SF_C(0, x_2)$ and

$$V_2(x_2) = E\big[U_2\big(T, X_2(T)\big)\big].$$

That is, $(H_2, 0)$ achieves the maximum in (10.16).

Similarly to Theorem 10.3.3, we can also establish:

Theorem 10.4.2. *If $L_2(y) < \infty$ and if*

$$E\big[|U_2\big(T, I_2(T, y\xi(T))\big)|\big] < \infty$$

for all $y \in (0, \infty)$, then the value function V_2 is given by

$$V_2(x) = K_2\big(G_2(x)\big)$$

where

$$K_2(y) = E\big[U_2\big(T, I_2(T, y\xi(T))\big)\big]. \tag{10.20}$$

Note K_2 is continuous and strictly decreasing for $0 < y < \infty$.

Also, if $U_2(t, y)$ belongs to $C^2(0, \infty)$ and $(\partial^2 U(t, y))/\partial y^2$ is nondecreasing in y, then the functions L_2, K_2 are also in $C^2(0, \infty)$ and $K_2'(y) = yL_2'(y)$ for $0 < y < \infty$.

Furthermore,

$$V_2' = G_2$$

implying that V_2 is strictly increasing in y and strictly concave.

Example 10.4.3. Again consider the utility function

$$U(T, c) = \exp\left(-\int_0^T \rho(u)du\right) \log c,$$

where ρ is bounded, real, and measurable. In this case

$$L_2(y) = \frac{a_2}{y},$$

$$G_2(y) = -a_2 \log y + d_2,$$

and

$$V_2(x) = a_2 \log\left(\frac{x}{a_2}\right) + d_2$$

with

$$a_2 = \exp\left(\int_0^T \rho(u)du\right)$$

$$d_2 = E\left[\exp\left(-\int_0^T \rho(u)du\right)\left\{\int_0^T \left(r(u) + \frac{1}{2}|\theta(u)|^2 - \rho(u)\right)du\right\}\right].$$

With $\rho(u) \equiv 0$ we have

$$I_2(T, y) = L_2(y) = y^{-1}.$$

Consequently, from (10.17),

$$X_2(T) = \left(G_2(x_2)\xi(T)\right)^{-1}.$$

In this example $G_2(x_2) = x_2^{-1}$ and

$$\xi(T) = \Lambda_T \beta(T)$$

with

$$\Lambda_T = \exp\left(-\int_0^T \theta(u)dW(u) - \frac{1}{2}\int_0^T \|\theta(u)\|^2 du\right).$$

Then

$$\beta(T)X_2(T) = x_2 \exp\left(\int_0^T \theta(u)dW(u) + \frac{1}{2}\int_0^T \|\theta(u)\|^2 du\right).$$

Recalling $dW(t) = dW^\theta(t) - \theta(t)dt$, we have

$$\beta(T)X_2(T) = x_2 \exp\left(\int_0^T \theta(u)dW^\theta(u) - \frac{1}{2}\int_0^T \|\theta(u)\|^2 du\right)$$

and, recognizing the right side as the terminal value of a P^θ martingale, we have from (10.18) that

$$\beta(t)X_2(t) = E^\theta[\beta(T)X_2(T)|\mathcal{F}_t]$$

$$= x_2 \exp\left(\int_0^t \theta(u)dW^\theta(u) - \frac{1}{2}\int_0^t \|\theta(u)\|^2 du\right)$$

$$= x_2 + \int_0^t \beta(u)X_2(u)dW^\theta(u).$$

Comparing this with (10.18) we see

$$H_2(t) \text{ must be } X_2(t)\sigma'(t)^{-1}\theta(t).$$

Example 10.4.4. For the utility function

$$U_2(T, c) = -\exp\left(-\int_0^T \rho(u)du\right)c^{-1}$$

we can show that

$$L_2(y) = a_2 y^{-1/2} \qquad G_2(y) = -a_2 y^{1/2}$$

and

$$V_2(x) = -\frac{a_2^2}{x}$$

with

$$a_2 = E\left[\exp\left(-\frac{1}{2}\int_0^T (\rho(u) + r(u))du\right)\Lambda_T^{1/2}\right].$$

10.5   Utility Maximization for Both Consumption and Terminal Wealth

We consider now an investor who wishes to both live well (consume) and also acquire terminal wealth at time $T > 0$. These two objectives conflict, so we determine the investor's best policy.

Consider two utility functions U_1 and U_2.

As in Section 10.3 the investor's utility from consumption is given by

$$J_1(x, H, c) = E\left[\int_0^T U_1(u, c(u))du\right].$$

The investor's terminal utility, as in Section 10.4, is

$$J_2(x, H, c) = E[U_2(T, X(T))].$$

Write $SF_D(0, x) = SF_B(0, x) \cap SF_C(0, x)$ for the set of admissible trading and consumption strategies. Then with

$$J(x, H, c) = J_1(x, H, c) + J_2(x, H, c)$$

the investor aims to maximize $J(x, H, c)$ over all strategies

$$(H, c) \in SF_D(0, x).$$

It turns out the optimal policy for the investor is to split the initial endowment x into two parts, x_1 and x_2 with $x_1 + x_2 = x$, and then to use the optimal consumption strategy (H_1, c_1) of Section 10.3 with initial investment x_1 and the optimal investment strategy $(H_2, 0)$ of Section 10.4 with initial investment x_2.

To see this consider an initial endowment x and a pair $(H, c) \in SF_D(0, x)$. Write

$$x_1 = E^\theta \left[\int_0^T \beta(u)c(u)du \right]$$

$$x_2 = x - x_1.$$

If $X(t)$ is the wealth process for (H, c),

$$X(t) = \beta(t)^{-1} \left[x - \int_0^t \beta(u)c(u)du + \int_0^t \beta(u)H'(u)\sigma(u)dW^\theta(u) \right]$$

and

$$J(x, H, c) = E \left[\int_0^T U_1(s, c(s))dt + U_2(T, X(T)) \right].$$

By definition $c \in \mathcal{D}(x_1)$ and $X(T) \in \mathcal{L}(x_2)$.

Now from Theorem 10.3.1 there is an optimal strategy $(H_1, c_1) \in SF_B(0, x_1)$ that attains the value

$$V_1(x_1) = \sup_{(H,c) \in SF_B(0, x_1)} J_1(x_1, H, c).$$

Also, from Theorem 10.4.1 there is an optimal strategy $(H_2, 0) \in SF_C(0, x_2)$ that attains the value

$$V_2(x_2) = \sup_{(H,c) \in SF_C(0, x_2)} J_2(x_2, H, c).$$

Now suppose X_1 is the wealth process corresponding to (H_1, c_1) and X_2 is the wealth process corresponding to $(H_2, 0)$. Then

$$X_1(t) = \beta(t)^{-1}[x_1 - \int_0^t \beta(u)c_1(u)du + \int_0^t \beta(u)H_1'(u)\sigma(u)dW^\theta(u)],$$

with $X_1(T) = 0$, and

$$X_2(t) = \beta(t)^{-1}[x_2 + \int_0^t \beta(u)H_2'(u)\sigma(u)dW^\theta(u)].$$

Consider, therefore, the wealth process $\overline{X}$ that is the sum of X_1 and X_2, and which corresponds to an investment strategy $\overline{H} = H_1 + H_2$ and consumption process $\overline{c} = c_1$. Then, with $x = x_1 + x_2$.

$$\overline{X}(t) = X_1(t) + X_2(t)$$
$$= \beta(t)^{-1}\left[x - \int_0^t \beta(u)\overline{c}(u)du + \int_0^t \beta(u)\overline{H}(u)\sigma(u)dW^\theta(u)\right].$$

However, for any initial endowment x, any decomposition of x into $x = x_1 + x_2$ and any strategy $(H, c) \in SF_D(0, x)$ we must have, because of the optimality of $V_1(x_1)$ and $V_2(x_2)$, that

$$J(x, H, c) \leq V_1(x_1) + V_2(x_2).$$

Consequently,

$$V(x) = \sup_{(H,c)\in SF_D(0,x)} J(x, H, c)$$
$$\leq V^*(x) := \max_{\substack{x_1+x_2=x \\ x_1\geq 0, x_2\geq 0}} [V_1(x_1) + V_2(x_2)].$$

We show that maximum on the right side can be achieved by an appropriate choice of x_1 and x_2. For such x_1 and x_2 there are optimal strategies (H_1, c_1) and $(H_2, 0)$ so the strategy $(\overline{H}, \overline{c})$ is then optimal for the combined consumption and investment problem. However, the maximum on the right is found by considering

$$\gamma(x_1) = V_1(x_1) + V_2(x - x_1).$$

The critical point of γ arises when

$$\gamma'(x_1) = 0,$$

that is, when

$$V_1'(x_1) = V_2'(x - x_1).$$

This means we are looking for the values $x_1, x_2, x_1 + x_2 = x$, such that the marginal expected utility from the consumption problem and terminal wealth problem is the same. From Theorems 10.3.3 and 10.4.2, $V_i' = G_i$ so this is when

$$G_1(x_1) = G_2(x_2).$$

Write z for this common value. The inverse function of G_i is L_i, $i = 1, 2$, so

$$x_1 = L_1(z) \quad \text{and} \quad x_2 = L_2(z).$$

For any $y \in (0, \infty)$ consider the function

$$L(y) = L_1(y) + L_2(y)$$
$$= E\left[\int_0^T \xi(t) I_1(t, y\xi(t)) dt + \xi(T) I_2(T, y\xi(T)) \right].$$

Here ξ is the 'deflator' of Definition 10.2.1.

Then L is continuous, strictly decreasing, and $L(0+) = \infty$, $L(\infty) = 0$. Write G for the inverse function of L. Then for the optimal decomposition:

$$x = x_1 + x_2 = L_1(z) + L_2(z)$$
$$= L(z),$$

and

$$z = G(x).$$

Consequently, the optimal decomposition of the initial endowment x is given by

$$x_1 = L_1(G(x)), \qquad x_2 = L_2(G(x)).$$

Consider the function

$$K(y) = K_1(y) + K_2(y)$$
$$= E\left[\int_0^T U_1(t, I_1(t, y\xi(t))) dt + U_2(T, I_2(T, y\xi(T))) \right].$$

Then K is continuous and decreasing on $(0, \infty)$ and from (10.15) and (10.20),

$$V(x) = V^*(x) = K(G(x)).$$

Summarizing the preceding discussion we state the following theorem.

Theorem 10.5.1. *For an initial endowment $x > 0$ the optimal consumption rate is*

$$\bar{c} = I_1(t, G(x)\xi(t)), \quad 0 \le t \le T,$$

and the optimal terminal wealth level is

$$\overline{X}(T) = I_2(T, G(x)\xi(T)).$$

There is an optimal portfolio process $\overline{H}$ such that $(\overline{H}, \bar{c}) \in SF_D(0, x)$ and the corresponding wealth process $\overline{X}$ is

$$\overline{X}(t) = \beta(t)^{-1} E^\theta \left[\int_t^T \beta(u) I_1(u, G(x)\xi(u)) du \right.$$
$$\left. + \beta(T) I_2(T, G(x)\xi(T)) \mid \mathcal{F}_t \right],$$

for $0 \leq t \leq T$. Furthermore, the value function of the problem is given by

$$V(x) = K\big(G(x)\big).$$

Example 10.5.2. Suppose $U_1(t,c) = U_2(t,c) = \exp\left(-\int_0^t \rho(u)du\right)\log c$. Then

$$L(y) = \frac{a}{y}, \qquad K(y) = -a \log y + b$$

and

$$V(x) = a \log (x/a) + b, \quad 0 < x < \infty.$$

Here $a = a_1 + a_2$, $b = b_1 + b_2$, where a_1, b_1 (resp., a_2, b_2) are given in Example 10.3.4 (resp., 10.4.3).

Example 10.5.3. Suppose $U_1(t,c) = U_2(t,c) = -\exp\left(-\int_0^t \rho(u)du\right)/c$. Then

$$L(y) = ay^{-1/2}, \qquad K(y) = -ay^{-1/2}$$

and

$$V(x) = -\frac{a^2}{x},$$

where $a = a_1 + a_2$ with a_1 as in Example 10.3.5 and a_2 as in Example 10.4.4.

Remark 10.5.4. In the case when the coefficients r, μ_i, and $\sigma = (\sigma_{ij})$ in the dynamics (10.1), (10.2) are constant, more explicit closed form solutions for the optimal strategies, in terms of feedback strategies as functions of the current level of wealth, can be obtained.

The solution of the dynamic programming equation can be obtained in terms of a function that is the value function of a European put option. Details can be found in [157] through [160].

References

[1] K.K. Aase and B. Oksendal. Admissible investment strategies in continuous trading. *Stochastic Process. Appl.*, 30:291–301, 1988.

[2] W. Allegretto, G. Barone-Adesi, and R.J. Elliott. Numerical evaluation of the critical price and American options. *European J. Finance*, 1:69–78, 1995.

[3] J.-P. Ansel and C. Stricker. Lois de martingale, densités et décomposition de Föllmer Schweizer. *Ann. Inst. H. Poincaré Probab. Statist.*, 28:375–392, 1992.

[4] P. Artzner and F. Delbaen. Term structure of interest rates: The martingale approach. *Adv. Appl. Math.*, 10:95–129, 1989.

[5] P. Artzner and D. Heath. Approximate completeness with multiple martingale measures. *Math. Finance*, 5:1–11, 1995.

[6] L. Bachelier. Theory of speculation. In P.H. Cootner, editor, *The Random Character of Stock Market Prices*, volume 1018 (1900) of *Ann. Sci. École Norm. Sup.*, pages 17–78. MIT Press, Cambridge, Mass., 1964.

[7] G. Barone-Adesi and R.J. Elliott. Approximations for the values of American options. *Stochastic Anal. Appl.*, 9:115–131, 1991.

[8] G. Barone-Adesi and R.J. Elliott. Pricing the treasury bond futures contract as the minimum value of deliverable bond prices. *Rev. Futures Markets*, 8:438–444, 1991.

[9] G. Barone-Adesi and R. Whaley. The valuation of American call options and the expected ex-dividend stock price decline. *J. Finan. Econ.*, 17:91–111, 1986.

[10] G. Barone-Adesi and R. Whaley. Efficient analytic approximation of American option values. *J. Finance*, 42:301–320, 1987.

[11] E.M. Barron and R. Jensen. A stochastic control approach to the pricing of options. *Math. Oper. Res.*, 15:49–79, 1990.

[12] B. Bensaid, J.-P. Lesne, H. Pagès, and J. Scheinkman. Derivative asset pricing with transaction costs. *Math. Finance*, 2:63–68, 1992.

[13] A. Bensoussan. On the theory of option pricing. *Acta Appl. Math.*, 2:139–158, 1984.

[14] A. Bensoussan and R.J. Elliott. Attainable claims in a Markov model. *Math. Finance*, 5:121–132, 1995.

[15] A. Bensoussan and J.L. Lions. *Applications of Variational Inequalities in Stochastic Control*. North Holland, Amsterdam, 1982.

[16] J.M. Bismut. Martingales, the Malliavin calculus and hypoellipticity under general Hörmander's conditions. *Zeits. Wahrsch. Verw. Gebiete.*, 56:469–505, 1981.

[17] F. Black and M. Scholes. The valuation of option contracts and a test of market efficiency. *J. Finance*, 27:399–417, 1972.

[18] F. Black and M. Scholes. The pricing of options and corporate liabilities. *J. Political Economy*, 81:637–659, 1973.

[19] N. Bouleau and D. Lamberton. Residual risks and hedging strategies in Markovian markets. *Stochastic Process. Appl.*, 33:131–150, 1989.

[20] P. Boyle and T. Vorst. Option replication in discrete time with transaction costs. *J. Finance*, 47:271–293, 1992.

[21] P.P. Boyle. Options: A Monte-Carlo approach. *J. Finan. Econ.*, 4:323–338, 1977.

[22] A. Brace, D. Gątarek, and M. Musiela. The market model of interest rate dynamics. *Math. Finance*, 7:127–155, 1997.

[23] A. Brace and M. Musiela. A multifactor Gauss Markov implementation of Heath, Jarrow, and Morton. *Math. Finance*, 4:259–283, 1994.

[24] M. Brennan, G. Courtadon, and M. Subrahmanyan. Options on the spot and options on futures. *J. Finance*, 40:1303–1317, 1985.

[25] M. Brennan and E. Schwartz. The valuation of American put options. *J. Finance*, 32:449–462, 1976.

[26] M. Brennan and E. Schwartz. A continuous-time approach to the pricing of bonds. *J. Bank Finance*, 3:135–155, 1979.

[27] P. Carr, R. Jarrow, and R. Myneni. Alternative characterizations of American put options. *Math. Finance*, 2:87–106, 1992.

[28] A.P. Carverhill. When is the short rate Markovian? *Math. Finance*, 4:305–312, 1994.

[29] M. Chesney, R. Elliott, and R. Gibson. Analytical solutions for the pricing of American bond and yield options. *Math. Finance*, 3:277–294, 1993.

[30] M. Chesney and R.J. Elliott. Estimating the instantaneous volatility and covariance of risky assests. *Appl. Stochastic Models Data Anal.*, 11:51–58, 1995.

[31] M. Chesney, R.J. Elliott, D. Madan, and H. Yang. Diffusion coefficient estimation and asset pricing when risk premia and sensitivities are time varying. *Math. Finance*, 3:85–100, 1993.

[32] M. Chesney and L. Scott. Pricing European currency options: A comparison of the modified Black–Scholes model and a random variance model. *J. Finan. Quant. Anal.*, 24:267–284, 1989.

[33] N. Christopeit and M. Musiela. On the existence and characterization of arbitrage-free measures in contingent claim valuation. *Stochastic Anal. Appl.*, 12:41–63, 1994.

[34] D.B. Colwell and R.J. Elliott. Discontinuous asset prices and nonattainable contingent claims. *Math. Finance*, 3:295–308, 1993.

[35] D.B. Colwell, R.J. Elliott, and P.E. Kopp. Martingale representation and hedging policies. *Stochastic Process. Appl.*, 38:335–345, 1991.

[36] A. Conze and R. Viswanathan. Path dependent options: The case of lookback options. *J. Finance*, 46:1893–1907, 1991.

[37] G. Courtadon. A more accurate finite difference approximation for the valuation of options. *J. Finan. Quant. Anal.*, 18:697–700, 1982.

[38] J.C. Cox and C.-F. Huang. Optimal consumption and portfolio policies when asset prices follow a diffusion process. *J. Econ. Theory*, 49:33–83, 1989.

[39] J.C. Cox, J.E. Ingersoll, and S.A. Ross. Duration and the measurement of basic risk. *J. Business*, 52:51–61, 1979.

[40] J.C. Cox, J.E. Ingersoll, and S.A. Ross. The relation between forward prices and futures prices. *J. Finan. Econ.*, 9:321–346, 1981.

[41] J.C. Cox, J.E. Ingersoll, and S.A. Ross. An intertemporal general equilibrium model of asset prices. *Econometrica*, 53:363–384, 1985.

[42] J.C. Cox, J.E. Ingersoll, and S.A. Ross. A theory of the term structure of interest rates. *Econometrica*, 53:385–407, 1985.

[43] J.C. Cox and S.A. Ross. The pricing of options for jump processes. Rodney L. White Center Working Paper 2-75, University of Pennsylvania, 1975.

[44] J.C. Cox and S.A. Ross. A survey of some new results in financial options pricing theory. *J. Finance*, 31:382–402, 1976.

[45] J.C. Cox and S.A. Ross. The valuation of options for alternative stochastic processes. *J. Finan. Econ.*, 3:145–166, 1976.

[46] J.C. Cox, S.A. Ross, and M. Rubinstein. Option pricing: A simplified approach. *J. Finan. Econ.*, 7:229–263, 1979.

[47] J.C. Cox and M. Rubinstein. A survey of alternative option-pricing models. In M. Brenner, editor, *Option Pricing, Theory and Applications*, pages 3–33. Toronto University Press, Toronto, 1983.

[48] J.C. Cox and M. Rubinstein. *Options Markets*. Prentice Hall, N.J., 1985.

[49] N. Cutland, E. Kopp, and W. Willinger. From discrete to continuous financial models: New convergence results for option pricing. *Math. Finance*, 3:101–124, 1993.

[50] N.J. Cutland, P.E. Kopp, W. Willinger, and M.C. Wyman. Convergence of Snell envelopes and critical prices in the American put. In M.A.H. Dempster and S.R. Pliska, editors, *Mathematics of Derivative Securities*, pages 126–140. Cambridge University Press, New York, 1997.

[51] J. Cvitanić and I. Karatzas. Convex duality in constrained portfolio optimization. *Ann. Appl. Probab.*, 2:767–818, 1992.

[52] J. Cvitanić and I. Karatzas. Hedging contingent claims with constrained portfolios. *Ann. Appl. Probab.*, 3:652–681, 1993.

[53] J. Cvitanić and I. Karatzas. Hedging and portfolio optimization under transaction costs: A martingale approach. *Math. Finance*, 6:133–165, 1996.

[54] R.C. Dalang, A. Morton, and W. Willinger. Equivalent martingale measures and no-arbitrage in stochastic securities market model. *Stochastics Stochastics Rep.*, 29:185–201, 1990.

[55] M.H.A. Davis and A.R. Norman. Portfolio selection with transaction costs. *Math. Oper. Res.*, 15:676–713, 1990.

[56] M.H.A. Davis, V.P. Panas, and T. Zariphopoulou. European option pricing with transaction costs. *SIAM J. Control Optim.*, 31:470–493, 1993.

[57] F. Delbaen. Representing martingale measures when asset prices are continuous and bounded. *Math. Finance*, 2:107–130, 1992.

[58] F. Delbaen. Consols in the CIR model. *Math. Finance*, 3:125–134, 1993.

[59] F. Delbaen and W. Schachermayer. A general version of the fundamental theorem of asset pricing. *Math. Ann.*, 300:463–520, 1994.

[60] L.U. Dothan. On the term structure of interest rates. *J. Finan. Econ.*, 6:59–69, 1978.

[61] L.U. Dothan. *Prices in Financial Markets*. Oxford University Press, New York, 1990.

[62] L.U. Dothan and D. Feldman. Equilibrium interest rates and multiperiod bonds in a partially observable economy. *J. Finance*, 41:369–382, 1986.

[63] R. Douady. Options à limite et options à limite double. Working paper, Courant Institute, New York, 1994.

[64] J.-C. Duan. The GARCH option pricing model. *Math. Finance*, 5:13–32, 1995.

[65] D. Duffie. An extension of the Black–Scholes model of security valuation. *J. Econ. Theory*, 46:194–204, 1988.

[66] D. Duffie. *Security Markets: Stochastic Models*. Academic Press, Boston, 1988.

[67] D. Duffie. *Futures Markets*. Prentice Hall, Englewood Cliffs, N.J., 1989.

[68] D. Duffie. *Dynamic Asset Pricing Theory*. Princeton University Press, Princeton, 1992.

[69] D. Duffie and C. Huang. Multiperiod security markets with differential information. *J. Math. Econ.*, 15:283–303, 1986.

[70] D. Duffie and C.-F. Huang. Implementing Arrow–Debreu equilibria by continuous trading of few long-lived securities. *Econometrica*, 53:1337–1356, 1985.

[71] D. Duffie and R. Kan. Multi-factor term structure models. *Phil. Trans. R. Soc. Lond. Acad.*, 347:577–586, 1994.

[72] D. Duffie and P. Protter. From discrete- to continuous-time finance: Weak convergence of the financial gain process. *Math. Finance*, 2:1–15, 1992.

[73] D. Duffie and H.P. Richardson. Mean-variance hedging in continuous time. *Ann. Appl. Probab.*, 1:1–15, 1991.

[74] D. Duffie, M. Schroder, and C. Skiadas. Recursive valuation of defaultable securities and the timing of resolution of uncertainty. *Ann. Appl. Probab.*, 6:1075–1090, 1996.

[75] N. Dunford and J.T. Schwartz. *Linear Operators, Part I.* Interscience, New York, 1956.

[76] E. Eberlein. On modeling questions in security valuation. *Math. Finance*, 2:17–32, 1992.

[77] N. El Karoui. Les aspects probabilistes du contrôle stochastique. In *Lecture Notes in Mathematics* **876**, pages 73–238. Springer-Verlag, New York, 1981.

[78] N. El Karoui and H. Geman. A probabilistic approach to the valuation of floating rate notes with an application to interest rate swaps. *Adv. Options Futures Res.*, 7:47–63, 1994.

[79] N. El Karoui, H. Geman, and V. Lacoste. On the role of state variables in interest rates models. Working paper, Université Paris VI, 1995.

[80] N. El-Karoui, H. Geman, and J.C. Rochet. Changes of numéraire, arbitrage and option prices. *J. Appl. Probab.*, 32:443–458, 1995.

[81] N. El Karoui, M. Jeanblanc-Picqué, and S. Shreve. Robustness of the Black and Scholes formula. *Math. Finance*, 8(2): 93–126, 1998.

[82] N. El Karoui and I. Karatzas. A new approach to the Skorohod problem and its applications. *Stochastics Stochastics Rep.*, 34:57–82, 1991.

[83] N. El Karoui, S. Peng, and M.C. Quenez. Backward stochastic differential equations in finance. *Math. Finance*, 7:1–71, 1997.

[84] N. El Karoui and M.C. Quenez. Dynamic programming and pricing of contingent claims in an incomplete market. *SIAM J. Control Optim.*, 33:29–66, 1995.

[85] N. El Karoui and J.C. Rochet. A pricing formula for options on coupon bonds. Working paper 72, SDEES, 1989.

[86] N. El Karoui and D. Saada. A review of the Ho and Lee model. *International Conference in Finance*, Paris, June 1992.

[87] R.J. Elliott. *Stochastic Calculus and Applications.* Springer-Verlag, New York, 1982.

[88] R.J. Elliott, L. Aggoun, and J.B. Moore. *Hidden Markov Models: Estimation and Control.* Applications of Mathematics **29**. Springer-Verlag, New York, December 1994.

[89] R.J. Elliott and M. Chesney. Estimating the volatility of an exchange rate. In J. Janssen and C. Skiadis, editors, *Sixth International Symposium on Applied Stochastic Models and Data Analysis*, pages 131–135. World Scientific, Singapore, 1993.

[90] R.J. Elliott and D.B. Colwell. Martingale representation and non-attainable contingent claims. In P. Kall, editor, *Fifteenth IFIP Conference*, Lecture Notes in Control and Information Sciences **180**, pages 833–842. Springer-Verlag, 1992.

[91] R.J. Elliott and H. Föllmer. Orthogonal martingale representation. In *Liber Amicorum for M. Zakai*, pages 139–152. Academic Press, 1991.

[92] R.J. Elliott, H. Geman, and R. Korkie. Portfolio optimization and contingent claim pricing with differential information. *Stochastics Stochastic Rep.*, 60:183–203, 1997.

[93] R.J. Elliott, H. Geman, and D. Madan. Closed form formulae for valuing portfolios of American options. Working paper, University of Maryland, 1996.

[94] R.J. Elliott and W.C. Hunter. Filtering a discrete time price process. In *29th IEEE Asilomar Conference on Signals Systems and Computers. Asilomar, CA, Nov. 1995*, pages 1305–1309. IEEE Computer Society Press, Los Alamos, Calif., 1996.

[95] R.J. Elliott, W.C. Hunter, and B.M. Jamieson. Drift and volatility estimation in discrete time. *J. Econ. Dynamics Control*, 22:209–218, 1998.

[96] R.J. Elliott, W.C. Hunter, and B.M. Jamieson. Financial signal processing. *Math. Finance (to appear)*.

[97] R.J. Elliott, W.C. Hunter, P.E. Kopp, and D.B. Madan. Pricing via multiplicative price decomposition. *J. Finan. Engineering*, 4:247–262, 1995.

[98] R.J. Elliott and P.E. Kopp. Option pricing and hedge portfolios for Poisson processes. *J. Stoch. Anal. Appl.*, 8:157–167, 1990.

[99] R.J. Elliott and P.E. Kopp. Equivalent martingale measures for bridge processes. *J. Stoch. Anal. Appl.*, 9:429–444, 1991.

[100] R.J. Elliott, C. Lahaie, and D.B. Madan. Filtering derivative security evaluations from market prices. In M.A.H. Dempster and S.R. Pliska, editors, *Mathematics of Derivative Securities*, pages 141–162. Cambridge University Press, New York, 1997.

[101] R.J. Elliott and D.B. Madan. A discrete time equivalent martingale measure. *Math. Finance (to appear)*.

[102] R.J. Elliott and R.W. Rishell. Estimating the implicit interest rate of a risky asset. *Stochastic Process Appl.*, 49:199–206, 1994.

[103] R.J. Elliott and J. van der Hoek. An application of hidden Markov models to asset allocation problems. *Finance Stochastics*, 3:229–238, 1997.

[104] D. Feldman. The term structure of interest rates in a partially observed economy. *J. Finance*, 44:789–811, 1989.

[105] H. Föllmer and M. Schweizer. Hedging by sequential regression: An introduction to the mathematics of option trading. *ASTIN Bulletin*, 18:147–160, 1989.

[106] H. Föllmer and M. Schweizer. Hedging of contingent claims under incomplete information. In M.H.A. Davis and R.J. Elliott, editors, *Applied Stochastic Analysis*, Stochastic Monographs 5, pages 389–414. Gordon and Breach, New York, 1991.

[107] H. Föllmer and M. Schweizer. A microeconomic approach to diffusion models for stock prices. *Math. Finance*, 3:1–23, 1993.

[108] H. Föllmer and D. Sondermann. Hedging of non-redundant contingent claims. In W. Hildebrandt and A. Mas-Colell, editors, *Contributions to Mathematical Economics*, pages 205–223. North-Holland, Amsterdam, 1986.

[109] A. Frachot and J.P. Lesne. Expectation hypothesis with stochastic volatility. Working paper, Banque de France, 1993.

[110] A. Frachot and J.P. Lesne. Modèle factoriel de la structure par terme des taux d'interêt théorie et application économétrique. *Annals d'Economie et de Statistique*, 40, 1995.

[111] M. Garman and S. Kohlhagen. Foreign currency option values. *J. Internat. Money Finance*, 2:231–237, 1983.

[112] H. Geman. L'importance de la probabilité "forward neutre" dans une approach stochastique des taux d'intérêt. Working paper, ESSEC, 1989.

[113] H. Geman and A. Eydeland. Domino effect. *Risk*, 8(4):65–67, 1995.

[114] H. Geman and M. Yor. Bessel processes, Asian options and perpetuities. *Math. Finance*, 4:345–371, 1993.

[115] H. Geman and M. Yor. The valuation of double-barrier options: A probabilistic approach. *Math. Finance*, 6:365–378, 1996.

[116] R. Geske. The valuation of corporate liabilities as compound options. *J. Finan. Quant. Anal.*, 12:541–552, 1977.

[117] R. Geske. The pricing of options with stochastic dividend yield. *J. Finance*, 33:617–625, 1978.

[118] R. Geske and H.E. Johnson. The American put option valued analytically. *J. Finance*, 39:1511–1524, 1984.

[119] J.M. Harrison. *Brownian Motion and Stochastic Flow Systems*. Wiley, New York, 1985.

[120] J.M. Harrison and D.M. Kreps. Martingales and arbitrage in multiperiod securities markets. *J. Econ. Theory*, 20:381–408, 1979.

[121] J.M. Harrison and S.R. Pliska. Martingales and stochastic integrals in the theory of continuous trading. *Stochastic Process. App.*, 11:215–260, 1981.

[122] J.M. Harrison and S.R. Pliska. A stochastic calculus model of continuous trading: Complete markets. *Stochastic Process. App.*, 15:313–316, 1983.

[123] H. He. Convergence from discrete-time to continuous-time contingent claims prices. *Rev. Finan. Stud.*, 3:523–546, 1990.

[124] D. Heath and R. Jarrow. Arbitrage, continuous trading, and margin requirement. *J. Finance*, 42:1129–1142, 1987.

[125] D. Heath, R. Jarrow, and A. Morton. Bond pricing and the term structure of interest rates: A discrete time approximation. *J. Finan. Quant. Anal.*, 25:419–440, 1990.

[126] D. Heath, R. Jarrow, and A. Morton. Bond pricing and the term structure of interest rates: A new methodology for contingent claim valuation. *Econometrica*, 60:77–105, 1992.

[127] T.S.Y. Ho and S.-B. Lee. Term structure movements and pricing interest rate contingent claims. *J. Finance*, 41:1011–1029, 1996.

[128] C.-F. Huang. Information structures and equilibrium asset prices. *J. Econ. Theory*, 35:33–71, 1985.

[129] C.-F. Huang and R.H. Litzenberger. *Foundations for Financial Economics*. North-Holland, New York, 1988.

[130] J. Hull. *Options, Futures and Other Derivative Securities*. Prentice Hall, Englewood Cliffs, N.J., 1989.

[131] J. Hull. *Introduction to Futures and Options Markets*. Prentice Hall, Englewood Cliffs, N.J., 1991.

[132] J. Hull and A. White. The pricing of options on assets with stochastic volatilities. *J. Finance*, 42:281–300, 1987.

[133] J. Hull and A. White. An analysis of the bias in option pricing caused by a stochastic volatility. *Adv. Futures Options Res.*, 3:29–61, 1988.

[134] J. Hull and A. White. Pricing interest-rate derivative securities. *Rev. Finan. Stud.*, 3:573–592, 1990.

[135] J. Hull and A. White. Valuing derivative securities using the explicit finite difference method. *J. Finan. Quant. Anal.*, 25:87–100, 1990.

[136] S.D. Jacka. Optimal stopping and the American put. *Math. Finance*, 1:1–14, 1991.

[137] S.D. Jacka. A martingale representation result and an application to incomplete financial markets. *Math. Finance*, 2:239–250, 1992.

[138] S.D. Jacka. Local times, optimal stopping and semimartingales. *Ann. Probab.*, 21:329–339, 1993.

[139] J. Jacod. *Calcul stochastique et problèmes de martingales*. Lecture Notes in Mathematics. **714**. Springer-Verlag, Berlin, 1979.

[140] J. Jacod and A.N. Shiryayev. *Limit theorems for stochastic processes*. Grundlehren der Math. Wissenschaften **288**. Springer-Verlag, New York, 1987.

[141] P. Jaillet, D. Lamberton, and B. Lapeyre. Variational inequalities and the pricing of American options. *Acta Appl. Math.*, 21:263–289, 1990.

[142] F. Jamshidian. An exact bond option pricing formula. *J. Finance*, 44:205–209, 1989.

[143] F. Jamshidian. Bond and option evaluation in the Gaussian interest rate model. *Res. Finance*, 9:131–170, 1991.

[144] F. Jamshidian. Forward induction and construction of yield curve diffusion models. *J. Fixed Income*, 62–74, June 1991.

[145] F. Jamshidian. An analysis of American options. *Rev. Futures Markets*, 11:72–80, 1992.

[146] R. Jarrow. *Finance Theory*. Prentice-Hall, Englewood Cliffs, N.J., 1988.

[147] R.A. Jarrow, D. Lando, and S. Turnbull. A Markov model for the term structure of credit risk spreads. *Rev. Finan. Studies*, 10:481–523, 1997.

[148] R.A. Jarrow and D.B. Madan. A characterization of complete markets on a Brownian filtration. *Math. Finance*, 1:31–43, 1991.

[149] R.A. Jarrow and G.S. Oldfield. Forward contracts and futures contracts. *J. Finan. Econ.*, 9:373–382, 1981.

[150] R.A. Jarrow and S.M. Turnbull. Delta, gamma and bucket hedging of interest rate derivatives. *Appl. Math. Finance*, 1:21–48, 1994.

[151] M. Jeanblanc-Picqué and M. Pontier. Optimal portfolio for a small investor in a market with discontinuous prices. *Appl. Math. Optim.*, 22:287–310, 1990.

[152] H. Johnson. An analytic approximation for the American put price. *J. Finan. Quant. Anal.*, 18:141–148, 1983.

[153] I. Karatzas. On the pricing of American options. *Appl. Math. Optim.*, 17:37–60, 1988.

[154] I. Karatzas. Optimization problems in the theory of continuous trading. *SIAM J. Control Optim.*, 27:1221–1259, 1989.

[155] I. Karatzas. *Lectures on the Mathematics of Finance*. CRM Monograph Series, Vol. 8. American Math. Soc., Providence R.I., 1996.

[156] I. Karatzas and S.-G. Kou. Pricing of contingent claims with constrained portfolios. *Ann. Appl. Probab.*, 6:321–369, 1996.

[157] I. Karatzas, J.P. Lehoczky, S.P. Sethi, and S.E. Shreve. Explicit solution of a general consumption/investment problem. *Math. Oper. Res.*, 11:261–294, 1986.

[158] I. Karatzas, J.P. Lehoczky, and S.E. Shreve. Optimal portfolio and consumption decisions for a "small investor" on a finite horizon. *SIAM J. Control Optim.*, 25:1557–1586, 1987.

[159] I. Karatzas, J.P. Lehoczky, and S.E. Shreve. Existence and uniqueness of multi-agent equilibrium in a stochastic, dynamic consumption/investment model. *Math. Oper. Res.*, 15:80–128, 1990.

[160] I. Karatzas, J.P. Lehoczky, and S.E. Shreve. Equilibrium models with singular asset prices. *Math. Finance*, 1:11–29, 1991.

[161] I. Karatzas, J.P. Lehoczky, S.E. Shreve, and G.-L. Xu. Martingale and duality methods for utility maximization in an incomplete market. *SIAM J. Control Optim.*, 29:702–730, 1991.

[162] I. Karatzas and D.L. Ocone. A generalized Clark representation formula with application to optimal portfolios. *Stochastics Stochastics Rep.*, 34:187–220, 1992.

[163] I. Karatzas, D.L. Ocone, and J. Li. An extension of Clark's formula. *Stochastics Stochastics Rep.*, 32:127–131, 1991.

[164] I. Karatzas and S.E. Shreve. *Brownian Motion and Stochastic Calculus.* Springer-Verlag, New York, 1988.

[165] I. Karatzas and X.-X. Xue. A note on utility maximization under partial observations. *Math. Finance*, 1:57–70, 1991.

[166] D.P. Kennedy. The term structure of interest rates as a Gaussian random field. *Math. Finance*, 4:247–258, 1994.

[167] D.P. Kennedy. Characterizing Gaussian models of the term structure of interest rates. *Math. Finance*, 7:107–118, 1997.

[168] I.J. Kim. The analytic valuation of American options. *Rev. Finan. Stud.*, 3:547–572, 1990.

[169] P.E. Kopp. *Martingales and Stochastic Integrals.* Cambridge University Press, Cambridge, London, 1984.

[170] D.M. Kreps. Multiperiod securities and the efficient allocation of risk: A comment on the Black–Scholes model. In J. McCall, editor, *The Economics of Uncertainty and Information.* University of Chicago Press, Chicago, 1982.

[171] N.V. Krylov. *Controlled diffusion processes.* Applications of Mathematics **14**. Springer-Verlag, Berlin, 1980.

[172] H. Kunita. *Stochastic partial differential equations connected with nonlinear filtering.* Lecture Notes in Mathematics. **972**. Springer-Verlag, New York, 1978.

[173] P. Lakner. Martingale measure for a class of right-continuous processes. *Math. Finance*, 3:43–53, 1993.

[174] D. Lamberton. Convergence of the critical price in the approximation of american options. *Math. Finance*, 3:179–190, 1993.

[175] D. Lamberton and B. Lapeyre. Hedging index options with few assets. *Math. Finance*, 3:25–42, 1993.

[176] D. Lamberton and B. Lapeyre. *Introduction to Stochastic Calculus Applied to Finance.* Chapman & Hall, London, 1995.

[177] J.P. Lesne. *Modeles factoriel de la structure par terme des taux.* Ph.D. thesis, Toulouse, 1995.

[178] F.A. Longstaff. The valuation of options on coupon bonds. *J. Bank. Finance*, 17:27–42, 1993.

[179] F.A. Longstaff and E.S. Schwartz. Interest rate volatility and the term structure: A two-factor general equilibrium model. *J. Finance*, 47:1259–1282, 1992.

[180] D.B. Madan and F. Milne. Option pricing with V.G. martingale components. *Math. Finance*, 1:39–55, 1991.

[181] D.B. Madan, F. Milne, and H. Shefrin. The multinomial option pricing model and its Brownian and Poisson limits. *Rev. Finan. Stud.*, 2:251–265, 1989.

[182] D.B. Madan and E. Senata. The variance gamma (V.G.) model for share market returns. *J. Business*, 63:511–524, 1990.

[183] M.J.P. Magill and G.M. Constantinides. Portfolio selection with transactions costs. *J. Econ. Theory*, 13:245–263, 1976.

[184] H.P. McKean. Appendix: A free boundary problem for the heat equation arising from a problem in mathematical economics. *Industr. Manage. Rev.*, 6:32–39, 1965.

[185] R.C. Merton. Lifetime portfolio selection under uncertainty: The continuous-time model. *Rev. Econ. Statist.*, 51:247–257, 1969.

[186] R.C. Merton. Optimum consumption and portfolio rules in a continuous-time model. *J. Econ. Theory*, 3:373–413, 1971.

[187] R.C. Merton. An intertemporal capital asset pricing model. *Econometrica*, 41:867–888, 1973.

[188] R.C. Merton. Theory of rational option pricing. *Bell J. Econ. Manage. Sci.*, 4:141–183, 1973.

[189] R.C. Merton. On the pricing of corporate debt: The risk structure of interest rates. *J. Finance*, 29:449–470, 1974.

[190] R.C. Merton. Option pricing when underlying stock returns are discontinuous. *J. Finan. Econ.*, 3:125–144, 1976.

[191] R.C. Merton. On estimating the expected return on the market: An exploratory investigation. *J. Finan. Econ.*, 8:323–361, 1980.

[192] R.C. Merton. *Continuous-Time Finance*. Basil Blackwell, Cambridge, 1990.

[193] P.A. Meyer. *Un cours sur les intégrales stochastiques*. Séminaire de Probabilités X. Lecture Notes in Mathematics **511**. Springer-Verlag, Berlin, 1976.

[194] F. Modigliani and M.H. Miller. The cost of capital, corporation finance and the theory of investment. *Amer. Econ. Rev.*, 48:261–297, 1958.

[195] M. Musiela. Stochastic PDEs and term structure models. *Journées Internationales de Finance, IGR-AFFI*, June 1993.

[196] M. Musiela. Nominal annual rates and lognormal volatility structure. Preprint, The University of New South Wales, 1994.

[197] M. Musiela and M. Rutkowski. *Martingale Methods in Financial Modelling*. Applications of Mathematics **36**. Springer-Verlag, New York, 1997.

[198] M. Musiela and D. Sondermann. Different dynamical specifications of the term structure of interest rates and their implications. Preprint, University of Bonn, 1993.

[199] R. Myneni. The pricing of the American option. *Ann. Appl. Probab.*, 2:1–23, 1992.

[200] J. Neveu. *Discrete-Parameter Martingales*. North-Holland, Amsterdam, 1975.

[201] D.L. Ocone and I. Karatzas. A generalized Clark representation formula with application to optimal portfolios. *Stochastics Stochastics Rep.*, 34:187–220, 1991.

[202] B. Øksendal. *Stochastic Differential Equations*. Springer-Verlag, New York, 4th edition, 1995.

[203] N.D. Pearson and T.-S. Sun. Exploiting the conditional density in estimating the term structure: An application to the Cox, Ingersoll and Ross model. *J. Finance*, 49:1279–1304, 1994.

[204] S.R. Pliska. A stochastic calculus model of continuous trading: Optimal portfolios. *Math. Oper. Res.*, 11:371–382, 1986.

[205] S.R. Pliska. *Introduction to Mathematical Finance. Discrete Time Models*. Blackwell, Oxford, 1997.

[206] S.R. Pliska and C.T. Shalen. The effects of regulations on trading activity and return volatility in futures markets. *J. Futures Markets*, 11:135–151, 1991.

[207] S. Port and C. Stone. *Brownian Motion and Classical Potential Theory*. Academic Press, New York, 1978.

[208] D. Revuz and M. Yor. *Continuous Martingales and Brownian Motion*. Springer-Verlag, Berlin, 2nd edition, 1996.

[209] R.T. Rockefellar. *Convex Analysis*. Princeton University Press, Princeton, N.J., 1970.

[210] C. Rogers and Z. Shi. The value of an Asian option. *J. Appl. Prob.*, 32:1077–1088, 1995.

[211] L.C.G. Rogers. Equivalent martingale measures and no-arbitrage. *Stochastics Stochastics Rep.*, 51:41–49, 1994.

[212] L.C.G. Rogers and S.E. Satchell. Estimating variance from high, low and closing prices. *Ann. Appl. Probab.*, 1:504–512, 1991.

[213] S.A. Ross. The arbitrage theory of capital asset pricing. *J. Econ. Theory*, 13:341–360, 1976.

[214] M. Rubinstein. The valuation of uncertain income streams and the pricing of options. *Bell J. Econ.*, 7:407–425, 1976.

[215] M. Rubinstein. A simple formula for the expected rate of return of an option over a finite holding period. *J. Finance*, 39:1503–1509, 1984.

[216] M. Rubinstein. Exotic options. Working paper, 1991.

[217] M. Rubinstein and H.E. Leland. Replicating options with positions in stock and cash. *Finan. Analysts J.*, 37:63–72, 1981.

[218] M. Rubinstein and E. Reiner. Breaking down the barriers. *Risk*, 4(8):28–35, 1991.

[219] P.A. Samuelson. Rational theory of warrant prices. *Ind. Manage. Rev.*, 6:13–31, 1965.

[220] P.A. Samuelson. Lifetime portfolio selection by dynamic stochastic programming. *Rev. Econ. Statist.*, 51:239–246, 1969.

[221] P.A. Samuelson. Mathematics of speculative prices. *SIAM Rev.*, 15:1–42, 1973.

[222] K. Sandmann. The pricing of options with an uncertain interest rate: A discrete-time approach. *Math. Finance*, 3:201–216, 1993.

[223] K. Sandmann and D. Sondermann. A term structure model and the pricing of interest rate options. *Rev. Futures Markets*, 12:391–423, 1993.

[224] W. Schachermayer. A Hilbert-space proof of the fundamental theorem of asset pricing in discrete time. *Insurance Math. Econ.*, 11:249–257, 1992.

[225] W. Schachermayer. A counterexample to several problems in the theory of asset pricing. *Math. Finance*, 3:217–230, 1993.

[226] S.M. Schaefer and E.S. Schwartz. A two-factor model of the term structure: An approximate analytical solution. *J. Finan. Quant. Anal.*, 4:413–424, 1984.

[227] S.M. Schaefer and E.S. Schwartz. Time-dependent variance and the pricing of bond options. *J. Finance*, 42:1113–1128, 1987.

[228] M. Scholes. Taxes and the pricing of options. *J. Finance*, 31:319–332, 1976.

[229] M. Schweizer. Risk-minimality and orthogonality of martingales. *Stochastics Stochastics Rep.*, 30:123–131, 1990.

[230] M. Schweizer. Option hedging for semimartingales. *Stochastic Process Appl.*, 37:339–363, 1991.

[231] M. Schweizer. Martingale densities for general asset prices. *J. Math. Econ.*, 21:363–378, 1992.

[232] M. Schweizer. Mean-variance hedging for general claims. *Ann. Appl. Probab.*, 2:171–179, 1992.

[233] M. Schweizer. Approximating random variables by stochastic integrals. *Ann. Probab.*, 22:1536–1575, 1994.

[234] M. Schweizer. A projection result for semimartingales. *Stochastics Stochastics Rep.*, 50:175–183, 1994.

[235] M. Schweizer. Risk-minimizing hedging strategies under restricted information. *Math. Finance*, 4:327–342, 1994.

[236] M. Schweizer. On the minimal martingale measure and the Föllmer–Schweizer decomposition. *Stochastic Anal. Appl.*, 13:573–599, 1995.

[237] M. Schweizer. Variance-optimal hedging in discrete time. *Math. Oper. Res.*, 20:1–32, 1995.

[238] M. Schweizer. Approximation pricing and the variance-optimal martingale measure. *Ann. Appl. Probab.*, 24:206–236, 1996.

[239] L. Shepp and A.N. Shiryayev. The Russian option: Reduced regret. *Ann. Appl. Probab.*, 3:631–640, 1993.

[240] H. Shirakawa. Interest rate option pricing with Poisson–Gaussian forward rate curve processes. *Math. Finance*, 1:77–94, 1991.

[241] A.N. Shiryayev. *Probability*. Graduate Texts in Mathematics. **95**. Springer-Verlag, Berlin, 1984.

[242] A.N. Shiryayev. On some basic concepts and some basic stochastic models used in finance. *Theory Probab. Appl.*, 39:1–13, 1994.

[243] A.N. Shiryayev, Y.M. Kabanov, O.D. Kramkov, and A.V. Melnikov. Toward the theory of pricing of options of both European and American types, I. Discrete time. *Theory Prob. Appl.*, 39:14–60, 1994.

[244] A.N. Shiryayev, Y.M. Kabanov, O.D. Kramkov, and A.V. Melnikov. Toward the theory of pricing of options of both European and American types, II. Continuous time. *Theory Prob. Appl.*, 39:61–102, 1994.

[245] S.E. Shreve. A control theorist's view of asset pricing. In M.H.A. Davis and R.J. Elliott, editors, *Applied Stochastic Analysis*, Stochastic Monographs, Volume **5**, pages 415–445. Gordon and Breach, New York, 1991.

[246] S.E. Shreve, H.M. Soner, and G.-L. Xu. Optimal investment and consumption with two bonds and transaction costs. *Math. Finance*, 1:53–84, 1991.

[247] C. Stricker. Integral representation in the theory of continuous trading. *Stochastics*, 13:249–257, 1984.

[248] C. Stricker. Arbitrage et lois de martingale. *Ann. Inst. H. Poincaré Probab. Statist.*, 26:451–460, 1990.

[249] M. Taksar, M.J. Klass, and D. Assaf. A dissuion model for optimal portfolio selection in the presence of brokerage fees. *Math. Oper. Res.*, 13:277–294, 1988.

[250] M.S. Taqqu and W. Willinger. The analysis of finite security markets using martingales. *Adv. Appl. Probab.*, 19:1–25, 1987.

[251] S.J. Taylor. Modeling stochastic volatility: A review and comparative study. *Math. Finance*, 4:183–204, 1994.

[252] S.M. Turnbull and F. Milne. A simple approach to the pricing of interest rate options. *Rev. Finan. Stud.*, 4:87–120, 1991.

[253] J. Van der Hoek and E. Platen. Pricing contingent claims in the presence of transaction costs. Working paper, University of Adelaide, 1995.

[254] P. van Moerbeke. On optimal stopping and free boundary problem. *Arch. Rational Mech. Anal.*, 60:101–148, 1976.

[255] O. Vasicek. An equilibrium characterisation of the term structure. *J. Finan. Econ.*, 5:177–188, 1977.

[256] R. Whaley. Valuation of American call options on dividend-paying stocks: Empirical tests. *J. Finan. Econ.*, 10:29–58, 1982.

[257] R. Whaley. Valuation of American futures options: Theory and empirical tests. *J. Finance*, 41:127–150, 1986.

[258] D. Williams. *Probability with Martingales*. Cambridge University Press, Cambridge, 1991.

[259] W. Willinger and M.S. Taqqu. Pathwise stochastic integration and applications to the theory of continuous trading. *Stochastic Process. Appl.*, 32:253–280, 1989.

[260] W. Willinger and M.S. Taqqu. Toward a convergence theory for continuous stochastic securities market models. *Math. Finance*, 1:55–99, 1991.

[261] P. Wilmott, J. Dewynne, and S. Howison. *Option Pricing: Mathematical Models and Computation*. Oxford Univesity Press, Oxford, 1994.

[262] P.G. Zhang. *Exotic Options: A Guide to Second Generation Options*. World Scientific, Singapore, 1997.

Index